AF262791

TATTOOS

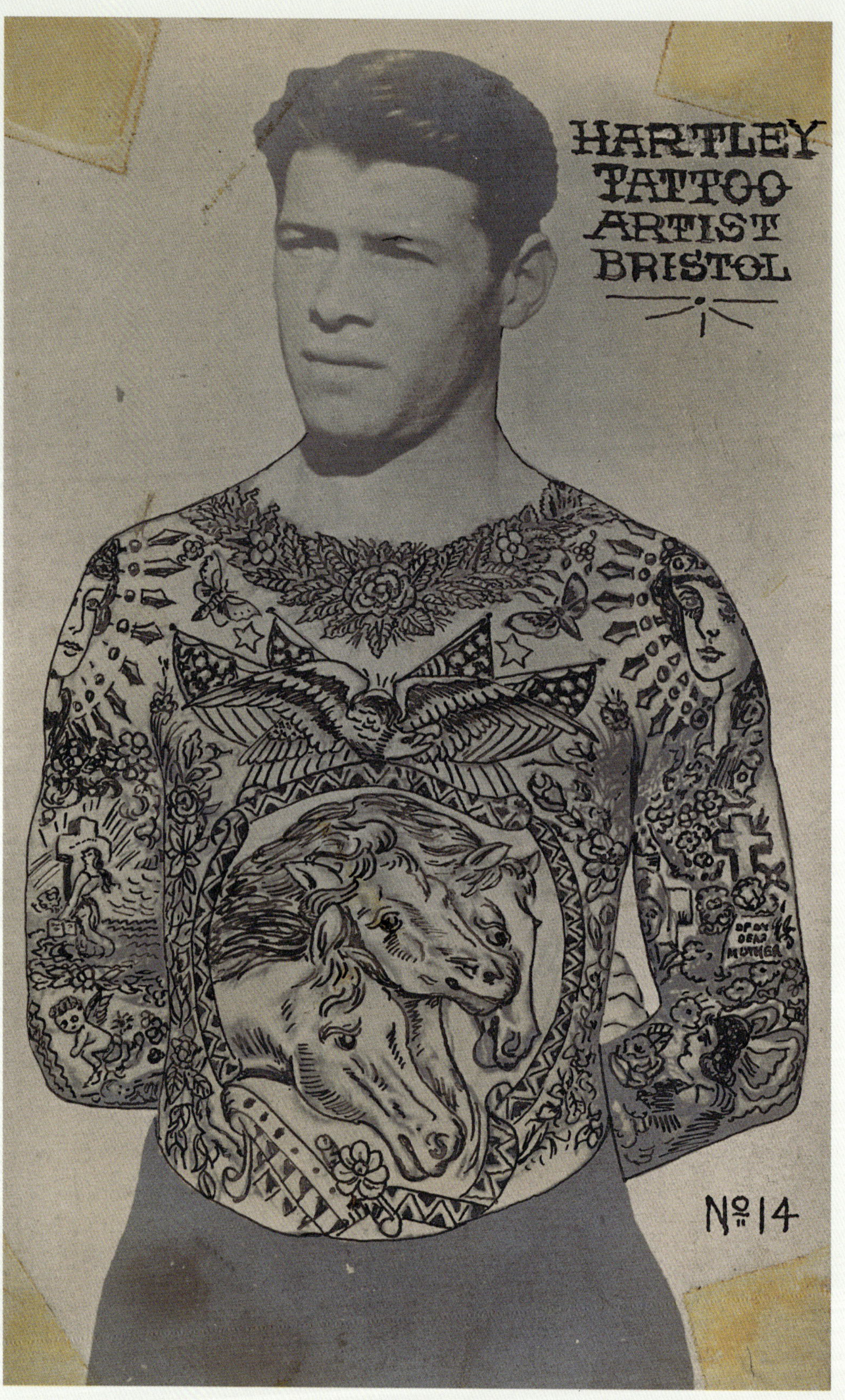

HARTLEY
TATTOO
ARTIST
BRISTOL
OF MY DEAR
MOTHER
No 14

TATTOOS

The Untold History of a Modern Art

Matt Lodder

Yale UNIVERSITY PRESS

New Haven and London

Published by Yale University Press
302 Temple Street
P.O. Box 209040
New Haven, CT 06520-9040
yalebooks.com/art

This book was designed and produced by
Quintessence Editions, an imprint of The Quarto Group,
One Triptych Place, London, SE1 9SH, United Kingdom

Senior Commissioning Editor	Eszter Karpati
Senior Editor	Emma Harverson
Copy Editor	Rachel Malig
Design	Jay Cross
Art Director	Gemma Wilson
Picture Research	Sarah Bell
Production Manager	David Hearn
Associate Publisher	Eszter Karpati
Publisher	Lorraine Dickey

ISBN 978-0-300-26939-0

Library of Congress Control Number: 2024940502

A catalogue record for this book is available from the British Library.

Printed in the United Arab Emirates

10 9 8 7 6 5 4 3 2 1

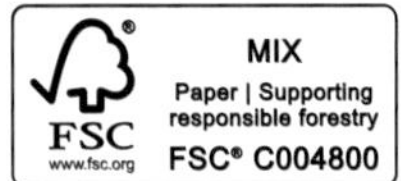

CONTENTS

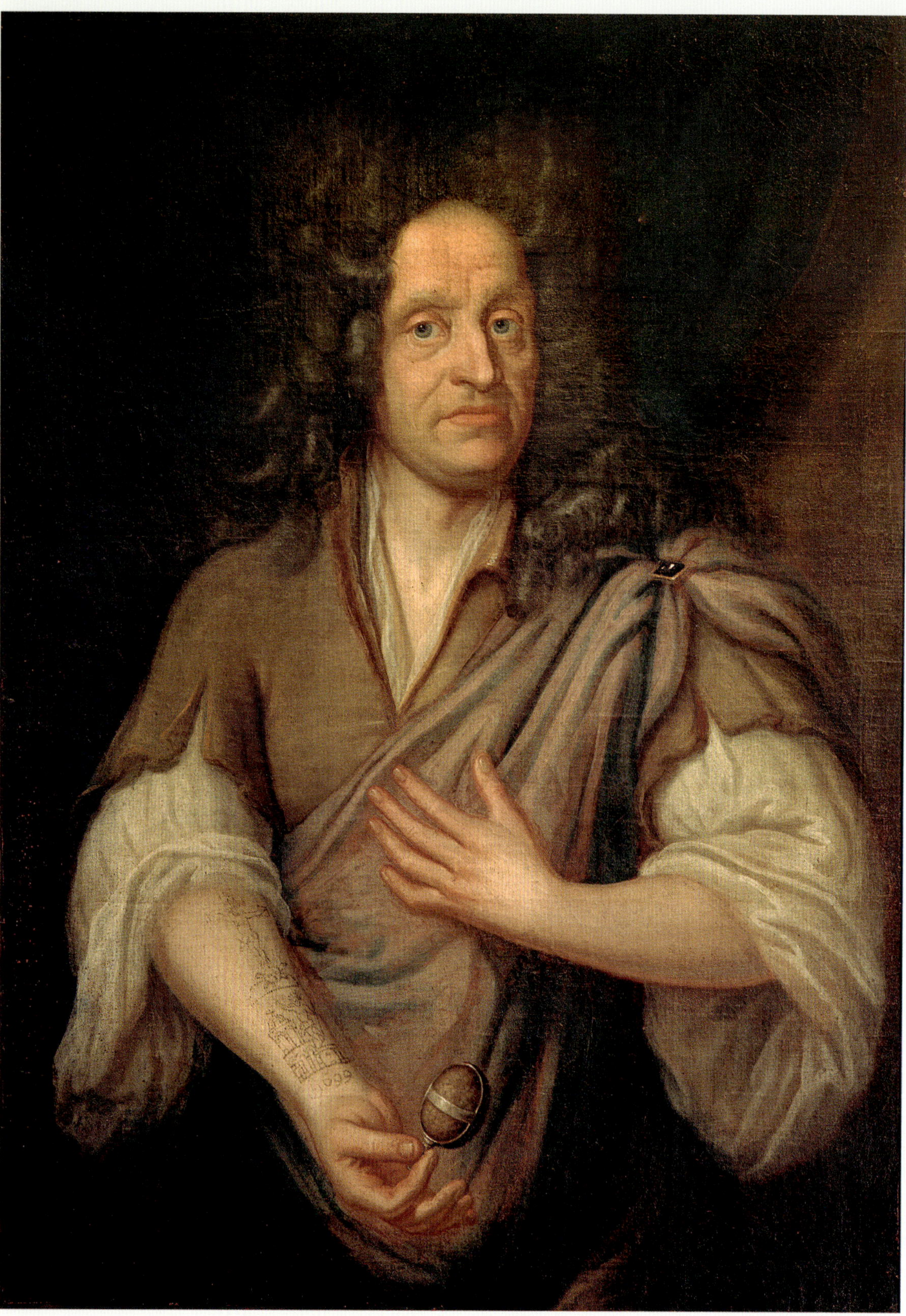

An Unworthy Subject

This book is the story of the Western tattooing profession, as it extends from 1719—the year of the earliest report yet found of an Englishman claiming to have made a business of pricking designs on skin—to the incalculable scale of the tattoo industry as it exists today, three hundred or so years later. Much tabloid ink has been cast over the centuries in describing the imagined transformation of a humble, intimate craft undertaken perhaps exclusively by sailors and incarcerated men, into a shiny, sanitized, cultural phenomenon, which is trendy, shorn of any true countercultural bite, and to be found on central shopping streets throughout the modern world. But, as we shall see, the mainstream of Euro-American culture has long suffered with a persistent amnesia about tattooing's history in the West, and has been consistently surprised and shocked by the repetitiously "novel" emergence of tattooing from what reporters imagined were its backstreet, shipyard origins into an "acceptable," fashionable fad.

Much of this amnesia results from a lack of access to good-quality information. Books such as this one, which combine academic research with hitherto-privileged information from within the tattoo trade, have long been difficult propositions for publishers. In May 1967, for example, photographer and corset-maker Roland Loomis received a disappointing letter from Wallace Exman, an editor at the World Publishing Company in Ohio. "Dear Mr Loomis," Exman wrote, "It goes without saying that the photographs [you sent] are of a very high quality and that they portray the subject quite well and in excellent taste. But the audience for a fairly expensive treatment on the art of tattoo is in our view an extremely limited one."

Loomis—later to become better known to the world as body-modification pioneer Fakir Musafar—

had pitched an ambitious publishing project entitled *Tattoo: A Photographic Essay* to every major publishing house in America, though received nothing but terse rejection letters in return. Originally conceived as *Tattoo: The Primitive Urge*, the book was to have been co-authored with Californian tattoo artist Davy Jones, who had recently produced an enormous blackwork tattoo across Loomis' back inspired by various indigenous tattoo traditions which had fascinated him since boyhood. The book's contents were to have been primarily a photographic presentation of studio portraits of tattooed people—including, perhaps, Satanist Anton LaVey—and candid shots of tattooers at work, peppered with short essays on the tattoo business, on the anthropology of tattooing, and on tattooing's personal impacts. It was, as the putative outline claimed, "born out of a disgust for academic prejudice toward a subject of social significance," as well as a sense that tattooing was an "unworthy subject," usually treated with a "negative attitude of sociologists, historians and others who should care."

It was never published, and the project was shelved. Loomis' ideas would (without Jones) eventually reach a global audience, to great impact, more than twenty years later, when they were compiled into V. Vale and Andrea Juno's book *Modern Primitives* (1989), but one can only speculate as to the impact they may have had were they to have been distributed more widely in the 1960s. In many ways, though, the gap in the market Loomis identified, and the disdain and confusion of academics and outsiders to the histories and presence of tattooing, still remain, even six decades since that original pitch.

A Much-Maligned and Belittled Subject

A decade later, in 1977, another pitch was landing at American publishers' desks. Also emerging from the Californian underground, and copyedited by a tattooer and piercer friend of Loomis' called Sid Diller, this book project was a rather different proposition to *The Primitive Urge*'s presentation of glossy, seductive photography bolstered by short essays. Instead, this was intended to be gargantuan in both size and scale: a 1200-page *Encyclopaedia of Tattooing* which would not only attempt to collate every academic article ever published on tattooing's history, technology, and social significance to date, but also to draw upon privileged information gleaned from industry figureheads which would expose the ingredients of tattoo inks, the secrets of tattoo-machine building, and even how much tattooers charged for their work. The initial outline also suggested the inclusion of profiles of great artists, and guest contributions from experts around the world. It was, essentially, to have been an academic reference tome, a comprehensive "history of tattooing," an overview of the psychology, sexology, and sociology of the marking of skin, a How-To guide, as well as a photographic documentation of the best of contemporary tattooing, all in one volume.

The lead author, Dr Andrew John Lemes, was not a tattooer, but a young psychiatrist recently out of med school. He had become fascinated by tattooing while acquiring an extensive full-body tattoo of a squid from seminal Californian artist Ed Hardy, and in his zeal to learn as much as he could about tattooing in the libraries and archives available to him, he found he consistently hit against absences and obstacles. As Loomis had realized a decade earlier, much research

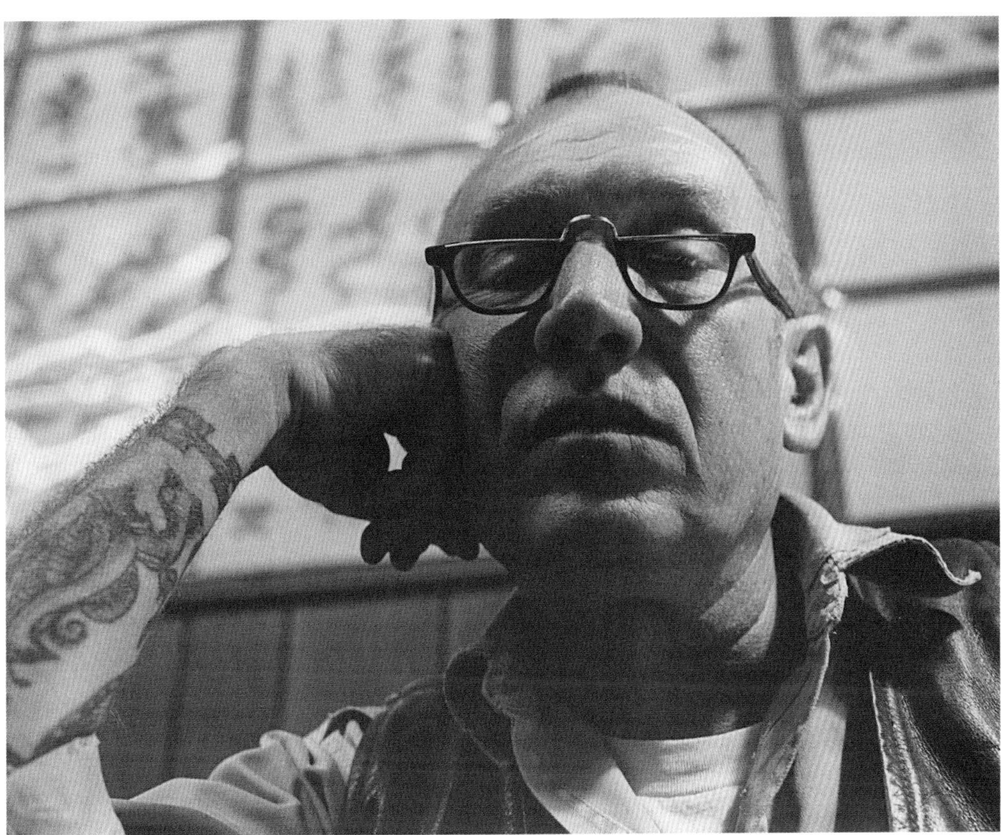

on tattooing simply hadn't been done, and that which had been done appeared obviously flawed to anyone who had really spent time getting tattooed. Moreover, much of the technical and historical detail on the industry of tattooing in Europe and America was simply not accessible to most people, shared only between those already inside the trade—as stories and secrets told in club newsletters, insider publications, and through hard-scrabble apprenticeships.

Lemes, messianic and arrogant, saw himself as the person to bring light into the dusky corners of the industry, wanting to turn his own manic curiosity into a book which would, in his own words "promulgate tattooing as an artform." From around 1973, he worked to compile every scrap of knowledge he could. He sourced copies of obscure journal articles by sending hardcopy requests to institutional libraries around the world. He wrote to luminaries including

Norman "Sailor Jerry" Collins, who politely but firmly told him that he had been lucky his letter had avoided the wastepaper basket, but welcomed his efforts to "throw light on a hitherto much maligned and belittled subject that is highly misunderstood by members of your own professions, as well as the layman in general." Lemes even lied to the poison control desk at Dupont Chemical's pigment division, claiming that a patient of his had swallowed their dalimar yellow powder—often used surreptitiously by tattooers—in order to evince from them a toxicity sheet.

Though initially supported by tattooers, including Hardy himself, and by prominent academics such as Arnold Rubin at UCLA, Lemes' zeal eventually drew the ire of professional tattooers, who did not want their trade secrets to be distributed so incautiously. Though tattooers had been publishing "How-To" guides at small scales for decades, the late 1960s and

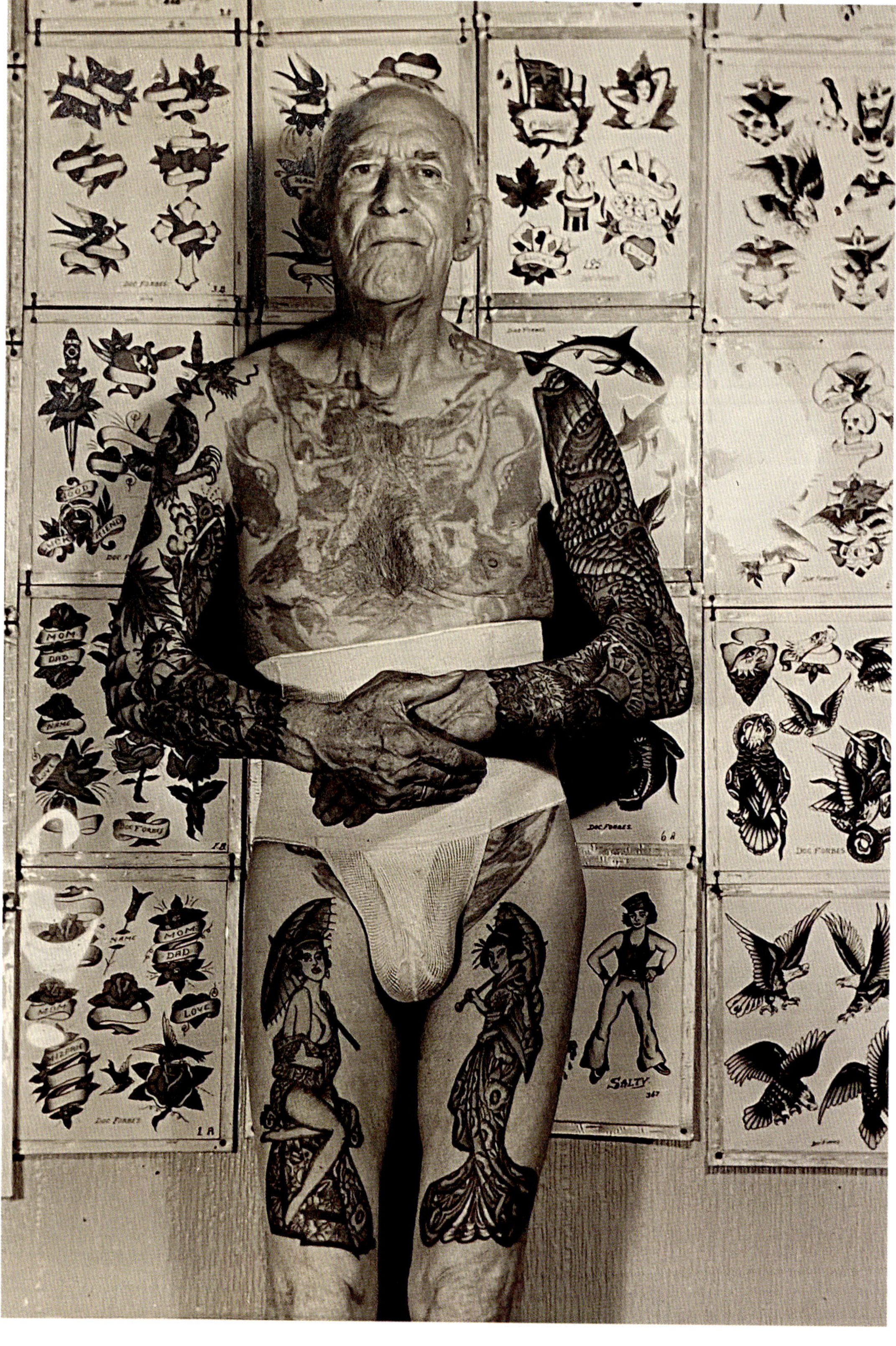

Tattooing through time and space
Eighty-two-year-old "Mr Brown," sporting
tattoos by turn-of-the-twentieth-century
British tattooer George Burchett, was
photographed in Vancouver, Canada,
by Doc Forbes Hendry in the 1960s.
As tattoos move through time with
their bearers, they are able to inspire
subsequent generations of artists and
collectors for decades.

early 1970s were a tense moment for the industry, with new regulations appearing rapidly. Any increase in amateurs trying to tattoo at home, with information learned from a book apparently endorsed by professionals, could be dangerous, and any resultant poor tattoos and adverse health outcomes would only look bad for the industry as a whole. Moreover, the idea of an outsider like Lemes taking it upon himself to become the centralized source for all information about tattooing "for decades to come" (as Lemes pitched) was rightly seen as presumptuous, pompous, and fundamentally unearned by industry figureheads, who turned against Lemes and the whole project.

Rubin eventually issued an open letter condemning the project and denying he had ever meant to support the endeavor, claiming that Lemes misled him as to the purpose of their correspondence. Hardy wrote to colleagues in dismay and disgust at Lemes' arrogance. Astonishingly, Lemes had narcissistically written to Hardy to explain that he planned to publish the collated material anyway, as "I feel it is in the best interest of the tattooing profession to allow the techniques to be disseminated freely."

Ultimately, *The Encyclopaedia of Tattooing* was never a viable commercial publication, given its scale and ambition. Without the backing of the industry, and amid personal issues, Lemes ran out of money for the book in around 1979, and the whole project collapsed, leaving behind only thirteen stuffed folders of notes, drafts, and letters. He did self-publish a smaller excerpt, called *Tattoo Trade Secrets*, which he sold through mail order for over twenty years, though in the face of open hostility against him, it barely made a ripple.

The Subject As It Really Is

There have been scarce few publications that have attempted to connect the development of professional Euro-American tattooing as an art form across history. The closest analogs to this current work are old indeed—Albert Parry's *Tattoo: Secrets of a Strange Art* (1933), Hanns Ebensten's *Pierced Hearts and True Love* (1954), and Captain R. W. B. Scutt and Christopher Gotch's *Skin Deep / Art, Sex and Symbol* (1974)—and all are limited insofar as they were unable to provide an overview of the complexity and breadth of the industry's professional networks.

This present book, then, will attempt to achieve some of the nobler goals of Lemes' project, without the pretence that it will either be the final word on the subject, nor be a guide for amateur tattooers. I have tried instead to heed some of Sailor Jerry's words to Lemes: "I hope you will do a great deal of research among the better class of tattoo artists before publishing any work on tattooing … If you do your homework, so to speak, you can do a great deal of good with your publication, giving the medical profession something to refer to that is not the ramblings of some sensation-seeking journalist, but rather the down-to-earth facts of the subject as it really is."

I want, here, to reset the scaffolding for a history of Western tattooing as a professional and commercial practice, which clearly demarcates it from its encounters and engagements with indigenous tattoo cultures throughout the Americas, Southeast and East Asia, North Africa, and Oceania; and from its vernacular, intimate, and amateur practice by sailors, incarcerated people, and those who pricked marks into others' skins but for whom tattooing did

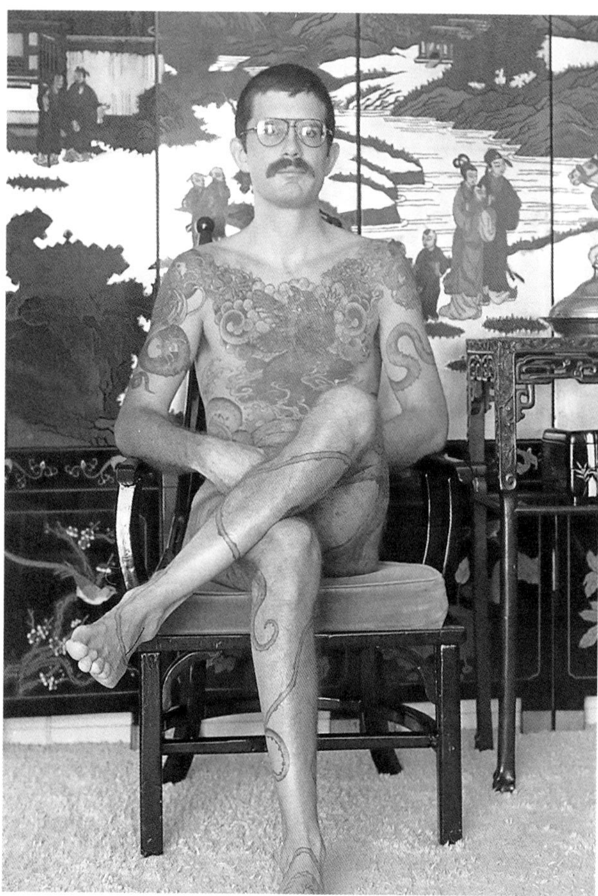

Forbidden knowledge Dr. Andrew Lemes, pictured here in the early 1970s, was tattooed by Ed Hardy. His large octopus tattoo (see page 144) has become iconic, and featured on the cover of Albert Morse's influential photobook *The Tattooists* in 1977. Lemes sought to use his academic skills to develop a definitive account of tattooing's history, culture, and techniques, but he was eventually ostracized by the industry, who resented his attempts to publish on a topic in which he had no expertise.

not form part of a commercial, public-facing trade. Where such cultures and subcultures are material to the development of commercial tattooing, they are of course accounted for, but the prurient gaze of the sociologist or the anthropologist is avoided. The specific details and delights of prison tattooing, sailor tattooing, biker tattooing, gang tattooing, and culturally and subculturally normative tattooing of all kinds are best discussed elsewhere. Importantly, I want to focus in this book almost exclusively on the artists themselves, and their influences, innovations, and interconnections, for while there is great value and interest in examining the lives and stories of clients—tattooed men and women throughout history—the specific work of the artists has been too often neglected in the understanding of tattooing beyond the industry itself.

I draw primarily on accounts from tattooers themselves, through newspaper and magazine interviews, private archive material, unpublished industry magazines, self-published books, and, in later chapters, interviews conducted with key figures over the course of my career. This approach strips back the muddled and incoherent secondary literature, and allows, again, an often untold story to emerge. The earliest chapters chart the rudimentary, stuttering beginnings of a commercial tattoo trade in Europe and North America. From the establishment of the first public-facing tattoo shop in the late 1850s through to the first real boom of the modern Western profession in the 1870s, 80s, and 90s, the book is structured by way of tracing the specific and often surprisingly tight-knit network of working artists with public visibility and influence in their trade. This approach doubtless leaves many wonderful and influential artists mentioned only in passing, or excluded altogether, and becomes impossible to sustain after the turn of the third

A sea full of sharks Known as "flash," these preprinted sheets of tattoo designs by "Doc" Forbes Hendry, Vancouver, Canada, 1964, were gifted to Swiss collector Rudi Inhelder. The seahorse at the right of the sheet was used as the basis for the logo of Inhelder's Tattoo Club of America, a central hub of the network of Western tattooing in the latter half of the twentieth century.

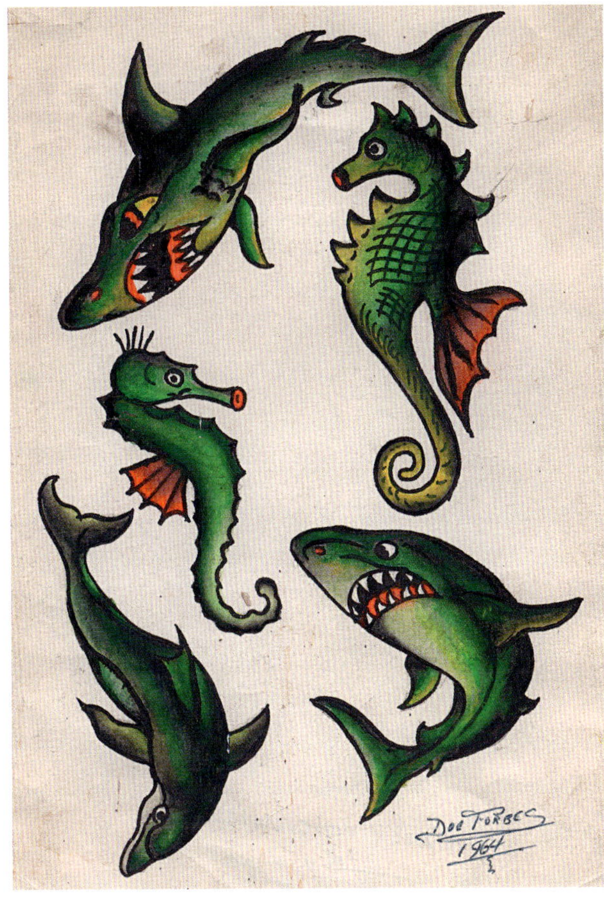

millennium. But it does allow a coherent and direct picture to be sketched of a passionate, creative, and sometimes fractious group of artists—largely, though by no means exclusively, men in California, London, and Germany—whose collective endeavors laid the foundations for the shape of the tattoo industry today, its working practices, and its design languages. These key figures knew each other, directly or indirectly, and a small number are central to the construction of the modern tattoo industry through friendships and rivalries. By tracing this network, a core of rapaciously intelligent individuals emerges—groundbreaking draftsmen, clever tinkerers and problem-solvers, and vivacious if often acerbic raconteurs and self-mythologizers. Many had very high levels of formal academic training in the arts, though there were just as many with no such pieces of paper. But the true, uniting feature of everyone cited here was

their unfailing enthusiasm for the irreplaceable magic of tattooing, and their desire to see it improve and be treated with respect as a true craft on its own terms.

I cannot claim, of course, that this short but richly illustrated text is a fully comprehensive account of tattooing, given the span of time and geography it tackles. As such, I take as my guide the words of legendary tattooer Jack Rudy, who wrote, "Some o'you reading . . . may remember things differently, too. But that's one o'the things that makes life so interesting. Don't ya think?"

Chapter One

Tattooing in Western Europe Before the Opening of Japan

−1858

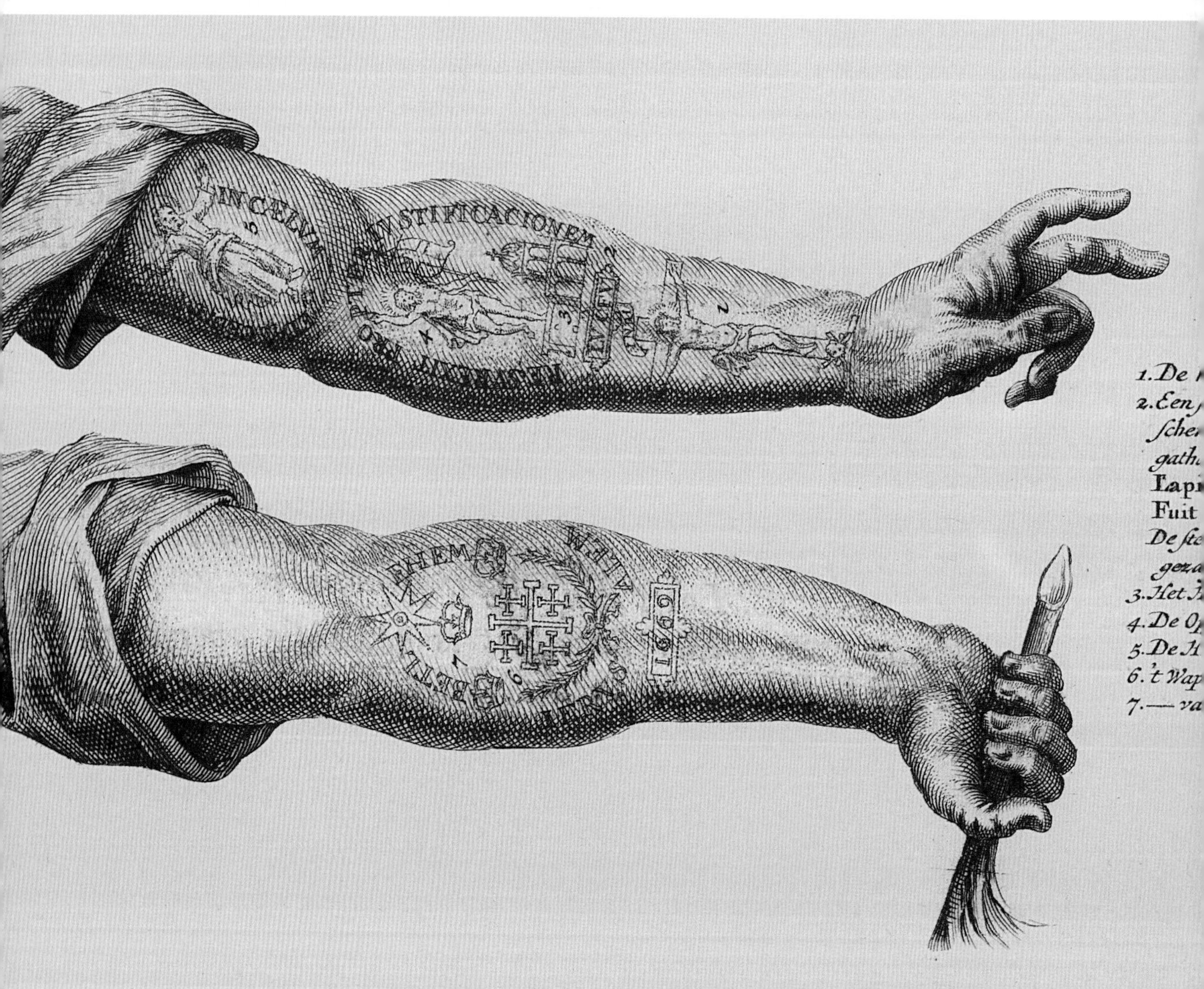

Literary Gazette, 1819

Signs of devotion A 1701 engraving showing the tattoos of German pilgrim Ratge Stubbe. Stubbe was tattooed in 1669, as attested by the date tattooed on his forearm, with the skull of Adam underneath an extensive Easter scene on his left arm. On his right arm he bears a Jerusalem Cross, as well as the names of both Bethlehem and Jerusalem.

n February 1719, John Woodward and Thomas Williams were convicted of housebreaking at London's Old Bailey and sentenced with transportation to the colonies. The two men had smashed the window of a private home in the City, one of them reaching through to snatch a silk scarf and lacerating himself in the process. Both were quickly apprehended—Williams on a nearby street corner, and Woodward while nursing his bloody hand over a pint in a local alehouse. When questioned, the men denied knowing each other, but the arresting police officer noticed that each bore the same ink mark on his arm: four crosses set around a larger cross in their center. The design is known as the Jerusalem Cross, a symbol of Christian proselytizing from the Holy Lands.

These pricked-in ink marks—not yet called tattoos—had by this point been common souvenirs on European pilgrims returning from sites that included not just Jerusalem, but also Bethlehem, Nazareth, and holy destinations such as Loreto in Italy, for over a century. Indeed, the technological innovation that led to a vibrant pilgrimage tattoo tradition may have even begun in Italy, as there is some evidence to suggest that the permanent creation of designs in the skin there dates to at least the 1550s. Polymath Gerolamo Cardano suggested in 1554 that razor-cuts made in the context of medicinal bloodletting could be rubbed with red or blue pigments to create letters or shapes in the skin, and Giambattista della Porta wrote in 1558 that such techniques were well known through tales of Greek antiquity.

The earliest records of pilgrimage tattooing in the Holy Lands stretch back to the 1560s. Eventually, this practice matured by the seventeenth century into a commercial enterprise where images were stamped onto the skin using design blocks carved from wood

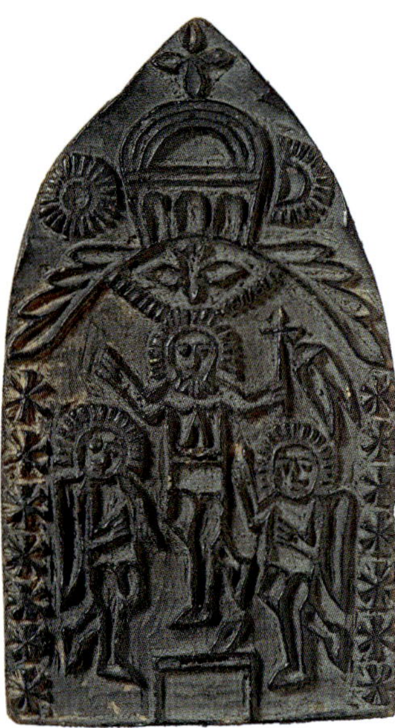 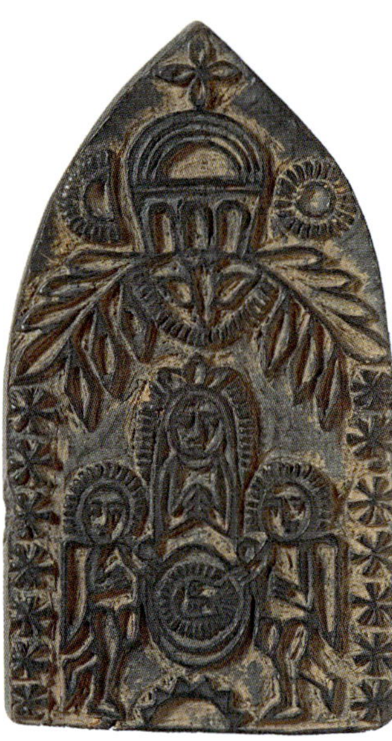

Wooden tattoo stamp These images show two sides of the same design stamp used for pilgrimage tattoos. Blocks like this one—collected in Armenia in the late nineteenth century—were used to place the outline of a design on the skin before being tattooed over. In this example, on the left Jesus is shown having risen from his tomb. The reverse side shows the miracle of Saint Veronica, who mopped Jesus's forehead with her veil while he was carrying his cross to Calvary. Subsequently, the veil bore a miraculous image of Christ's face. Such scenes of the Passion of Christ were frequent motifs for pilgrims to Jerusalem at Easter from the late sixteenth century onwards, and the practice continues in the city to the present day.

and then slowly and carefully pricked into the skin with a needle dipped in black ink. Such pilgrim marks served as a sign of religious devotion and, in providing souvenirs from long and meaningful voyages, they became a key part of the experience for those traveling to sacred sites. In one vivid account from 1658, French pilgrim Jean de Thévenot described how Christian tattooers "have several Wooden Moulds, of which you may chuse that which pleases you best, then they fill it with Coal-dust, and apply it to your Arm, so that they leave upon the same the Mark of what Is cut in the Mould; after that, with the left hand they take hold of your Arm and stretch the skin of it, and in the right hand they have a little Cane with two Needles fastened in it, which from time to time they dip into Ink, mingled with Oxes Gall, and prick your Arm all along the lines that are marked by the Wooden Mould."

Most accounts of these tattooing experiences come from the diaries and records of wealthy pilgrims who, like de Thévenot, had been able to make the trip, and whose records were notable enough to have been published, so surviving through the centuries. The presence of such marks on local metropolitan housebreakers is fascinating because they reveal that the habit had likely spread beyond those able to make a pilgrimage directly, to become a more vernacular, everyday custom back home. Most intriguing of all, the brief Old Bailey record reports that one of the defendants had claimed it was "his Business" to make the mark.

Prior to the mid- to late-nineteenth century, we can be sure that plenty of Europeans and European-Americans were tattooed outside the bounds of mainstream cultural practice. As well as those who were tattooed abroad as pilgrims, for example, some

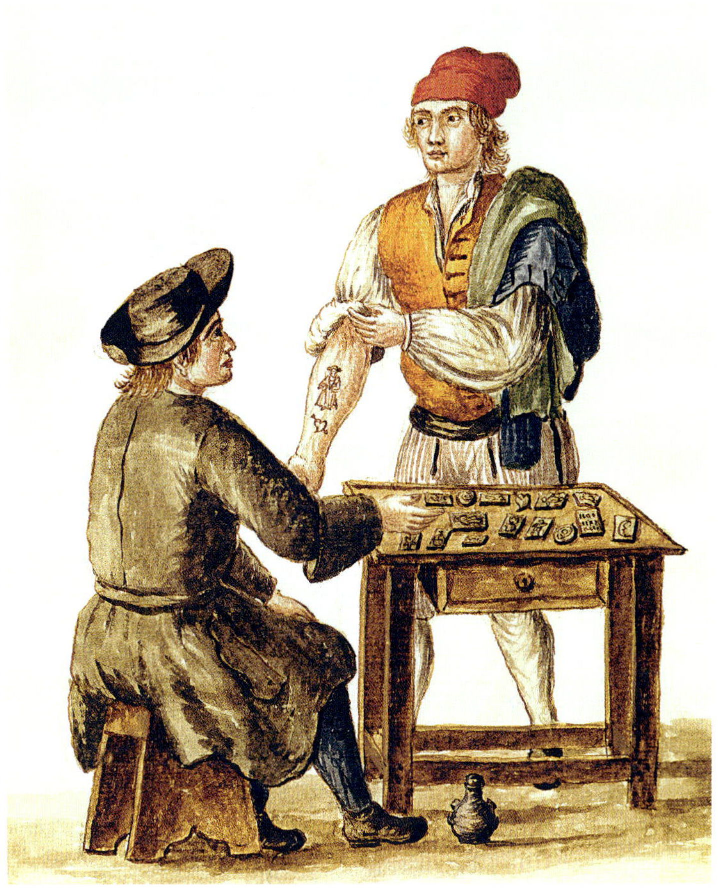

Venetian tattooist In the latter half of the eighteenth century, Flemish painter Jan van Grevenbroek was commissioned by a Venetian patron to document the clothing and daily life of people in the city. Among the various ordinary occupations depicted, van Grevenbroek illustrated a tattoo artist called Giovanni Tebaldino, with a customer showing off his newly completed design. Strikingly, Tebaldino is transferring designs to skin using carved wooden stamps, as had been used at pilgrimage sites for over a century by this time. The brief accompanying description explains that according to this artist, the Italians had learned the practice from Greeks a century before. "Almost every sailor and soldier," Grevenbroek explains, "suffered the scars of sharp needles."

tattooing was clearly undertaken in early modern Europe for more practical reasons, such as the marking of foundling children in Italian hospitals during the late sixteenth century to ward against one infant being surreptitiously swapped for another. In mid-eighteenth-century Austria, juvenile migrant workers were tattooed in such a way that their parents could identify them when they returned home from many years of labor on German farms. Most Western tattoos prior to the late nineteenth century were produced within the intimate context of the military, boarding schools, places of work, or among friends and family members.

Even if it was not their primary profession, some individuals would have been known in such communities for making permanent marks in the skin. Yet there was no formal tattooing industry in the Western world—certainly not as we would recognize it today. You could not generally walk into a permanent place of business and pay money to a stranger to be permanently marked with ink. There is currently no evidence to suggest that any professional tattooing activity of this kind was happening in the United States prior to the 1850s, nor in the United Kingdom prior to about the 1880s. There were no tattoo studios, parlors, or salons.

Still, the mention of Woodward and Williams' "business" indicates that, by the early eighteenth century, even though it was not happening in a demarcated premises, something more commercialized was going on, allowing people who had not undertaken a pilgrimage to nevertheless receive a meaningful mark. In a similar vein, an illustrated survey of the habits of Venetians made around 1753, depicts a tattoo artist working in a style reminiscent of that recorded by pilgrims in the Holy Land, his table laid out with design stamps carved into wooden blocks.

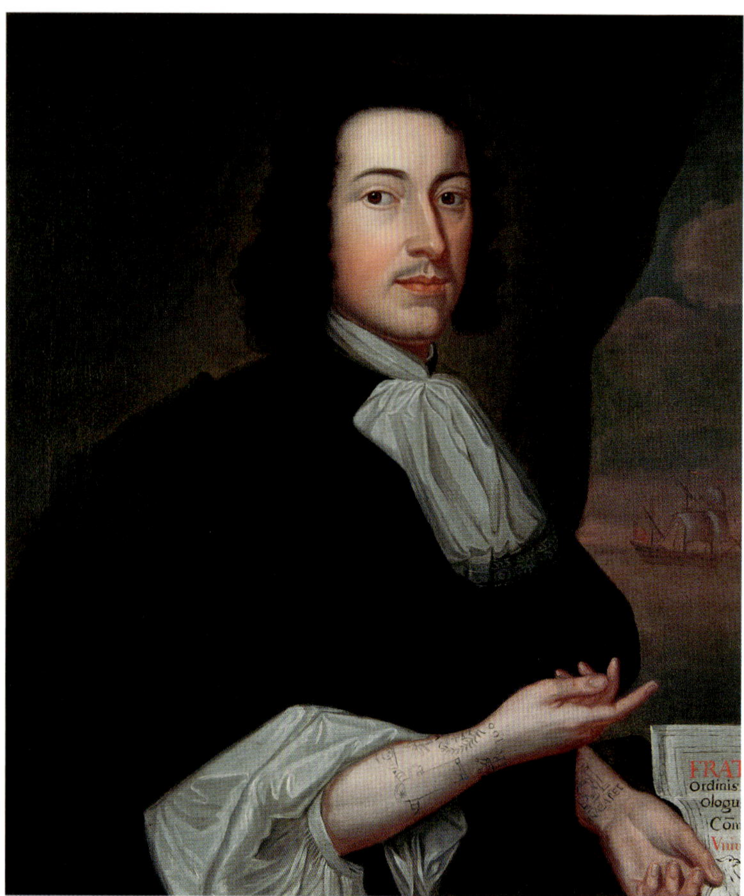

Recurring motifs (*left*) This enigmatic portrait is one of only three known depictions of tattooed pilgrims from the seventeenth century. The man, likely a French or German merchant, bears marks similar to those shown in one of the other extant portraits, that of Heinrich Ludolf—a Jerusalem cross, the date of his pilgrimage, and the skull of Adam. Additionally, he has been tattooed with the floorplan of the Holy Sepulchre.

Connected traditions (*right*) While eighteenth-century Italians claimed to have learned the practice from Greeks, they also acknowledged the long parallel history of religious tattooing in the Holy Lands. Grevenbroek explains that Maronite Christians were permanently marked when traveling to Jerusalem so that when they died, they could be afforded a Christian funeral. This 1778 depiction of tattoos on an Italian sailor shows a combination of maritime and such pilgrimage marks.

Disputed Origins

There has been much discussion about the Pacific voyages of Captain James Cook, Louis-Antoine Bougainville, and others in the late 1760s and early 1770s, and the extent to which their discoveries influenced tattooing traditions in the West. Skin-marking was already well known, both from antiquarian writing and from the practices of populations across the American and Asian continents, but it was during these expeditions that Western explorers first encountered the indigenous tattooing traditions of the Polynesian islands of Tahiti, Samoa, and Fiji, and of Aotearoa/New Zealand.

Indeed, it is from the Tahitian word for marking of the skin—*tatau*—that the word "tattoo" assimilated into the English language in the aftermath of Cook's first voyage. Since the middle of the seventeenth century, the onomatopoeic word "tattoo" in English had denoted a military drumbeat, its syllables matching the tempo of rhythmic tapping—Ta! Too!—and as Tahitian tattooing is produced by rapidly tapping a kind of mallet against a needled tool, it is likely that "*tatau*" similarly arises from an account of its sound. Once English writers heard Cook speak of "*tatau*," the word quickly took on the already familiar English spelling.

The limited archival lens through which we must view early modern tattooing does mean that it is primarily the marks on surveilled populations that were recorded at all—populations studied by anthropologists; those in military service; those under the control of the penal system; or, in the case of pilgrims, those who were significant and literate enough to leave diaries which would end up in libraries.

Enormous swathes of early modern tattooing are thus invisible to history. Nevertheless, there is still plenty of evidence of "marks" being made using

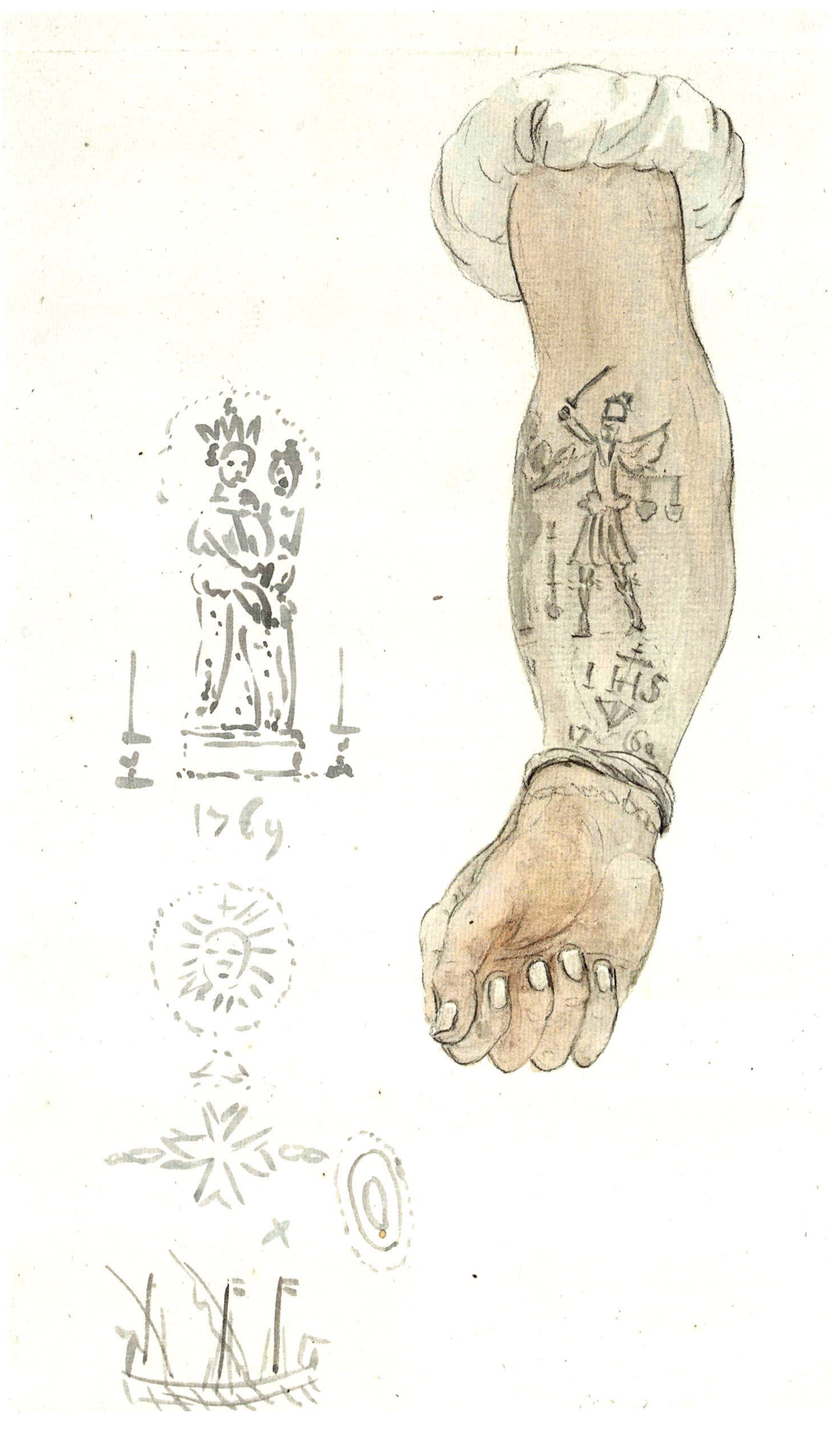

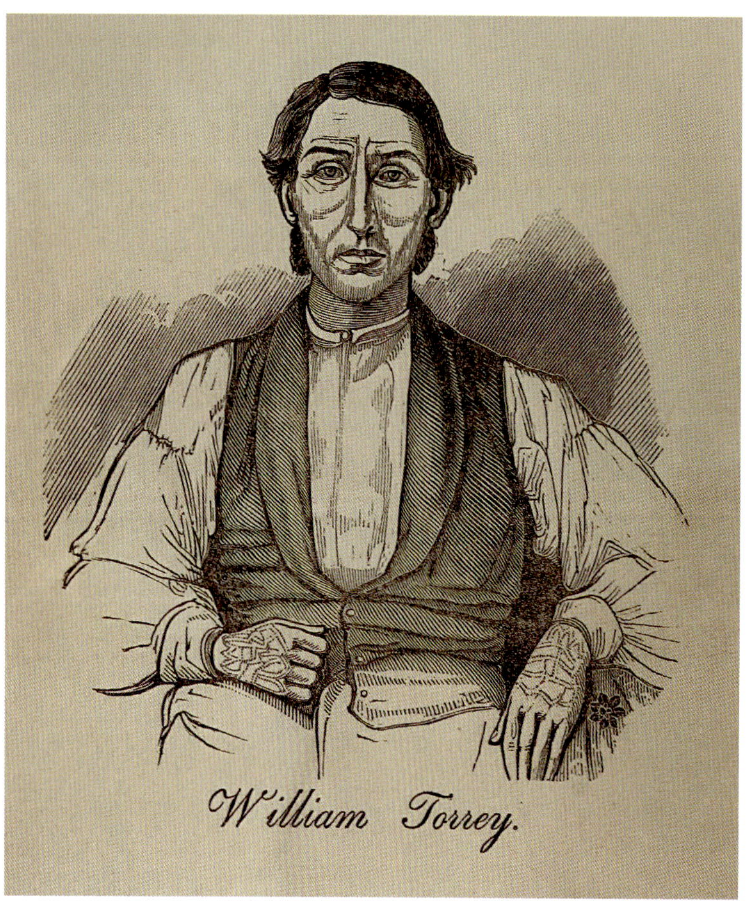

Coerced tattooing In 1835, William Torrey was shipwrecked on an island in the Marquesas, where he claimed to have subsequently been captured by "cannibals," who forced him to be tattooed in order to "join the tribe." Many similar narratives of tattooed so-called "transculturites" (European men who were extensively tattooed in local fashions in the Pacific and in the Americas), were published throughout the nineteenth century. In these stories, tattoos tend to serve as indications of "savagery" and the otherness of indigenous populations, even as authors like Torrey speak of the welcome and care given to them while they were stranded.

Indian ink or gunpowder in the decades immediately preceding the Pacific voyages and back through pilgrim accounts to the early seventeenth century.

Importantly, not only was there evidence of tattooing in western Europe prior to the 1760s, but in the decades immediately following the Pacific voyages records exist of anthropologists of the period actually comparing these newly encountered indigenous traditions with both similar habits in the New World and with familiar Western maritime and pilgrim marks. In 1813, for example, German naturalist Georg Heinrich von Langsdorff noted in his accounts of the Marquesas Islands in the southern Pacific Ocean that tattooing there was reminiscent of the tattooing he knew about from elsewhere. "It is undoubtedly very striking," he wrote, "that nations perfectly remote from each other, who have no means of intercourse whatever . . . should yet all be agreed in this practice.

Among Europeans, that is to say pilgrims to the Holy Sepulchre, and the sailors of almost all the nations of Europe . . . among the nations of both the northern and southern hemispheres, both of the east and the west, in the old and the new world, are to be found traces of this custom; in some places more, in some places less, but among all and in a certain degree."

Aside from marked pilgrims, there are mentions of marked Englishmen and Irishmen throughout the early decades of the eighteenth century, in such places as dockworker description books, criminal reports, and newspaper advertisements seeking the whereabouts of escaped servants in the colonies. One striking example is that of twenty-one-year-old Irishman Francis Power, an indentured servant in the American colonies, who ran away from his masters Thomas Barnsley and Herman Vansant in August 1766. To try and secure his return, the men took out an advertisement in the

Recorded for posterity (*top right*) One of the reasons for the persistence of the idea that tattooing was primarily a habit "confined to criminals and sailors" is simply that these were the kinds of marks which were systematically recorded for history. Among such surveilled populations, the documentation of tattooing allowed easier identification of repeat offenders or escapees. From the nineteenth century onward, tattoos were often listed by way of simple description, though occasionally, such as in this detail from a ledger of prisoners at Bodmin Gaol in Cornwall, an artistically inclined warden might choose to draw the distinguishing marks instead.

A criminal habit (*bottom right*) Elaborate depictions of criminal tattoos were often also drawn on intake forms and behavioral logs, which afforded more space to depict designs than the ledger books. Here, a gaoler at Suffolk County Gaol in the east of England has elaborately illustrated the tattoos on one particularly extensively marked prisoner, logged into his sentence on July 2, 1842.

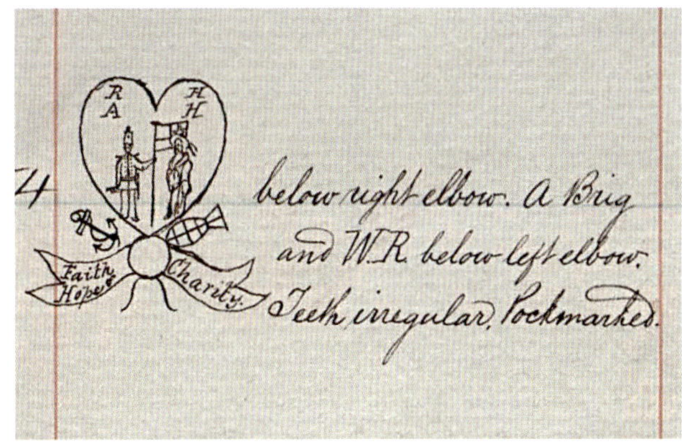

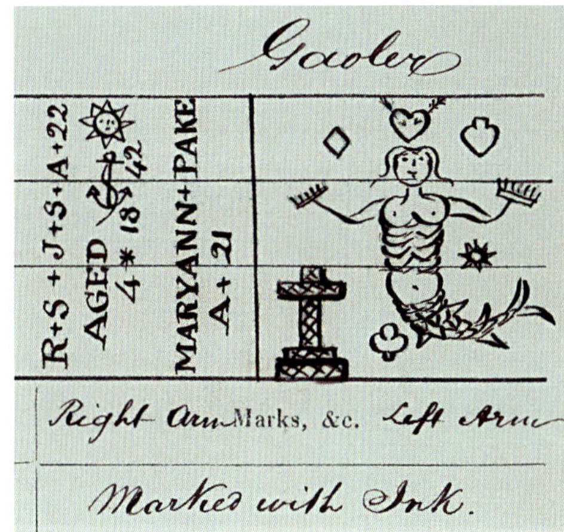

Pennsylvania Gazette offering a reward for his successful capture. In the brief advertisement, Power is described as "5 feet 6 inches high, short light colored hair, pock-marked, a little hook nosed, [with] a stoop in his shoulders, [he] is a great lover of strong drink [and] has been aboard a man of war." Fascinatingly, Power was "marked with Indian ink, or gunpowder on both arms, under his shirt, with the figure of our Savior crucified, and the upper part of his right thumb has the date of the year 1761 on it." Another Irishman escaped in the colonies gets us even closer in date to connecting tattooing before and after the Cook voyages—Johan Abbott, a transported convict, escaped in Virginia in January 1769 just three months before Cook's fleet arrived in Tahiti. Abbott had his initials, JA, marked with Indian Ink on his left arm—a practice commonly described in maritime records and gaol logs throughout the nineteenth century.

Dominant Styles

It is the case that a small number of curious members of the officer class had tattoos of an indigenous nature. They included Cook's draftsman Sydney Parkinson, and the famed botanist and his scientific officer on the voyage Joseph Banks. Both men had been tattooed by local tattooers during the trip. Infamously too, many of William Bligh's crew on the mutinous voyage of HMS *Bounty* were tattooed in the Tahitian style during their bucolic five months there in 1789. And there are also several more well-documented narratives of so-called "transculturites"—European men who were extensively tattooed in local fashions in the Pacific and in the Americas. Reasons for wanting these tattoos range from base curiosity to a desire to integrate into indigenous cultures having deserted their naval positions.

But European sailors were not inspired to take up the indigenous tattooing traditions of the South Seas—

"Tribal" tattoos (*below*) In his book *The New Zealanders*, John Rutherford recounts having been captured by Ngāpuhi Māori in New Zealand in 1816, and tattooed against his will. Given that the extensive facial tattooing he wore could only have been completed over several days, and given that facial moko is considered a particularly important mark of status, it is unlikely that Rutherford's claims to unwillingness are credible.

Political scandal (*right*) The fishwife in this 1773 cartoon by William Austin prominently displays "WL 45" on her wrist. Here the tattoo mark serves, as they often do in fiction, as indicatory shorthand of principled true beliefs, as well as suggestions as to the class and status of their bearers.

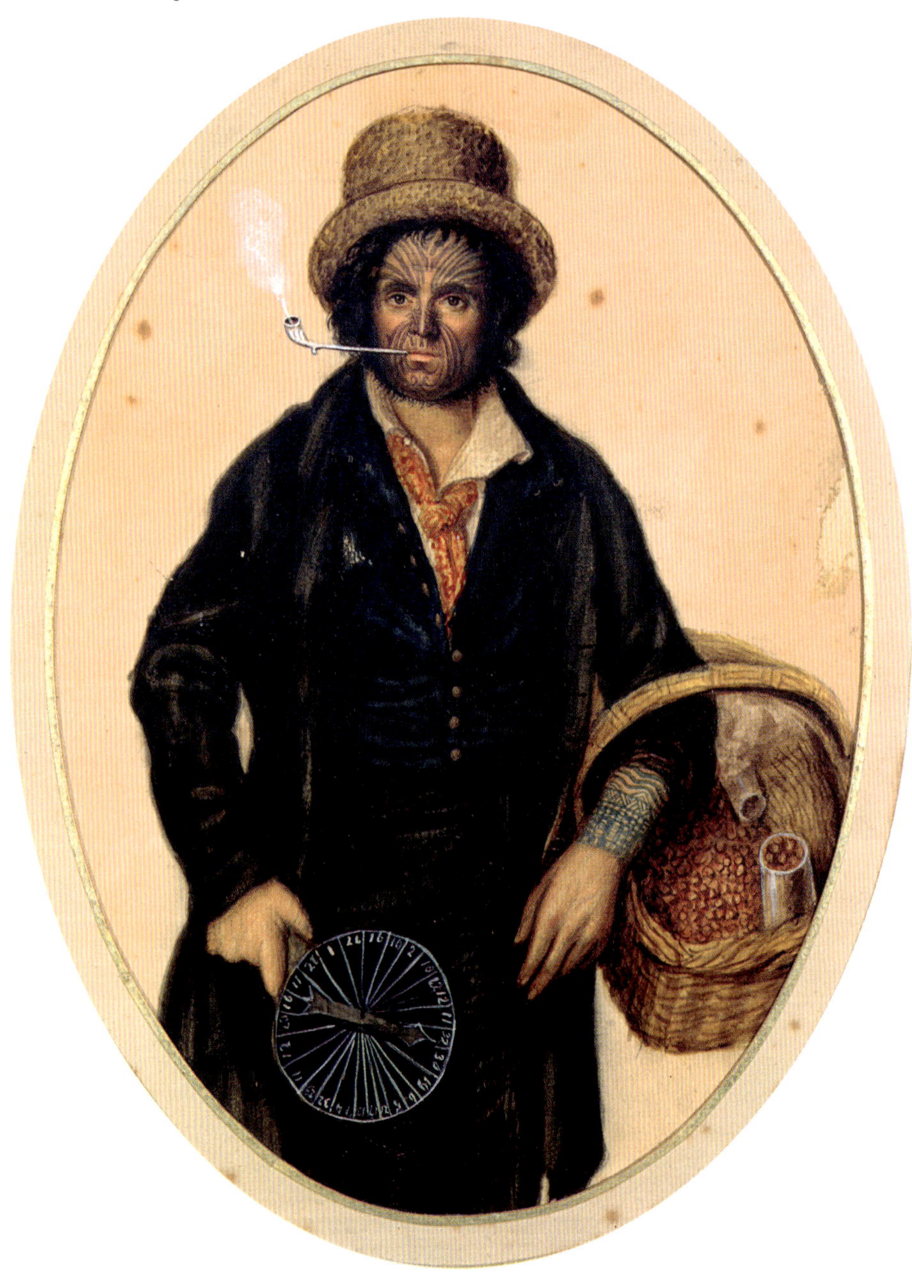

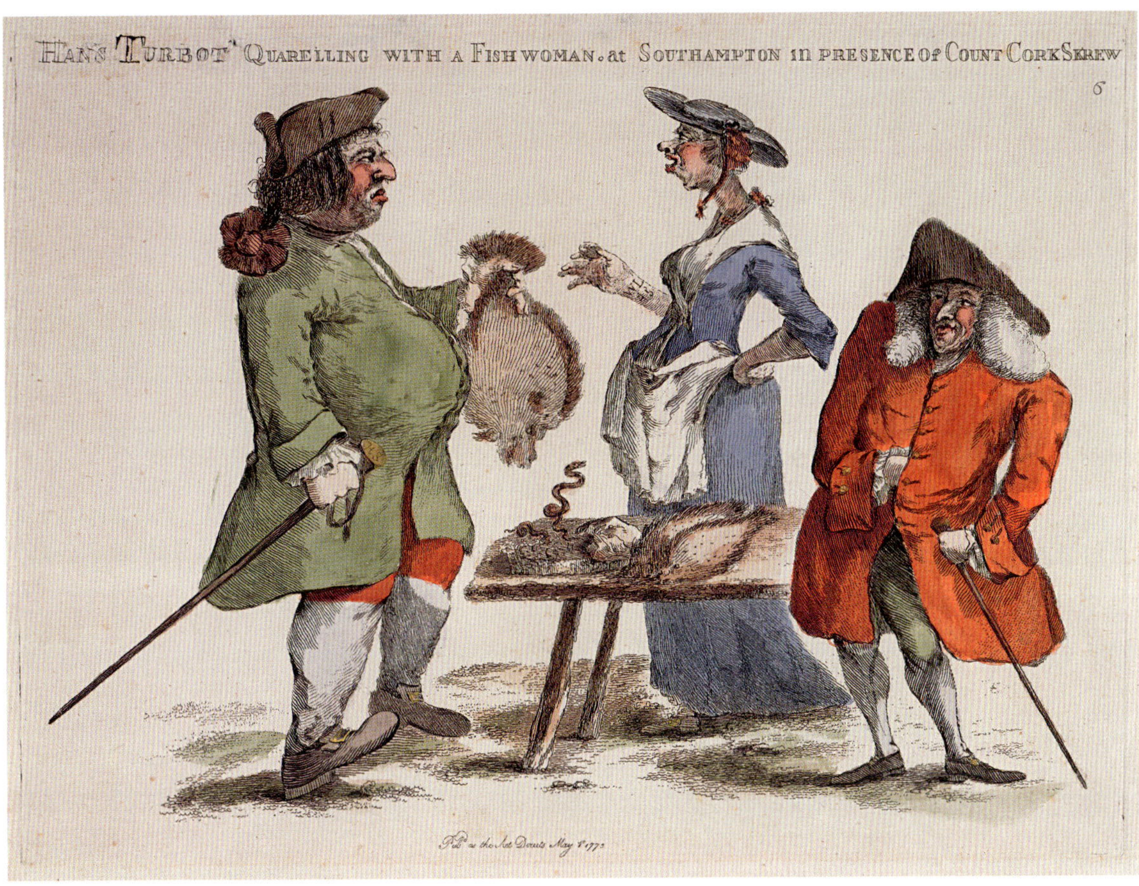

the tattoos that become visible during the increasingly comprehensive records taken during the Napoleonic Wars of the early 1800s remained religious, naval or romantic, unchanged in design, size, and location from those that had been sparsely documented before the encounters in Polynesia. Designs recorded from the early seventeenth through the late nineteenth centuries are drawn from the visual cultural lexicon of Christian and seafaring communities, and include crosses and images of saints, pierced hearts, anchors, ships, mermaids, stars, and moons, as well as names, inscriptions, and portraits.

As we should perhaps expect, European tattoos are lifted from, and mirror, the visual cultural contexts from which they emerge. To illustrate, we can compare Francis Power's tattoos from 1766 and the designs shown on the Venetian tattooer's table from 1753 with those from the years immediately following Cook's

voyages. In 1773, for example, a satirical broadside by William Austin depicts a fisherwoman with initials and a date tattooed on her wrist, a likely reference to a political scandal of the day. "WL 45" is likely a reference to a loud political slogan at the time: "Wilkes, Liberty, and Number 45!" Issue 45 of radical journalist John Wilkes' political freesheet *The North Briton*, published in 1763, caused a major scandal, as it successfully called for the resignation of Prime Minister Bute over what Wilkes understood to be weaknesses during the Seven Years War with the French, and by implication, the failures of King George III himself. Wilkes was censured by parliament for libel, leading to enormous and persistent protest and debate as to the freedom of the press. Austin's joke here is rather inscrutable to a modern audience, but given that fishwives were notorious in caricature for being angry and verbose, the choice to inscribe a homage to a biting satire which became a rallying cause for freedom of speech advocates is apt.

In 1797, a man named Thomas Maley was convicted in London of high treason and piracy, with his criminal record listing a number of tattoos, including the iconic pierced heart—which also appears on the arm of the Venetian's customer from half a century earlier—as well as a crucifix and a mermaid. By 1808, Royal Navy captain Edward Rotherham recorded that a quarter of the men aboard his ship were tattooed with marks that included, like Power's, crucifixes, names, dates, and initials, as well as elaborate scenes of things like centaurs. There are no records of Samoan- or Maori-inspired designs.

In another vivid example—one of the rare few from the period that are illustrated—we can see direct connections between Power's tattoos and those on runaway convict Miles Confrey, whose three-quarter portrait in an edition of *Punch* magazine published in 1854 shows a crucifix, initials, and dates, alongside motifs of tall ships and a chest design seemingly depicting an armed robbery. And in 1844, another discharged sailor was described in court as having his arms tattooed "with the figure of our Savior, and representations of the sun, moon, and various stars."

In short, therefore, prior to the nineteenth century, and certainly before the Pacific encounters of the late eighteenth century, European tattooing is hard to spot in the historical record. Though present, it was clearly not a widespread trend, and it had no major public visibility. The practice has no single name, being called "pricking" and "staining" in English, as well as "marking." Most tattoos were hidden by clothing, and it was not common to show much of your body in public at the time—tattoos rarely appear in paintings and drawings for the same reason. The lives of the lower and middle classes were not systematically recorded, or, if they were, those records were not preserved. There is as yet no good account from an English source that describes the actual techniques or any cultures of pre-Cook marking, despite increasing discoveries of sources that mention the presence of designs. So, there is a great deal we do not know about Western tattooing in this early modern period, and our knowledge of the practice during the late medieval centuries is nonexistent. Nevertheless, we can be sure that the design languages of Western traditional tattooing, dominated as they are by religious, sentimental, and mythological images, form a continuous and essentially unbroken connection going back more than four hundred years from the present day.

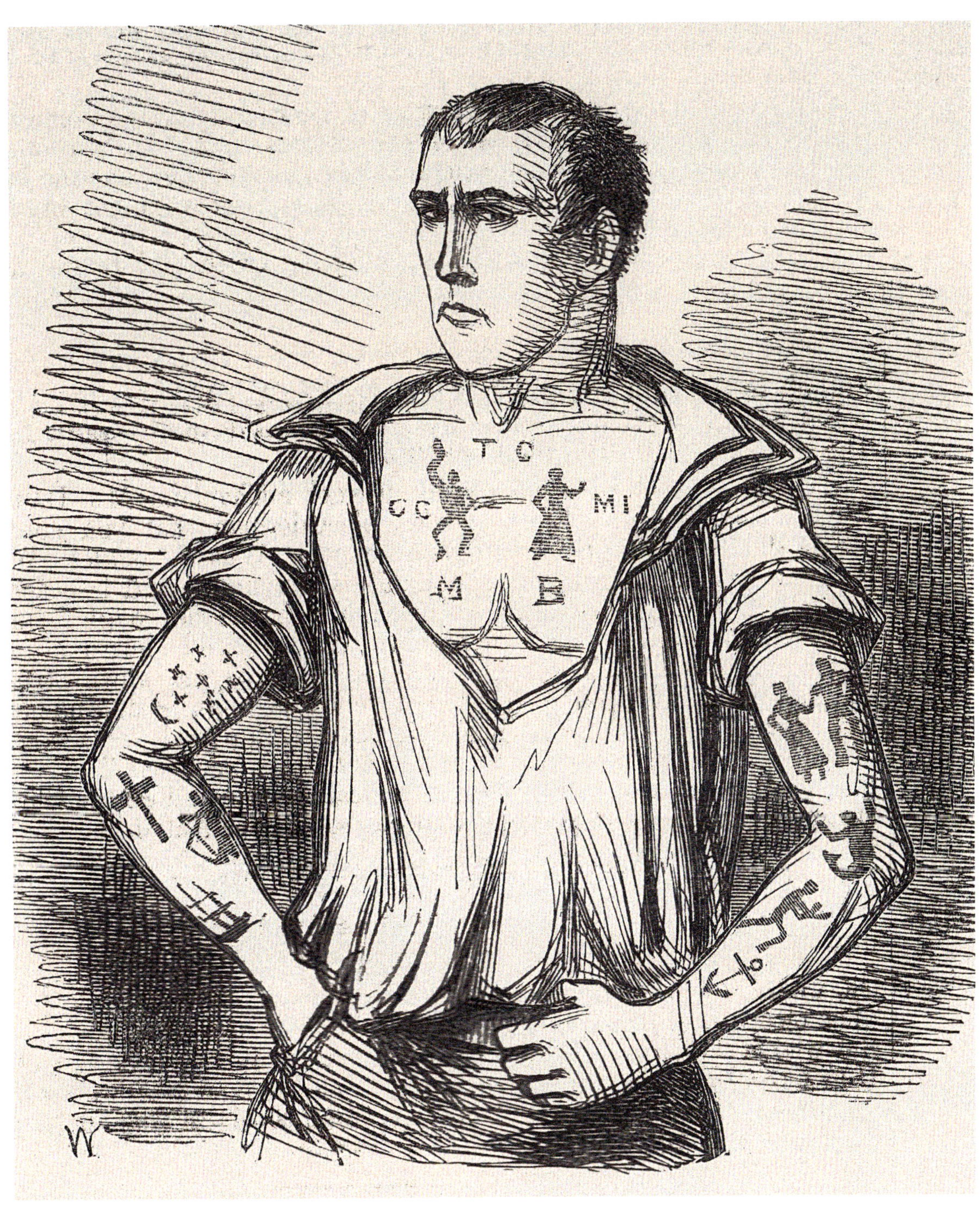

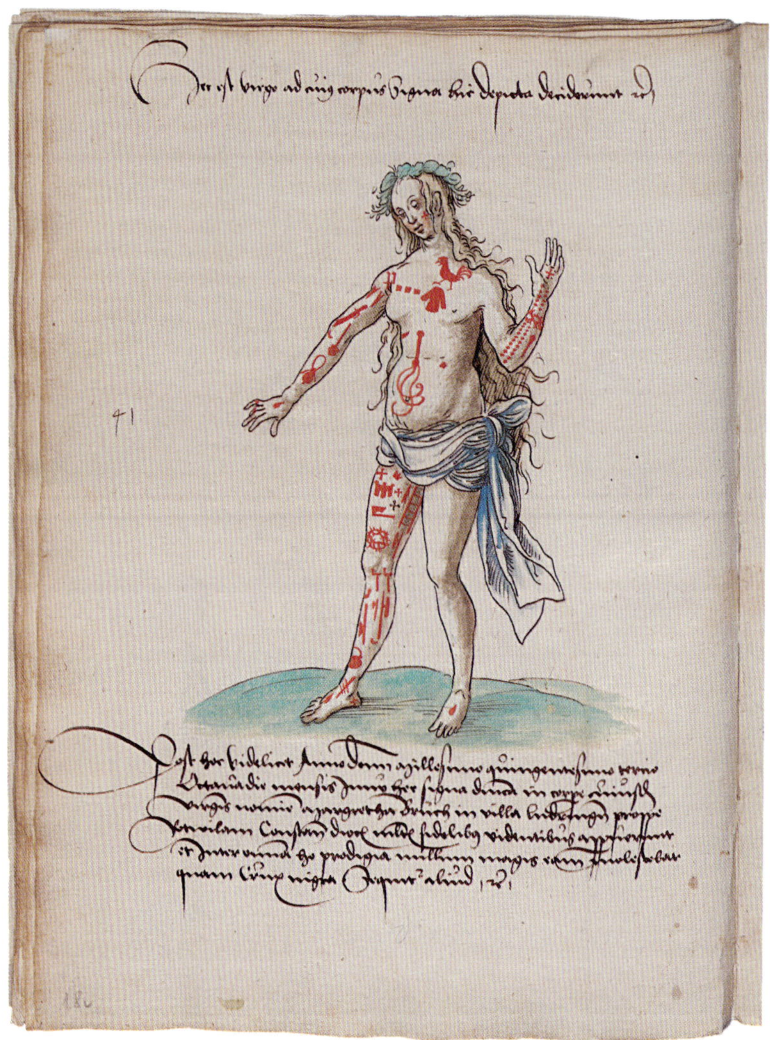

De Signis, portentis atque prodigiis … ("Miraculous Signs"), Jakob Mennel, 1503

This early-sixteenth-century image does not illustrate tattoos, but rather the miraculous marks which appeared on several German stigmatics, including the strange case of Margaretha Bruch, a teenage girl from Leidringen in Southern Germany. According to contemporary reports, Margaretha was blessed with stigmata—miraculous wounds reflecting and empathizing with Christ's suffering on the cross. Beyond the marks of nails on her hands and feet, on her forehead was the mark of a crown of thorns, on her chest, a flagellating whip, and on her thigh, a ladder by which Jesus would have been hoisted to his crucifixion. This early-modern fascination with religious designs on the body prefigures the emergence of deliberate mark-making with religious designs in the following decades.

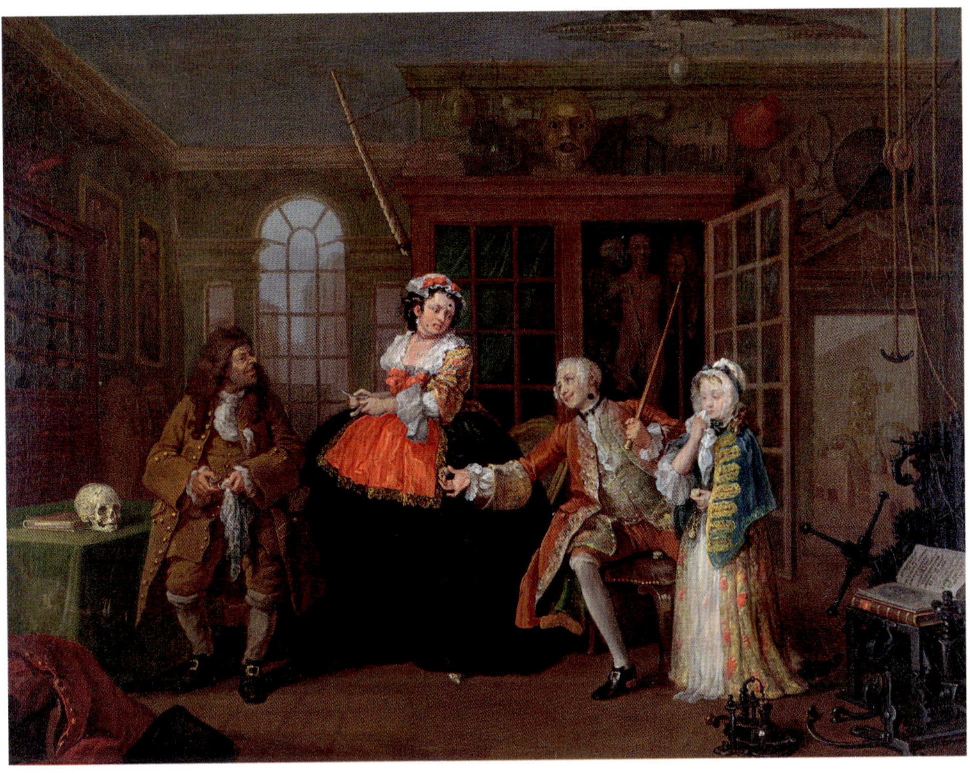

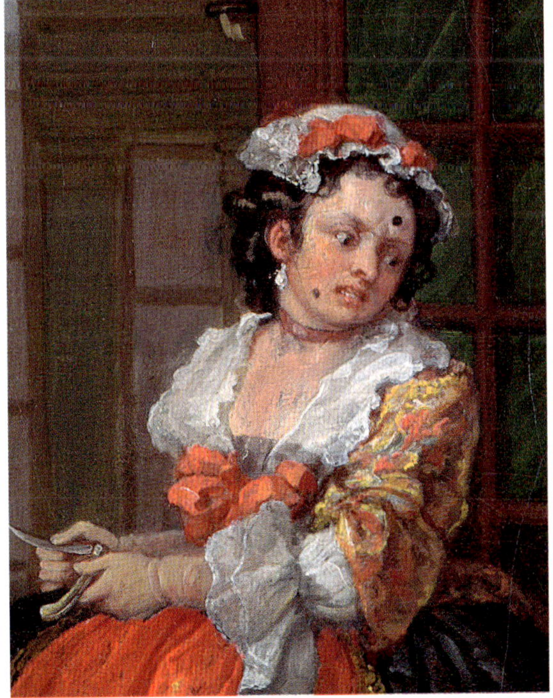

The Inspection, William Hogarth, 1743

The third image in William Hogarth's sequence "Marriage-a-la-mode," *The Inspection* shows a young nobleman visiting a quack physician. Of interest here is the older woman in the center of the image wielding a knife, who sports a faintly inscribed blue tattoo of two initials on her chest, E (or maybe F).C. Hogarth himself claimed to have forgotten the precise meaning of the details in this picture, and art historians are divided on this woman's role, but in every interpretation, she is hardly a sympathetic and upstanding character. Though some have suggested that the "F.C" means she is marked as a "female convict," this is incorrect, as such punitive tattooing was not undertaken in England. Where initials were tattooed in the period, they were likely a reference to the wearer's own name, or the name of a lover. Here, it has been suggested that Hogarth is referencing Fanny Cook, the daughter of an auctioneer Hogarth knew, or, most convincingly, Elizabeth "Betsy" Careless, an infamous sex-worker, brothel-owner, and courtesan to London's aristocracy at the time. Alternatively, "E.C" additionally works as a pun for "easy," a critique of the character's loose virtue.

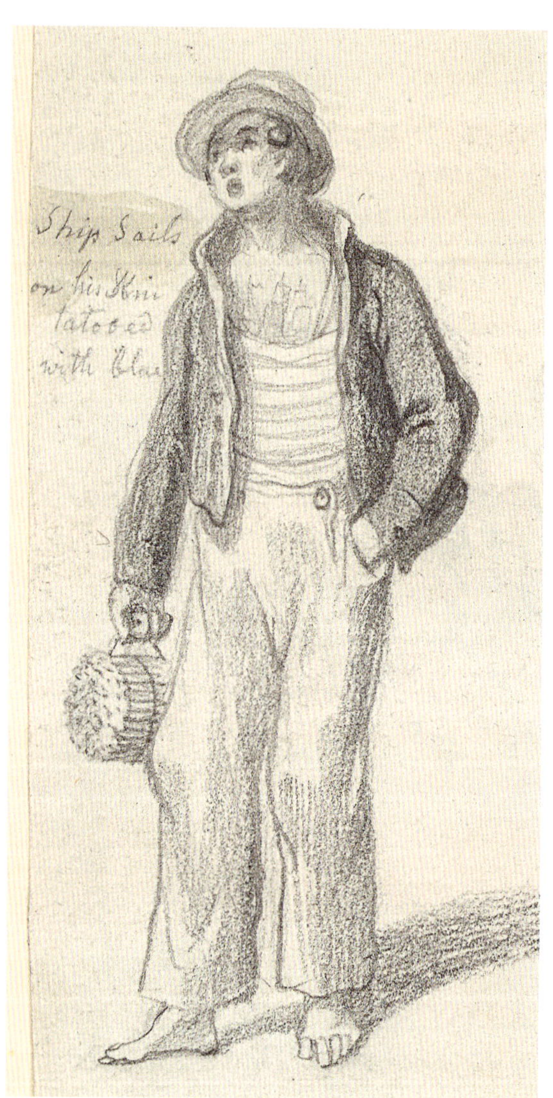

***Tattooed Georgian Sailor*, George Scharf, 1833 (*left*)**

Even before the era of professional tattoo shops and electric machines, designs could still be large in scale, as attested by the full chestpiece of a rigged galleon peeking out of the young man's vest. During this period, it has been estimated that over a quarter of enlisted sailors had at least one tattoo.

***Interieur d'une Chambre Militaire* ("Interior of a Military Baracks"), Baron Louis Albert Guislain Bacler d'Albe, 1818 (*top right*)**

Among the various activities being undertaken by the soldiers in this military barracks, including making their beds and having a haircut, one man is adding to his mate's collection of tattoos. Prior to the establishment of a professional tattoo trade, most tattooing in Europe was of this kind—intimate, and between confidants. As Napoleon's personal mapmaker, d'Albe spent a long period of his life embedded on military service, and the scene is therefore likely representative of a common habit among French forces during the Napoleonic Wars. Due to health concerns, the French Navy quixotically attempted to ban tattooing several decades later.

***Bellerophon Doves, Sailors' Encampment before Sebastopol*, H. Mandeville, 1854 (*bottom right*)**

The "Bellerophon Doves" were a naval crew who manned guns ashore which had been removed from HMS *Bellerophon*. This image depicts the happy gunners preparing for the infamous Siege of Sebastopol during the Crimean War in 1854. One can imagine that the ability to stay on dry land was particularly appealing, hence the relaxed countenances. On the sailors' arms, revealed by their rolled-up sleeves, are typical naval tattoos of the period.

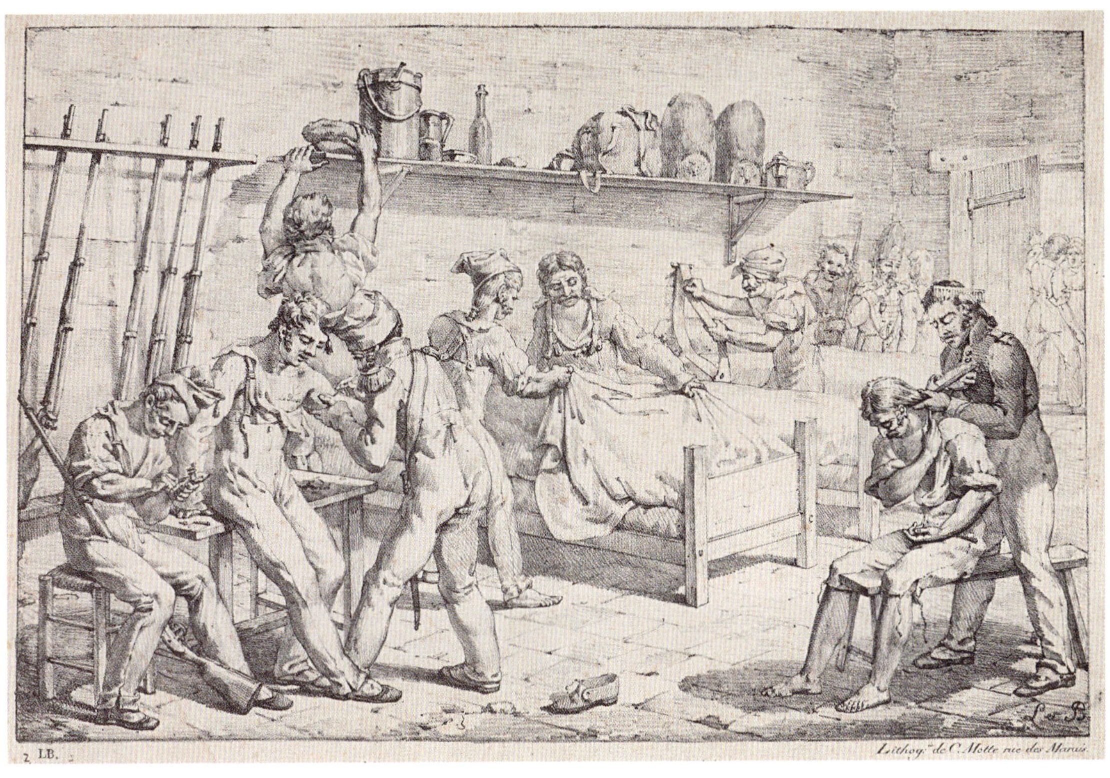

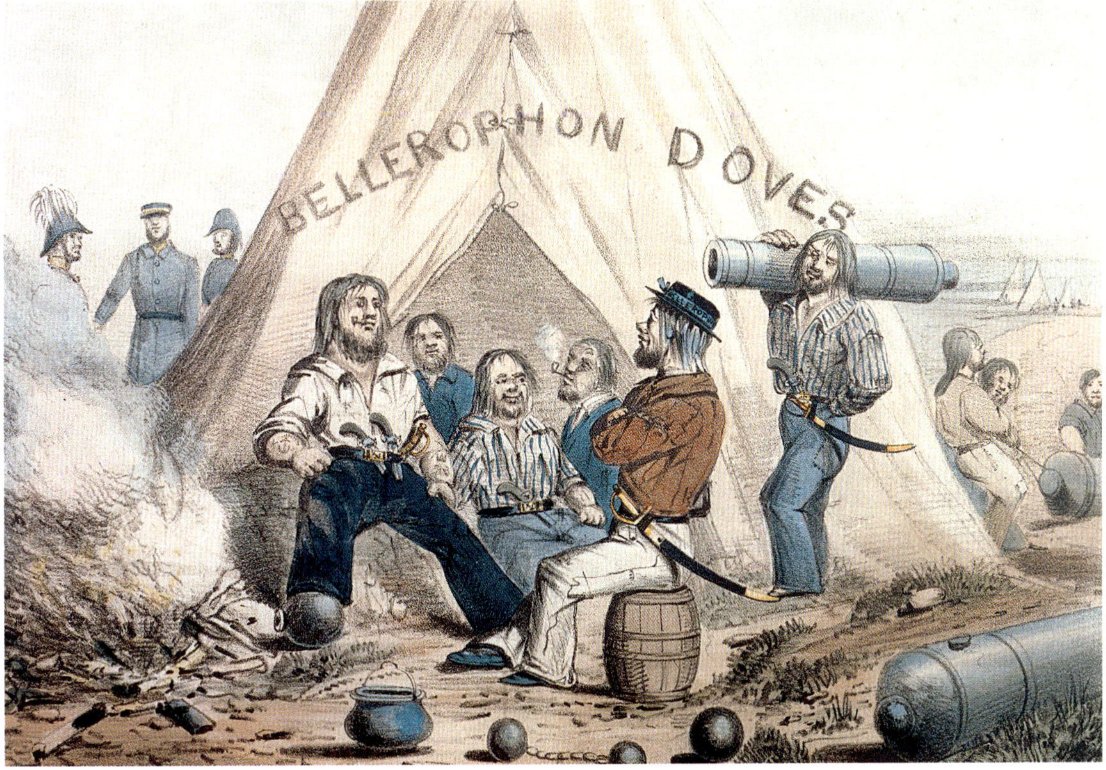
BELLEROPHON D OVES

The Birth of the Professional Era

1858–1880

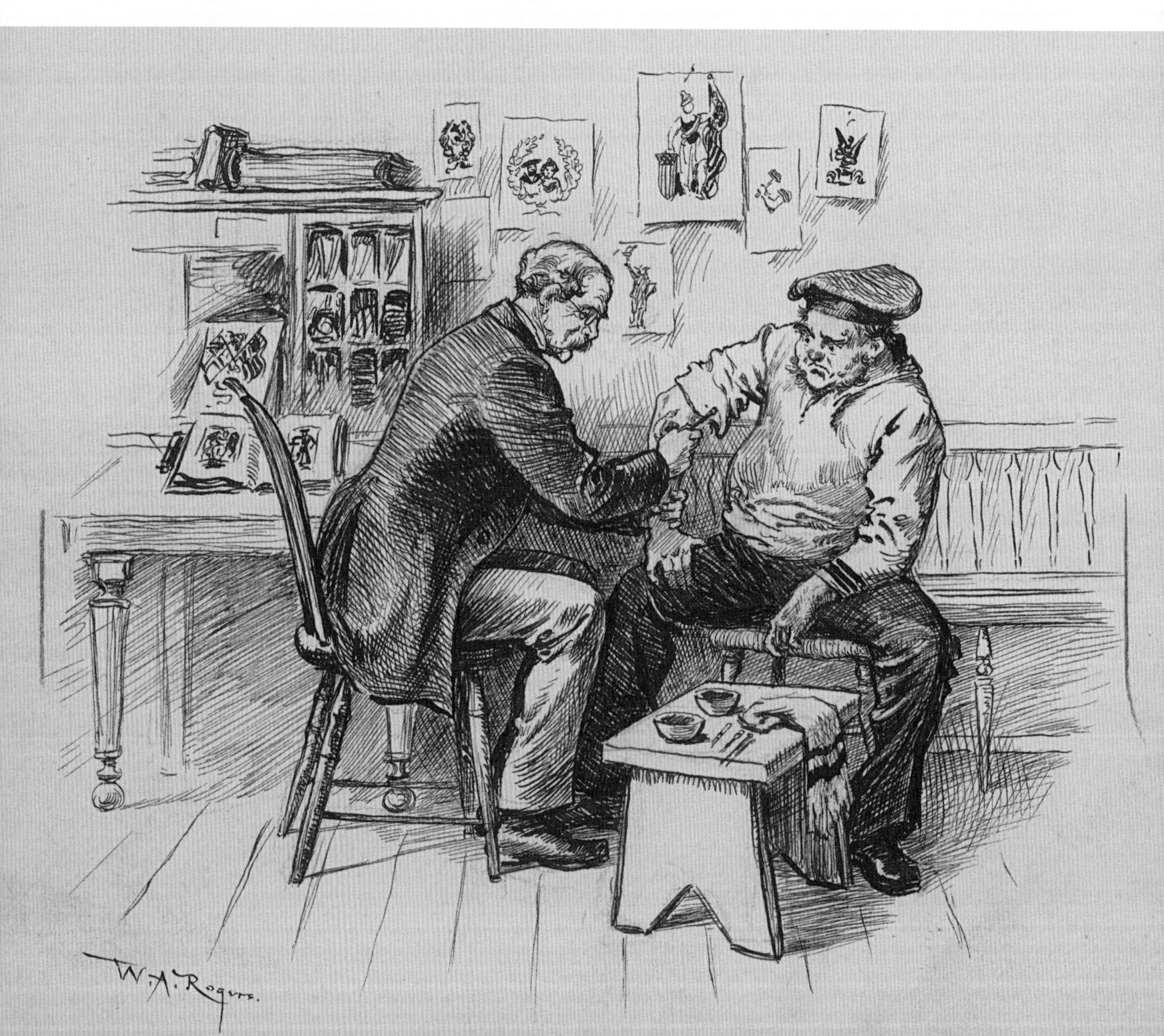

> "This Metropolis is addicted to short-lived hobbies.
> They are born almost every month, and about the
> time they become passably introduced are displaced
> for a later attraction. The latest fashionable fallacy
> I discovered [the] day before yesterday. It is tattooing."
>
> *The New York Times*, 1882

Professional rivalry Edwin Thomas was Martin
Hildebrandt's main rival for the New York tattoo trade
through the 1880s. This scene unfolds on South Street
in New York's Lower East Side, where Thomas boasts
of a genteel business "tattooing elderly and well-to-do
merchants and ladies in silk attire."

Martin Hildebrandt, an eloquent, mustachioed
German immigrant to the United States, is
widely considered to be the first professional
tattooer in the Western world. "Hildebrandt, Martin.
Tattooing" was listed in the *New York Directory* for the
year ending May 1859. His address, 361 Water Street,
was a notoriously insalubrious boarding and drinking
house in a violent, pier-side neighborhood known as
Slaughterhouse Point. This unremarkable directory
entry, packed in amid the workaday streetscape of
New York's grocers, carpenters, and laborers, marks,
perhaps, the moment at which the ancient, intimate,
and vernacular art of tattooing emerged into the full
light of public commerce in the Western world.

As we have seen, tattooing had already enjoyed
a long and continuous existence in Europe and the
United States by this time. However, the practice,
though not entirely unremunerated, was confined
primarily to private spaces among shipmates,
cellmates, schoolboys, and friends, or was carried
out commercially on pilgrimages to the Middle East.
Now, with New York expanding rapidly, its harbor
came to welcome more passenger ships than every
other port in the country combined. For the first time,
there were sufficient numbers of potential customers in
one place, so making tattooing a viable, public-facing
trade. Hildebrandt himself had learned tattooing from
a fellow "salt" while serving in the navy in the 1840s,
and had tattooed aboard ships for nearly twenty years.
He, too, was covered in designs from shoulder to
toes by the time he made it his "exclusive profession"
in around 1866, by his own account. Even in 1870,
though, his street directory entry at 43 Oak St lists
him as "painter," suggesting a wider use of his artistic
talents than simply just on skin.

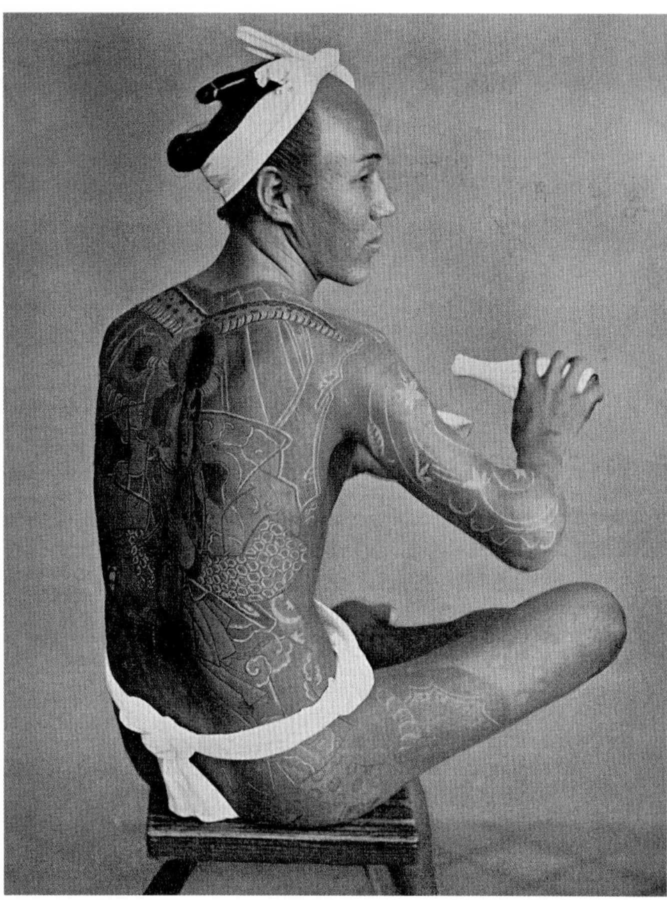

A modern art (*left*) Though tattooing became emblematic of traditional Japanese culture, when Europeans forced the opening of the country the practice of large-scale, pictorial tattooing—Irezumi—was not much more than a century old. Most heavily tattooed men, such as this unnamed man from the nineteenth century, were from the lower orders of society, including firefighters, craftsmen, mail-carriers, and members of chivalrous street gangs called Otokodate. Their large tattoos often imitated finer garments worn by fashionable merchants.

Cross-cultural encounters (*right*) Japanese men, including a heavily tattooed figure on the left, encounter European visitors in *View of Miyozaki in Yokohama* (Miyozaki Yokohama ichiran) by Utagawa Yoshimori (1860). Yoshimori was fascinated by these kinds of cross-cultural encounters at a moment of rapid and unsettling cultural change, and these pictures became a style of their own, known as *Yokohama-e*. Japanese audiences were enthralled by the strangeness of foreigners, and for foreign visitors tattoos represented authentic, old Japanese culture.

A Growing Reputation

The seminal moment for Hildebrandt, and for Western tattoo history more broadly, was the opening of Japan after the Meiji Restoration. Japan had been largely closed off to foreign trade and visitors since the early seventeenth century but, in 1853, an American flotilla under the command of Commodore Matthew Perry sailed into Japanese waters with firm insistence that the military Japanese government open the country's borders to trade or face a conflict they were certain to lose. Hildebrandt often claimed (perhaps mendaciously) of being aboard one of the ships in the squadron.

The cultural aftermath of this encounter drove an overwhelming fascination for all things Japanese in the Western world. Most surprising of all were the extensive, elaborate tattoos worn by actors, mailmen, firemen, and others in Japan's eastern capital Edo (modern-day Tokyo), that were far removed from the familiar European tattoos in both scope and aesthetic execution. It is from this first encounter between the elaborate Western maritime tattooing tradition and the decorative tattooing of the East that the raging inferno of contemporary tattooing arose.

The growing influence of Japanese art and design on tattooing in Europe, the United Kingdom, and the United States is discussed in more detail in the next chapter. For Hildebrandt, initially at least, his client base on land was not all that different from the rough-hewn enlisted men he would have tattooed at sea. The American Civil War of 1861–1865 interrupted his trade at a listed premises—and the advancement of the profession—though he continued to make a living as a traveling artist, tattooing soldiers on both sides of the conflict. In these first, stuttering moments of professional tattooing, very little was novel in terms

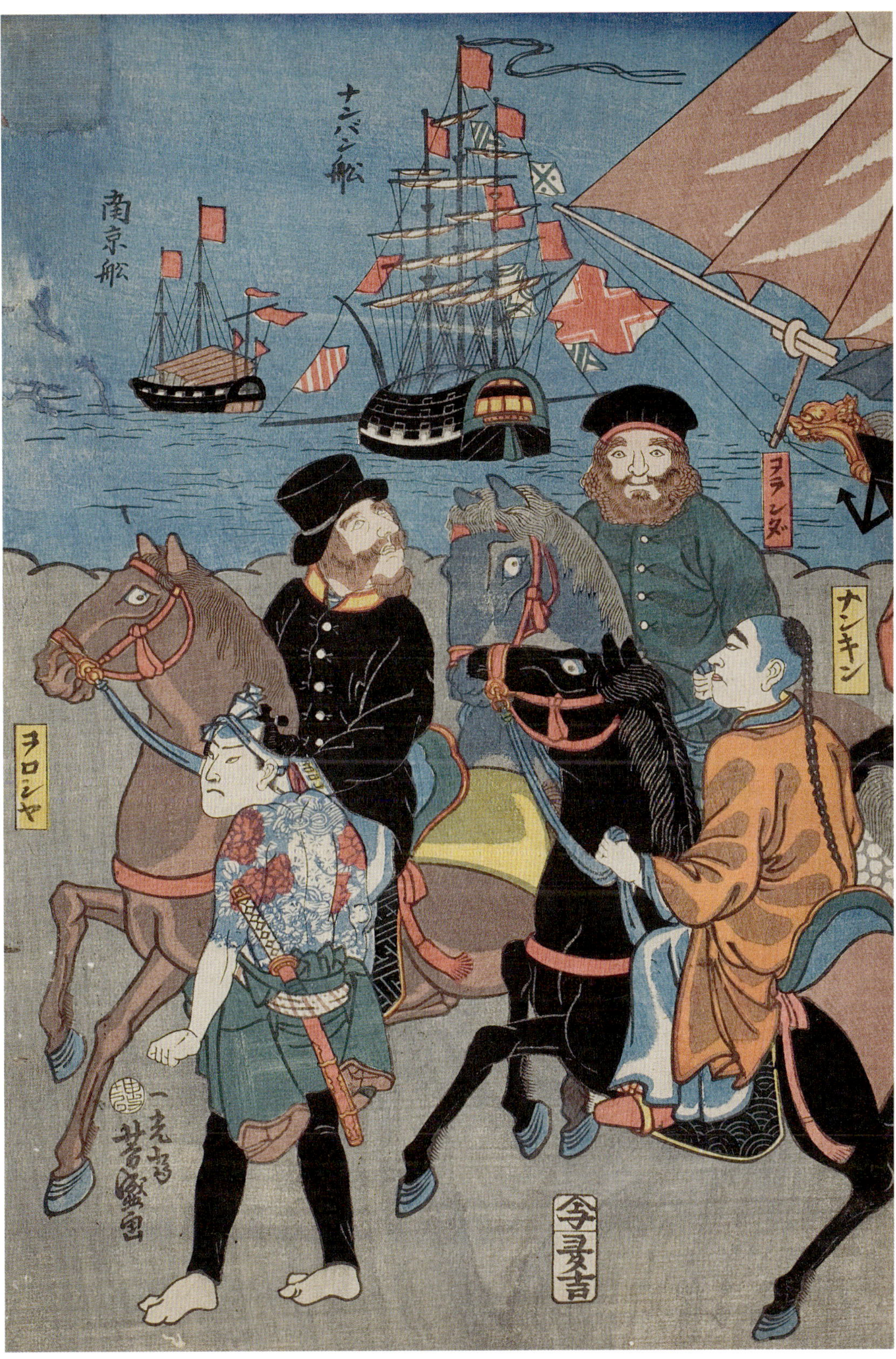
ナンバン船
南京船
ヲロシヤ
ヲランダ
ナンキン
今戎吉
一光斎芳盛画

A bare-skinned imposter Sir Roger Tichborne (*opposite, left*) was skinny and rakish when lost at sea in 1854. When he returned a decade later (*opposite, right*), he was mysteriously much larger, and had little memory of his early life. A famous set of tattoos helped to explain what had really happened.

of demographics or designs when compared to those of the previous century and a half.

By 1872, however, things were changing. By this time Hildebrandt had established himself on Oak Street, tattooing discreetly from a studio inside a drinking saloon, though by now surrounded by paintings of odalisques, and with sufficient fame and reach to merit celebratory articles in the city's press. The *New York Sun* went so far as to call his work "beautiful," and besides his tanned mariner clients, he boasted of "many highly respectable gentlemen" who had called upon him to tattoo their club emblems on them. The *New York Times* called him a "distinguished master of the art," in comparison to lesser "bungling" competitors in Boston, Philadelphia, and Chicago, and described an exquisite design book full of images to choose from, including flags, religious scenes, and a plethora of pinups, ballerinas, and weeping widows. Modern tattooing had truly begun—indeed, Hildebrandt incorrectly predicted that tattooing would continue to become popular until the millennium, by which time "we will all be a pure white, with not a disfiguring mark upon us."

Tattoos for All?

Before the establishment of the professional tattoo industry, tattooing was carried out on a fairly ad-hoc basis among close-knit groups in the privacy of their own lodgings, although it is clear the designs being acquired were not small or insignificant. One report from 1873 describes "on the breast of a bronzed and stalwart seaman in her Majesty's service, in fine dark blue etching, a full-rigged three-decker, with her portholes, guns, mast, spars and rigging, correctly

drawn, while a somewhat disproportionate cable from the same ship passed over his shoulder and down his broad back, where she was securely anchored." In another example, a "well-marked" shoplifter arrested in Liverpool in 1880 was reported to have had body and limbs "tattooed all over with the outlines of nearly every known animal, amongst the number being a lion, tiger, leopard, elephant and monkey, all of whom are said to have been delineated with surprising fidelity."

Moreover, even before tattoo studios were common, the art was already sufficiently widespread that popular magazines published tips and recipes for their removal. Pleas for advice on removing tattooing and helpful recipes for tinctures to do so were not uncommon, but their prevalence suggests that even in the glow of royal patronage, tattooing was something many people wanted to efface. In 1865, *Reynolds's Miscellany* suggested that readers "blister the part with a plaster, a little larger than the mark; then keep the place open with a green ointment for a week; finally, dress it to get it well." Though we should be skeptical that this method is effective, the piece did gleefully assert, implausibly, that "as the new skin grows, the tattoo will disappear." The stigmatizing tattooing of deserters from the British Army was practiced until 1871, and there was also an unfortunate spate of "practical jokes" played in the British Navy in 1867, whereby young midshipmen would be lashed to a mast, an arrow shape cut into their nose, and gunpowder rubbed into the wound, leaving a permanent tattoo. Presumably the poor victims of these pranks would have been willing to try anything to return their faces to some kind of unblemished state. That same year, the *English Mechanic* shared a query from a subscriber seeking tattoo

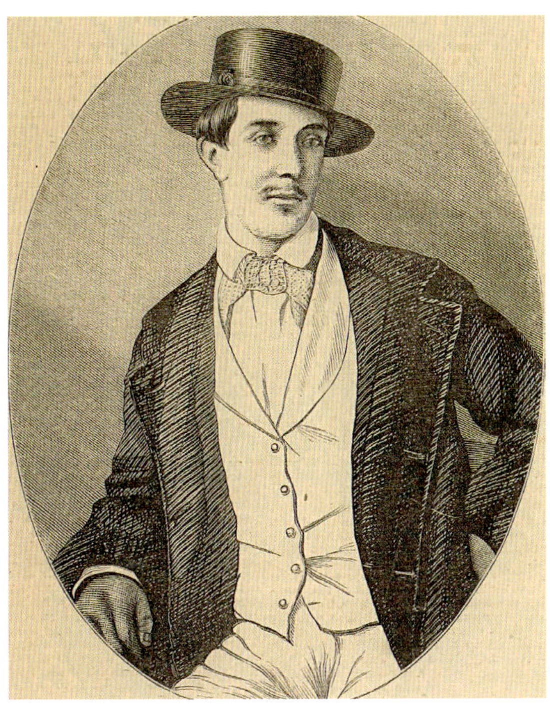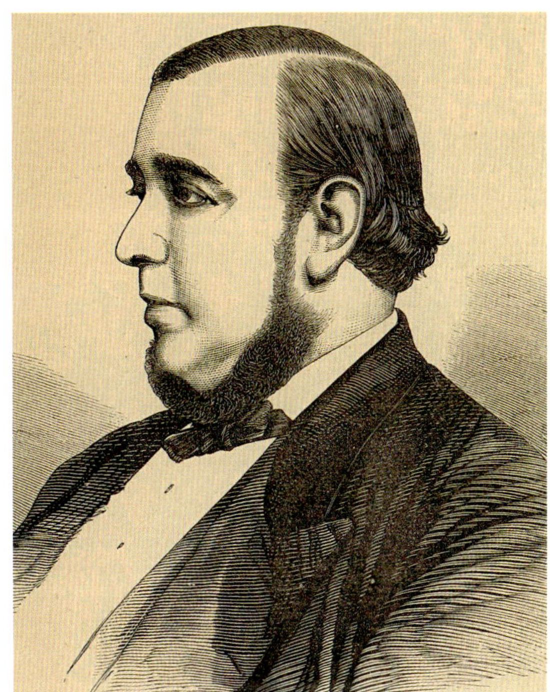

removal advice—perhaps he had been a victim of just this kind of tomfoolery.

The final nudge that took tattooing from the seedy corners of New York's Fourth Ward and the intimate environs of British naval bases onto the society pages of both the *Times* and the *New York Times* came from the events that unfolded spectacularly in the British courts through 1871 and into 1872, with the celebrated Tichborne Trials.

In 1854, a young aristocrat named Sir Roger Tichborne was shipwrecked off the coast of Brazil and never seen again. By 1862, he was officially pronounced dead, and his wayward younger brother was set to inherit the family fortune and titles, much to the chagrin of the boys' mother, Dowager Baroness Henriette Tichborne. Henriette simply could not accept that her beloved Roger had died, and she undertook a global search to try and find him. Eventually, in

1865, word arrived from Australia that, miraculously, Roger had indeed survived a watery grave, and had been working as a butcher in a small New South Wales outpost town called Wagga Wagga under the name of Tom Castro. With the aid of some determined lawyers, keen for their slice of Roger's rightful inheritance as a finders' fee, and to great public fanfare, Castro traveled back to London in order to reclaim his title and lands.

The decade since his sinking had clearly played havoc with his memory, and Castro—now insisting he again be called Roger—had forgotten how to speak French, Roger's mother tongue, and did not recognize any of his old schoolfriends or family staff. They did not recognize him either, though he was by this point remarkably corpulent in comparison to the rakish lad he had been when he had first disappeared. The wider Tichborne family was skeptical that this man was indeed their long-lost relative, and the Claimant,

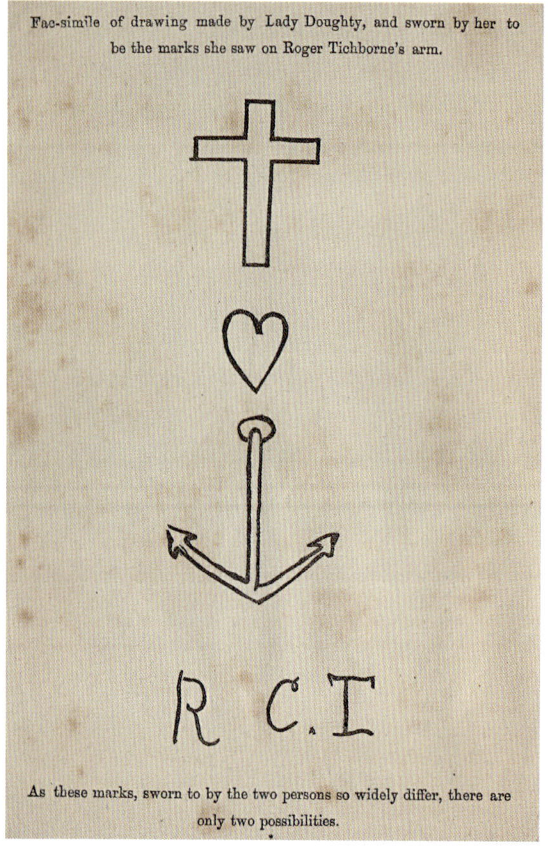

Fac-simile of drawing made by Lady Doughty, and sworn by her to be the marks she saw on Roger Tichborne's arm.

As these marks, sworn to by the two persons so widely differ, there are only two possibilities.

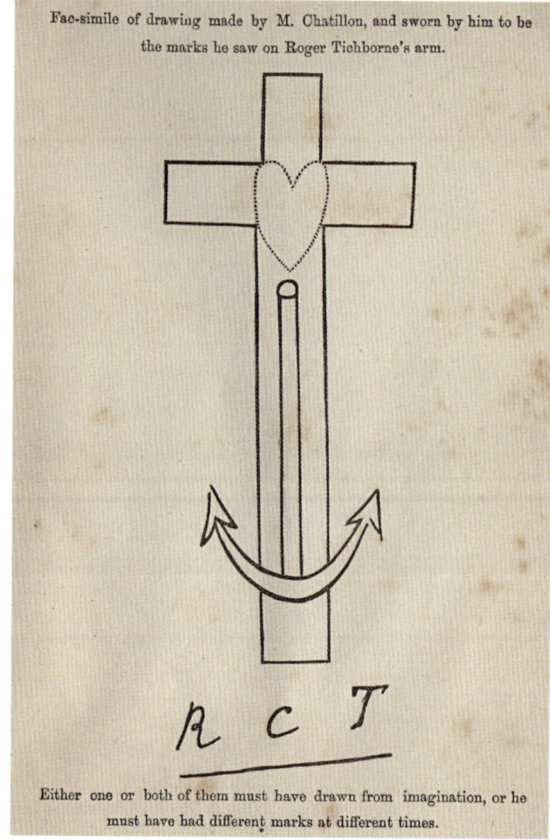

Fac-simile of drawing made by M. Chatillon, and sworn by him to be the marks he saw on Roger Tichborne's arm.

Either one or both of them must have drawn from imagination, or he must have had different marks at different times.

as he became known, was forced to take them to court in order to release the fortune owed to him. The long, arduous trial came to a dramatic end in March 1872, when the lawyers for the Tichborne family revealed that they had proof that this man in the dock could not be their long-lost Roger, and that he was most certainly an imposter. Sir Roger, a schoolfriend attested, had tattooed arms—he had been marked "like a common sailor" with his initials, a heart, an anchor, and a cross while attending an exclusive public school. The man in the dock—who turned out to have been a butcher's son from Wapping, London, all along—had entirely unblemished arms!

The revelation that British aristocrats bore tattoos (and, I suppose, that butchers' sons did not) caused public astonishment around the world. In the immediate aftermath of the trial, the first adverts for semi-professional tattooers appeared in the London papers, with at least two entrepreneurial classified advertisements promoting tattooing services out of residential premises after usual working hours. These were not quite yet fully recognizable modern studios, as their occupants were working in ways which suggest more the opportunistic monetization of a hobby rather than a profession per se, and their advertisements appeared alongside those of other ad hoc service providers such as music teachers. Nevertheless, the adverts of "Professor Thomas" of Clerkenwell in 1873, published during Castro's subsequent criminal trial, and of Mr. Wiffin of St. Pancras in 1878 (which repeats much of the language of Thomas's advert) appear as clear indicators of the key role played by Tichborne mania in creating the circumstances for the establishment of the modern tattoo industry.

Given the similarity in language, and that several Mr. Thomas Wiffins lived and worked in the area at

Varied recollections Sir Roger Tichborne's tattoos were recalled by childhood friends during the trials of his imposter. Supporters of the Claimant wove detailed conspiracy theories about the way these images came to play such an important role in the trial, noting that (as depicted here) the recollections of the designs varied between individuals, and that some of the witnesses appeared to have been coached in their testimony by the prosecution.

the same time, it is likely that "Professor Thomas" and "Mr. Wiffin" are one-and-the-same person. Both advertisements used a refrain popularized in headlines during the trial—"Tattooing, tattooing, tattooing"— as the lede and claimed, like Hildebrandt in America, "long experience in Japan." Interestingly, Thomas was already styled as a "professor" at this early stage, indicating a self-presentation as someone who wished to be taken seriously. Many tattooers over the following century would style themselves similarly, understanding that a learned title, even if unearned, added a certain gravitas to their sometimes roguish trade. Furthermore, like Hildebrandt in New York, Thomas made claims to artistic expression, tattooing "in three colours," and in echoes of the specific designs presented at the trial, specifically advertised "Monograms, initials, designs . . . indelible," clearly aiming his business at those who would seek to follow in Sir Roger's wake.

This desire of middle-class citizens to be tattooed like Sir Roger was not just fueled by voyeuristic curiosity, but also the rising tone of moral panic in the press. In London, the *Saturday Review* wrote provocatively, "Before long, we expect to see an advertisement in all the papers: 'Do you tattoo your children yet?'," and *Cassell's Magazine* explicitly linked the "perfection" of Japanese tattooing in the Western imagination with the "cause célèbre" of the Tichborne Trials. In the British parliament, one MP suggested that every member of the army be tattooed as a means of identification, and by 1879, tattooing was accepted as a "new custom." That year, a young girl eloped from London with her boyfriend, and in an advertisement offering a reward for her safe return, her father noted that, among other defining characteristics,

she was "tattooed on the left leg." (The advert actually described the young woman, Linda, as being tattooed with a cross on her right leg!) At the time, the *New York Times* noted, "it is very evident that in England, it was customary and proper to tattoo the youthful feminine leg." Inspired by the advert, in November of 1879, an intrepid reporter for the US *National Police Gazette* set out to discover if this girlish whim had yet reached the United States.

In Philadelphia, one writer had already reported that so many young women had been inspired by the story, and now sported similar tattoos, that the mention of such a mark would hardly be of use anymore for identification purposes. Following up on these stories, the *Gazette* embarked on a gonzo mission to find out just where these tattoos were being performed.

Remarkably, the artist responsible for this "feminine freak" turned out to be a woman operating from an "unpretentious house in a respectable locality." Her name is sadly lost to history, as she refused permission to the reporter to print her details. We know from the *Gazette*, however, that she was "pleasant-faced," and "attired becomingly," her fingers stained with black ink from a day's tattooing. An accompanying image shows her in a grand living room, tattooing by hand using a short-handled tool. With needles in one hand, and stretching her client's skin taut with the other, she is hunched over the leg of a young woman extravagantly dressed in a frilly dress and high wig, wafting a fan over her decolletage. Her clients, said the lady tattooer, were frequently from the "best families," though most could best be described as "demi-monde"—disreputable and salacious young women. The tattoos ranged from crosses, in imitation of Linda, to snakes coiled around

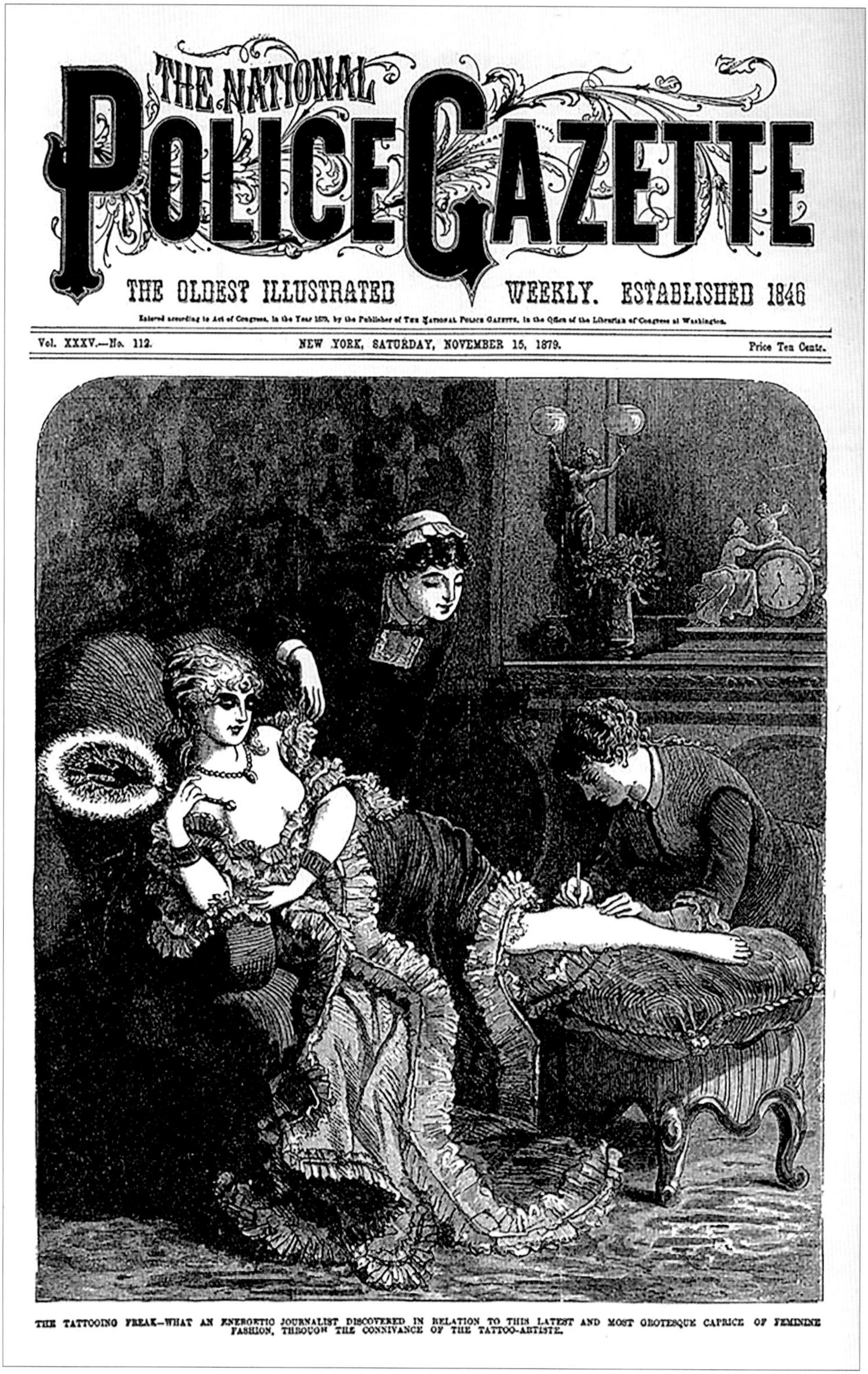

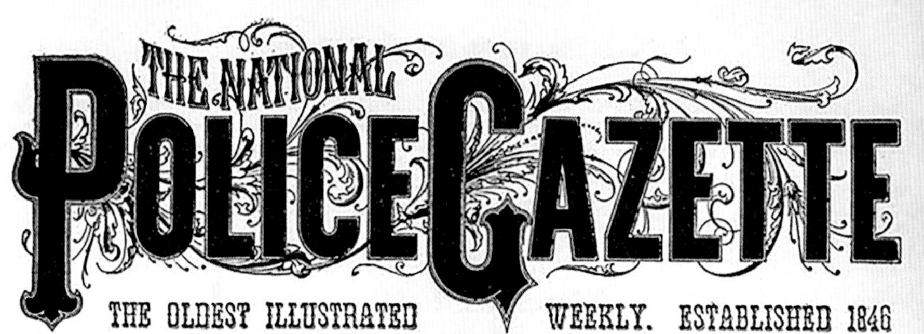

THE TATTOOING FREAK—WHAT AN ENERGETIC JOURNALIST DISCOVERED IN RELATION TO THIS LATEST AND MOST GROTESQUE CAPRICE OF FEMININE FASHION, THROUGH THE CONNIVANCE OF THE TATTOO-ARTISTE.

Gonzo journalism On November 15, 1879, the cover of *The National Police Gazette* illustrated "The Tattooing Freak." The piece is told as a remarkable feat of gonzo journalism, as the intrepid reporter follows local whispers in Philadelphia in order to discover the truth of this "fantastic fashion" and "grotesque conceit of the capricious fair, having their limbs disfigured by odd devices indelibly pricked in India Ink."

their thighs. Many clients had the names of lovers tattooed on them, and embarrassingly, she reported, two young women came in on consecutive days asking to be permanently marked with the name of the same local politician. The second client was so furious that she demanded that the tattoo be inscribed on her foot, "so that I can express my contempt for him!", rather than on her arm, as initially requested. "The rumors of the practice of this art," the *Gazette* concluded, "were not without foundation."

Toward a High-Class Trend

By 1881, Hildebrandt was described as a "fine artist," his client base of sailors having been displaced by increasing numbers of tradesmen, firemen, and eminent foreign visitors. A pair of long-time customers had also begun earning good livings as tattooed exhibits at Coney Island. One of them, Harry Decoursey, traded a career as a jeweler to work as a sideshow performer, proudly bearing his chest tattoo of the Washington Monument. Hildebrandt's customer base, however, included very few women. "One of the illustrated papers represented me and an assistant tattooing a roomful of ladies once," he confessed, "but it was all untrue. I don't average ten lady visitors a year."

In 1882, though, Hildebrandt had suddenly become responsible for a "mania" of tattooing, "the latest fashionable fallacy." In the course of a year his client base had become—reportedly, at least—"predominantly women," and so popular was his trade among trend-setting folks that he was considering a move away from the shabby environs of Oak Street to a "fashionable throughfare" up town. Favoring floral and faunal designs, Hildebrandt told the *Times* he was busy and making a very good living indeed, earning as much as $30 per tattoo—an amount close to $800 in terms of purchasing power today. Given the contrast to the story he told just the previous year, however, it seems possible that he was embellishing his circumstances a little for the purposes of publicity—perhaps he was advertising the tattoo business he wanted, rather than the one he actually had. The author of this latest piece in the *Times* imagined that this was but a short-lived hobby, set to disappear quickly, but as we shall see, whatever the truth of Hildebrandt's own circumstances, this was only the beginning for tattooing as a fully fledged, high-class trend in Europe and America.

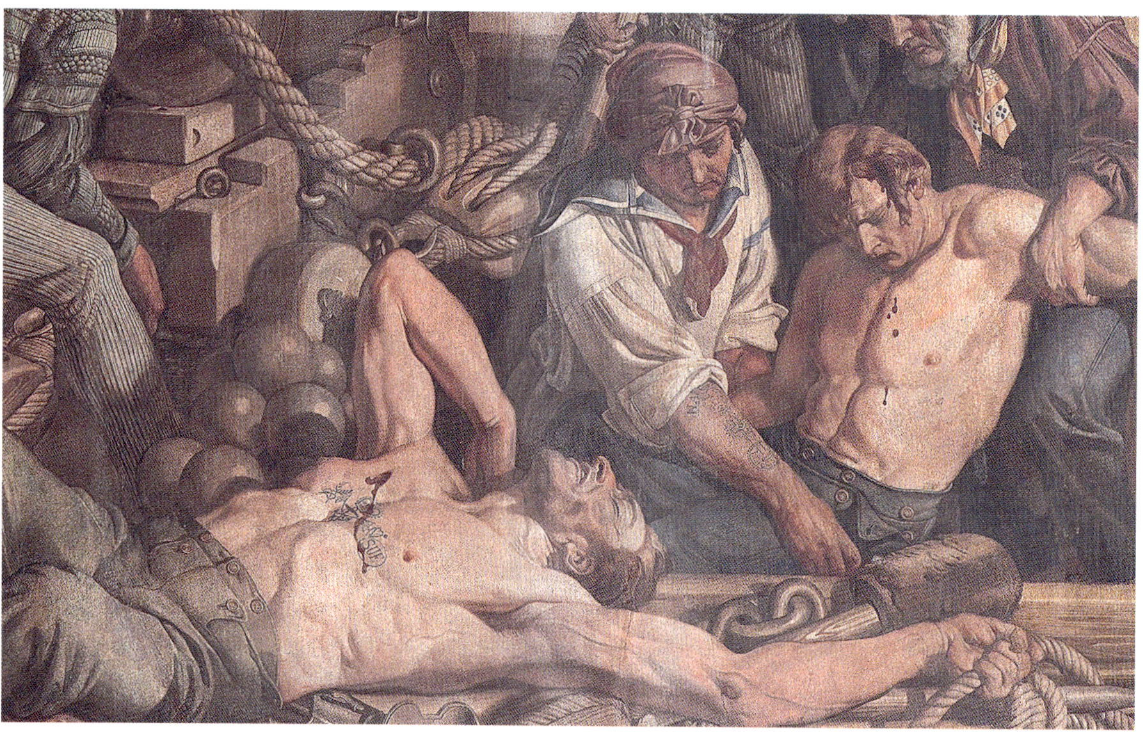

The Death of Nelson, Daniel Maclise, 1866

Outside of official records, images of pre-professional tattoos in England are rare indeed. One particularly important exception is the vast array of tattoos on display in Daniel Maclise's waterglass murals of the battles of Waterloo and Trafalgar. Many of the serving men prominently bear sentimental, patriotic, and religious marks on their arms and chests. Maclise was known for his attention to period accuracy, and it is possible that he studied real tattoos on surviving pensioners from the Napoleonic Wars. The huge murals are installed in a central gallery of the House of Lords, placing heroic tattooing at the heart of parliamentary London —and perhaps ensuring that tattoos never became quite as stigmatized in England as they would be on the Continent.

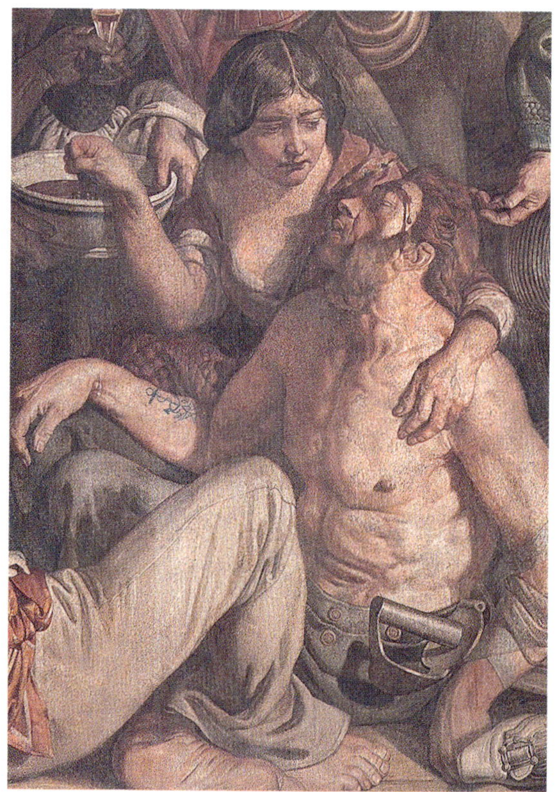

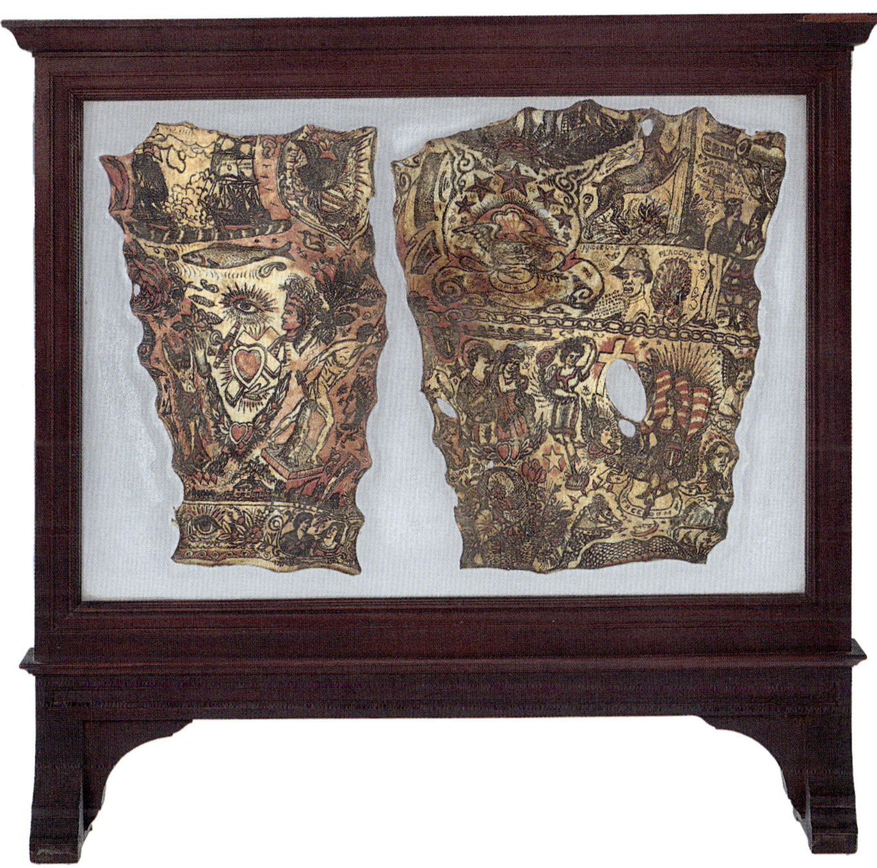

Preserved tattooed skin, University of Edinburgh, tattooed c.1870 and preserved before 1892

In 1892, an anatomist called Dr. J. Biggs presented a remarkable specimen to the regular meeting of the Anatomical Society of Great Britain and Ireland—the "tattooed Skin from an Irish American, æt [aged] 29." The unnamed man, Biggs claimed, had been tattooed from boyhood in the 1860s. Between the ages of four and seven he had been used by his elder brother as a practice canvas, resulting in elaborate coverage. Through to the early 20th century, authorities in New York documented several tattooers learning and honing their trade on children in this way, rather than on paying adult customers. Such anatomical collections were common in the days before regulations constrained what pathologists should do with body parts that interested them.

À propos d'Étrennes ("About that New Year's gift"), Alfred Grévin, *Le Petit Journal pour Rire*, 1870

This image was a cover gag for French satirical magazine *Le Petit Journal pour Rire*, 1870, offering a cynical twist on the standard implications of a romantic commitment tattoo. The decorated officer is presenting his lover with his new tattoo as a New Year's gift, telling her that whatever happens to their relationship during the coming year, at least the mark will be permanent …!

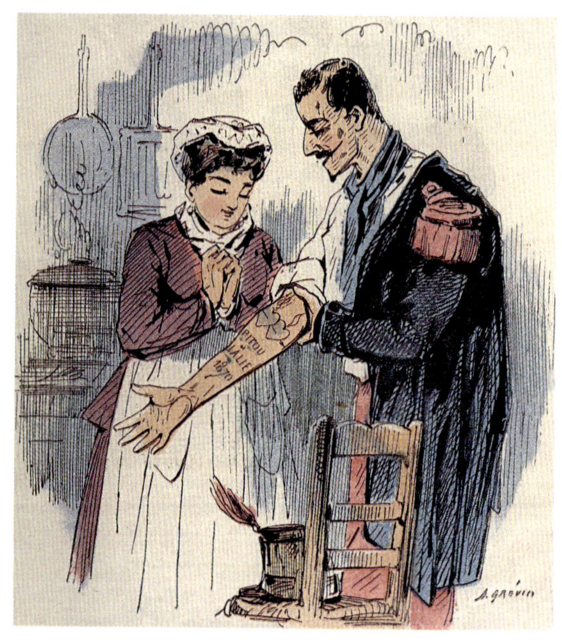

Irene Woodward, cabinet photo, photographer unknown, 1880s

Martin Hildebrandt is also said to be the artist behind the creation of the first ever "tattooed woman," Irene Woodward, though she claimed that she had been decorated by her father in the Wild West. Woodward (born Ida Levina Lisk) was actually from Philadelphia, and was hired by George Bunnell, the same promoter who had represented Harry DeCoursey. Her debut appearance in 1882 was such a sensation that it made the *New York Times*. She later toured Europe with P.T. Barnum's Greatest Show on Earth, becoming so famous that at least thirty-eight museums commissioned waxworks of her.

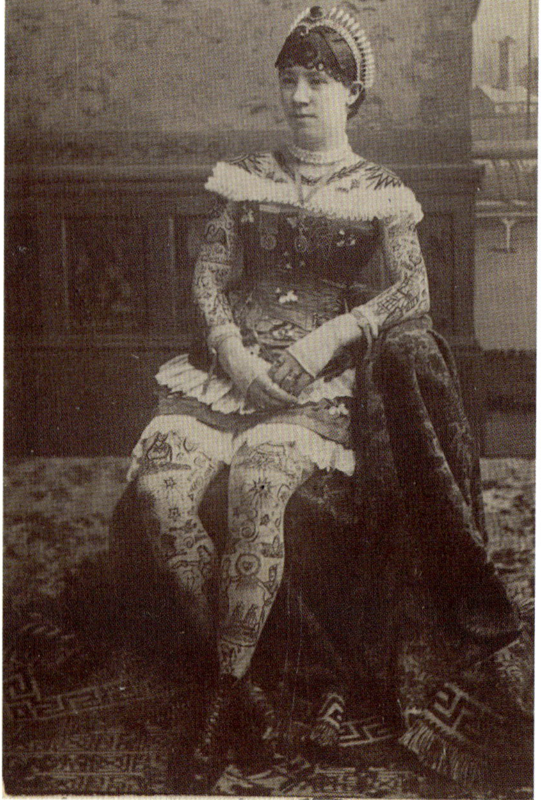

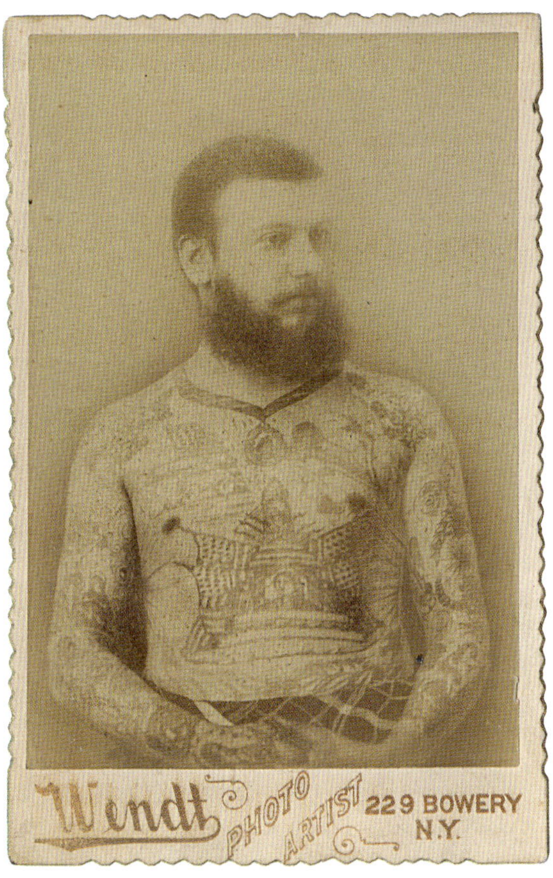

Harry DeCoursey, cabinet photo by Charles Eisenmann, New York, c.1880s

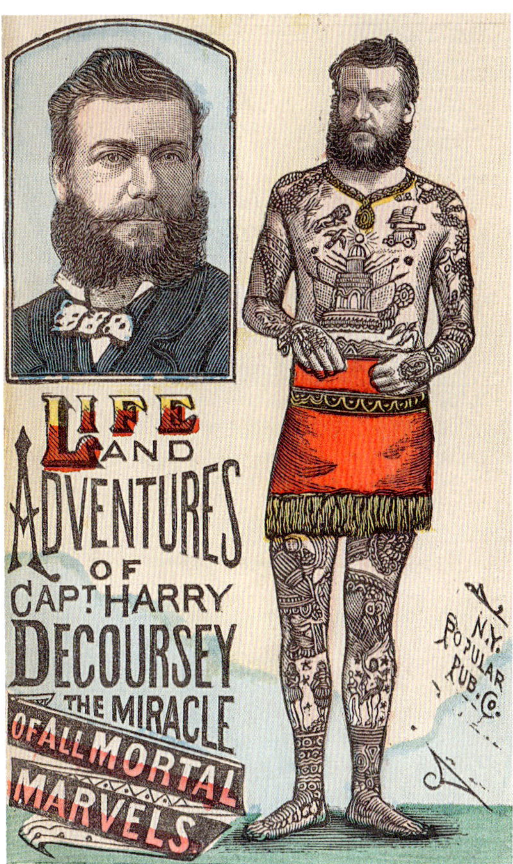

"The Life and Adventures of Captain Harry DeCoursey" flyer, 1883

Captain Harry DeCoursey (born William Denny) was Martin Hildebrandt's most famous client. DeCoursey had been a jeweler in Brooklyn, but eventually came to make a living performing as "The Miracle of All Mortal Marvels" from 1880, showing off his extensive tattooing to curious crowds at a dime museum in New York. The bare fact of being heavily tattooed was often sufficient to serve as a performing tattooed man or woman, though many performers added increasingly tall and salacious tales to their self-presentations in order to wow their crowds. Some even turned to feats of strength, juggling, sword-swallowing, or other circus skills to hold punters' interest. P.T. Barnum had already made waves in the city by exhibiting "Captain Costentenus," the infamous tattooed Greek Albanian who claimed at performances across Europe, the UK, and America to have been tattooed against his will in Burma. DeCoursey was thus the all-American counterpart to this trope, and was such a sensation that he was briefly able to quadruple his jeweler's salary to $40 per week.

In his pitch book and his show, performing tattooed man DeCoursey boasted of Martin Hildebrandt's great artistic talents (and those of Hildebrandt's apprentice, Stephen Lee). Nevertheless, even DeCoursey needed to exaggerate his story to create a compelling narrative: while he acknowledged that Hildebrandt had tattooed him, his pitch book fantastically claimed that their fearsome captors in Peru had actually forced Hildebrandt to produce the work under duress.

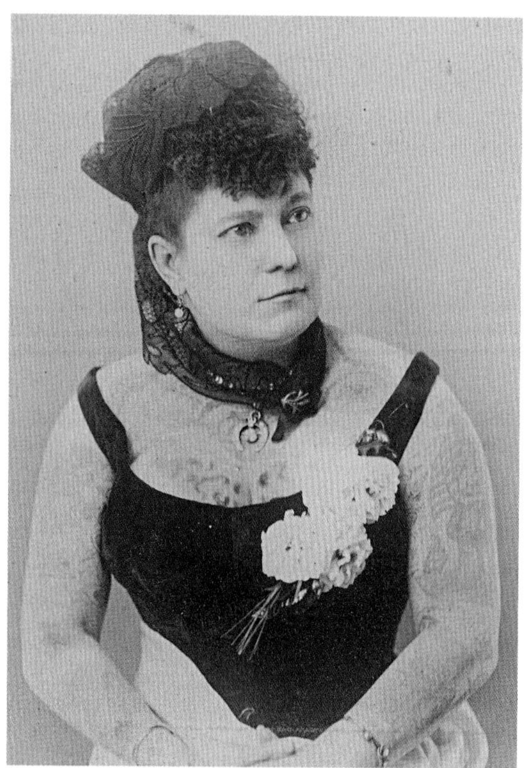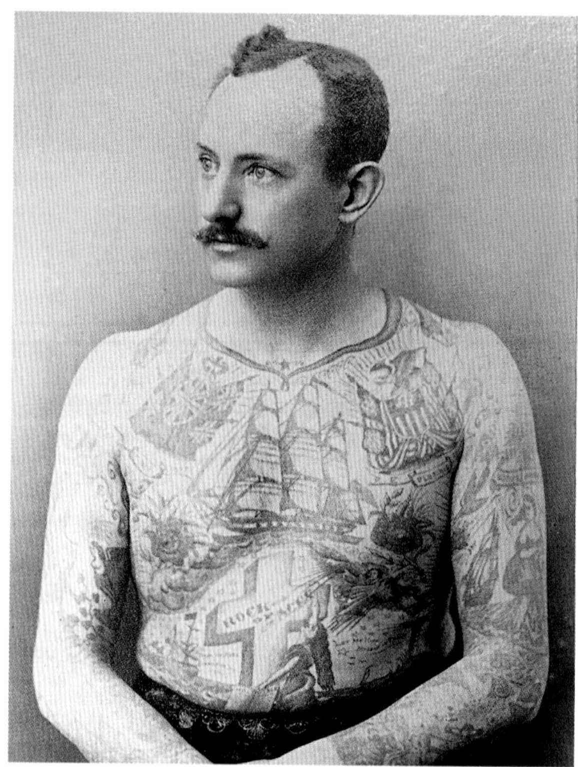

Nora Hildebrandt and Jacob Gunther, cabinet photos, photographer unknown, 1890s

Nora Hildebrandt (*left*; born Nora Keatin) claimed to have been born in Australia, but was actually English. She was married to Martin Hildebrandt some time before 1882, when he tattooed her extensively. After their relationship broke down (and Nora had Martin committed to an asylum), she continued to work prominently in New York. She later married a tattooed barber named Jacob Gunther (*right*), who took her surname and also performed alongside her. It is assumed that Jacob's tattooing was carried out by Martin—and that perhaps the couple met while Jacob was being worked on by Martin. Nora and Jacob's showbusiness career was cut short in April 1893, when Nora died from influenza, just three years after the death of Martin. Following Nora's death, Jacob retired from the limelight.

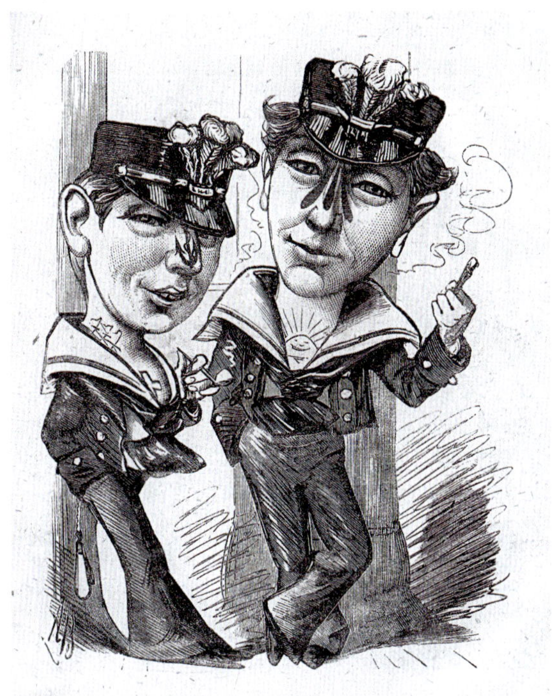

Cartoon of Princes Albert Victor and George,
Entr'Acte, **January 24, 1880**

Rumors swirled in Britain in 1880 about the apparent
tattooing of Princes George and Albert Victor, abroad in the
West Indies. Stories such as the one depicted in this cartoon
suggested they had been tattooed on their noses, and their
mother, the Queen, even wrote to them to admonish their
stupidity. It was, however, not true—the black marks had only
been some dirt. Both princes were tattooed for real, however,
in 1881. In Japan, George—later to become King George V—
received a dragon, and Albert Victor, a stork. These tattoos
were so famous that they directly drove sufficient interest to
kickstart the professional tattoo industry. A scene of George
being tattooed even featured in a commemorative newspaper
account on the occasion of his marriage.

**Tattoo design claimed to be copied from George
V's arm by Tom Riley, 1898**

Several entirely different sketches of future King
George V's dragon tattoo were circulated throughout
the 1880s and 90s by tattooers who had claimed to
have seen it. Many tattooers in London and elsewhere
also claimed to have added to his collection, but there
is no evidence he was tattooed anywhere other than
in Japan and Jerusalem. The most famous tattooer
in Japan, Hori Chiyo, also claimed to have been the
man who tattooed the princes, though that too is
considered unlikely.

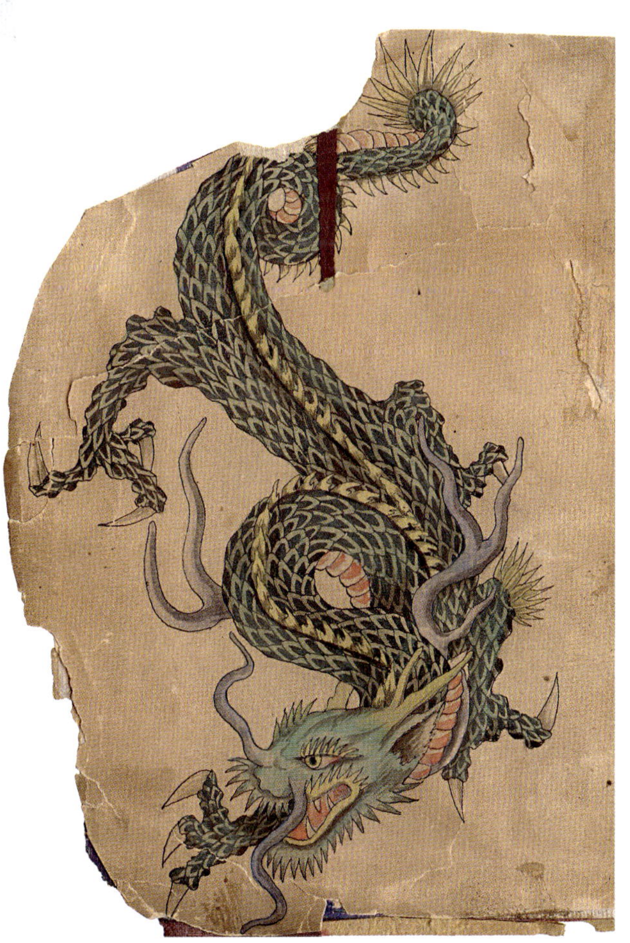

Chapter Three

Tattooing in High Society

1881–1914

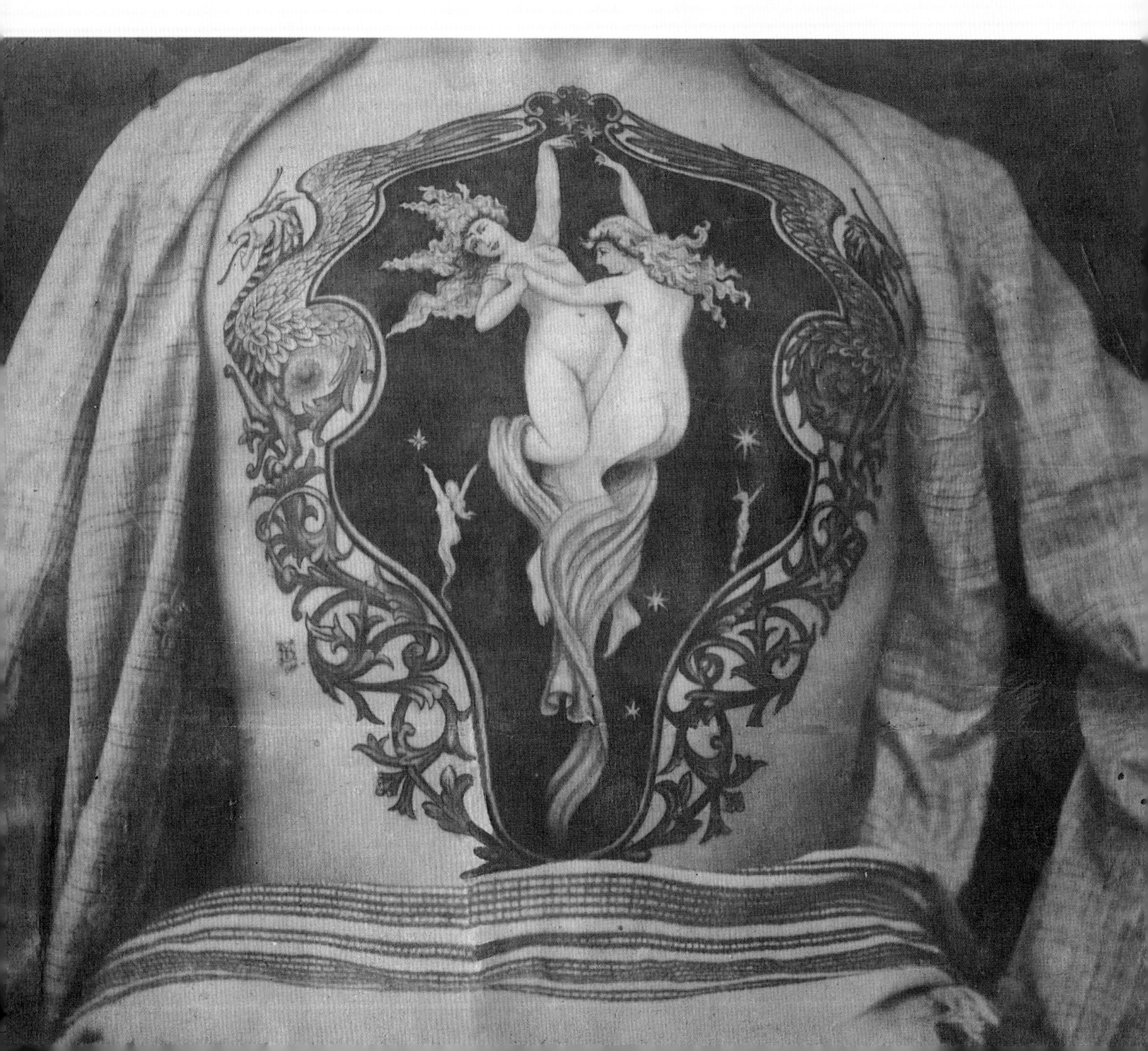

"Tattooing is on increase. Habit not confined to seamen only."

The New York Times, 1908

Twin stars Sutherland Macdonald recreated Spanish salon painter Luis Falero's *Twin Stars* (1881) on the back of a Mr Wertheim—perhaps art dealer Mari Paul Johan Wertheim. The Falero composition is augmented with filigrees taken from Victorian decorative art books. Note Macdonald's use of negative space to form the tattoo—something more common in large-scale Japanese tattooing than the conventional European practice at the time. Macdonald's signature is also visible.

If we define the term "professional tattooer" as someone to whom a member of the public pays money to receive a tattoo, then Martin Hildebrandt is reasonably understood as the first full-time professional tattooer in the United States. Operating from a specific address, his first adverts appear in the late 1850s, and he claims to have been a full-time tattooer from about 1866. But where might the United Kingdom find its first professional tattooer? Were there professionals before the tentative home operation of Professor Thomas in 1873?

George Burchett's *Memoirs of a Tattooist*, published in 1958, is purportedly a firsthand account of the most important UK tattoo artist of the first half of the twentieth century. It is also, perhaps, the most frequently cited book for evidence of tattooing's early professional history in Britain. In the book, Burchett states: "I believe the first British professional of any standing was David Purdy. He had a booth in Holloway in the 1870s." Although this is categorically untrue, an examination of Purdy's tattoo career provides a fascinating lens through which to examine the early decades of professional tattooing in Britain.

Purdy's status as the first professional tattoo artist has been accepted as fact since *Memoirs of a Tattooist* was published. However, far from being a version of Burchett's own writings, *Memoirs* is largely comprised of press clippings about tattooing, hastily compiled by a journalist following Burchett's death, with Burchett's wife's blessing but with little fact-checking or independent research. Given the status that has been placed on the book for so long, its claim for Purdy has since been cited with authority by later sources.

Purdy is elusive in the historical record, save for a small booklet he authored entitled *How to Tattoo, What to Use and How to Use Them*, dated 1896, a rare surviving copy of which sits in the British Library.

The booklet is a marvelous piece of self-publishing. Purdy, who claims to have had "a vast amount of practice and experience in Tattooing," outlines across twenty or so pages the methods of tattooing by hand— that is, without the use of an electric machine. The book gives advice on designs ("have something done which will be a novelty to you, such as a picture, or some well-known person's likeness"; "it would not be amiss to take the Tower Bridge, for instance, or the Great Wheel at Earl's Court, or the Imperial Institute, or one of Her Majesty's Battleships, and the Houses of Parliament,") and offers some comparative analysis of global tattoo practices, but focuses primarily on detailed accounts of tools, with accompanying information on how to acquire them, and technique. "The better the ink, so the better it looks," Purdy explains. "You will require two very fine pens . . . and the finer the pen you purchase, so the better the work. Most important, of course, are the needles: three or four packets of 'No. 7' needles, bound into groupings of various sizes depending on the level of detail in your design, lashed with thread to short pieces of wood."

Purdy's advice on "sketching" is sage: "If you don't draw the figure to your liking at first, you must rub it out until you do get a good figure; no doubt you would get tired of rubbing it out, but it is better to rub out two or three times than to prick it in and wish it off." And his description of the "pricking and sponging" process, whereby the tattooist holds their client's freshly shaved skin taut with their left hand while wielding the needle tool in the right, is remarkably close to that still used by professional hand-tattooers today. Only the hygiene protocols are radically different from tattooing in the twenty-first century. Purdy advises that "you do not

want to buy new needles for every piece of Tattooing you do," suggesting that his students instead clean blood from their needles with a piece of rag or flannel before using them again!

The booklet was sold via mail-order adverts in local newspapers including the *Lincolnshire Echo* and the *Swindon Advertiser*, and came with a kit comprising all the necessary equipment for tattooing from home. This clearly indicated an entrepreneurial spirit. It is evident from reading the booklet that Purdy was familiar with tattooing techniques, fashionable with his design choices, and cautious with his knowledge, steering people away from the urge to tattoo themselves, for example. And yet there are, curiously, no records of an established practice that might place Purdy at the wellspring of professional tattooing in Britain. The domestic address on the booklet's title page, which also appeared in the mail-order ads— 23 Ringcroft Street, Holloway—accords with Burchett placing him in Holloway, but diligent combing of street directories, censuses, and records of births and deaths reveals no possible candidate for a David Purdy old enough to have begun tattooing here in the 1870s. Indeed, the booklet itself is registered not to David Purdy, as Burchett has it, but simply to a Professor D.W. Purdy. Who was this mysterious individual? What was his role in the early moments of professional British tattooing?

The address in Holloway where Purdy was based in 1896 and 1897 was registered to a Maurice Rowland, a printer's inkmaker, and his family. It was a private home and not a commercial premises in which tattooing the public could reasonably have been practiced. By following the copyright registration forms

CONFIDENTIAL.

SUTHERLAND MACDONALD.
Artist in Tattooing.

Has had the honour of Tattooing:—

H.M. THE KING OF ENGLAND.

H.M. THE KING OF NORWAY.   H.M. THE KING OF DENMARK.
H.I.H. THE GRAND DUKE MICHAEL ALEXANDROVITCH OF RUSSIA.
H.R.H. PRINCE HENRY OF PRUSSIA.   H.R.H. THE COUNT OF TURIN.
H.S.H. PRINCE SCHAUMBERG LIPPE.
H.R.H. PRINCE JAIME DE BOURBON.
H.S.H. PRINCE VICTOR OF HOHENLOHE.
H.S.H. PRINCE FRANCIS OF TECK (The late).
H.S.H. PRINCE CHRISTIAN VICTOR OF SCHLESWIG HOLSTEIN (The late).
H.H. THE SULTAN OF JOHORE.   H.H. THE MAHARAJA OF BIKANER.
H.H. THE MAHARAJA OF PATIALA.
H.H. PRINCE HUSSIEN KEMEL-EL-DINE OF EGYPT.
T.H.'s PRINCE, AND PRINCE SERGE, BELOSERSKY-BELOSERSKY.
H.H. PRINCE VLADAMIR ORLOFF.
H.H. PRINCE COLERADO-MANSFIELD.
THE DUKE OF PENARANDO.   THE DUKE D'ARION.
THE DUKE DE MACQUEDE.   THE DUKE DE ALBERQUERQUE.
ETC.   ETC.   ETC.

STUDIO—76, JERMYN STREET (HAMMAM TURKISH BATHS) LONDON.

for Purdy's booklet, however, the mystery resolves itself: Purdy was not David, as *Memoirs* has it, but Daniel.

Daniel William Purdy was born in Heigham, Norfolk, c.1871, a date that immediately precludes him from having run a professional tattooing operation in the 1870s. He was tattooed himself—his World War I service records account for tattoos of a ship on his chest, a Britannia and another female figure on his right arm, a female figure and a flower on his left arm, and the bust of a man on the back of his left hand. But Purdy was, alas, no professional tattooer of any note. At the time his booklet was produced, "Professor" Purdy was working as a postman (1894–1901), having recently left the Norfolk Regiment. Later in life, he worked around North London as a fishmonger (1911) and a valet (1914), before a short stint in the army as a relatively old recruit left him shunted between regiments, cited for untidiness, and subject to an eventual discharge in 1915 for mental deficiency. He seems to have ended his life homeless, in and out of the workhouse during the 1920s, before dying in 1931. From the clarity of his descriptions of the tattooing process, it seems certain that Purdy was a proficient practitioner and did tattoo, but it is unlikely that his base at Holloway ever functioned as a tattoo studio.

A Tattooing Boom in Britain

If not Purdy, then who was the UK's first professional tattoo artist? The semi-professional practice of Professor Thomas in the 1870s, or even the itinerant Jerusalem mark-making in London a century and a half earlier, are important parts of the evolution of tattooing into an industry, but they do not quite rise to the level of a permanent, public-facing premises of the kind Hildebrandt was running. And so, I suggest that the most reasonable candidate is Sutherland Macdonald,

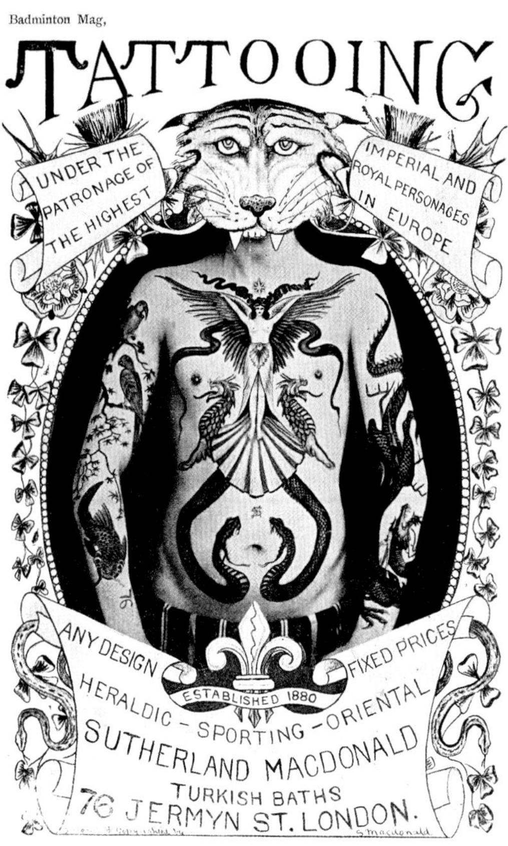

Any design, fixed prices (*left*) Macdonald circulated this card among potential customers. Note the range of designs he claims to offer—"Heraldic, Sporting, Oriental." Macdonald frequently advertised in the pages of society magazines such as *Badminton*. This particular image never appeared in print, though the addition of the magazine's name on the front of this card suggests it had perhaps been inserted into the periodical's pages when it was sent out to subscribers.

The height of taste (*right*) Reginald A. Loyd was the son of Oxford-based Member of Parliament Archie Kirkman Loyd. A qualified barrister, Loyd later became Land Tax Commissioner for Berkshire. Such wealthy, educated, and trendy men were clearly Macdonald's most favored clients. Loyd's tattoos are a striking, thrilling hybridization of Japonesque dragons and snakes with an allegorical figure drawn in the style of French salon paintings of the period. The various components have been skilfully assembled so as to augment Loyd's body, and featured in Macdonald's advertising (*left*).

born in Leeds in 1860, raised in Guildford by a middle-class couple, and, according to his publicity, a tattooer from around 1880 onward. That year, Mac (as his friends called him) was on the verge of a discharge from the Royal Engineers, with whom he had served as a telegraph operator in the Anglo–Zulu War of 1879. He quickly began working at the Aldershot garrison. In 1887, his marriage certificate gave his profession as "chiropodist."

Macdonald first appears as a tattooist in the press in 1889, and he is certainly the first English tattoo artist to establish a widespread reputation as a public-facing "professional." Macdonald even claimed, not entirely truthfully, to have coined the term "tattooist," a contraction of "tattoo artist," to distinguish his practice from that of a mere "tattooer," which he thought made his profession sound too much like an unfashionable job such as plumber or bricklayer.

Sociologist Herbert Spencer, writing around the time Macdonald was beginning to forge a professional identity for tattooing, explained that professions serve to enhance and augment quality of life, and do not meet basic needs. Of professional artists in general, Spencer says "those who carry on the plastic arts—the painter, the sculptor, the architect—excite by their products pleasurable perceptions and emotions of the aesthetic class, and thus increase life." Spencer himself considered Maori tattooing as one of the earliest iterations of an artistic profession, but Macdonald's push to be seen as a professional serves not only to demarcate his own practice as of particular quality, but also to signal a novel development in approach and context to a practice with such ancient roots.

The Post Office Directory for London in 1894 created the category of "Tattooist" for Macdonald, listing him as the only one in town. His premises

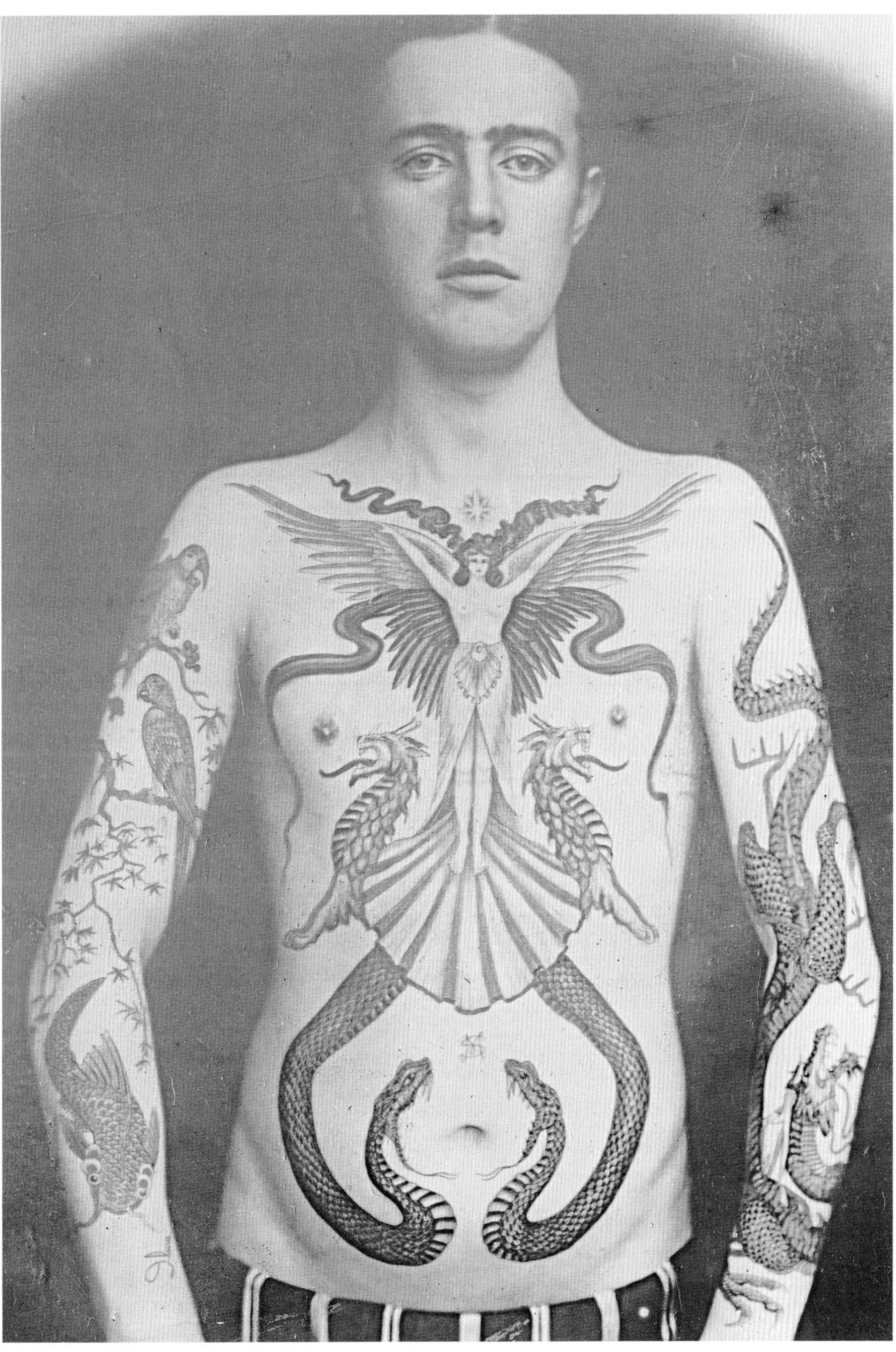

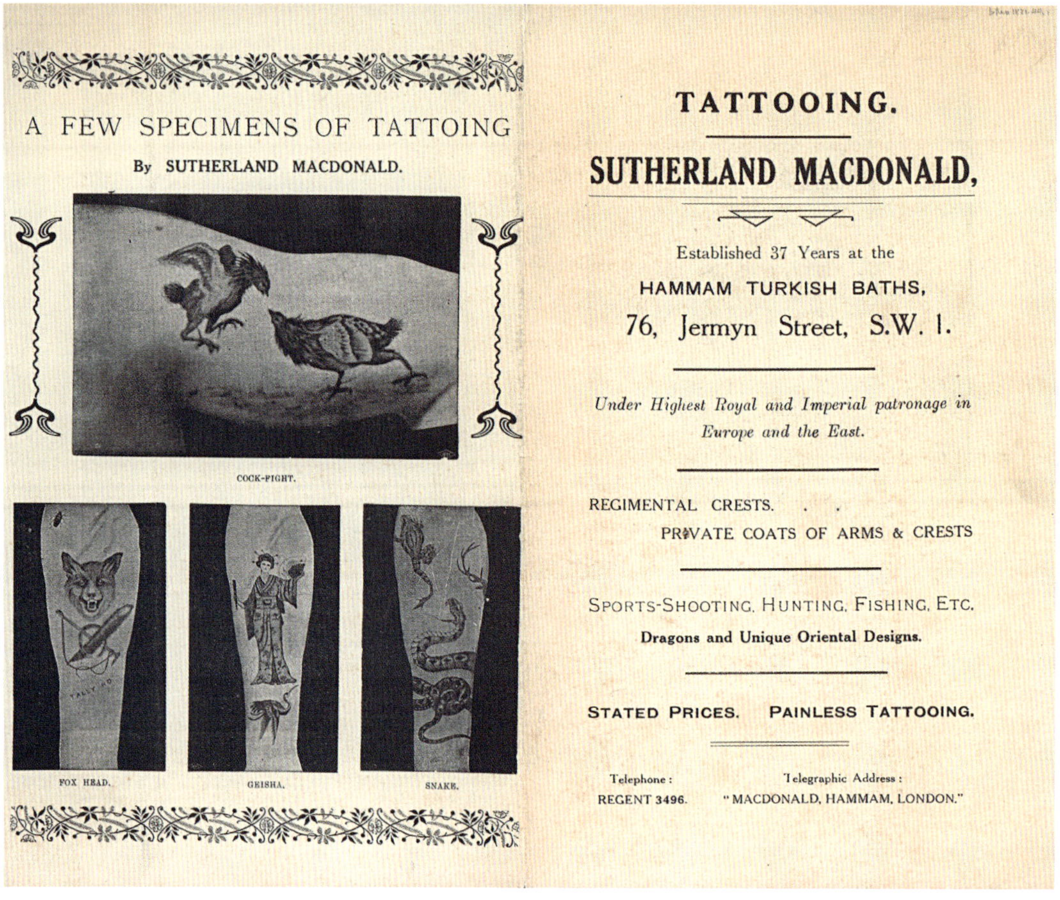

were in the basement of the ornate Turkish Baths at 76 Jermyn Street, a locale known for its parade of gentlemen's clubs and fashionable shops. Macdonald had been working as the baths' manager, drawing on skills learned growing up (his father had owned Guildford's Turkish Baths) and tattooing customers out of hours. Such was the demand for his work, however, that he was eventually able to move to tattooing full time. He worked in a large, square room in the basement of the baths, down a series of dark passageways. The studio was sumptuously outfitted, much as a Japanese studio might have been, with luxurious cushions and a divan, with cigarettes and drinks made available for clients. As one visitor recalled: "the thrilling melody of caged songsters filled the air with shrill music, and there was an odor of cigarettes and brandy, mixed with a slight aroma of drugs about the place." (By "drugs," the visitor meant pharmaceuticals and cleaning chemicals, although Macdonald was known to regularly use cocaine injections to numb his clients' pain!)

Around the same time as Macdonald was becoming established, Professor Williams, a tattooed performer who had arrived home after a period working in America, was carrying out tattooing on patrons at London's Royal Aquarium—a venue which had hosted performances of tattooed men and women since 1878. Even in Macdonald's first published interview from 1889, he mentions other unnamed "members of my profession." Records attest to contemporaneous tattooers in Cardiff—James Cross and "Professor" Welsh, for example—and in 1890, the *Daily Graphic* visited a tattooing "atelier" in Portsmouth run by an artist called Baltser. Interestingly, like the inkings on Woodward and Williams more than a century and a half earlier, Baltser was transferring designs to skin

Stated prices, painless tattooing (*left*)
Another of Sutherland Macdonald's
advertising flyers, c.1927, demonstrates
how Mac stuck firmly to the branding
he established early in his career as
the tattooer to the "Highest Royal
Personages," even as tastes changed
around him.

Tattooing at all price points (*right*) While
Macdonald aimed his services at a high-
end clientele, Londoners could obtain
cheaper tattoos at the Royal Aquarium.
Though initially opened to display
exotic fish and to serve as a place of
education, the Aquarium became a space
of popular entertainment, with the huge
fishtanks instead used to stage theatrical
recreations of naval battles. On other
stages variety and music hall acts proved
popular, including tattooed performers.
As well as watching tattooed men and
women perform, patrons could go home
with a tattoo themselves. As such, the
opportunity to ply their trade became a
source of great rivalry between tattooers.

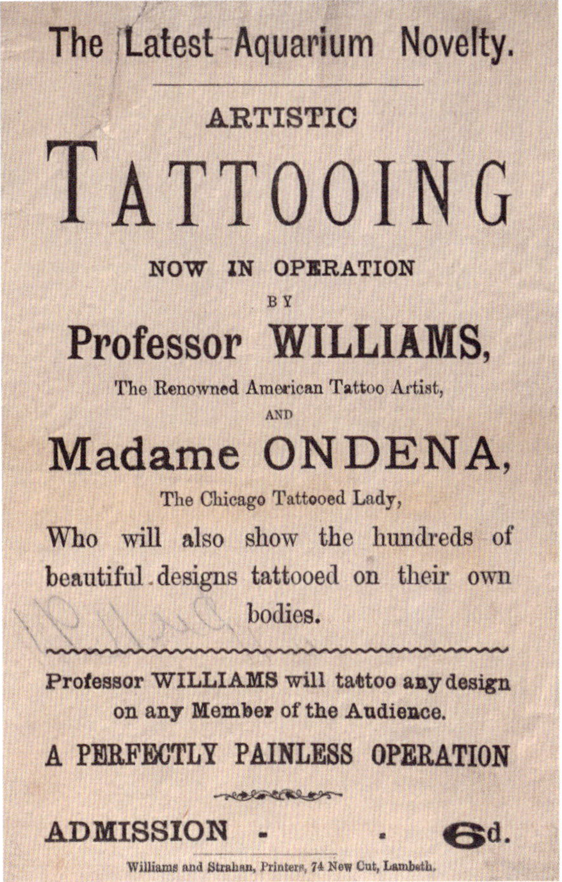

using carved wooden blocks like the ones used for the pilgrims' tattoos in the Middle East.

A primary driver for the explosion of tattooing in Britain through the 1880s links directly to the interest in tattooing that followed the opening of Japan in the 1850s, and, specifically, the British royal family's embrace of the art in Japan, which stemmed from visits to the country following the Meiji Restoration. Prince Alfred, Duke of Edinburgh, was tattooed while staying at the Enryokan Palace in Tokyo in 1869, and every royal visitor from then on was tattooed, right through to the 1920s. In particular, and most famously, Prince George, Duke of York (and future King George V), and his brother Albert Victor, Duke of Clarence, were both tattooed in 1881—George with a dragon, of course, and Albert Victor with a stork. (Their father, Edward VII, had been tattooed in Jerusalem as a pilgrim in 1862, and the young princes were directly and proudly following in his footsteps, further acquiring their own Jerusalem Crosses when they visited the Holy Lands on their return journey.) But the story of their tattooing adventures in Japan became so well known that an illustration of George under the needle was part of the commemorative news coverage during his marriage to Mary of Teck.

Tattooing had been rather unsuccessfully banned in the French Navy in 1861 following concerns from medical professionals, ensuring that in France, at least, tattooing remained more salacious and taboo than in the Anglophone world. But the desire of wealthy clients to ape the fashions of the British royal family undoubtedly fed the boom in professional tattooing across Europe and America through the 1880s. Newspapers on both sides of the Atlantic reported breathlessly on various minor aristocrats and members of high society seeking out the finest artists to acquire

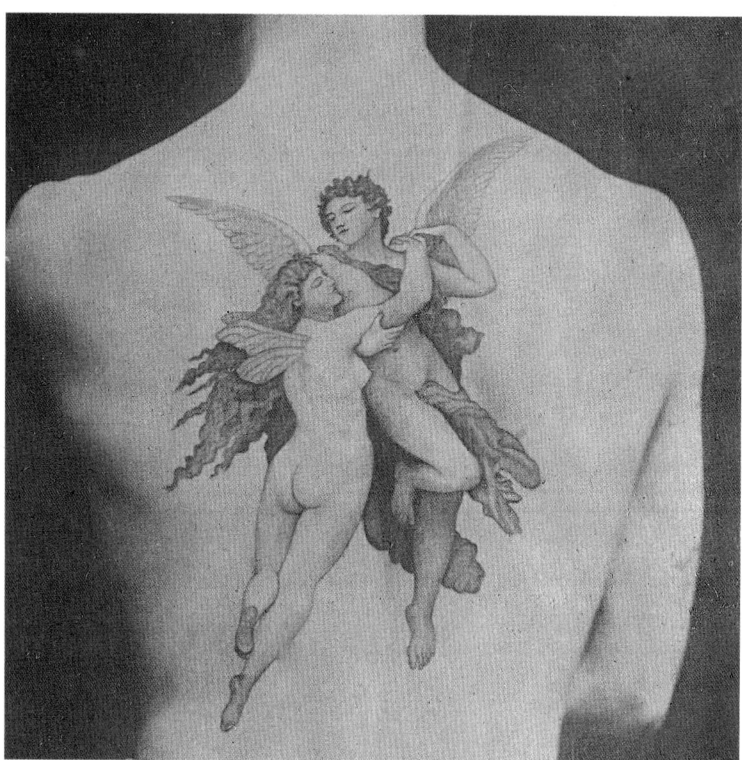

A living art gallery (*left*) Salon paintings like William-Adolphe Bouguereau's *Cupid and Psyche* (1899) were popular choices for tattoo designs in the Victorian period. Bouguereau's art was sneered at by critics at the time as being cloying, commercialized, and silly, but its aestheticism, gentle eroticism, and pretension to seriousness were precisely what made it such excellent subject matter for tattooing.

New rivalries (*right*) Charlie Wagner (b. Wiegner)—pictured here tattooing a female customer in c.1905—worked in New York City near to Samuel O'Reilly. Wagner was credited with his own patent for a new style of machine, which oriented the coils vertically. Bitter rival, "Electric" Elmer Getchell, derisively called him an "amateur."

Japanese-style tattoos, and even copies of their favorite French salon paintings.

In Japan itself, tattooing was made illegal for citizens in 1869, and so Japanese artists had an incentive to seek out foreign clients both at home and abroad. Several left Japan to advertise their services in places such as Singapore and Hong Kong; others traveled on the invitation of Western tattooers to work in Paris, London, New York, and San Francisco. Those who remained in Japan began to tailor their work for European and American clients. At the high end, this meant that wealthy foreign visitors, enticed by adverts in English-language guidebooks, could seek out some of the greatest tattoo artists in the country. Aimed at sailors arriving in Japan aboard English, Russian, French, or American naval vessels, design books from tattoo artists in Nagasaki show an eclectic, cross-cultural melange of European and Orientalist designs

of all tastes. (Note here the use of the term Oriental*ist* —these designs function as generically and fictively "Oriental" in the flattening, patronizing distortions of the European gaze, shedding cultural specificity in the process.) Very quickly, even English naval tattooers began to incorporate fashionable Japanese motifs into their repertoire.

Touristic tattoos abroad, and those they inspired back in Europe and the United States, were qualitatively distinct from the designs seen in previous generations—a difference that did not go unnoticed in English-language guidebooks to Japan. In the hands of Japanese tattooers, writer Basil Chamberlain exclaimed in 1891, tattooing "has become an art indeed—an art as vastly superior to the ordinary British sailor's tattooing as Heidsieck Monopole [champagne] is to small beer. Birds, flowers, landscapes of marvelous finish and beauty—thoroughly Japanese withal in style and conception—are now

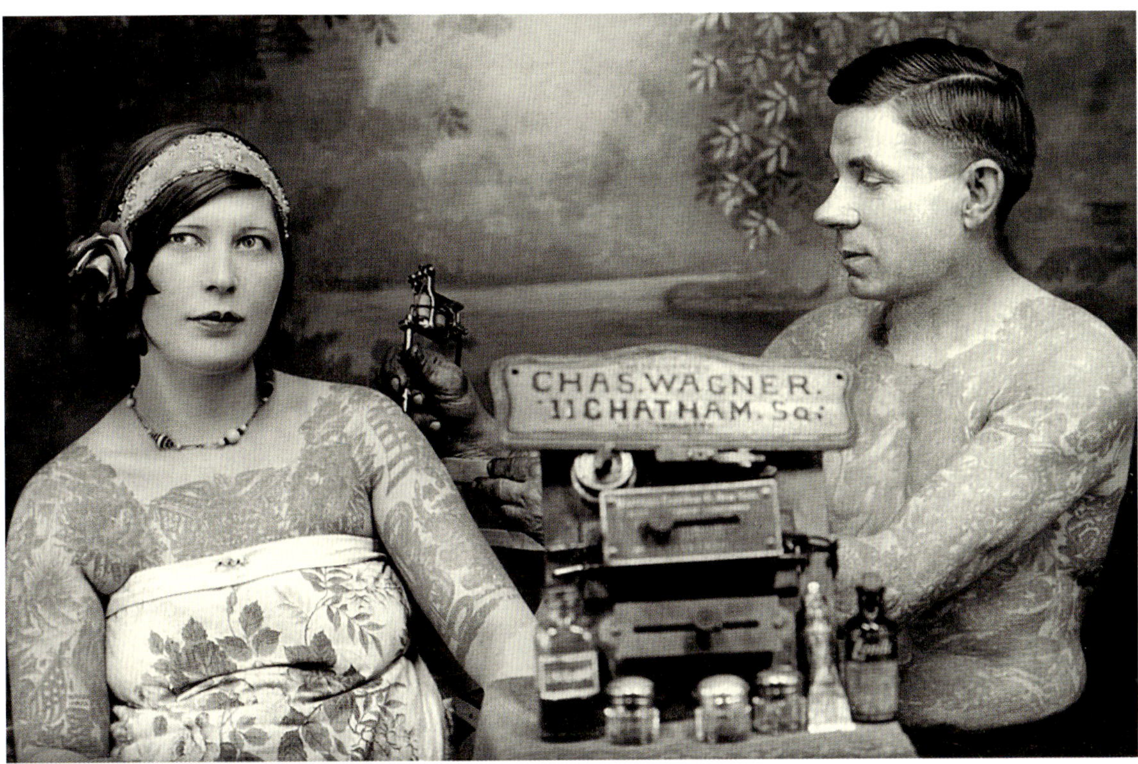

executed, some specimens being so minute as almost to render the aid of a microscope necessary in order properly to appreciate them."

Tattooing Innovations

As the demand for tattoos grew, increasing numbers of artists established tattoo shops in the major cities of Britain and the United States. Increased business led to greater competition, driving innovations among artists seeking commissions from the highest-paying customers. For example, first in the United States and then later in England, tattooers began to adapt modern electrical appliances into tools for their trade. Anything that could produce a reciprocating motion was converted, as it would allow tattooers to work more quickly, and thus more profitably. Dental pluggers for filling holes in teeth were the first handheld electrical devices to be patented. Toward the latter half of the

1880s, tattooers were using these tools to speed up the laborious process of pricking in ink by hand. The first patent for a tattoo machine, awarded in 1891, was granted to New York tattooer Samuel O'Reilly for a device adapted from Thomas Edison's reciprocating engraving pen, originally designed for making stencils for document reproduction.

In England, Sutherland Macdonald had been using an electric machine since 1891 and was granted a patent for it in 1894; his rival Alfred South (b. Alfred Schmidt), an Austrian immigrant to London, patented a tattoo machine derived from a doorbell chime in 1900. American tattooer and performer Frank Howard sold electric machines to the public in the United Kingdom in 1898 as part of his traveling show.

Innovation also spread to colored tattooing inks. Prior to the electric era, tattooing inks were almost exclusively blue-black or red. In the Victorian period,

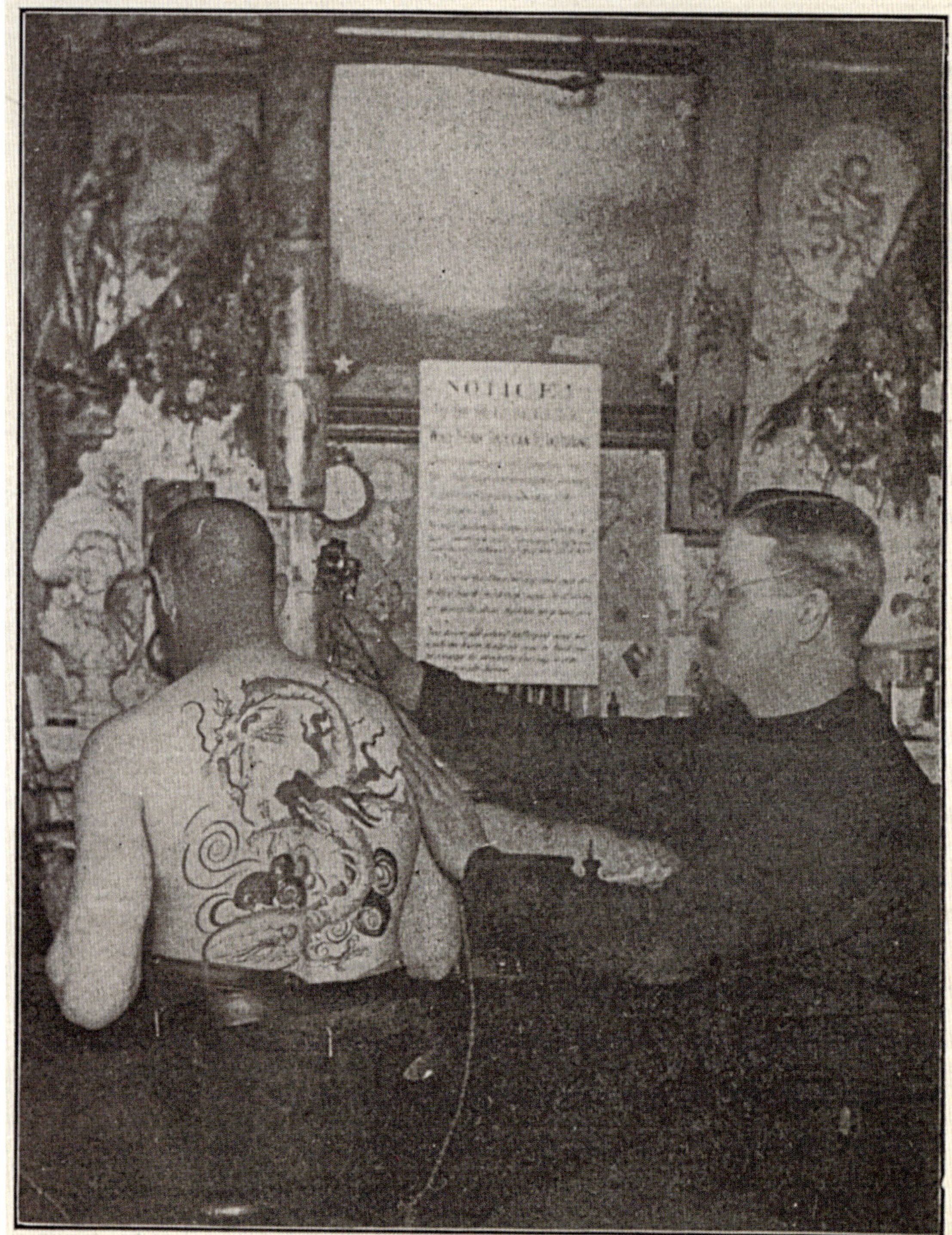

PROF. O'REILLY AT WORK.

The interior of an electric tattooing shop.

Power to the people (*left*) Samuel O'Reilly was the first person to hold a patent for an electric tattoo machine, which he obtained in 1891. O'Reilly worked in New York from around 1885 onward, claiming to have trained with Martin Hildebrandt. He narrowly escaped prison time for tattooing minors in the early twentieth century, and generally cultivated a reputation as a "professor" of some standing (see page 37). His shop on Chatham Square became a key hub for tattooing on America's east coast, and played home to several of the most famous tattooers of the period.

A crowded marketplace (*right*) The three big names of the late nineteenth- and early twentieth-century industry often sparred through the medium of adverts in key periodicals read by the upper-middle classes, including *Country Life*, *Sporting Times*, and *Badminton*. Each claimed (with varying degrees of puffery) royal patronage, global reputation, technical innovation, and hygienic technique.

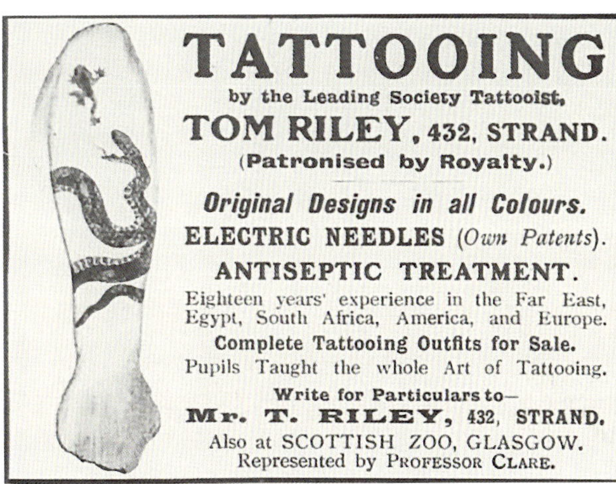

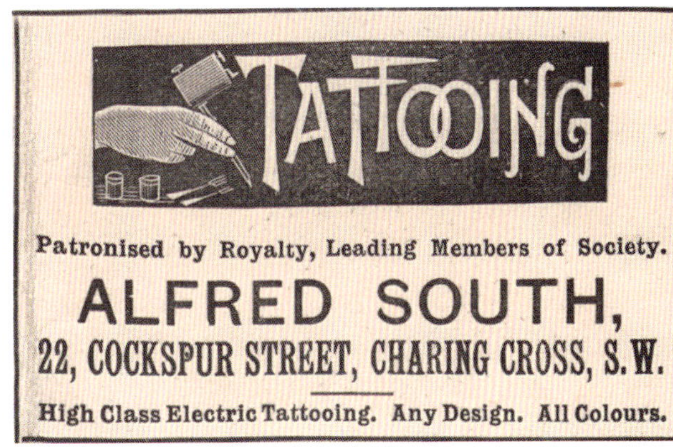

Macdonald began to experiment with colored mineral pigments that would heal in the skin, introducing browns, greens, and pinks in rapid succession. Only yellow eluded him—at one point, whatever substance he was experimenting with caused such an awful toxic reaction that he reports having to cut chunks of flesh away from his body!

Professional Rivalry

The tattooing boom also led to hostility and rivalries, as artists fought for prominence, fame, and even prime locations in order to ensure a steady stream of wealthy clients. In America, O'Reilly ended up in court, sued by fellow New York tattooer Elmer Getchell over who really deserved the electric machine patent. Getchell also testified against one of O'Reilly's colleagues, Charlie Wagner, when Wagner was accused of tattooing children. In London, Macdonald took on a tattooer called Tom Riley (b. Thomas Clarkson) in the pages of the London press, squabbling over which of them had tattooed particular members of the royal family. Each furiously laid claim to having tattooed Prince George, even though there is no evidence that the future king was ever tattooed again, following his return to England. In turn, Riley feuded with rival Alfred South over the prime tattooing pitch at the Royal Aquarium, by the 1890s London's premier venue for the edgier end of music-hall entertainment. Their rivalry became so heated that they resorted to a fist fight over who was the better artist, and who had more right to tattoo punters at the Aquarium. Each also engaged in absurd publicity stunts of questionable veracity. Riley claimed to have tattooed a water buffalo in Paris; South posed for pictures while tattooing a tiger tamer inside the tiger's cage. In spite of all this drama, however, urban, professional tattooing retained a veneer of class, albeit

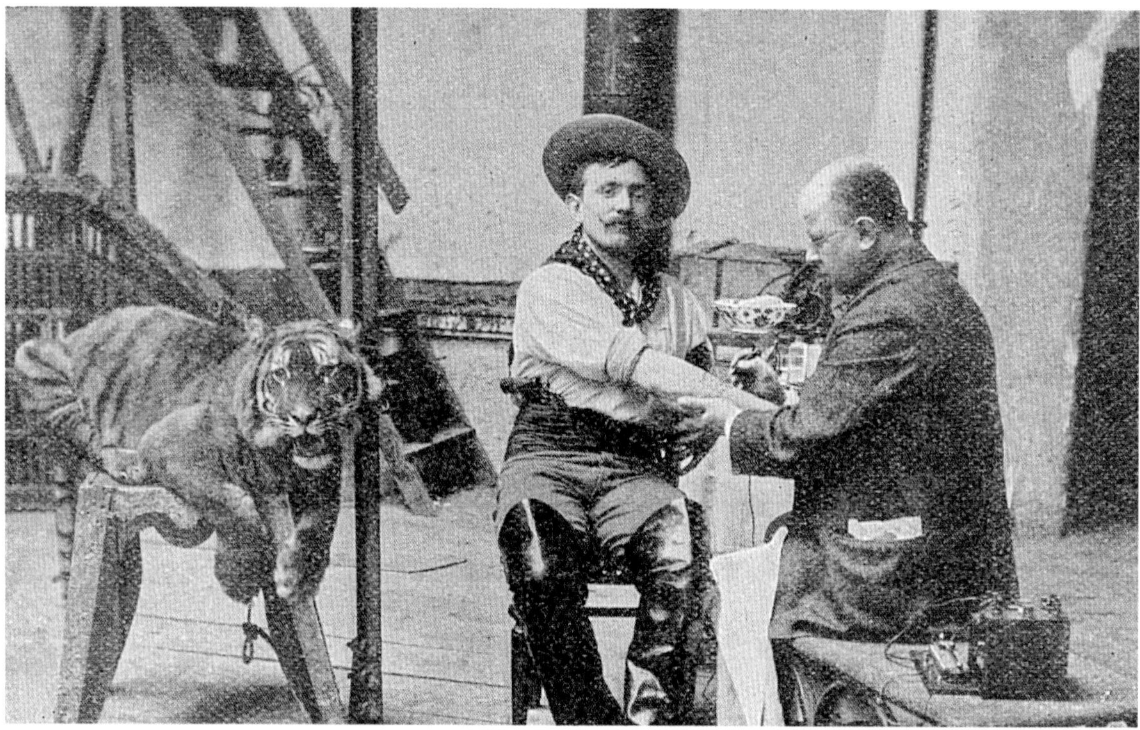

one always viewed with suspicion by the mainstream sections of society.

Through the late 1800s and in the years leading up to World War I, tattooing was able to exist in a way that rather transcended social status. On the one hand, the art was celebrated in the most fashionable members' clubs. Certain tattooers were patronized by actors, members of parliament, and minor royals, while others worked at the stuffy Crufts dog show, lest owners wanted souvenir portraits of their dogs. Tattoo artists worked at world fairs and, in London at least, had studios on the most monied streets in the city. On the other hand, even the trendiest tattooers were treated more as eccentrics than central members of the artistic establishment, and eager youngsters who had been tattooed were regularly condemned as foolish: in 1881, a young girl called Marinella was admonished in the pages of *The Girl's Own Paper* that "your efforts to

remove tattoo marks are quite thrown away, inasmuch as the cure would be worse than the disease . . . Wear long sleeves, or mittens, or gloves."

Some tattooers did forge social statuses commensurate with some prestige—Macdonald was gifted a cigarette case by a baronet; South was a member of the Freemasons—but this never fully blossomed into a complete sense of legitimacy. As often as tattoo art was celebrated, it was condemned—as a health hazard, a foolish fad, or even as creeping barbarianism. Even as some headlines raved about this new fine art, others reported on the occasional deaths of some customers as a result of unsanitary practices: in 1880, a maritime tattooer from the West Indies, Thomas Chapman, "a professor of the art of tattooing," and likely the first Black tattoo artist recorded in Britain, was charged and ultimately acquitted in relation to the death of a Liverpudlian boiler-maker,

Publicity stunts (*left*) Tattooers took to increasingly bold and implausible stunts to grab headlines and customers. Tom Riley claimed (without evidence) to have tattooed a water buffalo, and here Alfred South is tattooing a Viennese tiger tamer in the circus ring. "Halfway through the sitting," the report claims, "the brute broke loose and attacked the tattooist." South, of course, escaped the vicious beast just in the nick of time, and was able to complete the tattoo.

Man's best friend (*right*) Aside from hunting and shooting, Victorian and Edwardian high society also had a fascination with dogs. Sutherland Macdonald advertised in the program at the famous Crufts dog show in 1904; Tom Riley was once photographed tattooing identification marks onto a customer's puppy; and Alfred South made headlines for his canine portraits, pictured here.

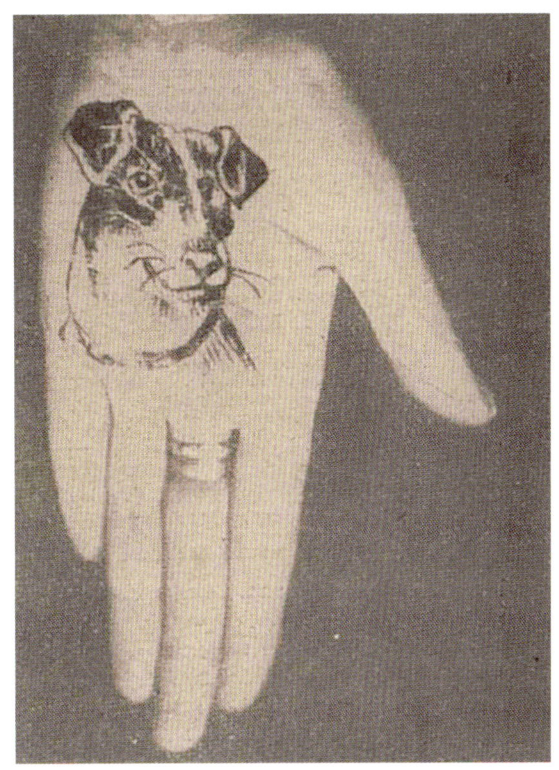

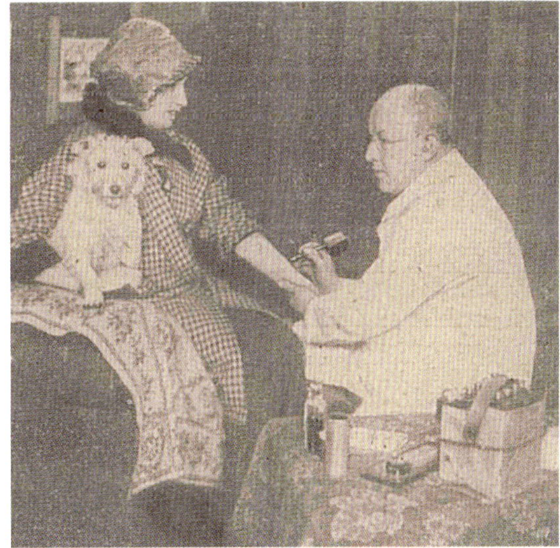

Robert Willey, after Willey's tattoos became infected; in 1899, Alfred South was charged but also acquitted of the death of one of his customers, who had died under similar circumstances.

As with all trends initiated by the upper classes, those customers with the greatest wealth eventually tired of tattooing and moved on to other things, leaving the art to slip slowly down the social strata. It is typical of upper-class tastemakers to abandon their fashions and habits once they are adopted by those on lower social rungs and thus lose their air of exclusivity and refined taste. Gone was the time when Victorian aristocrats sat for dozens of hours over several sittings to buy expensive, custom dermal artwork, tattooed for the most part by hand. Now, middle- and lower-class Edwardian consumers, who couldn't afford work at such quality and scale, began to get tattoos that were smaller, less elaborate, and less unique.

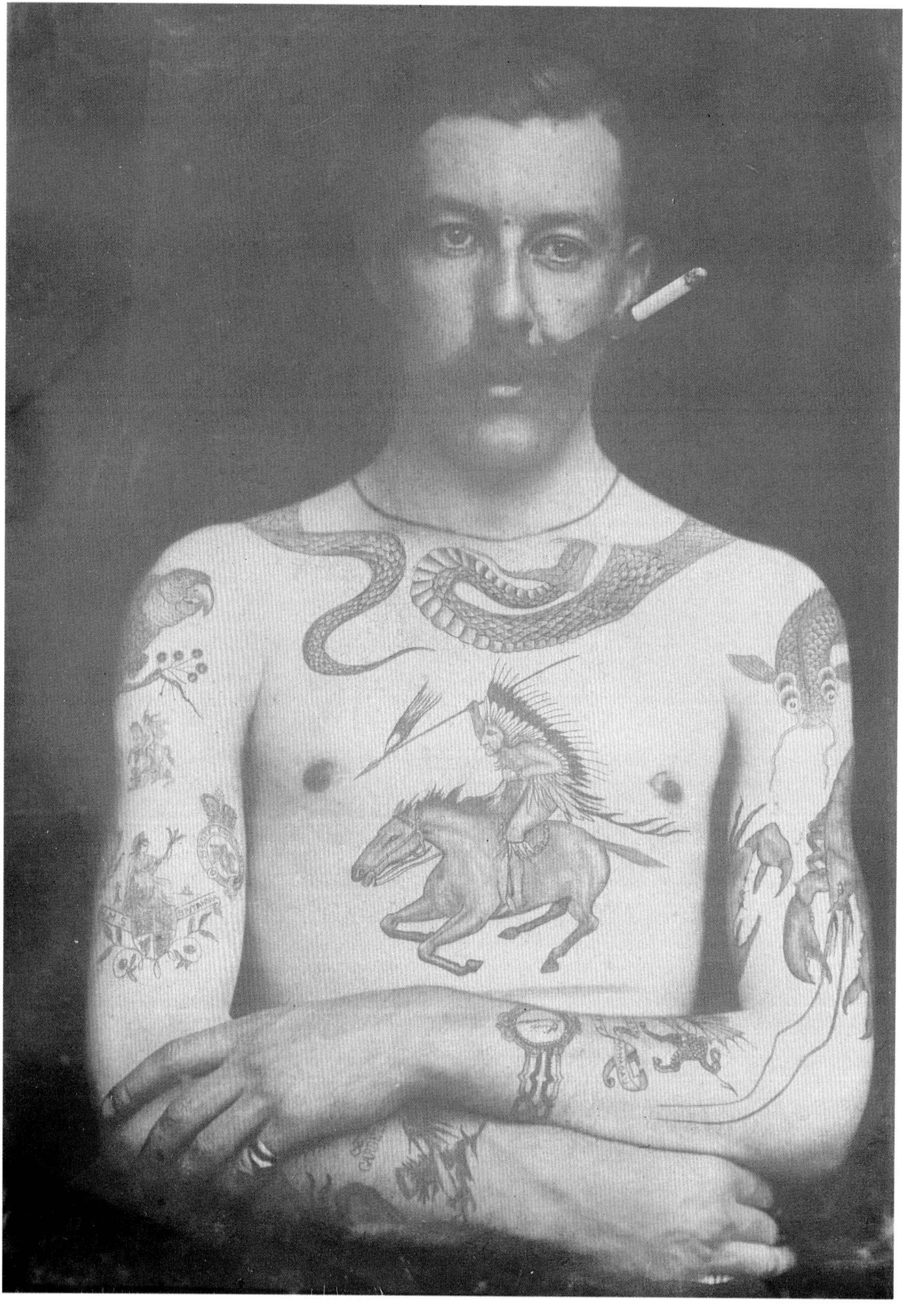

Indian on horseback tattoo by Sutherland Macdonald on The Hon. George Edwardes, 1905 (*left*)

Despite roguish appearances, this client of Macdonald's is George Edwardes, son of prominent Member of Parliament William Edwardes, 4th Baron Kensington. George was later promoted to the rank of Major. Like many of Macdonald's celebrity clients, Edwardes sports a combination of European and Japanese designs, including a catfish on his left arm which is traced directly from Hokusai (see below).

Snake and frog tattoo by Sutherland Macdonald on unknown customer, 1905 (*right*)

The frog pictured here bears great resemblance in composition to one drawn by Hokusai (see below), which featured in *A Grammar of Japanese Ornament and Design* (1880), by Thomas W. Cutler. Macdonald drew upon such books frequently in composing his larger projects.

Hokusai, page from *Ryakuga haya-oshie*, 1814 (*below, left*); Hokusai, page from *Random Drawings by Hokusai*, 1850–59 (*below, right*)

Katsushika Hokusai's manga drawings are hailed as one of the key drivers of the popularity of Japanese design in Europe following the opening of Japan. Designers, printmakers, and artists used Hokusai's humble graphic designs as the basis for their own work on paper, glass, ceramic, silverware, and textiles. Tattooers, too, lifted Hokusai's designs to add an air of Japonesque authenticity to their practice. The frog, in particular, has had a remarkable afterlife as an extremely popular tattoo design.

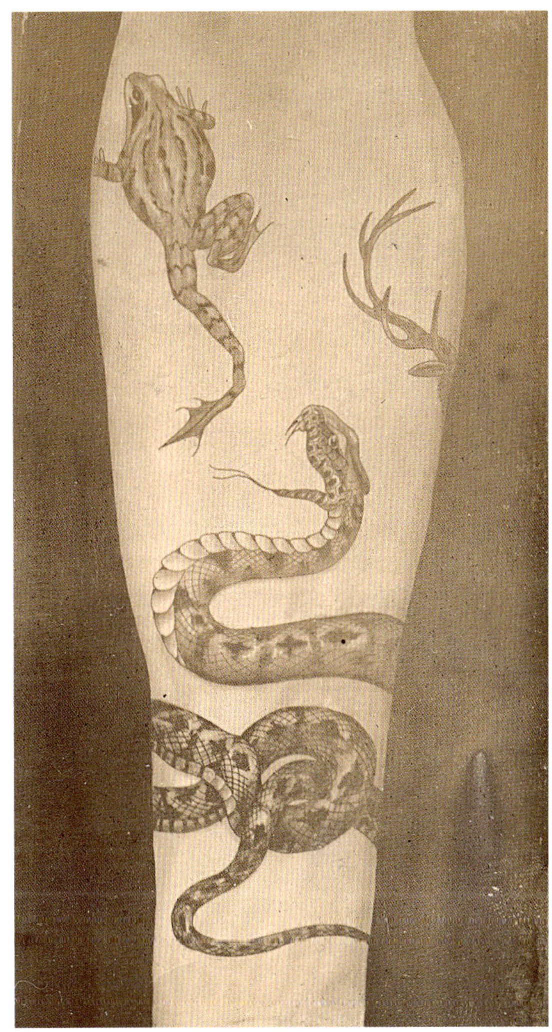

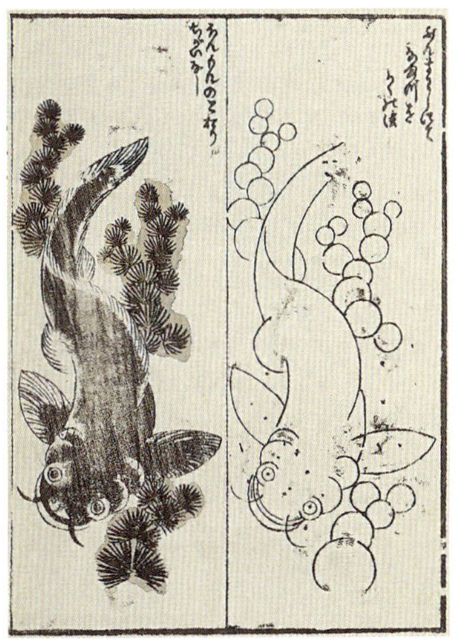

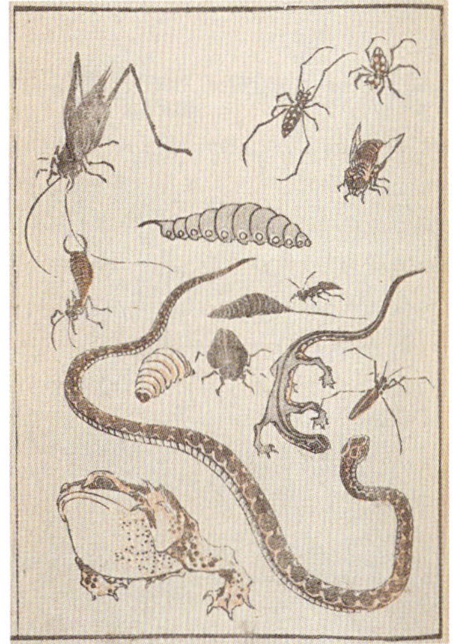

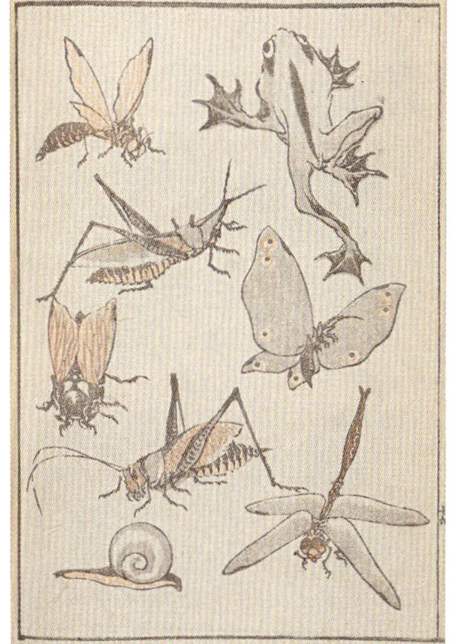

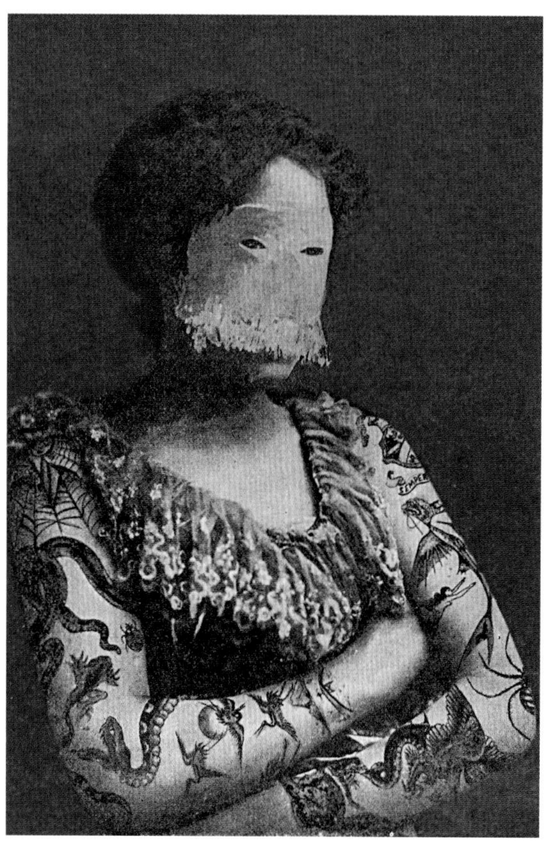

"A German Lady Well Known In Society," *English Illustrated Magazine*, **1903**

This mysterious woman appeared in an article called "Pictures on the Skin" from 1903, illustrating the work of London tattooer Tom Riley. The reason for her mask is unclear, but there are two possible reasons. The first is that this woman is not, in fact, a well-known German lady, as the caption attests, and Riley is simply intending to give the impression of a better-heeled client-base than he actually possessed. The second is that this woman really is of high standing, and wished to keep the knowledge of her tattoos discreet. Among her distinctive collection of European and Japanese designs, note the frog, again referenced from Hokusai (see page 61), on her right arm.

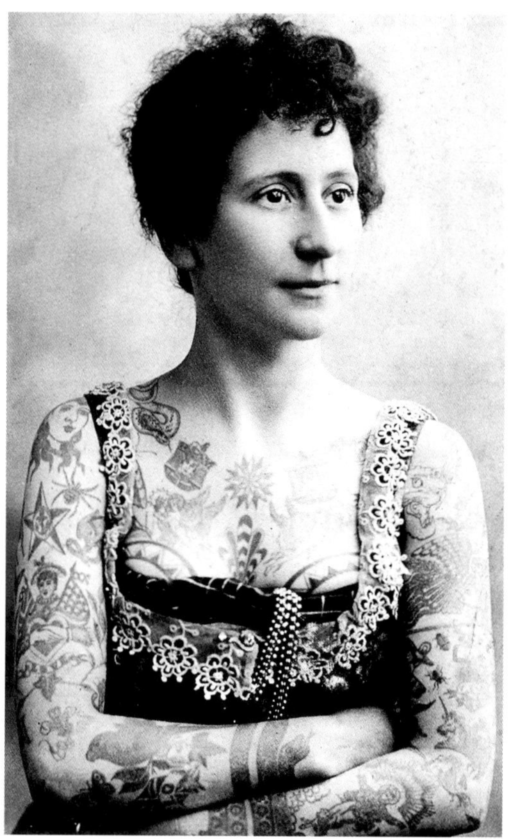

Flo Riley, The Living Picture Gallery, 1903

Tom Riley's wife Florence performed at the Royal Aquarium and elsewhere as a "Living Art Gallery." Riley often performed tattooing live on stage as part of his act. She and Tom separated in the early 1900s, and she briefly carried on her show as "Mademoiselle Flo" alongside her new partner, American escapologist Fred Cady.

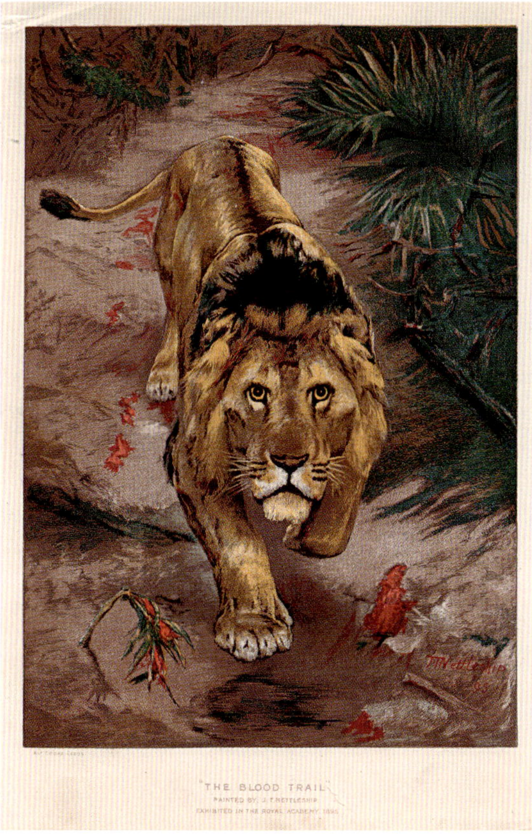

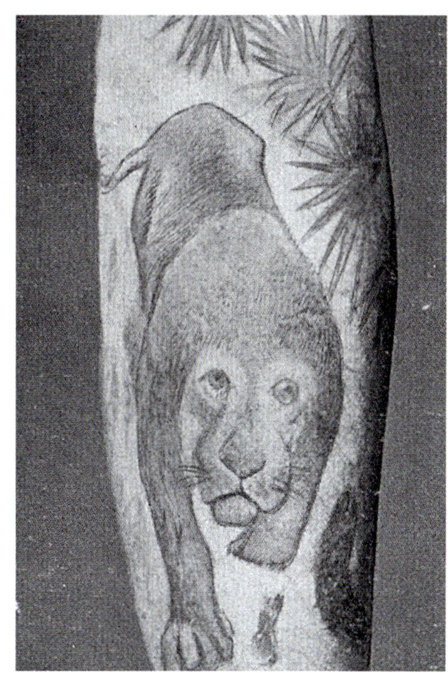

Detail from "The Gentle Art of Tattooing" article, *Tatler*, 1903 (*above*)

Alfred South was the third of the prominent tattooers of Victorian London, and sadly perhaps, the least technically adept. Though, like Macdonald and Riley, he advertised in high-society magazines like *Tatler*, it is clear that he lacked some of the technical finesse of his rivals. The saggy-looking lion, for example, is an awkward rendition of the cover of a *Boy's Own* magazine (*above*). Nevertheless, he boasts in his *Tatler* advert of having tattooed over 15,000 people.

Alfred South leaflet cover, 1904 (*right*)

South was multilingual, and like his rivals cultivated customers across the world, hence his advertising card here in French and German as well as English. Note the self-designation as "artist," and the claim for copyright on the design, which was officially lodged with the Stationer's Office.

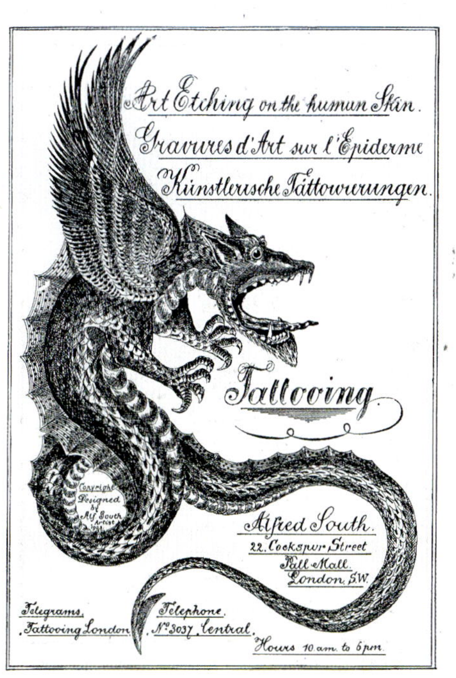

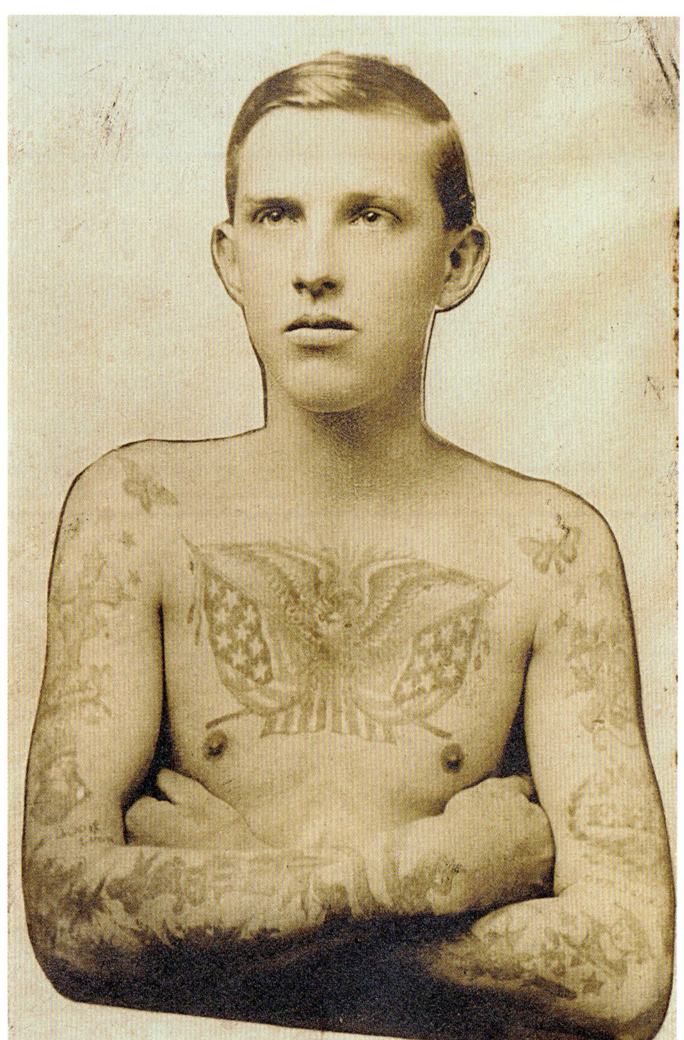

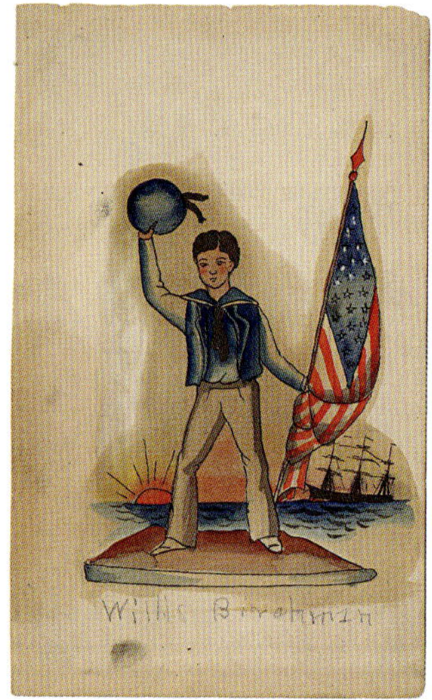

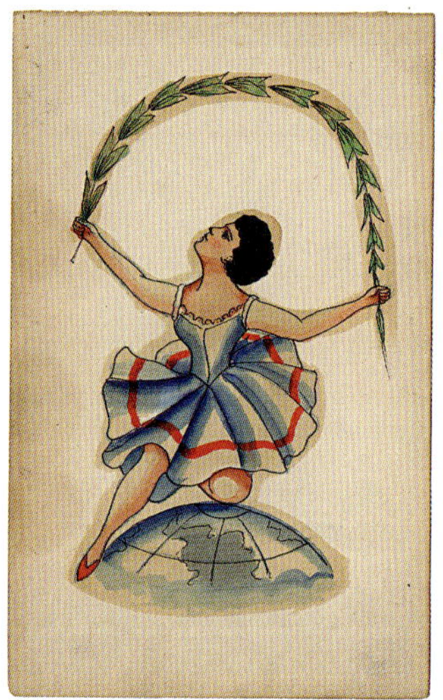

Young American, perhaps tattooed by Samuel O'Reilly, late nineteenth century

Though tattooers in New York boasted of high-end clients, artists like O'Reilly generally had a lower class of customer than seen in England. New York's key status as a naval port as well as an urban metropolis meant that tattooers there had a much steadier supply of young sailors seeking new work on their skin, with popular designs thus taking on a much more militaristic flavor. The text visible on the boy's left arm is in a typographic style often used by O'Reilly.

Flash designs attributed to Samuel O'Reilly, late nineteenth century

O'Reilly owned a large volume of hand-painted designs in watercolor and ink. Such designs, called "flash," were available for customers to choose from. Originally painted into books through which customers could flip, it is unclear if these designs are by O'Reilly himself, or someone with whom he worked. The page with the boy doffing his cap, for example, is marked on the front with the name "Willis Birchman," the son of one of O'Reilly's collaborators, Arthur Birchman. Birchman was a "lightning cartoonist," who sketched theater patrons live on stage, and could thus be the artist here.

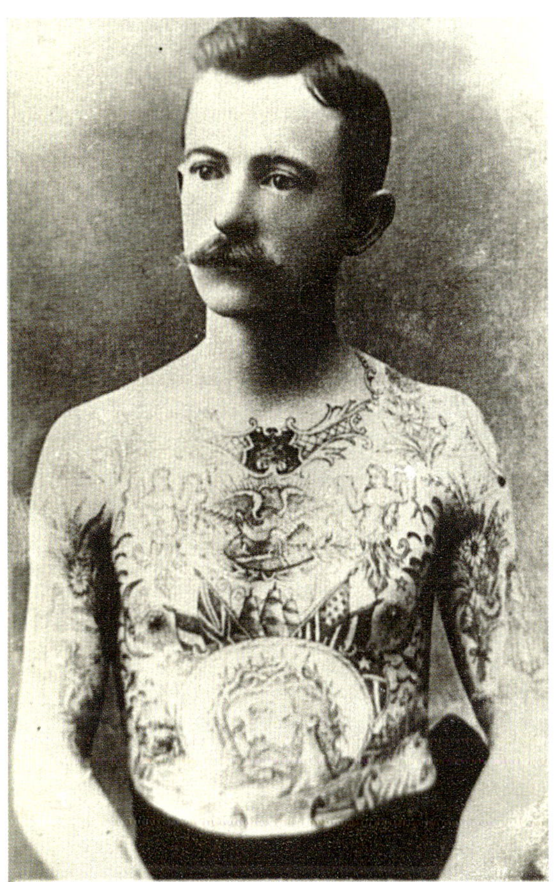

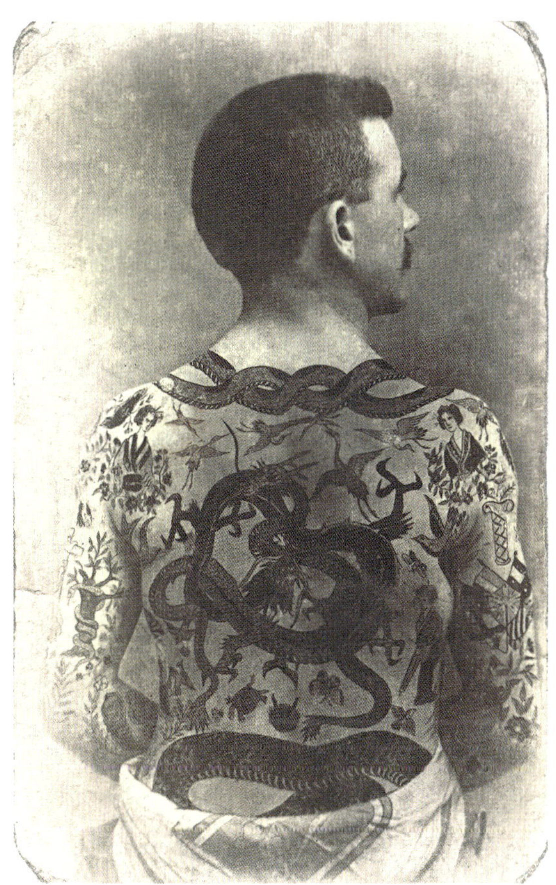

Tattooed men, early twentieth century

On the left is American performing tattooed man Frank
La Ramo. Tattooed extensively across his body, La Ramo
wore an enormous tattoo of a Civil War naval battle on his
back. The extensive backpiece on the right was tattooed by
Liverpool tattooer William Turner, who began working in
the city around 1904.

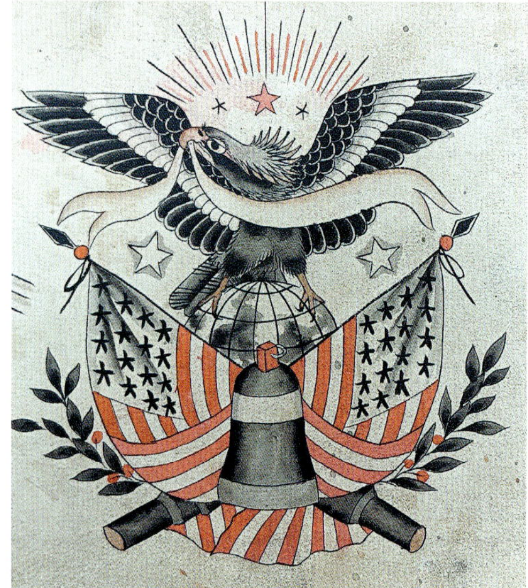

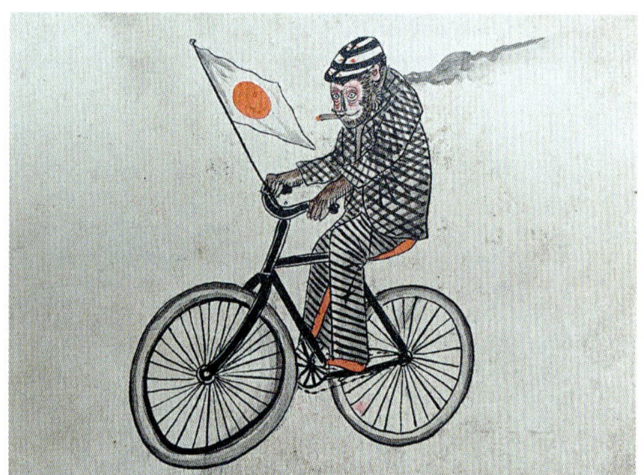

Tattoo flash designs by O. Ikasaki, c.1908

Across several small, vibrant sketchbooks, Nagasaki-based tattooer Ikasaki offers a remarkably eclectic mix of tattoos specifically tailored toward European clients. Alongside dragons and other familiar Orientalist motifs, Ikasaki has drawn amusing caricatures, including a monkey riding a bicycle; Westernized "pinups"; Japonesque takes on popular sailor tattoos such as eagles, gravestones, and pierced hearts; and even figures carrying empty flags, presumably to be customized depending on the wearer's allegiance. As such, they do not resemble traditional Japanese Irezumi in style or scale, but instead comprise a hybrid form which adopts European tastes to produce tattoos that could be completed relatively quickly. These design books are utterly unlike any common imagination of Japanese tattooing at the turn of the 20th century, and demonstrate the mutual paths of influence between Europe, the United States, and Japan. Japanese tattooing was changed by Western influence and taste, just as Western tattooing was changed by the opening of Japan.

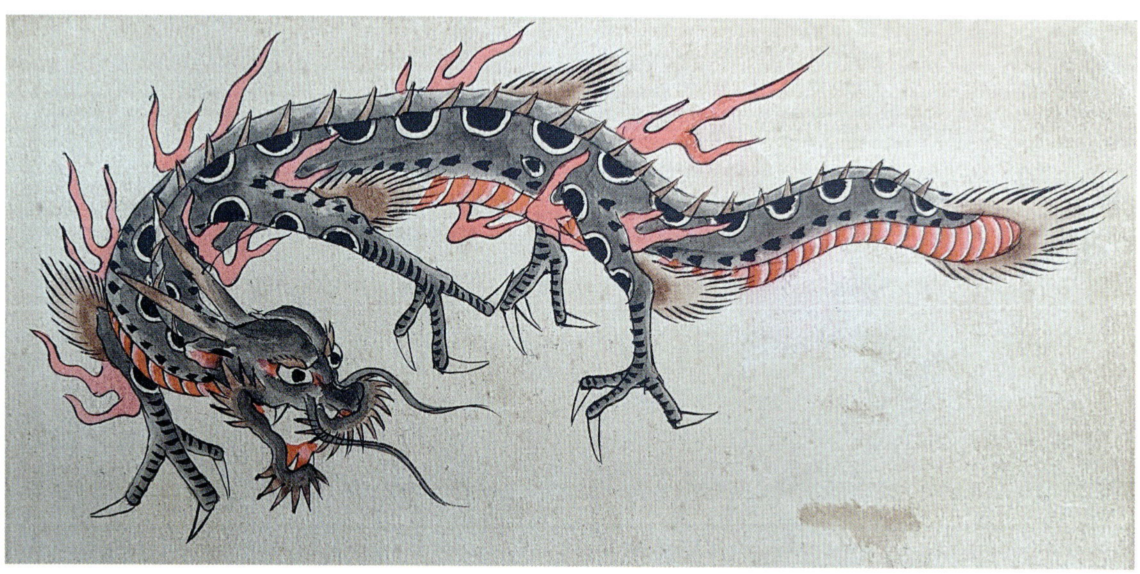

Tattoo flash designs by O. Ikasaki, c.1908

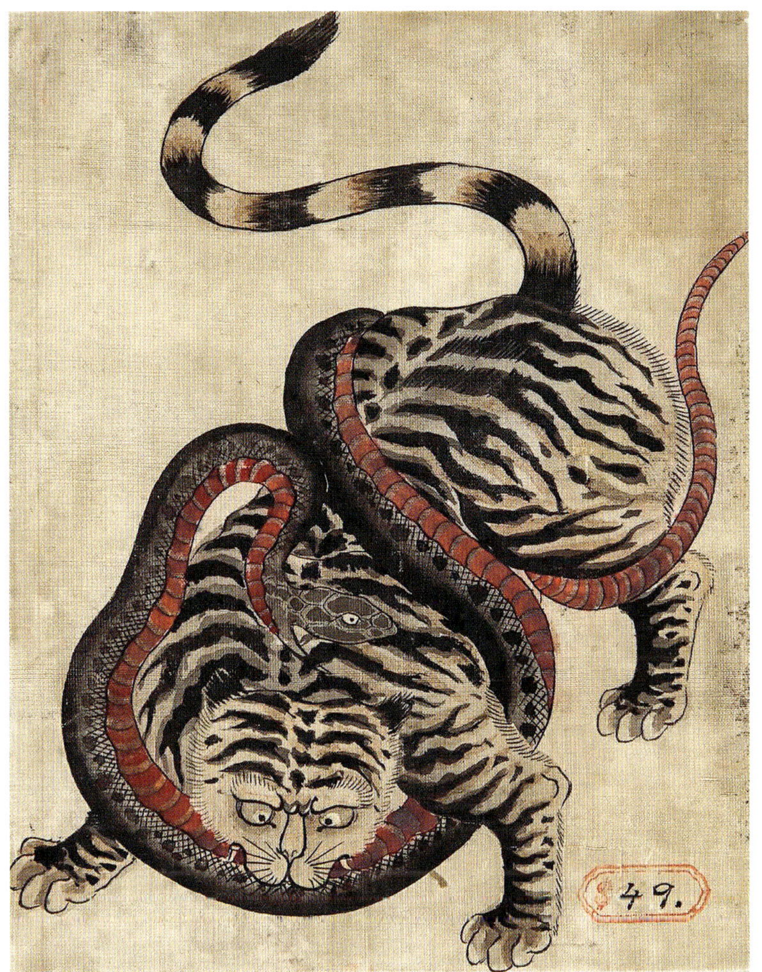

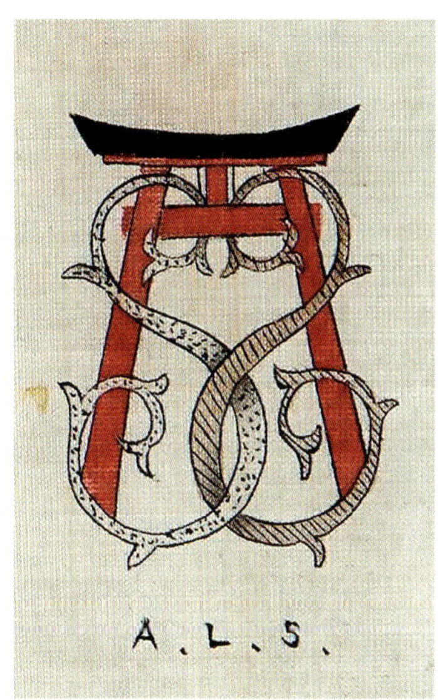

Designs by Hori Chiyo, early twentieth century

Though his contemporaries did not think highly of his workmanship, Hori Chiyo (b. Miyazaki Tadashi) was internationally famous as the man who purportedly tattooed the Royal Princes George and Albert Victor when they visited Yokohama in 1881. Though this claim has been convincingly disputed, Chiyo capitalized on this reputation, with his name becoming a byword globally for excellence in the art of tattooing. While many of his designs are large, and in the Japanese style, Chiyo's surviving drawings include a large set of monograms, created for visiting European aristocracy. The large design here shows "battle royale," a common motif of mortal combat between fearsome beasts. The theme of disparate animals locked in an unwinnable, balanced impasse serves to remind viewers of the cosmic clashes of good and evil, light and dark. It is also interesting to note that while tigers are common in Japanese art, there are no wild tigers in Japan. This perhaps explains why Chiyo's tiger here looks more like a tigerskin rug than an actual, living beast.

Tattooing During and After Wartime

1914–1939

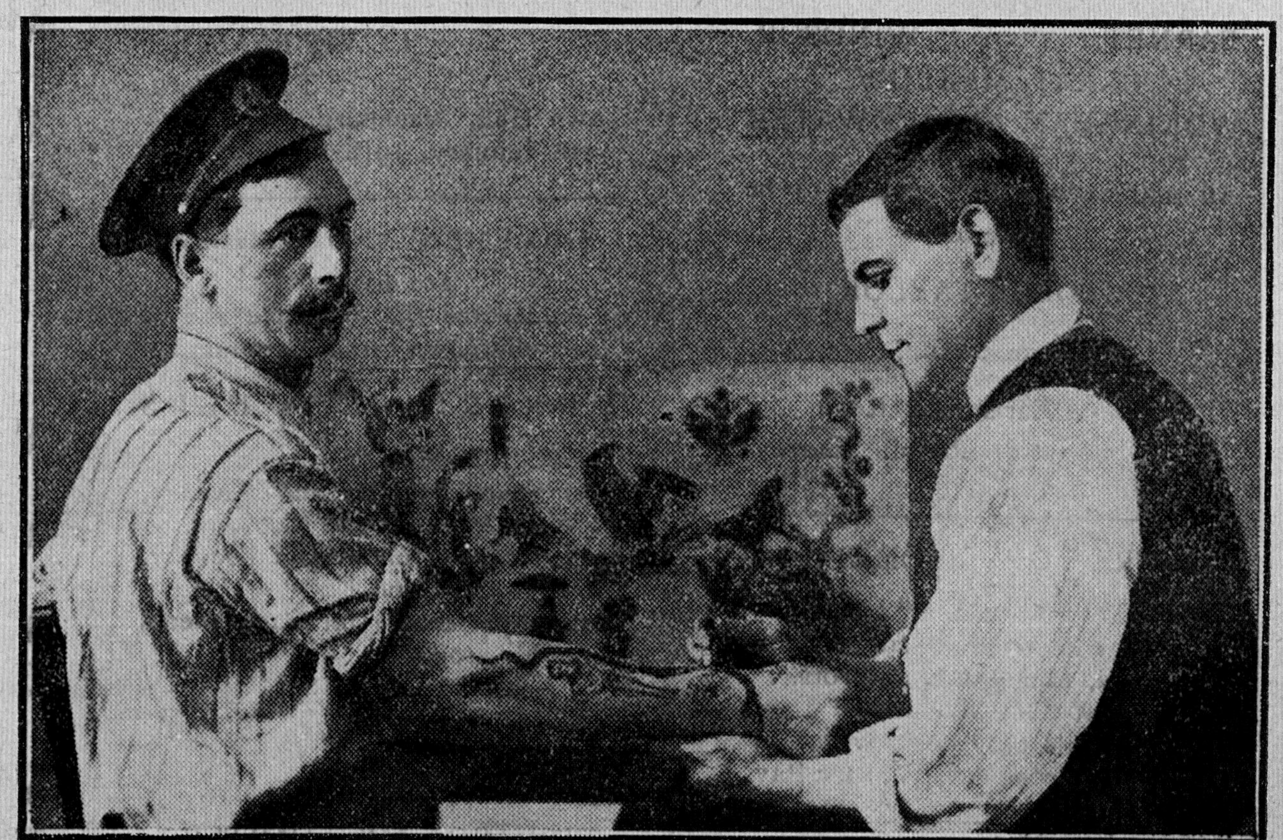

One of the results of the great war has been the revival of the ancient art of tattooing and our photograph shows Professor Pat Kilbride, one of the foremost followers of this art at work in the Agricultural Hall, Islington. Professor Pat Kilbride is the artiste who is responsible for the clever designs on Miss Queenie

Revival of an "ancient art" Professor Joe Kilbride, also known as Pat, was a peripatetic tattooer and stage-set painter from Bradford, UK. Shown here tattooing a soldier at a 1916 agricultural show in London as the "great war revived the ancient art of tattooing," Pat can be traced to have worked at fairs, shows, and theaters across England and Ireland from 1901, though he boasted even then a fifteen-year prior career. Intriguingly, the 1911 census records his occupation as "labourer" and his wife Hannah's as "tattooist." It was common for women to work alongside their husbands, boyfriends, and fathers in the industry, though they were rarely recognized as artists in their own right.

n November 1915, the *North Star* newspaper in Darlington, an industrial town in England's northeast, reported on the "tattooing craze," showing its readers an image of a young woman being tattooed on her right forearm, as her soldier boyfriend bends over the tattooer's table to get a better look. "The latest in tattooing," the caption reads, "is to have the 'best boy' tattooed on the arm, and many artists who make a specialty of this are doing great business."

World War I had brought a boom to tattoo shops across Britain, as men heading to the front stood in line to have marks of love, patriotism, and home tattooed on their skin. Lovers and family members joined them, creating intimate images that could never be lost during the turbulence into which the world had been thrown. With the shift in clientele from the high-society customers of the late-nineteenth century to less wealthy patrons, designs grew smaller, cheaper, and could be more quickly applied. Popular designs included simple names, regimental emblems, patriotic insignia, and flags, as well as sentimental tokens of love and memory—a return, of sorts, to the vernacular design language of Anglo-American tattooing before the eighteenth century. Regular enlisted men and officers were keen to be tattooed, but the specific circumstances of war also drove, according to the *North Star*, "numbers of girls and women who in ordinary times did not dream of being tattooed" into tattooers' salons.

The *Hull Daily Mail* imagined with horror these tattooed women as stylish young debutantes with enormous spiders and birds tattooed on their necks, and apparently trendsetting black beetles on their arms. But the general trend for women was more conventional. Photographs survive of women working in munitions factories, for example, proudly displaying the names of their sweethearts tattooed on

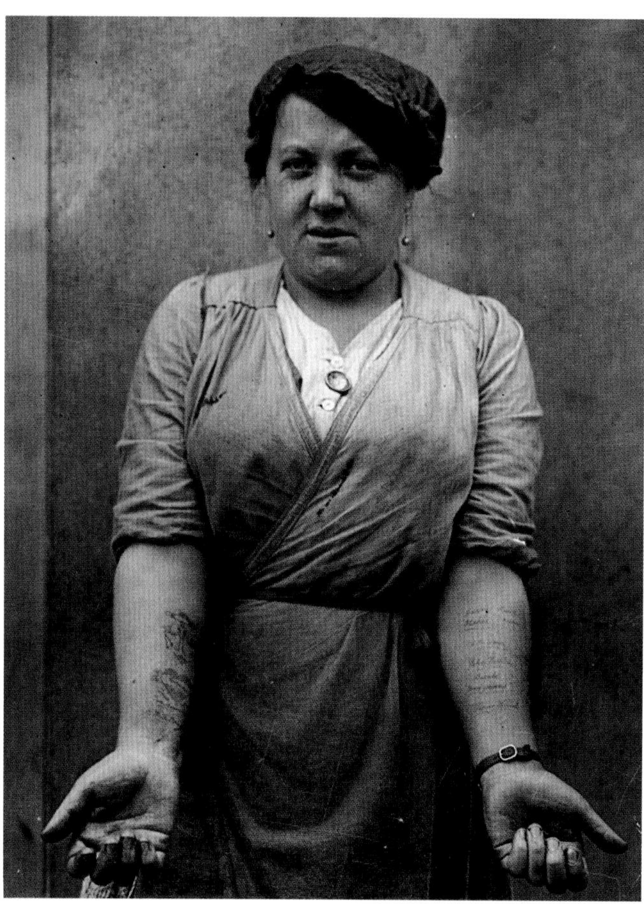

Working women (*left*) The history of tattooing among working-class women is hard to trace, given the archival scarcity of good records of their lives. Nevertheless, as with men, we can be sure much more tattooing was hidden under clothing than has usually been acknowledged. This woman displays her memorial and patriotic designs during a break from work at a munitions factory in 1917.

In the colonies (*right*) George Burchett and Professor John Thomson Clark outside their studio in Johannesburg, South Africa. Despite the date of 1910 enscribed on the photo, this image was likely taken in late 1911.

their arms alongside memorial crosses added later to commemorate their untimely deaths at the front. That said, sometimes the indelibility of tattooing meant the marks outlasted the relationships that they were intended to commemorate—readers of a newspaper were presumably amused by the 1915 tale of a fickle East End belle, who had been "distinctly unfortunate with her lovers in the services, and is declared to have had no fewer than a dozen names obliterated from her arm." Later in the war, *Punch* magazine imagined an embarrassed girl in a similar predicament, telling the tattooer that she needed her regimental badge tattoo covered up, as her boyfriend had "transferred into another regiment."

In the late nineteenth and early twentieth century, a few enterprising tattooers had started selling equipment and stencil designs by post and at exhibitions. The trade was of sufficient volume by 1912 for San Francisco tattooer Louis Morgan to advise readers of his pamphlet *Modern Tattooist* to ensure they purchased their designs only from professional tattoo artists. While any talented draftsman could produce a good stencil, only the best and most experienced tattooers could really understand which images would prove popular with customers.

During the Edwardian period and into the war, tattoo machines were even sold over the counter at a London department store called Gamages. Novelties Ltd, a firm from Norwich in England, advertised and possibly manufactured tattooing equipment and supplies alongside "novel toys and fancy goods," with customers as far away as South Africa. The company even distributed an anonymously penned "How-To" guide, which also featured a potted (if inaccurate) history of the trade. In France, as his biographer recalled, Pablo Picasso himself was practicing with tattooing

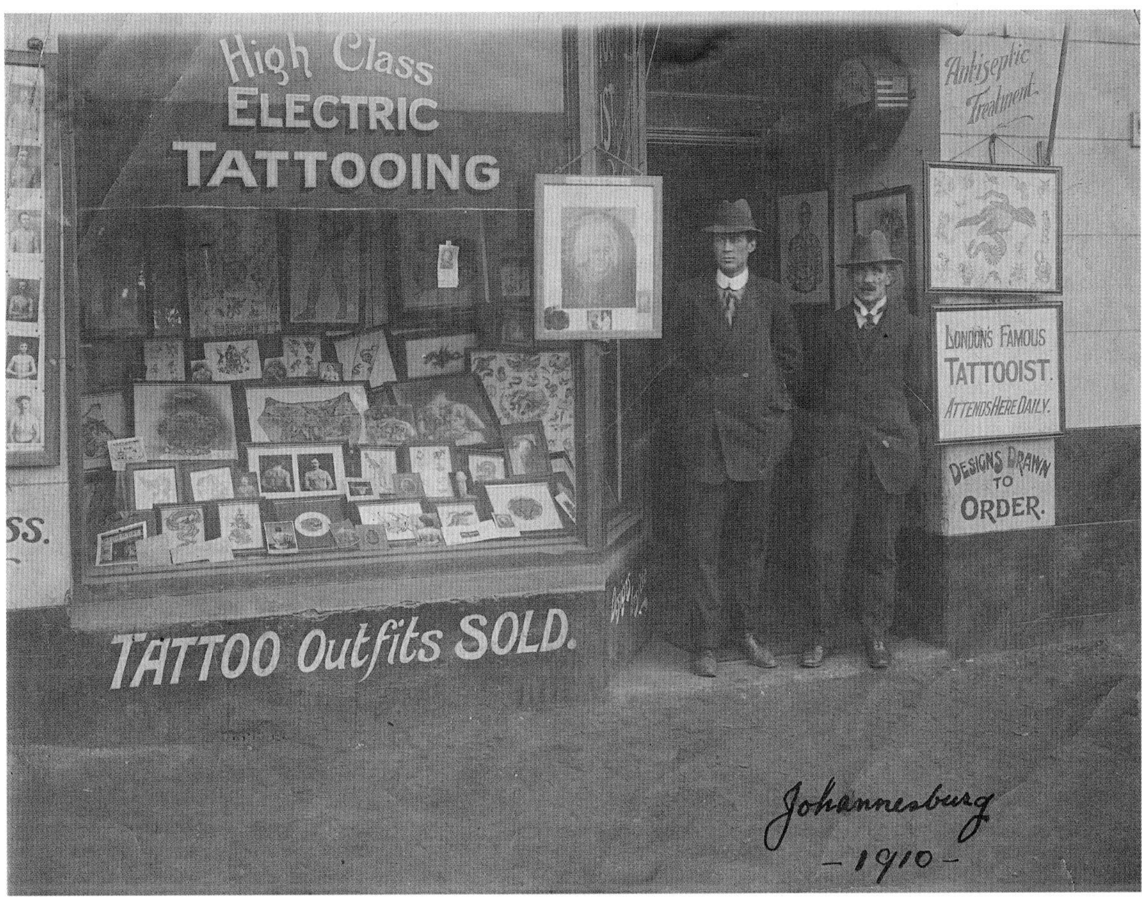

equipment around 1917. But as tattooing increased in popularity, some, including George Burchett's brother Charles Davis, realized there was also a ready market to sell tattoo removal tinctures through mail order. Aside from the ignominy of a permanent reminder of a failed relationship, for some soldiers the indelibility of tattoo marks made desertion rather more difficult, should they have wished to skip their service.

Throughout the war, the *Police Gazette* listed the names of men who had abandoned their positions from the British Army, accompanied by helpful descriptions of their tattoo marks. The systematic records of tattoo marks on enlisted men also made the identification of dead bodies easier. When the body of a young sailor washed up in Southend in July 1917, the police were only able to identify him based on the extensive tattooing that covered his arms and chest. Some tattooed men were darkly teased, in fact, that were

they to be blown up by enemy bombardment, they would make excellent jigsaw puzzles.

More than twenty tattoo artists worked in London alone during the years leading up to World War I, including those arriving from elsewhere to make their living leaving their work on skin. American tattooer Gus Wagner claimed to have visited England in 1915, specifically to seek the tutelage of Sutherland Macdonald. Many more worked across the country: Prince Vallar in Glasgow, for example, was feted not only as an artist, but also "Nowdays," wrote *Thompson's Weekly* in 1910, "a beauty doctor," as comfortable tattooing "the daintiest designs that appeal to ladies" as seasonally appropriate images including plum puddings at Christmastime.

Central to the English boom was George Burchett of the aforementioned *Memoirs*. Burchett had been tattooing since the late 1890s, but in 1904 he had

Bavarian romanticism Karl Rödemich tattooed in the port city of Hamburg, Germany. Trained and celebrated as a porcelain painter, Rödemich seems to have begun tattooing in the 1870s, before the establishment of permanent studios in what would become Germany's tattoo capital. In 1934, folklorist Adolf Spamer published his account of tattooing in the German ports, and was particularly complimentary in his descriptions of design sheets by Rödemich, noting their "old, Bavarian romanticism."

opened a tattooing premises near Waterloo Station. He briefly moved to South Africa, tattooing alongside an artist called Professor John Thomson Clark, but in 1914 returned to London, running his next shop at 72 Waterloo Road, usefully located opposite the Union Jack Services Club. Men poured into London from across the country, and from Waterloo out to barracks from whence they would be despatched to the front. As one illustrated paper described it: "With the aid of electricity, the tattooer does his swift, skilful work— for Tommy and Jack feel underdressed without some designs tattooed on their arms or chest."

Burchett was forty-two years of age at the outbreak of the war. Avoiding the call to duty, he was able to work at his shop for the duration. There was plenty of work, and dozens of men plied their tattooing trade across the United Kingdom, particularly out of key military towns and dockyards such as Glasgow, Liverpool, Portsmouth, Dover, Chatham, Belfast, and Cardiff. Alongside the men, in 1917, the South London street directory even lists a female tattooer, Mrs. Annie Kitteridge, briefly holding the fort for her tattooer husband Josiah.

Further Afield

The patrons were not just Tommies and Jacks (men enlisted in armies and navies). Port towns across northern Europe became hubs for the tattoo trade as European fleets maneuvered through the edges of the old empires. Denmark, in particular, was buzzing with the noise of electric tattoo machines, and in fact the Western world's oldest still-functional tattoo shop continues to thrive at Nyhavn 17 in the Copenhagen docks. That space, first operated by the artist Gustav

Bechmann in 1884 underneath a bar, became so popular as a tattooing shop during World War I that it would become exclusively dedicated to the art in 1919.

The first professional tattoo artists in Germany were also established over the first decades of the twentieth century, with busy tattoo shops springing up in Hamburg in particular. Estimates suggest that more than twenty tattooers were active in the port between the end of the nineteenth century and the 1930s, frequently working inside other businesses, such as pubs, as well as in more conventional tattoo studios on occasion. Before the war, German artists such as Karl Rödemich and Karl Finke included designs in their flash books which, like those of their counterparts in Japan, catered as much to sailors from Britain and America as to locals.

German tattooers traded designs with American and British counterparts, too, and tattooed performers made good livings working at venues in Germany as well as in the Anglophone world. But as hostilities began, newspapers in England reported that British sailors were forgoing German artists.

Though the United States was removed from the immediate horrors of the Western Front, major urban centers and ports were thronging not only with sailors, but also with migrants from home and abroad seeking work in the new, busy factories, amusement in bars and circuses, and lodging in flophouses. Tattooing thrived in places with enormous naval bases such as Norfolk, Virginia, but also in cities like New York and Boston, where seafarers were at close quarters with new urban populations of all kinds. With dwindling work opportunities in the European variety and circus scene, due to both practicality and the fading of the

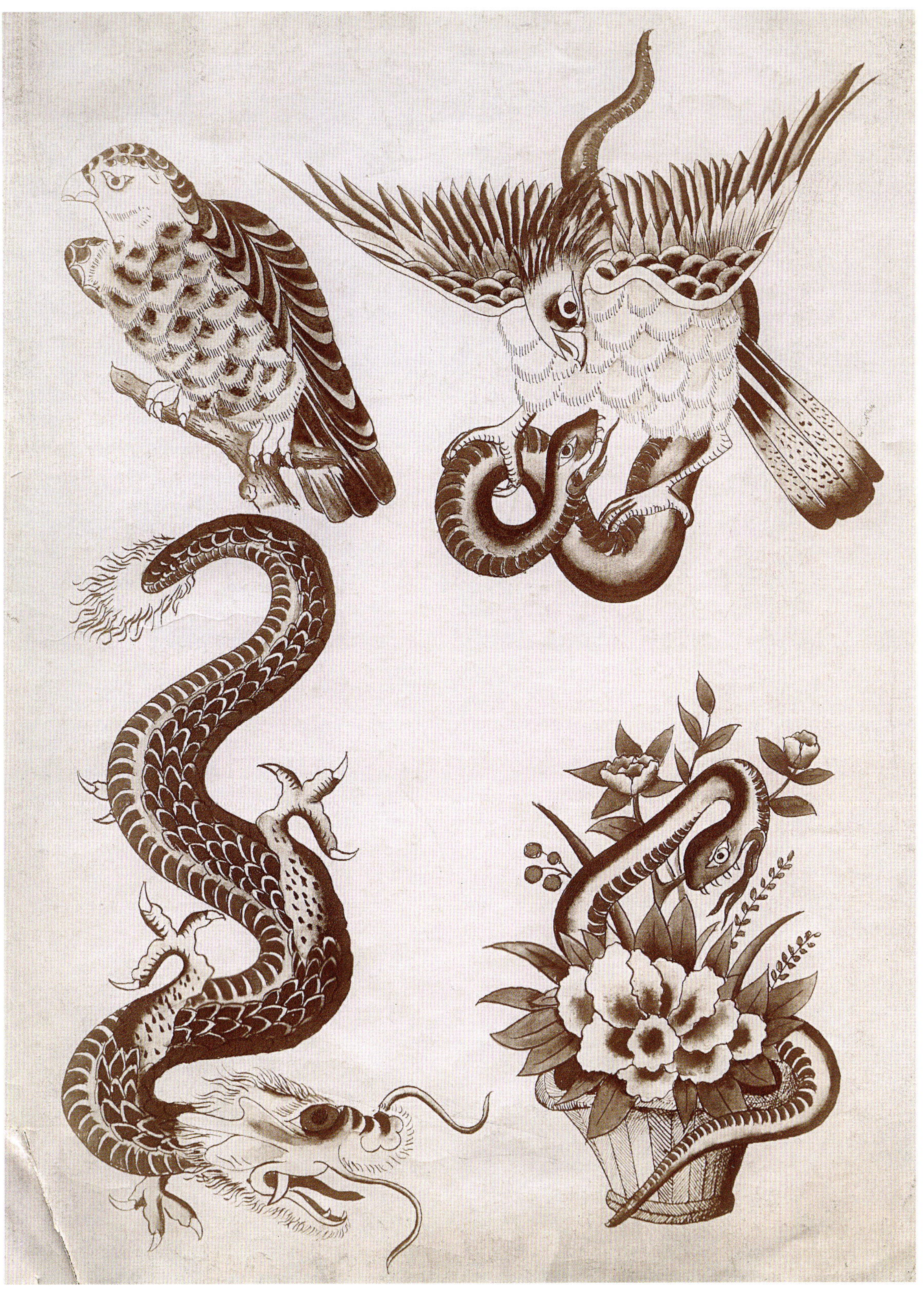

Power couple Samuel "Deafy" Grassman tattooing his wife Edith "Stella" Grassman, c.1930s. Both Deafy and Stella were tattoo artists—working in locations including Philadelphia and New York City from the 1920s onwards, the pair forged a strong reputation as something of a power couple, advertising themselves jointly as "The Original Deafy and Miss Stella." The quality of tattooing on Stella's body marks out Deafy as one of the finest artists of his era.

Victorian appetite for sideshows, tattooed American performers such as Frank Howard, who had made global headlines for his performances with Barnum & Bailey, made the move to become permanently established tattoo artists in their own right.

Such was the appetite for tattooing during World War I that, even at the front, tattooers were in high demand. Newsreels show gaggles of assembled young men, smiling and stripped to the waist, waiting eagerly outside a tent at an encampment as a tattooer pricks "I Love Alice" by hand into a recruit's arm. Throngs of British soldiers were also pictured being tattooed by local artists in Egypt. Trench magazines featured adverts for tattoo artists—one Sergeant Heslop of the 8th Reserve Battalion proudly proclaimed that he would tattoo "any design" from his hut, with prices starting at just one shilling. And an unnamed artist who claimed to have been trained by Burchett was celebrated in the *Guardian* as having taken tattooing with him to the front "as a hobby" before turning it into a profitable sideline:

> "There are men who say they would rather lose an arm or a leg than the picture that the soldier-artist has written for them . . . Many men were most anxious to have photographs of mothers or sweethearts copied in electric-needle pricks, and were delighted with the result. Others chose the old-fashioned tombstone design, or a scroll with 'In Remembrance,' while others chose heroic subjects. The Lusitania was a very favourite subject, but one could not learn whether any chest bore the cathedral of Rheims. Some of the men took advantage of their leisure hours to become perfect picture galleries, with angels, crucifixes, dragons and faces all elegantly disposed, and one man had such an elaborate design that the proud artist had to use 143 different shades before the handsome thing was completed."

Tragically, the story concludes, the artist was blinded while serving, and many of his masterpieces thus remained forever unfinished.

Typical Motifs

Since tattooing inevitably reflects the visual cultures from which it emerges, it is unsurprising that the design language of military tattooing reflected the designs sailors and servicemen were making and collecting in handicraft media. The swallows, love-hearts, and odes to wives, brothers, and the king that filled the design books of tattooers were also to be found embroidered onto cloth, etched into tobacco tins, printed on Christmas cards, and even scribbled on hardtack biscuits, as they provided better drawing surfaces than sustenance. But as the war ground interminably onward, design tastes in tattooing began to change, with imagery more specifically reflecting the ferocity and industry of modern warfare. By 1918, names and flags had given way to starker representations of everyday life during the militarized conflict, such as pictures of tanks, planes, and machine guns. And at the Armistice, tattooing proved a powerful way for people to memorialize their wartime friendships and traumas, again driving customers to tattoo shops. One young soldier had the names of every battle in which he had served inscribed down his arm.

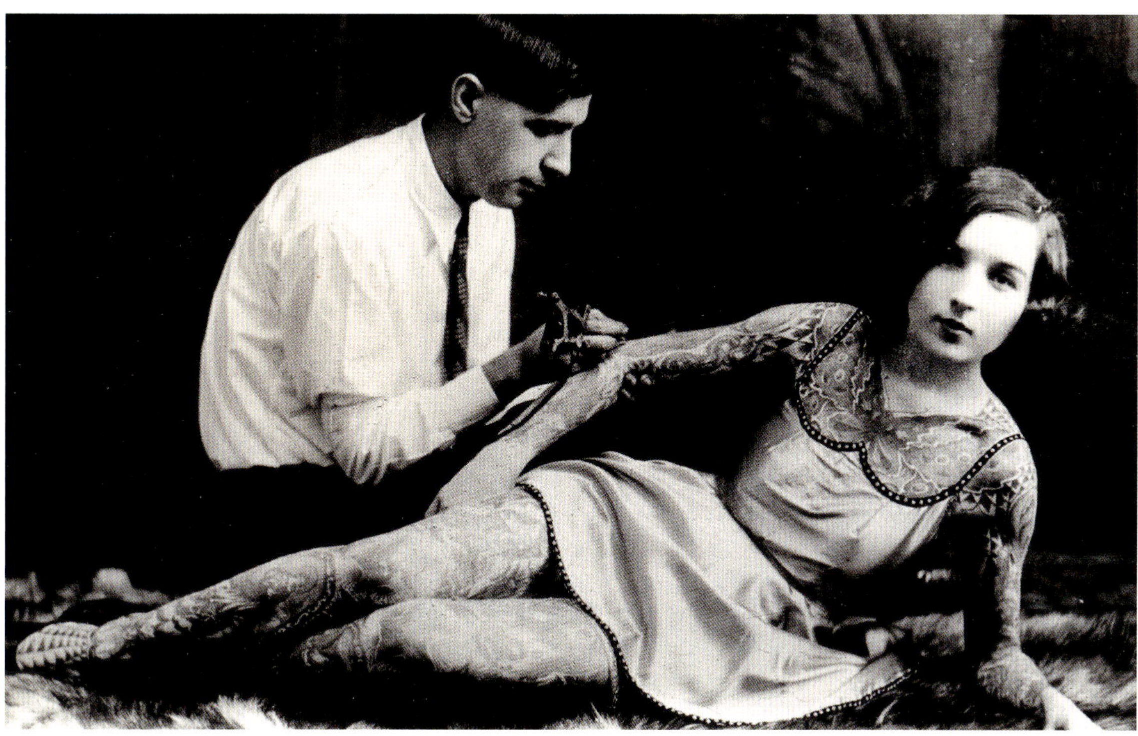

A Respite

The brief decades between the end of World War I and the beginning of World War II allowed western Europe a short breath of liberty from conflict. The nascent women's movement, which won limited women's suffrage in England in 1918, resulted from, and was in turn propelled by, young women seeking to push the boundaries of patriarchal behavioral norms, asserting autonomy and freedom in the form of fashion, behavior, and, of course, tattoos. For young middle-class women in metropolitan centers like London, Paris, New York, and Berlin, "flapper" subcultures eagerly took to tattooing as a way of expressing rebellion and sensual, even sexual, femininity simultaneously. Throughout the 1920s, reports lit up newspapers of new fashions for butterfly tattoos, tattooed stocking garters, coiling snakes, and "weird, fantastic designs." As in the 1890s, the so-called "trend" appeared to skip back and forth across the Atlantic, as American fashionistas and European socialites seemed to ape each other. By 1931 Sutherland Macdonald was complaining to friends that the large-scale Japanese-inspired work he had become famous for in the late nineteenth century was so unpopular that he was hardly bothering to go into his studio. Instead, smaller, cheaper tattoos were utterly "à la mode," and the general impression of the tattoo artist was as a dandy as much as an old "salt". By the end of the decade, tattooing was so fashionable for women that tattoo designs found their way onto contemporary knitwear in Paris, with Elsa Schiaparelli's 1929 summer collection boldly featuring swimsuits stitched with emblems lifted directly from maritime tattooers in French ports.

Even the men's corner of the fashion press could not resist telling its readers just how fashionable a small tattoo was: "Tattooing has passed from the savage to

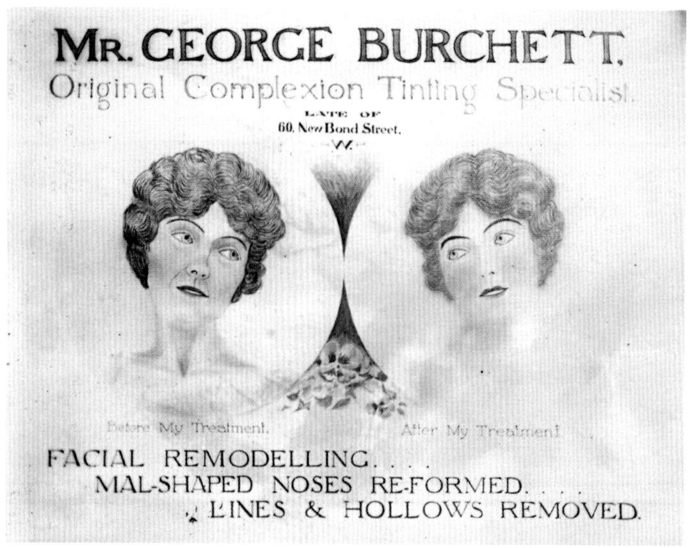

Facial remodeling (*left*) Metropolitan tattooers in Britain often advertised cosmetic services alongside their more conventional trade. Services included cheek rouging, the application of permanent makeup to the lips and eyes, and the tasteful addition of beauty spots. George Burchett worked under the brand-name Kosmeo for his cosmetology work, operating a private studio in an apartment in London's trendy West End as a counterpart to his servicemen-oriented shop on Waterloo Road. For this clientele, though also offering tattooing, he advertised as "the well-known Bond Street Beauty Specialist." His wife Edith worked with him, offering electrolysis.

Fashionable reveals (*right*) Lady Edith Vane-Tempest-Stewart, Marchioness of Londonderry, had been tattooed on the legs in Japan in 1904. As skirt heights began to rise with the fashions of the 1930s, her tattoos were revealed to the world, causing global press headlines.

Sheer beauty (*far right*) There is a constant interplay between fashions in clothing and tattooing. This woman sports embroidered stockings, which were all the rage in the 1910s and 20s. The stockings resemble the leg tattoos which had also become trendy during this time.

the sailor, from the sailor to the landsman, and is now to be found beneath many a tailored shirt," wrote *Vanity Fair* in 1926. Just as in London, old-school American tattooers were by then bemoaning the capricious and uncultured tastes of youngsters, with one artist despairing that he had to tattoo small pictures based on cute popular prints on customers, when in previous decades he was producing, by his own estimation, exquisite works of art. "It is too bad to have to tattoo diving girls and Venus rising from the sea, when you have it in you to do things like these, ain't it?" said the tattooer. "But I've got to live . . . It ain't wot it was," he sighed. "In my day, they wanted dragons."

The Wall Street Crash of 1929 caused a stumble for the best-regarded artists in New York, whose most prestigious clients among the city's white-collar professions such as banking and law had lost so much money on the markets that they could no longer afford

their tattoo habits. The middle market continued to be popular right into the 1930s, however. Over the course of the decade, tattooing was variously "the rage in London society" and a "vogue," and the increased liberalization of clothing for women, particularly the introduction of shorter skirt lengths, also had the side-effect of revealing, for the first time, tattoos on older ladies that had been acquired in the early days of professional tattooing. In one vivid example, Edith Vane-Tempest-Stuart, Marchioness of Londonderry, was spotted at a fashion show in 1938 with a huge dragon tattoo on her legs peeking through her sheer stockings. The tattoos had been done in Japan more than thirty years earlier, but the revivified revelation that minor aristocrats were concealing tattoos beneath their clothes again caused imitators to rush to tattooers.

The first half of the twentieth century thus cements paradoxically erroneous conceptions of tattooing in

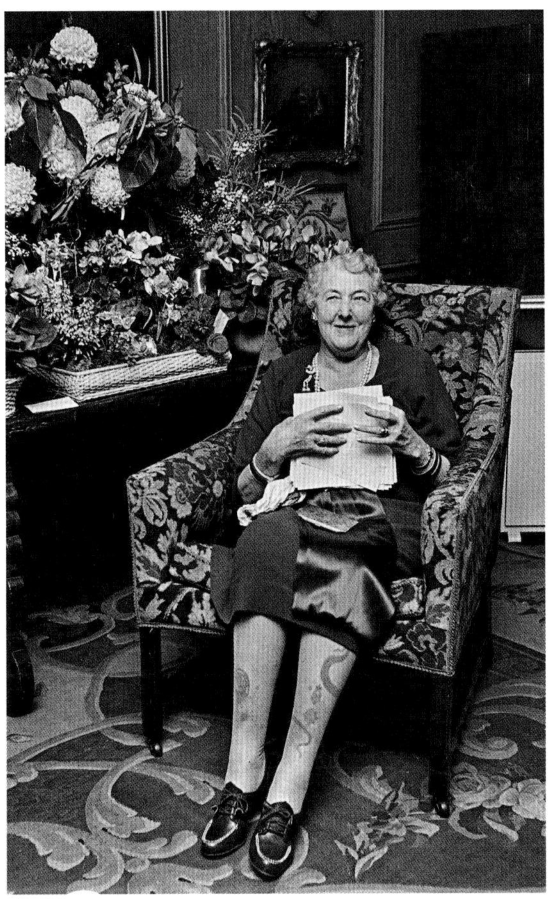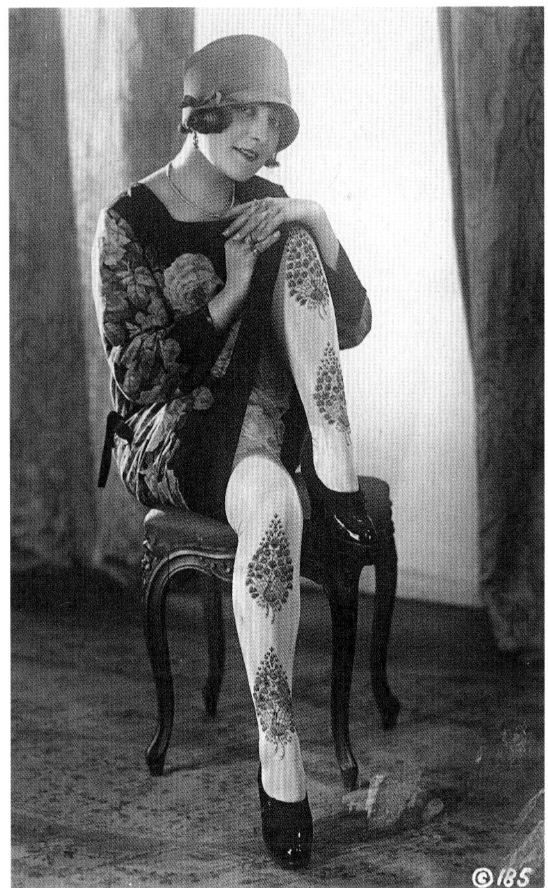

the mainstream imagination. On the one hand, the popularity of tattooing in the military, both at home and abroad, meant that the artform had become inseparable from our stereotypes of sailors and soldiers. On the other hand, the period also created social and technological changes that ensured tattooing remained increasingly fashionable and patronized by both men and women across all social classes. However, despite being fashionable, tattooing was not elevated to a level of comfortable cultural acceptance. In turn, this ensured that, for more than a century, the mere existence of tattooed women and tattooed lawyers has been, and perhaps will forever continue to be, a source of tabloid titillation.

Alexander (Alec) Colville Gordon in his studio in Paddington, c.1950

Alexander Colville Gordon is one of the most important, but also one of the most unknown, figures in the graphic development of tattooing in Britain. Born in the US, he grew up working on cattle ranches before taking up tattooing around 1905. By 1908, he had moved to London, putting down roots into a thriving tattooing scene. Gordon is shown here late in his career.

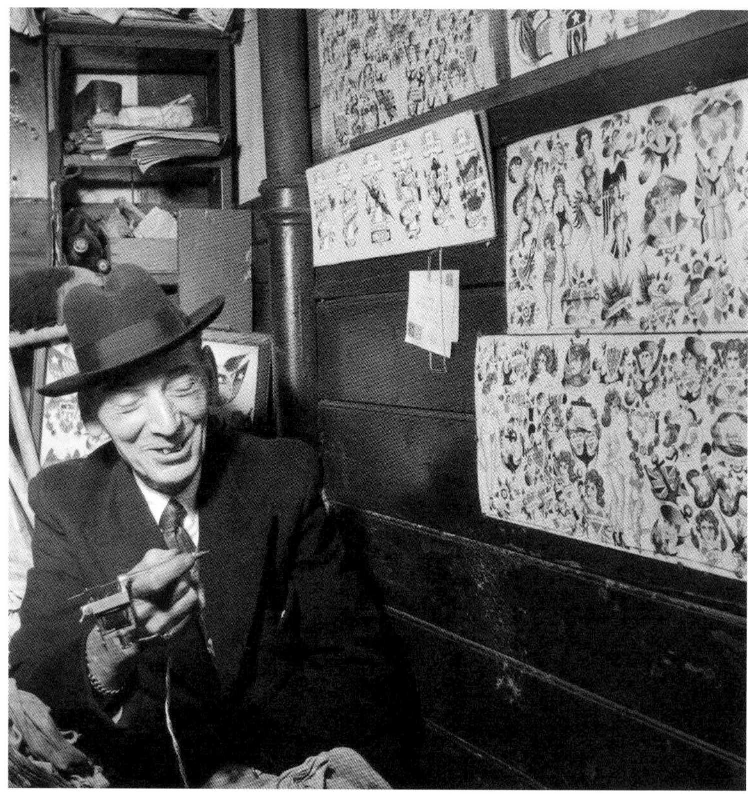

Harry Battell Jr. tattooing in London, photography by Nigel Henderson, c.1955

As Gordon sold "flash" (a generic term used to describe preprinted sheets of tattoo designs) to artists around the south of England and beyond, his work has often been mis-attributed to its buyers including Cecil Rhodes (Dover), Charlie Knight (Southampton), and Charlie Parnis (Malta), largely obscuring his talent and name from canonical histories of the industry. To add to the confusion, after Gordon died in 1950, neighboring artist Harry Battell Jr., pictured here, adopted his name, using it, he said, in tribute to his old friend.

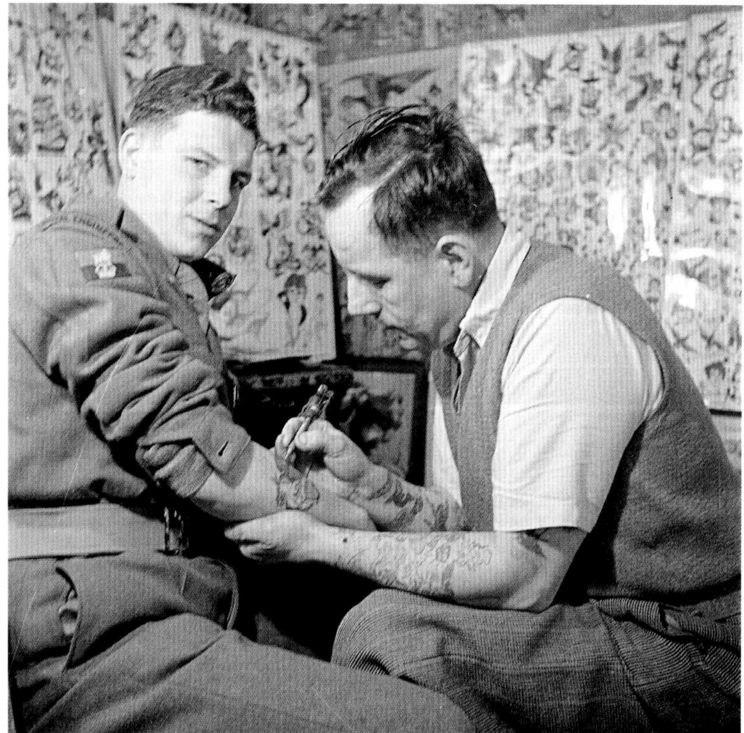

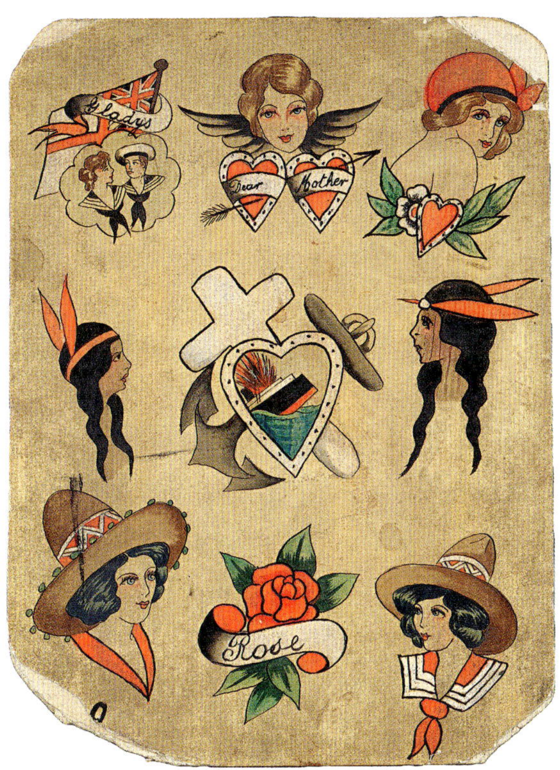

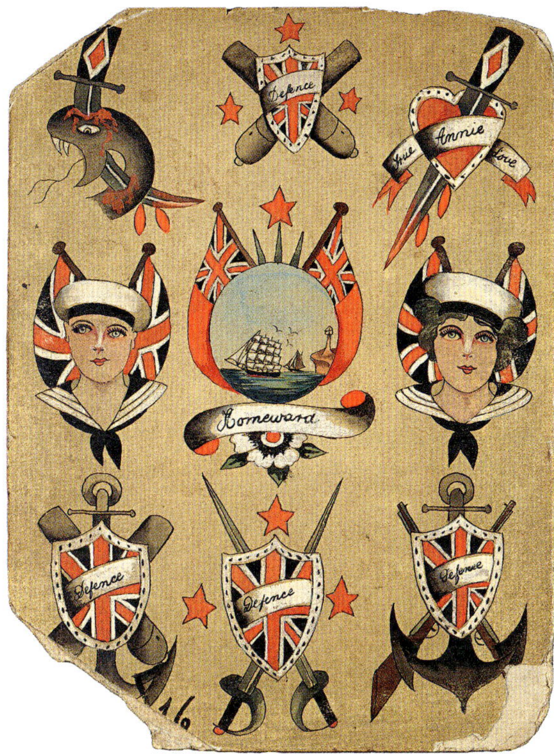

Hand-painted flash on cardboard by Alexander Colville Gordon, c.1914–18

Gordon arrived from the US at a time when tattooing was falling out of favor with wealthy collectors in London, but was increasingly enjoyed by the hoi polloi, who demanded smaller, fresher designs than those often offered by stuffy Victorian tattooers. His style was perfectly aimed at this new demographic: bold, graphic, and resolutely modern, though still firmly rooted in the folk traditions of maritime, religious, and orientalist motifs. Gordon's influence has been felt through his voluminous production of beautiful hand-painted flash sheets. His work in both watercolor and oil is some of the finest of the era.

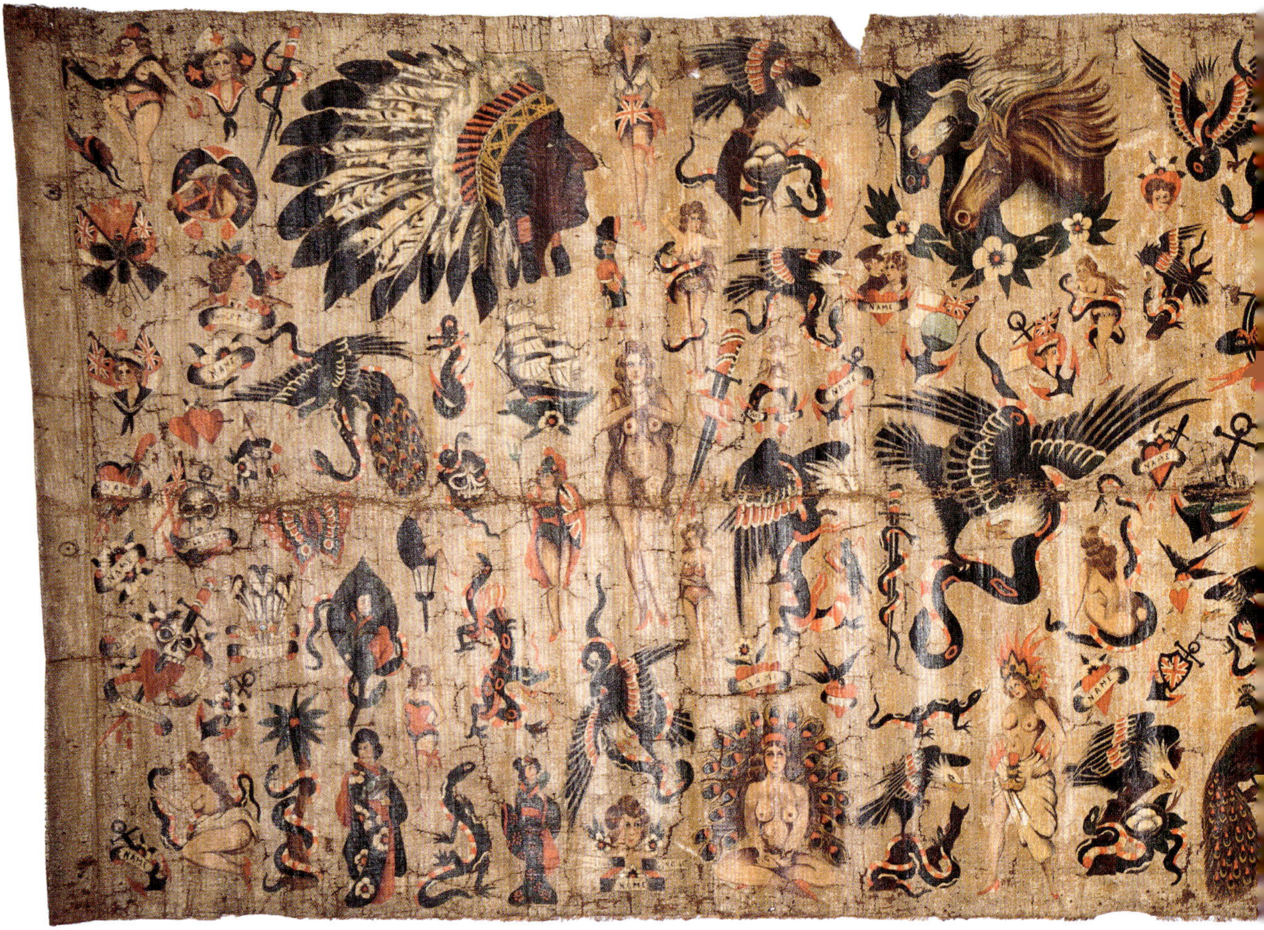

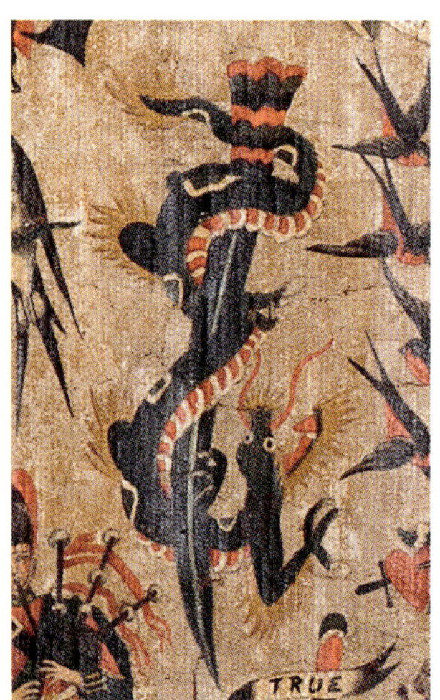

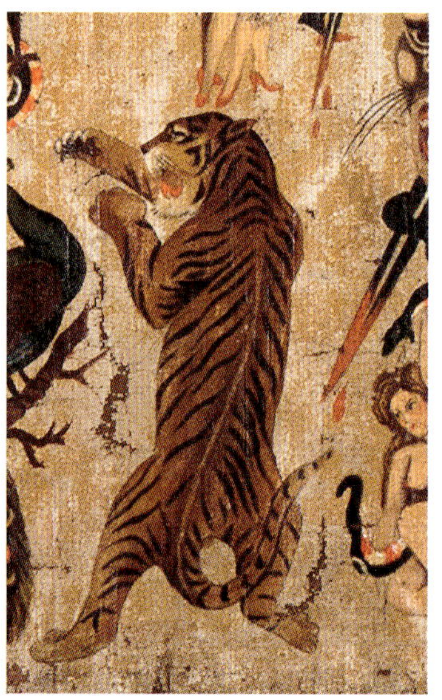

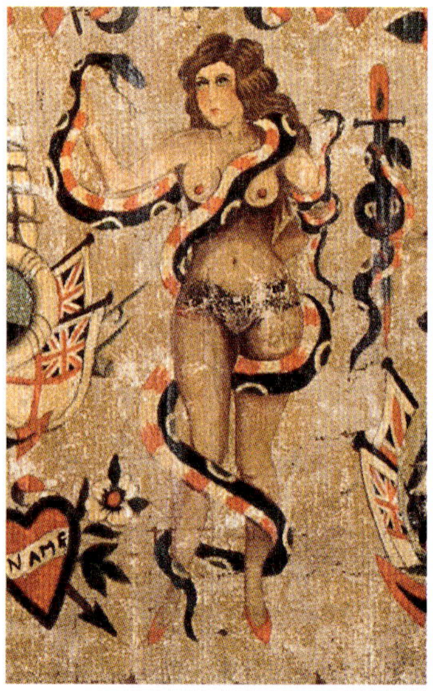

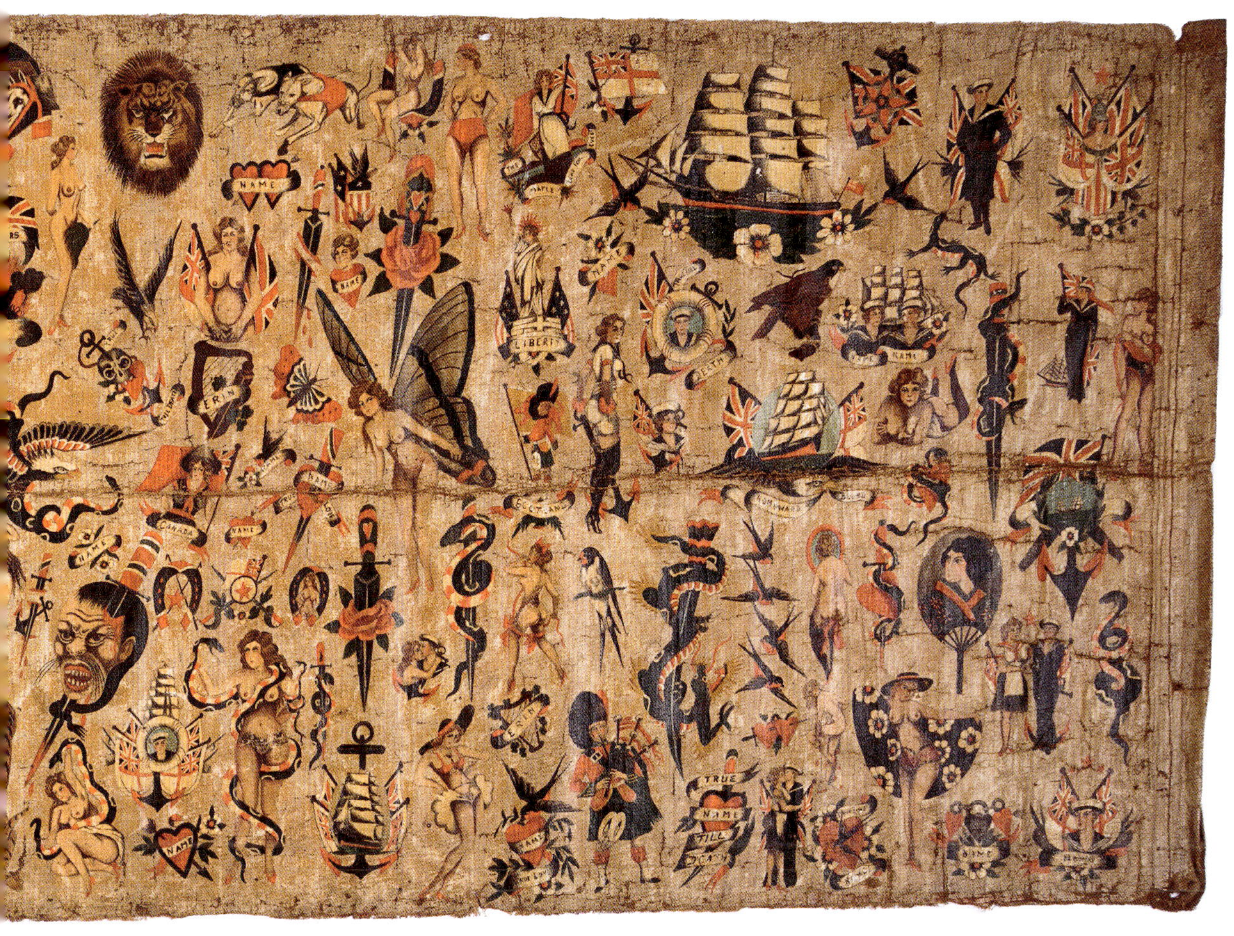

Canvas banner by Alexander (Alec) Colville Gordon, c.1914, with details (*left*)

This enormous banner by Gordon is arguably the most beautiful work of painting by a British-based tattoo artist yet to surface. Hundreds of designs are meticulously rendered on thick canvas stock. The banner could be unrolled on a dockside when a new ship had arrived, allowing the tattooer to vividly advertise his services. This banner was owned by Charlie Knight, who tattooed in Southampton and in the Welsh port of Barry in the second decade of the twentieth century. Subsequently, it passed to his daughter Jessie, also a portside tattooer, and she guarded it jealously from rivals. It is now in a private collection.

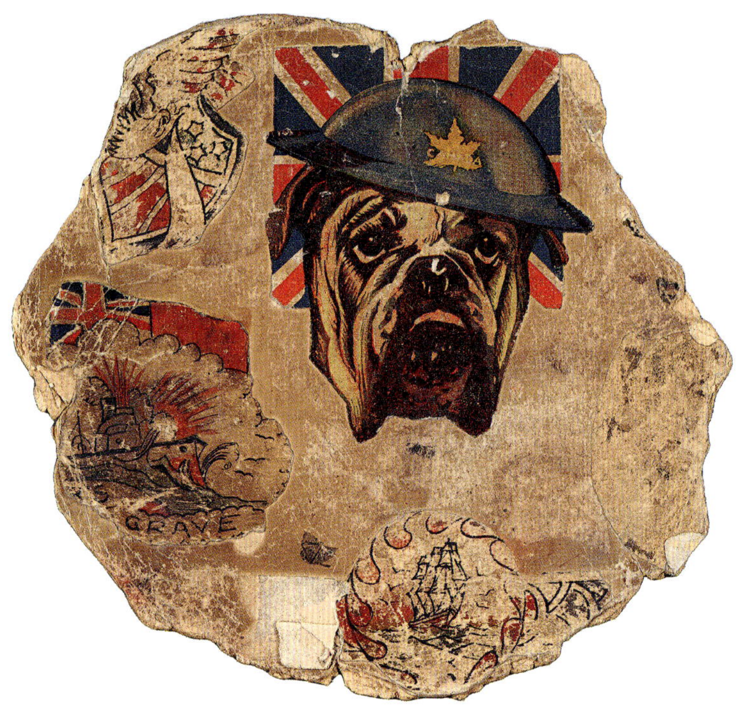

Flash sheet of collaged images pasted to board, c.1914–18 (*left*)

This sheet is by an unidentified artist working in the early twentieth century, and is part of Jessie Knight's collection of ephemera inherited from her father. Patriotic designs including American insignia and a helmeted British Bulldog sit alongside updated classics.

Production flash by Joseph Hartley, 1920s (*below*)

Note the demarcation lines between the individual motifs on this mass-produced, hand-colored sheet of designs by Joseph Hartley. Hartley sold these sheets uncut, such that they could be displayed on a shop wall, but they were also sized to be easily cut out and stuck into artists' sketchbooks, the more easily to be used by itinerant tattooers.

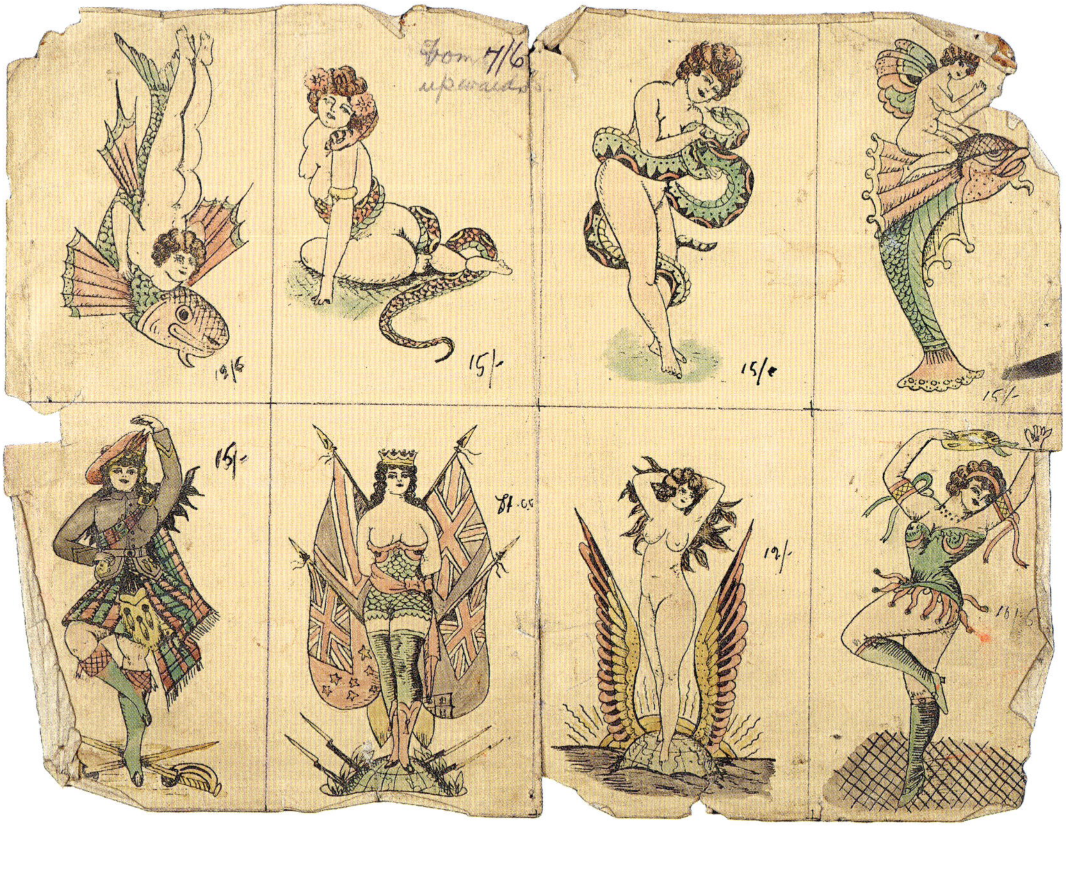

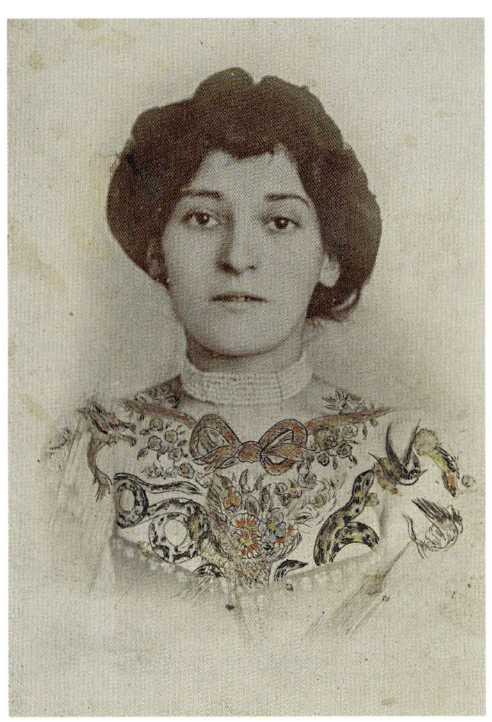

Overpainted photograph by George Burchett, c.1930s (_left_)

Photographs like this one show George Burchett's habitual overdrawing technique. Burchett would add tattoos in pen and ink on top of portrait shots, perhaps as a sketch for an envisioned tattoo, or as a simple conceptual drawing exercise. This woman has recently been suggested to be Annie, a performing tattooed lady married to Tom Riley's apprentice, Jim Wilson.

Overpainted photograph by George Burchett, c.1930s (_right_)

In some early photographic processes, tattooing does not show on the body particularly prominently. Here, Burchett has overdrawn the tattoo designs in ink, making them more visible. Tattoo artists also used this technique to conceptualize future work, or even to outright fabricate designs for publicity purposes.

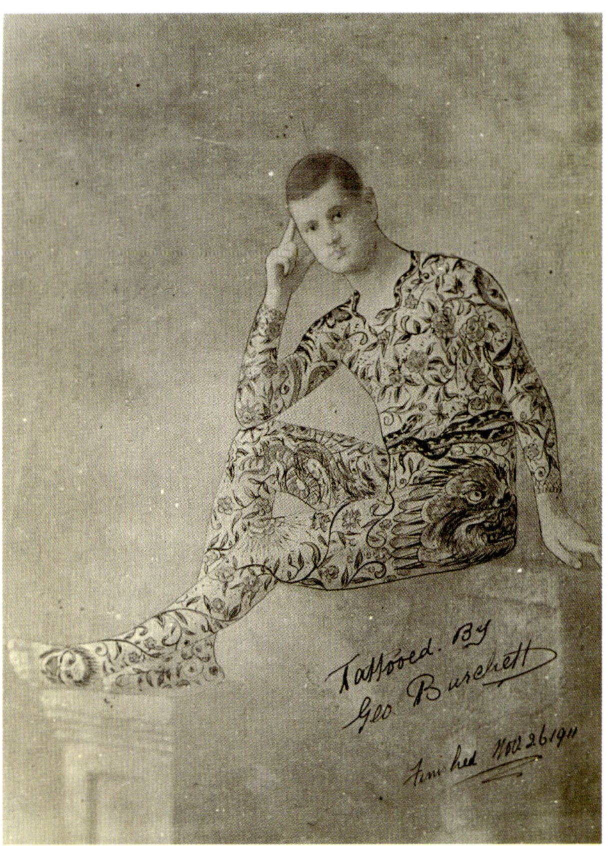

Chapter Five

Tattooing During World War II

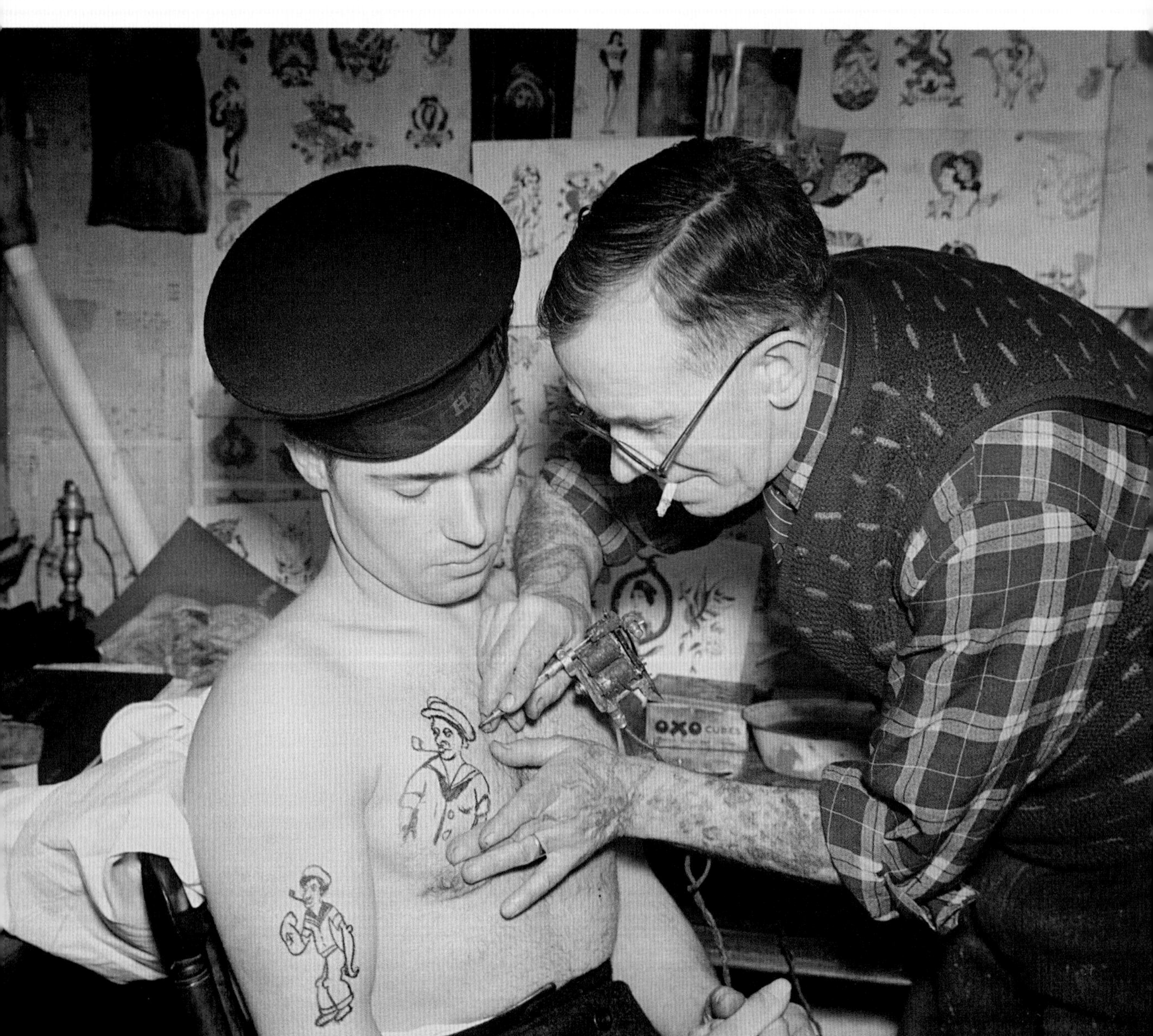

"The demand for tattooing is quite brisk . . .
The girls have a preference for having
men's names, flowers, and butterflies
tattooed on their arms and legs."

Nottingham Evening Post, 1945

"Our best customers" Kent tattooer Charlie Bell
adds to the collection of a British sailor in 1945.

In November 1940, just over a year into World War II, tattooing had again been "revived," according to the *Auckland Star*. Of course, it had never really gone away. Tattooing is the craze that is always new.

The driver for this particular moment, the article claimed, was a surge in interest among sailors mobilized for combat. The 1920s and 30s had seen tattooing find favor among fashionable women in urban centers, with (per *Life Magazine*) an estimated 10 percent of Americans having a tattoo in 1936, and (per British service newspaper *Salt*) reaching a "zenith" that same year. The 1940s retrenched the association of the art form with the stereotypical blue-armed sailor (soldiers, sailors often joked, weren't tough enough to really get into tattooing). "Sailors are still our best customers," a tattooer told the paper. "Tattooing is traditional in the Navy, and more popular than ever to-day . . . Sailors are a sentimental lot. The first thing many of them have

tattooed on their arms is the word 'Mother'—especially the boys just joining up." Just as in World War I, George Burchett saw lines of people at his tattoo shop on Waterloo Road in London. "The barbaric custom of tattooing is spread by British war hysteria," screamed the *Philadelphia Inquirer* in 1938, as conflict loomed.

Against expectations, perhaps, the interviewee for the *Star* article was not one of the old, cynical professors so often interviewed in the interwar period, who had been plying their trade since the nineteenth century. Rather, it was a woman—twenty-year-old Grace Bell, tattooing out of a premises in Chatham, Kent, near to a naval dockyard. The article claimed that Grace was the niece of the shop's owner Charlie Bell, though genealogical research suggests that the two were not actually related. Charlie had been tattooing since the Edwardian period, working in towns including Portsmouth. He was also a showman, traveling the

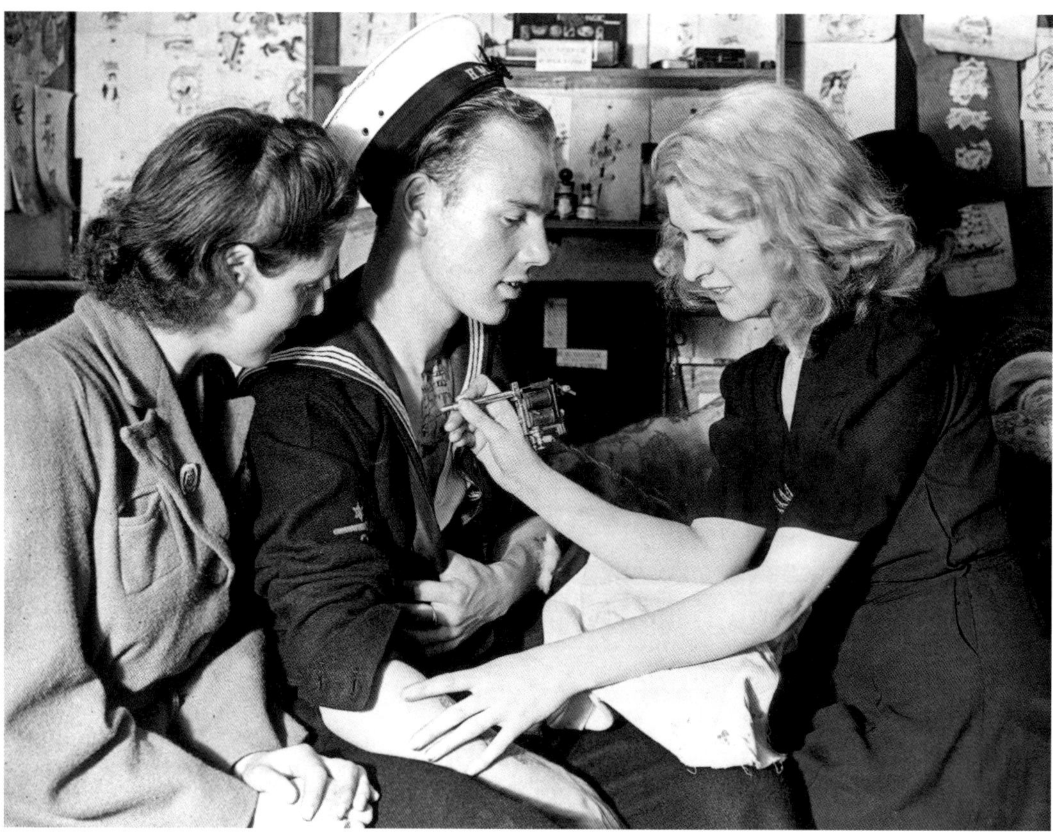

country with his wife, "Princess Cristina," a performing tattooed lady born Christine Violet Duncan. When Christine died in 1936, Grace stepped in briefly to help support the business. When people have imagined tattoo studios, their minds will often have conjured pictures of grubby tattooers working in just the kind of dockside hole where Grace found herself. Rarely, though, would that imagination have led to a young woman in the artist's chair. Even in this most stereotypically evocative of moments, the naval tattoo shop was something beyond the instinctive imagination. Paying careful attention to the historical detail thus reveals a richer and more complicated reality in terms of artists, customers, and designs than the standard picture of the time might suggest.

By 1944, there were reportedly 163 full-time working tattooers in Britain, based on government tax records. As well as Grace Bell, a few other young women supported their husbands, fathers, or family members as business boomed, including Joyce Derrick in Bristol, working with her father, H.G. Derrick, in a tattooist-cum-barbershop. Derrick worked largely from design books he had acquired from early twentieth-century pioneer Joseph Hartley, who had retired in the late 1930s. Beyond the more traditional images of hearts, flowers, and bluebirds for the princely sum of five shillings, Derrick also boasted of tattooing designs such as Churchill's head on the body of a bulldog, swastikas pierced with daggers, and, on women, spiders, portraits of handsome bomber pilots, and, in at least one case, a portrait of Hitler on her posterior so that she could "sit on him whilst turning out parts for Lancaster bombers." For larger work—should his customers have fancied being tattooed all over—he charged by the hour. And, just as Edwardian clients had in the previous generation, women in the 1940s

All hands on deck! (*left*) Joyce Derrick tattooing a sailor in Bristol in 1942, as his girlfriend looks on. Derrick worked for her father—as trade boomed, many tattooers roped in their wives and daughters to help deal with the demand.

Mutual decisions (*right*) Tattoo studios are often busy, vibrant spaces, particularly when lovers and friends crowd the customer as they choose their design. As sentimental and romantic designs were a common choice for the sailor heading abroad and his partner remaining at home, the experience of being tattooed became a shared one.

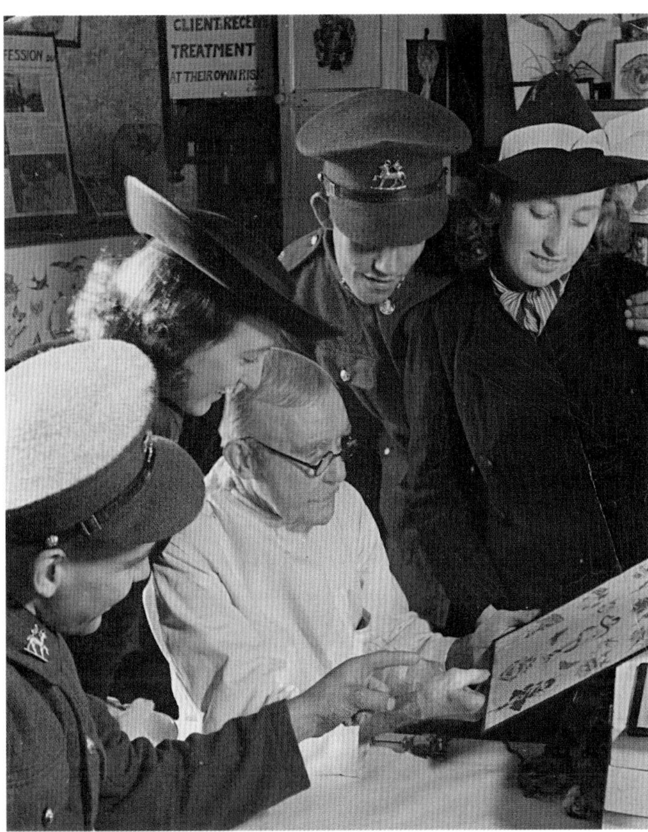

were also often tattooed with permanent makeup, rouging their cheeks or adding beauty marks. "Now many an English bobby-dazzler tattooed effectively where her mouth curls," one naval paper reported in 1942. "But then, they don't call it tattooing. They call it 'beauty culture.'"

A Sailor's Life for Me

There was some anxiety among the British officer class that particularly distinctive regimental or identificatory tattooing might inadvertently provide information on things like troop movements, were tattooed men to be captured by the Nazis. And some recruits did push the boundaries of acceptability—one lad even had "I hate the Navy" tattooed on his saluting hand. But while the 1940s did see the introduction of some bylaws in the United Kingdom to regulate the general sanitation of tattooing premises, in general there was little official regulation of tattoo designs in the British armed forces In the United States, however, well-documented naval regulations more strictly limited the design choices of new recruits. Anyone with "indecent or obscene" tattooing had been barred from enlisting in the United States Navy since at least 1890, but hopeful servicemen with such decadent marks were offered the opportunity to have them amended in line with the military's expected standard of decency.

Popular designs of nude female figures had long proven problematic for recruiters, and reports of the addition of swimsuits to tattoos based on Paul Chabas's controversial painting of a bathing nude—*September Morn*—even inspired the plot of a comedy film as far back as 1914. Into World War II, though, older Americans wanting to re-enlist still had to make their tattoos more demure, even if they had been carried out decades earlier. In the early 1940s, one veteran was

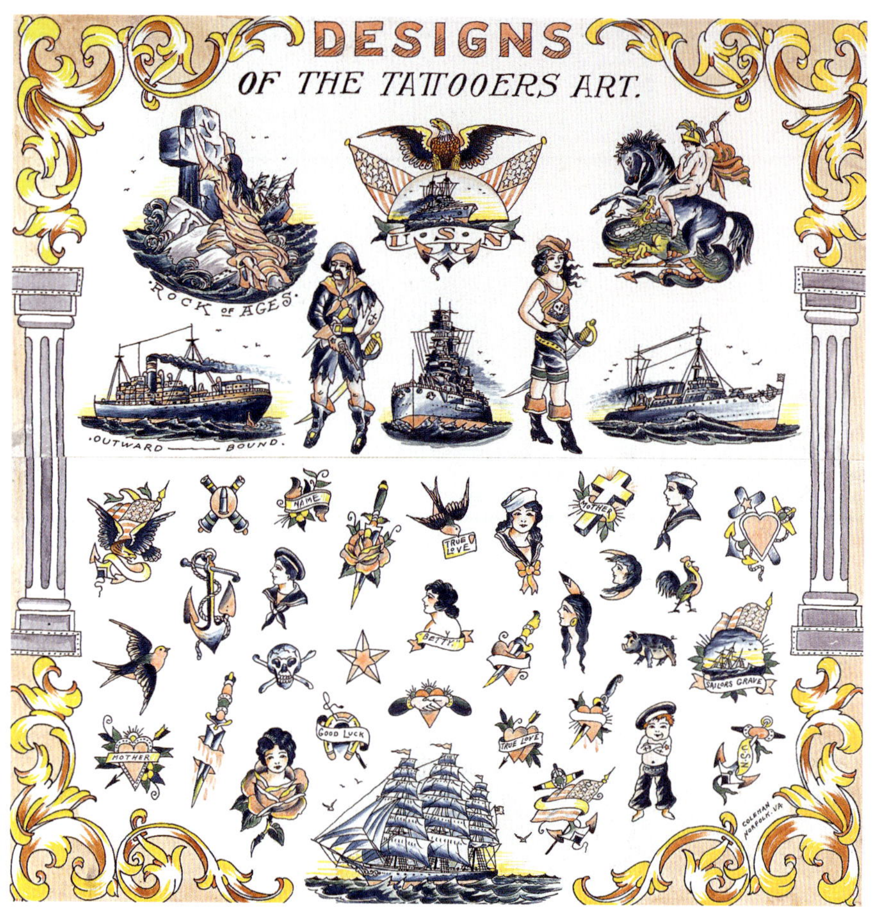

forced to add a bathing suit to the by then twenty-five-year-old September Morn tattoo on his leg before being allowed to serve in the navy. As one chronicler put it at the time, "Female nudes are out; displays of bathing suits unadorned must now be furnished with swimsuits or at least flowing tresses must be discreetly draped about their persons in order to bring them within the classification of 'all the nudes that's fit to print.' The gay blade who has a pair of twin propellers tattooed upon that part of the anatomy which, were he a ship, would be designated as the stern, may have difficulty in selling the navy officials on his particular brand of humor!"

With salacious pinups and bawdy jokes banned for serving sailors—or "Jacks," as they were known—other designs rose in popularity. Some artists boasted of offering over 1,500 different options for customers to choose from, with the classic repertoire of patriotic, sentimental, and military designs augmented with images lifted directly from popular culture, including Disney cartoons traced straight from the funny pages of daily newspapers.

In Norfolk, Virginia, a naval town steeped in tattoo history and home to legendary artists including August "Cap" Coleman, one report described this war-time visual culture of tattooing particularly vividly:

"In the modest shop window of the 'studio' are displayed scores of designs, ranging from intricate Japanese dragons and American battleships in five colors designed for 'chest pieces' which cost all the way from $50 to $100 and consume four to five hours to execute, down to small daggers thrust through bleeding hearts that can be etched upon the forearm in a few minutes and cost only a couple of bucks. A glance over the standard designs may not give

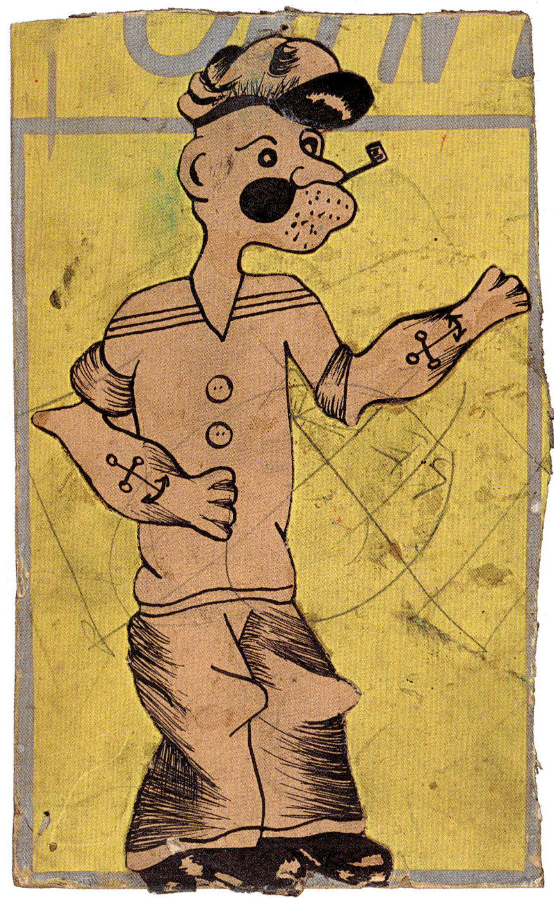

convincing proof of Jack's esthetic tastes, but they do tell something about his temperament. For the serious-minded a variety of gravestones inscribed 'Mother,' crosses and thorns, sentimental floral wreaths and madonnas are available. The patriotically disposed have their choice of interwoven flags, spreadeagles and United States shields, interspersed with such characteristically national symbols as Indians, cowboys, wild horses and buffaloes. To the naughtically inclined is submitted a snappy line of mermaids and bathing beauties, with and without [sic]. Behind a low partition two artists are messily at work under the absorbed gaze of a crowded house. By means of an electrically operated instrument from which dyeing fluid oozes, the artist sits on a low stool opposite his customer—all right, then, patron—and tattoos a small Mickey Mouse upon his arm; comic-strip characters are prime favorites and do not cost much. The other patron is having a small pig tattooed upon one foot and a rooster upon the other; they are the ancient naval talismans for warding off death by drowning and defeat in battle. Social security numbers tattooed upon the person cost as little as four bits."

This rise in popularity of comic books as source designs also had an interesting impact on the style of Western tattooing. Tattooing always intersects with the visual cultures from which it emerges, and it is in the intersection of tattooing and print culture that we can understand a stylistic change that emerges in Euro-American tattooing as the mid-century loomed. Early professionals used small needle groupings to reproduce images, often traced from periodicals, which

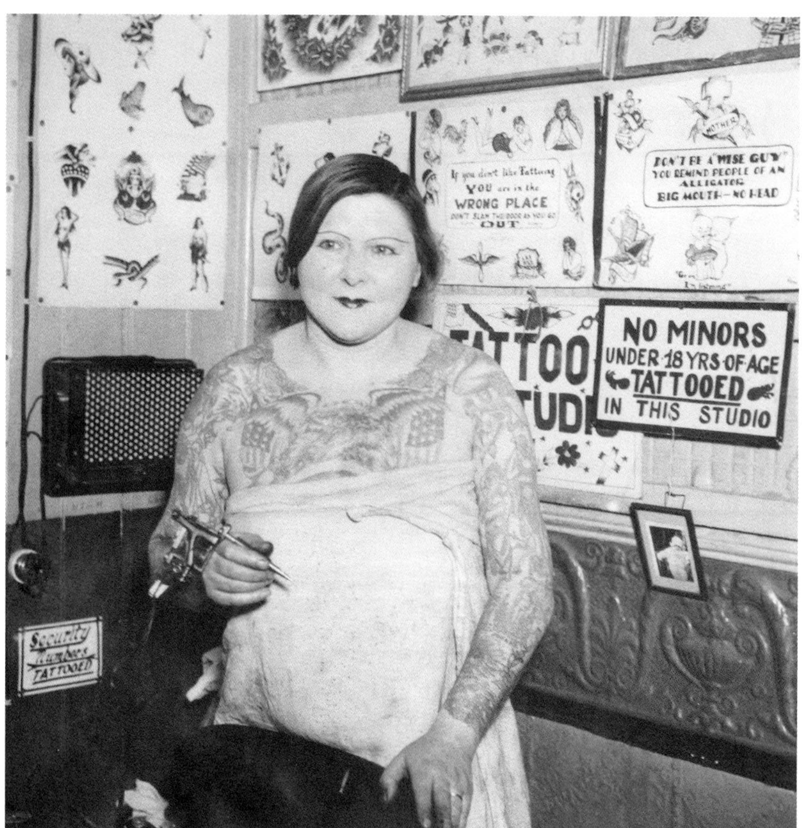

had been engraved from oils or watercolor or even pastel originals. Images in print were thus frequently characterized by delicate line work stuffed with detail and drafted with soft gradations of shading. In turn, the reproduction of such images by tattooers produced fine, intricate tattoos.

But Cap Coleman and others of his era worked in ways that produced tattoos with thick linework and bold, solid color. To understand why this shift occurred, we can look at the change in print sources by which tattoo clients were inspired.

Cheap, mass-market printing of comic books required a four-color printing process, with black, yellow, magenta, and cyan plates being printed separately in order to build the full multicolored image. For comic book inkers whose job it was to turn the main artists' pencil work into bold and legible heavy line work, this necessitated the deployment of a particularly thick line work in order to mitigate the effects of "misregistration," where one plate was not printed precisely in line with another. Thick black outlines ensured that small misregistrations did not result in figures being colored outside the lines. As tattooers traced these designs to skin, fidelity dictated that they copy the heavy line work too, establishing a new style of tattooing in the process that we now call "Traditional." Of course, heavy comic-weight lines leave a tattooer the same latitude in perfection when applying shading and color as they do their printmaking brethren, and the particular specificity of the tattooing medium also means that bolder lines work better in the skin as it ages than more delicate ones.

The Flash to Get the Cash

Tattoo artists were also forced to evolve their public images in order to appeal to the changing tastes of a

Selective clientele (*left*) Mildred "Millie" Hull, seen here in 1940, carved out a stubborn niche on the Bowery in New York despite jealousy from some rival male tattooers. It is interesting to note her advertising, variously refusing to tattoo minors, reminding patrons not to be "wise guys," and pointedly asking people who don't like tattooing to "get out."

Not just for sailors (*right*) While enlisted men were frequent customers of New York's tattooers, the taste for tattoos also pervaded the local culture. Here, a very heavily tattooed cook serves customers at a flop house on the Bowery, 1947. This man's tattooed hands would have marked him out as unusually heavily covered for the time.

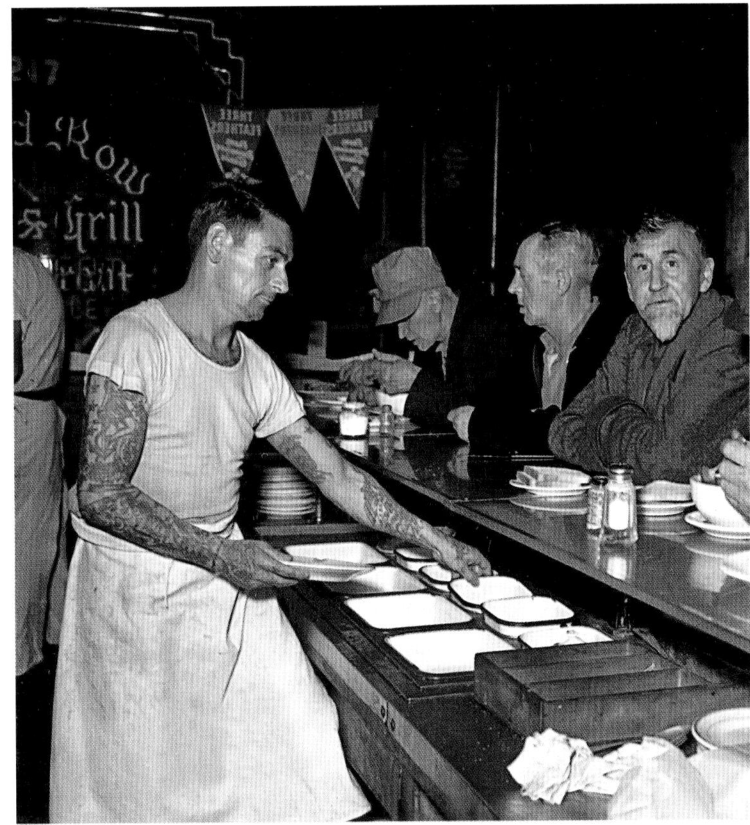

new generation of customers, much to the chagrin of some veterans of the profession. In New York, the birthplace of professional tattooing in the Western world, artist Mildred Hull, America's pre-eminent female tattooer, took to advertising in her Bowery shop window that her customers should avoid being ripped off by "old has-beens." She was referring to the industry's elder statesmen, who struggled to keep up with the volume of demand and the thirst for an expanded range of images, and to stand out in an increasingly crowded marketplace. Hull had initially taken to tattooing after being encouraged by a boyfriend, who saw her prowess with an embroidery needle and thought she would be able to turn her hand to work on skin instead. Working from the backroom of a barbershop, she was able to establish a diverse set of customers that included, by her own telling, "the white-collar class as well as the longshoremen and stevedores."

One artist in Australia found that his gimmick to bring in trade almost came back to bite him—literally: Lindsay Vane had set up his tattoo studio to illegally bootleg booze to customers, but when he was raided by constables looking for illicit liquor, they also found a box of twelve venomous snakes he had bought as part of a sideline he had established, selling them to collectors and zoos! Worse, a drunken customer stole one—a three-foot-long tiger snake—and was apprehended waving it around in the lobby of a nearby hotel.

This rapid expansion through the late 1930s and into the 1940s, combined with the development and increasing availability of mass-printing, did, however, present a commercial opportunity that could help artists work more quickly and with greater range than had ever been possible before: flash!

"Flash" is the generic term used to describe pre-printed sheets of tattoo designs which artists could buy

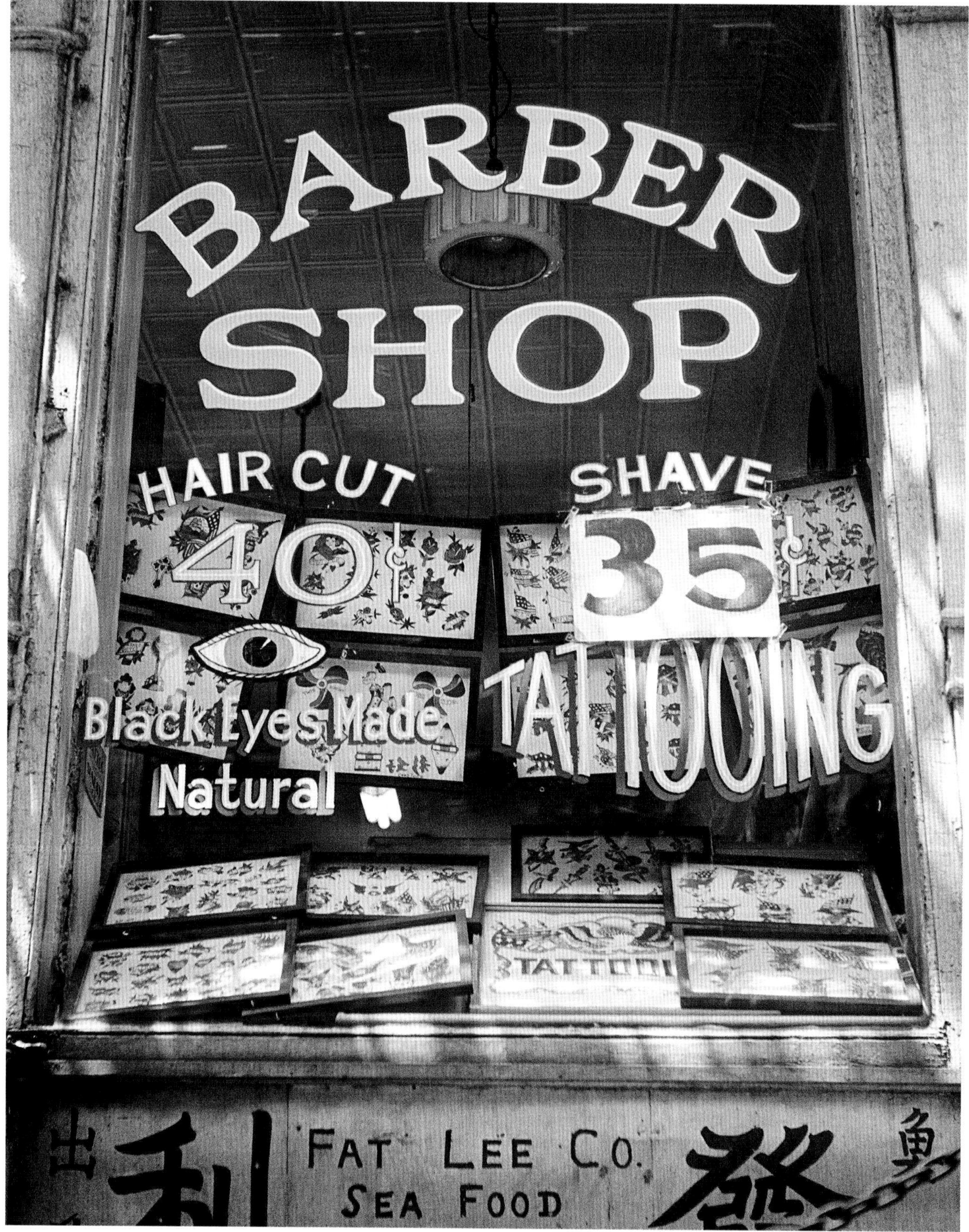
BARBER
SHOP
HAIR CUT
40¢
SHAVE
35¢
Black Eyes Made
Natural
TATTOOING
TATTOO
出 利 FAT LEE CO. 發 魚
SEA FOOD

Shiners (*left*) Tattooing often formed part of a suite of services offered to patrons at a single location. Some tattoo shops incorporated bars, others served as photographic studios. This New York shop combines tattooing with barbering, and offers to make "black eyes natural." Showing up for work with a black eye was likely to result in dismissal, and so some tattooers offered their clients a way to minimize the results of last night's drunken fights—hot towels and leeches applied to the bruise, followed by a discreet dab of makeup.

Sweetheart (*right*) This hand-painted watercolor flash was produced by an unknown artist in around 1940. Flash was often painted in black and the three colors of red, yellow, and green, as these were the cheapest and most easily available colors of tattoo ink. Some shrewd artists such as Cap Coleman would even sometimes lie to customers, telling them that any colors other than red would cause allergic reactions, allowing them to tattoo designs more quickly and cheaply than if they were to deploy a full palette of pigments.

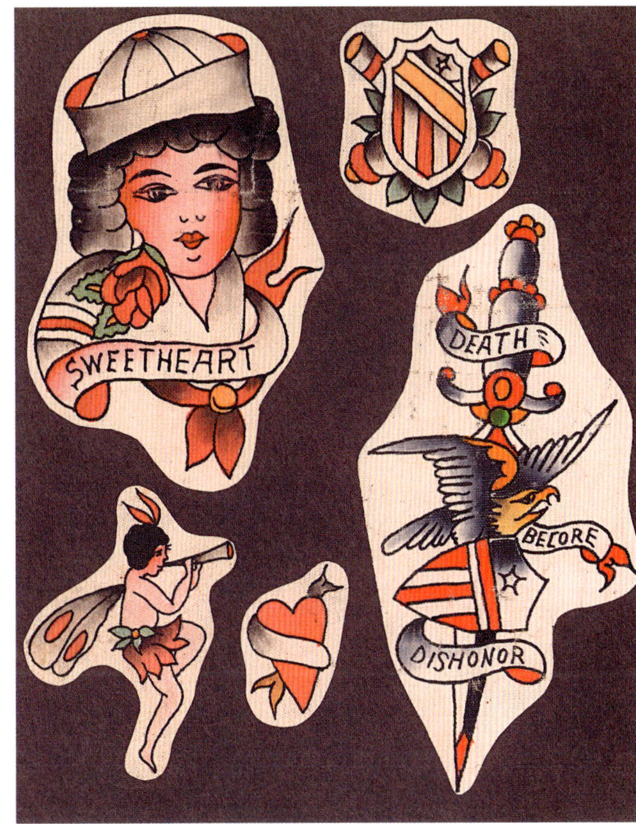

wholesale and display on their shop walls for customers to choose from. Mass-produced flash removes the need for tattooers to spend time drawing and creating their own designs, and allows them to buy in sheets with new iterations on popular designs as tastes change. Good flash could be the difference between a busy shop and a dead one, and the best-selling designs even became known as "pork chop sheets," as they'd earn an artist enough money to eat handsomely at the end of the week. The term "flash" itself originates from bookmaking, where a turf accountant would display their "flash part," a gaudy banner advertising their services and prices at the racecourse, drawing a crowd. Flash—as in "flashy"—ostentatious, and enticing, such sheets could fill a tattoo shop window to lure cautious potential customers over the threshold. The term also holds connotations of rapidity, and reflects what was known as "flash language," the slang and vernacular of thieves and criminals in the late nineteenth and early twentieth centuries.

The particular features of tattoo flash originate in the design books of late-nineteenth-century Japanese artists, and are produced with very specific drawing techniques which aim, as far as is possible, to replicate the specificities of the tattoo medium on paper. As seminal late-twentieth-century tattooer Ed Hardy wrote, "Flash strives to represent how the tattoo will appear in skin, and is painted in ink and watercolor, usually using a round tip lettering pen for the lines. This evokes the circular cluster of needles used for outlining, ideally producing a consistent line no matter which way the machine tracks." The shading is produced using watercolor and a spit-moistened brush, as "all colors are more or less fugitive in the skin."

As we saw in previous chapters, tattooers had been selling design sheets, stencils, and kits by mail order

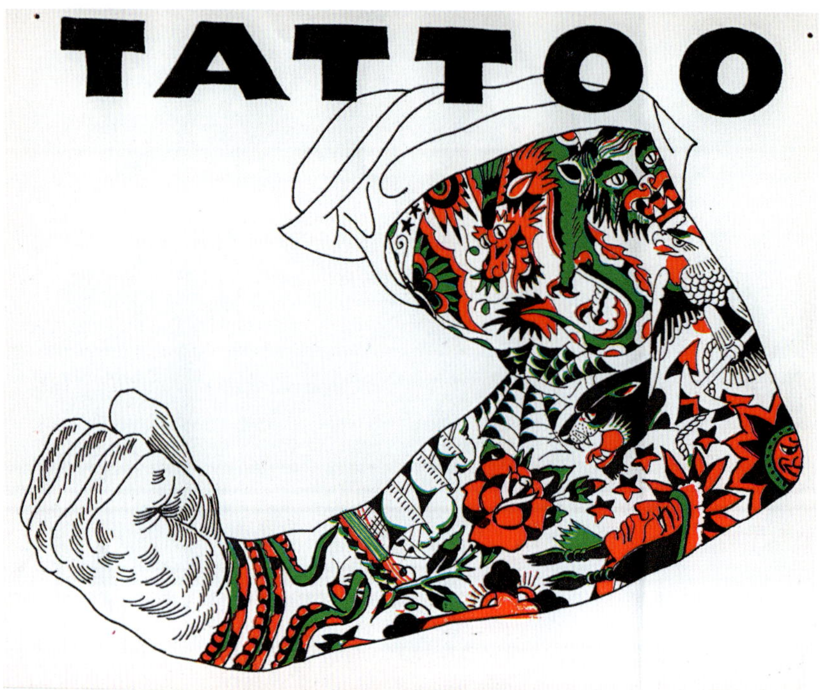
TATTOO

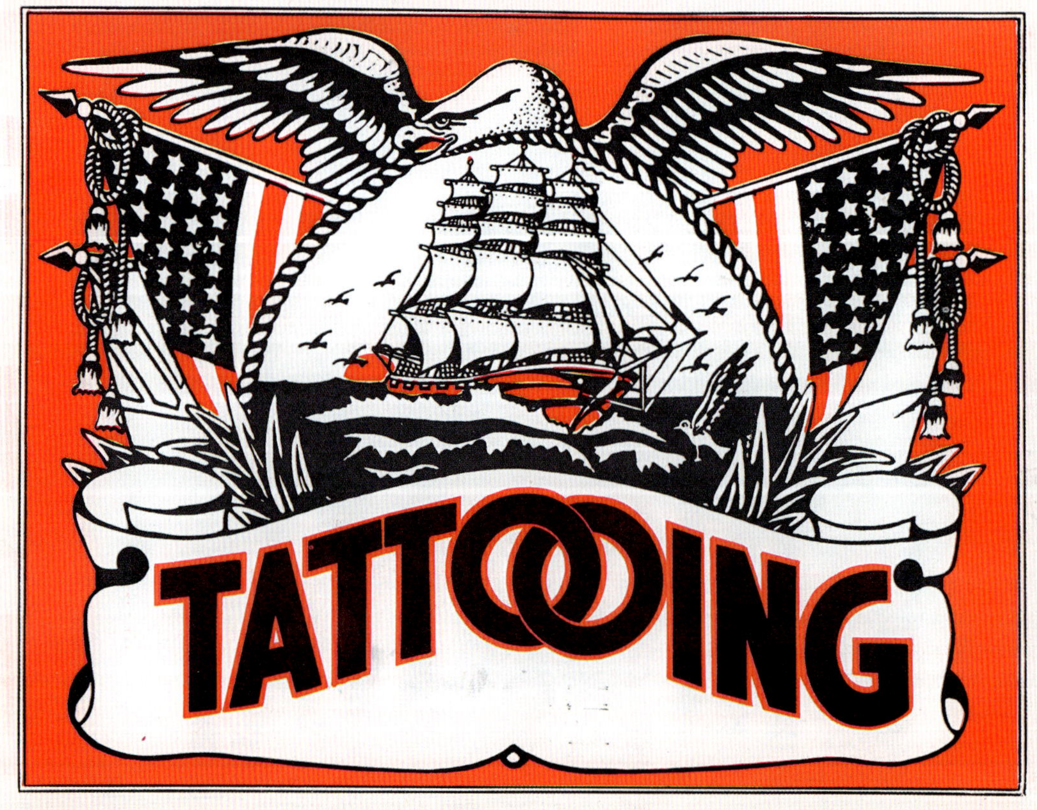
TATTOOING

Window dressing (*left*) Milton Zeis not only supplied machines and flash designs, but also signs for tattooers to advertise their services in their shop window. These examples date from the late 1940s.

Spreading the word (*right*) *Tattooing the World Over* is perhaps best described as the first magazine dedicated to tattoos, though it only ran for two (frequently reprinted) issues. The first edition was published in 1947, and distributed to customers of Milton Zeis's supply business. This second edition, from 1951, compiles contemporary and historical photographs of tattooed people alongside short annotations by Zeis.

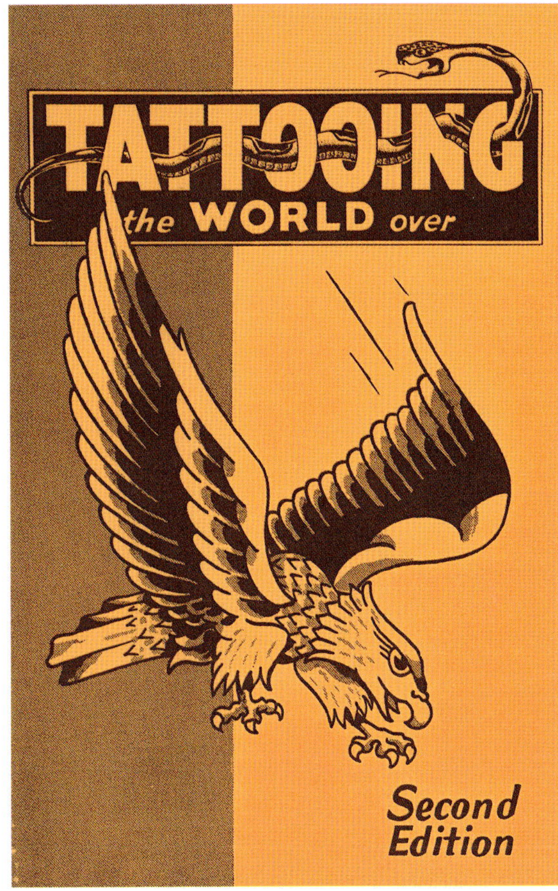

since the late nineteenth century on a small scale. It is an American wallpaper designer-cum-tattooer, Lew "the Jew" Alberts (born Albert Kurzman), though, who is popularly credited with the first mass-production of flash sheets. In 1905, Alberts began commercial production of designs by other artists—there is some historical argument about whether or not he had their permission to do so! And through the 1920s and 30s, several tattoo artists established supply companies, including Percy Waters in Detroit and Joseph Hartley in Bristol, and this network saw machines, how-to guides, and designs sold throughout the world.

There is, of course, something of a circle of cause and effect here. Changing tastes and economic circumstances led to tattooers offering smaller, simpler, and cheaper designs. These changes accelerated the use of flash, as premade designs were efficient as well as eye-catching. In turn, the ubiquity of flash sheets

resulted in a new set of implied limits for tattoo shop customers, with even the best tattooing understood to be generally done at the small scale of individual motifs, as opposed to the large-scale pieces that had been seen in previous generations. Such implied limits then generated their own trends.

In 1936, inspired directly by Waters, peripatetic entrepreneur, showman, and tattooer Milton Zeis established his eponymous mail-order business, The Zeis Studio, selling tattoo designs, machines, ink, and equipment from Illinois to customers all over the United States. Zeis took Waters' rather staid business model and supercharged it, with bold, professional adverts, sheets featuring designs by many of the best tattooers in the country printed in multiple colors, a zippy "How to Tattoo" course, and, by the late 1940s, the first industry-specific tattoo history magazine, *Tattooing the World Over*. During the war, Zeis was even

Cultural contact This man is likely an Iban member of the Sarawak Rangers, a paramilitary force of Indigenous men recruited by the British Army during the conflicts in Malaya and Indonesia from the late 1940s through to the 1960s. His cap badge suggests he was associated with the Gordon Highlanders, probably during the 1963 Konfrontasi with communist rebels in Borneo. The Dayak are a variety of populations indigenous to Borneo, many groups of whom are traditionally tattooed. In 1945, during World War II, Sarawak Rangers had also joined with Australian special forces as guerrillas to liberate the jungles of northern Borneo from Japan. Australian soldiers have written of trading tattoos with their Iban comrades.

able to fulfil his customers' ration-busting need for new equipment by melting down spoons and turning them into tattoo machines. Simultaneously, largely through Zeis's huge popularity, quality, and reach, the range of designs available to artists increased enormously, but with the effect of standardizing, homogenizing, and solidifying the kind of tattoos Western customers were acquiring, and further ossifying customer choices at the small scale of the stencil, as compared with the elaborate ornamental backpieces of the previous generations. With Zeis's sheets on display in tattoo studios throughout the world, the familiar forms of the most popular motifs became global staples for a generation to follow. "Most tattooers," Hardy says, "through lack of skill, inclination, or necessity worked from what the customer had to choose from."

Tattooing Foreign and Domestic

Paradoxically, perhaps, as flash standardized Western tattooing and made it much more familiar through the first half of the twentieth century, it also, as a response, allowed non-Western tattooing to become re-exoticized as something rather distinct from the kind of thing sailors were indulging in. Western tattooing had shifted into the domain of fashion and was visible in many urban centers as the fads and fashions of Anglo-European tattoo styles drifted away from the Orientalist modes which had characterized much of the first wave of professional tattoo art, and thus public and industry perceptions of tattooing had become much more prosaic. If not entirely faded, the instincts of commentators to connect tattooing habits in London and New York with "primitivism," "savagery," and the practices of colonized populations across the Americas,

North Africa, Asia, and the Pacific were greatly dampened during the decades in which tattooing was primarily discussed as a youthful folly and the designs lifted almost exclusively from familiar modern European sources.

During World War II, though, as innumerable swathes of people from Europe and the United States found themselves stationed with battalions and fleets in distant corners of the globe, intimate encounters with local tattoo traditions became a common leitmotif of the reportage sent home. In India, Burma, Jerusalem, and even Hawaii, tattooing became another consistent signifier of the strangeness of the experience and the utter novelty of the places and people among which these young white servicepeople found themselves. Just as tattooing had become familiar, it became strange again: inspired by cartoonish depictions of Ancient Egypt, a British soldier in Gibraltar joked in pseudo-mystic prose about the exotic TATT-U-WIST who "armed himself with a weapon which was named NEE-DELL and did plunge it into the arms of men of ENG, IRE, SCOT and other lands," joking that faith in this magical scholar and wise man would save you from the false prophet ENOCHU-LATION. The TATT-U-WIST, you see, "will inscribe writings and ye will not be stricken with sickness."

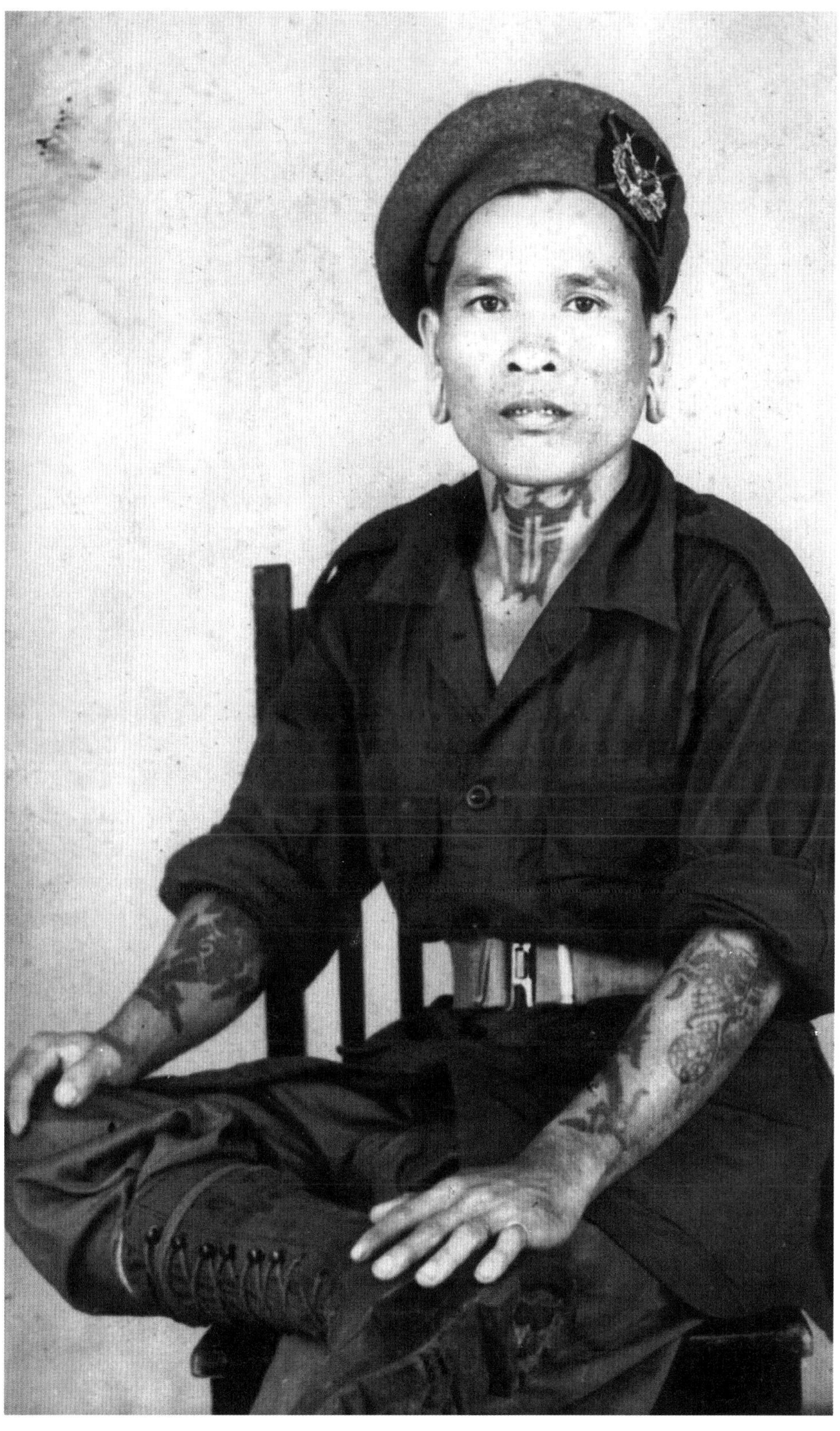

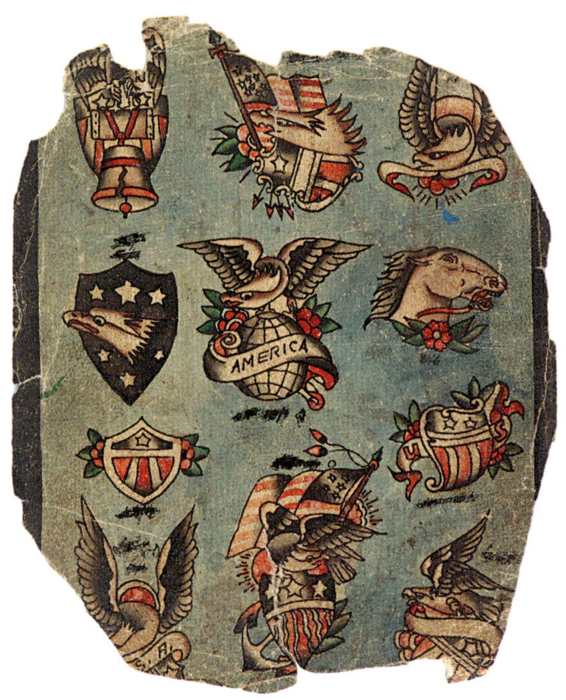

Hand-painted American flash sheet, c.1939–45

This hand-painted design sheet shows extensive signs of use, with ripped corners from having regularly been taken off the wall, and crossed out prices indicating the march of inflation and the sharing of the sheet between countries. Clearly intended for an American audience given the patriotic eagles and flags, this sheet found its way into the collection of a tattooer in the UK.

Chicago Tattoo Supply House production flash sheet by William "Frisco Bill" Moore, c.1931

This mass-produced design sheet was created by William "Frisco Bill" Moore in the early 1930s for his Chicago Tattoo Supply House. The sheet, found in Jessie Knight's collection in the UK, was included as part of eight sets of designs sent with a "how to tattoo" guide and marketed worldwide. Moore started his business as a way to boost profits in the latter years of the Depression, and ran it successfully right up until World War II. These ubiquitous, salable designs remained staples for decades—Knight copied several into her book of favorite stencils, which she used through to the late 1960s.

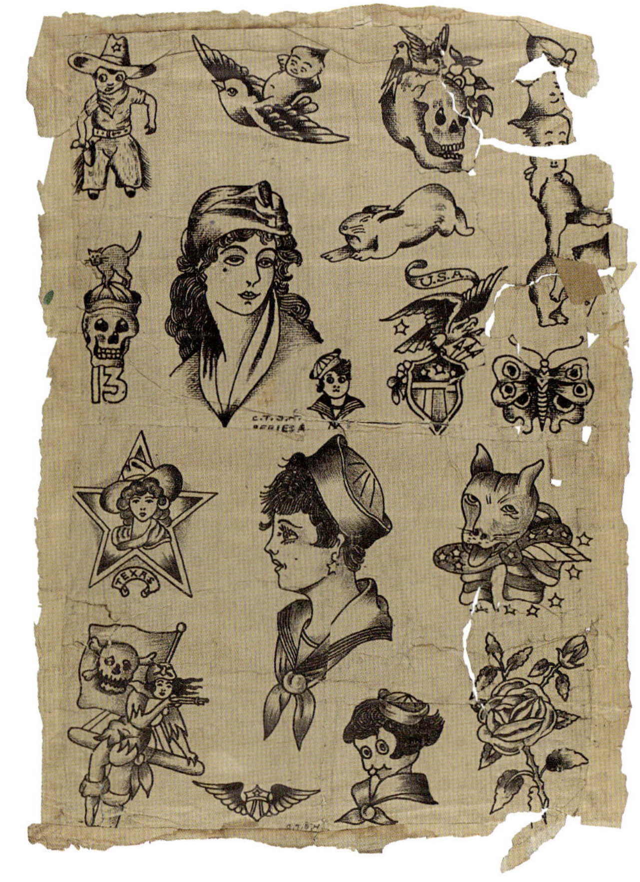

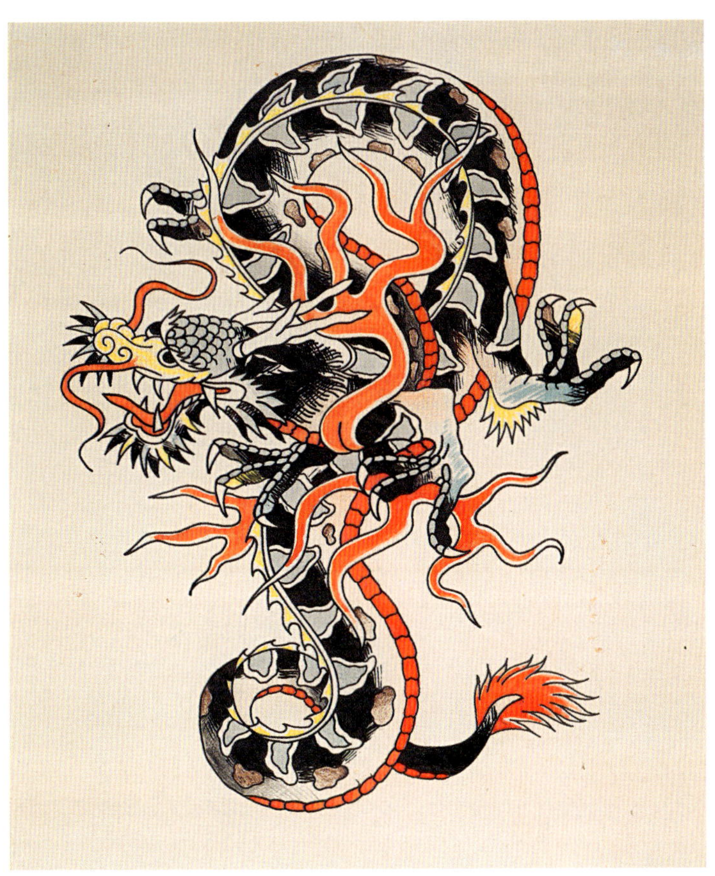

Flash tattoo designs by August "Cap" Coleman, c.1937

American flash of this period became starker and bolder, in line with changing tastes. Coleman was an enormous influence on future generations of tattooers as copies of his designs circulated for decades. Both these designs, for example, were later sold as production sheets for backpieces by Huck Spaulding and Paul Rogers.

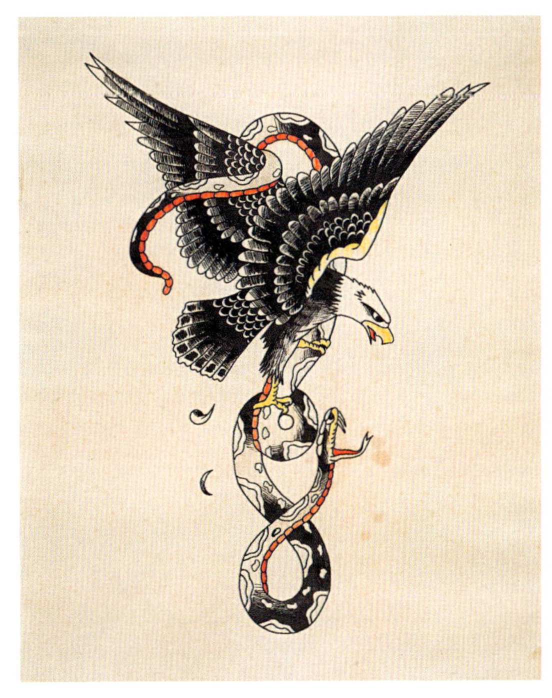

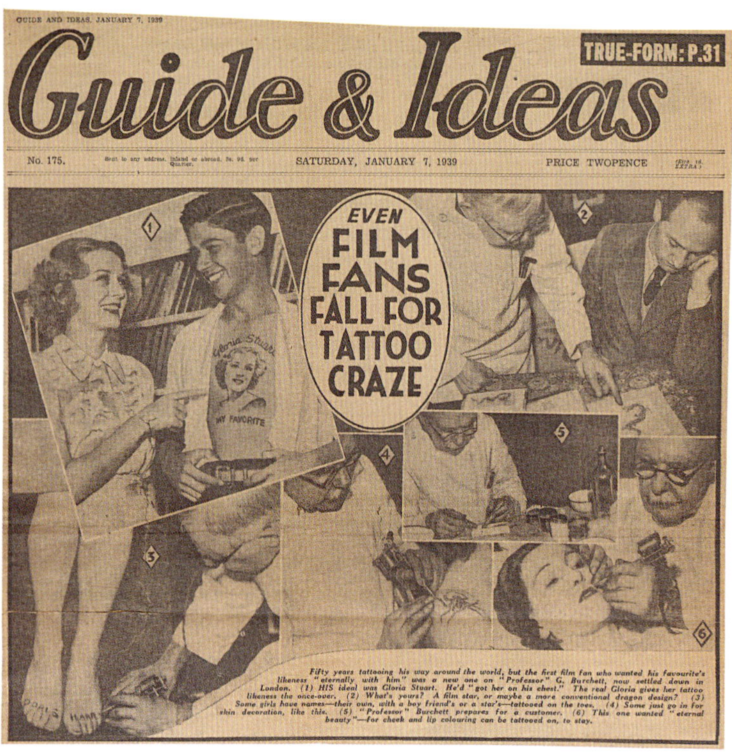

Interior of Cecil Rhodes' tattoo shop in Dover, England, 1941 (*right*)

Dover was a key staging post for British troops into the European theaters, and thus saw a booming tattoo trade as war escalated. Cecil Rhodes began tattooing in 1898, initially in London. Pictured here near the end of a long career, he boasted of having amassed so many designs that he could "tattoo an entire ship's company without repeating himself." The shop was destroyed by German shelling in September 1944, forcing Rhodes to end his career tattooing out of his house, or a nearby pub.

"Even Film Fans Fall for Tattoo Craze," *Guide & Ideas,* **January 7, 1939 (*above*)**

Though stereotypes of midcentury Western tattooing focus predominantly on sailors and criminals, tattooers' customers spanned all walks of life. This 1939 article shows young men and women choosing portraits of film stars like Gloria Stuart over pierced hearts and swallows. Burchett once also tattooed someone with a portrait of Cary Grant.

"In the blacksmith's shop," **May 14, 1942 (*right*)**

This blacksmith claimed to be "the most tattooed man in the British Army." The man's tattoos are intriguing: his backpiece is a copy of the famous frontpiece copy of Luis Falero's painting *Twin Stars,* tattooed by Sutherland Macdonald at the turn of the century (see page 46). A photograph of Mac's tattoo was circulating among artists.

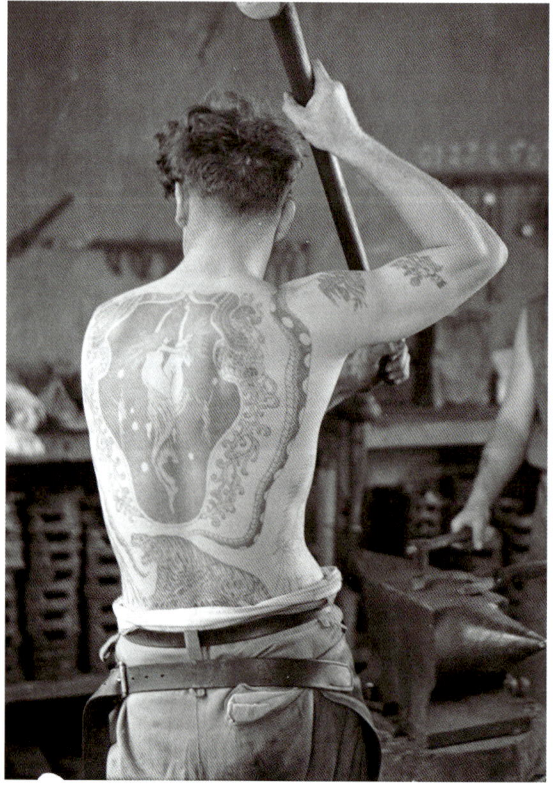

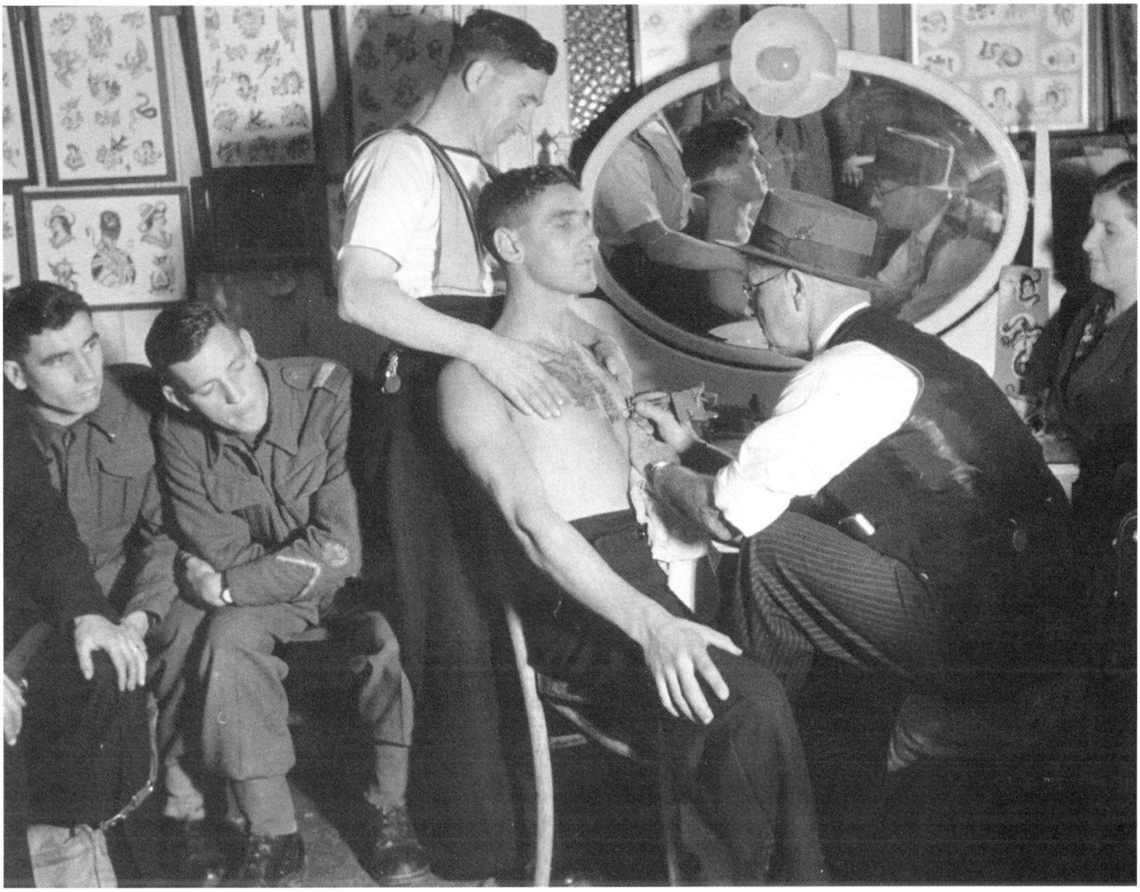

Christian Warlich removes tattoos with his secret method, c.1936 (*right*)

Hamburg tattooer Christian Warlich developed a revolutionary method of tattoo removal in the 1930s. As tattooing became increasingly taboo under Nazi rule, many Germans sought ways to efface the usually permanent marks. His tincture—a secret blend of mineral acid and ether—was applied to the design, which was then left to work for a period of time (up to twelve days). Eventually, the tattoo could be peeled away whole, preserving it as a specimen.

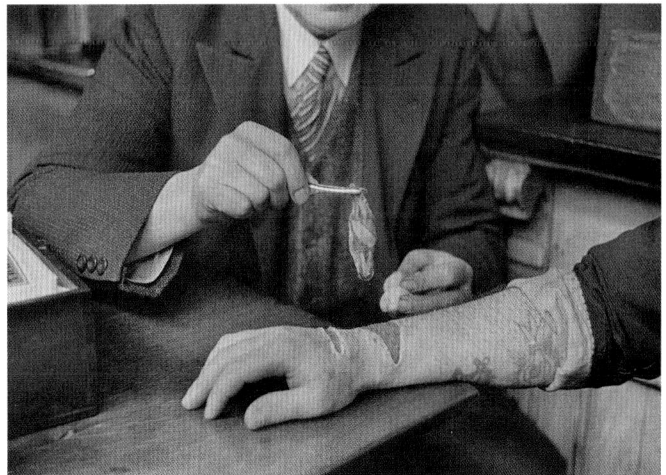

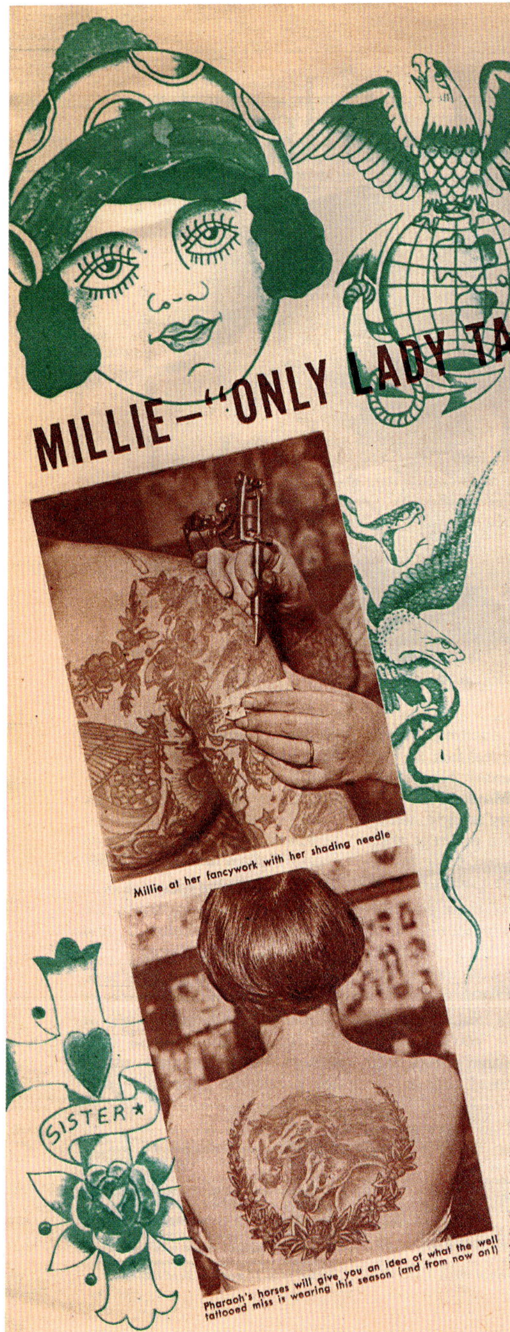

Millie at her fancywork with her shading needle

Pharaoh's horses will give you an idea of what the well tattooed miss is wearing this season (and from now on!)

MILLIE—"ONLY LADY TATTOOIST"

BY MABEL De La MATER SCACHERI

PHOTOGRAPHS BY MARIO SCACHERI

"NO, it isn't a handicap to be a woman in the tattooing business."

That's the opinion of Mildred Hall, whose business notice at 16 Bowery, New York City, announces that she is "Millie, the only lady tattooist."

She should know, for she has been a professional tattooist for five years, after she decided that tattooing was more interesting than embroidery. She is an expert embroiderer and has been clever at copying designs ever since she was a child.

"I say it isn't a handicap," she adds, "but you know how men are in any business. Always sort of jealous if a woman does as well as they do. Some of the men tattooists along the Bowery are now cutting prices to try to put me out of business. But I get plenty of customers just the same— fourteen or fifteen a day. I think men rather like the idea of having a woman tattoo them. They think a woman is likely to be more careful.

"Of course, to be fair to my men competitors, I must say that not all of them have worked against me. Some have been very nice about showing me the tricks of the trade—how to keep the needles in good condition, and so on. Business is picking up lately. Of course, it isn't like it was before the depression, when it was easy to make sixty to eighty dollars a week tattooing. The seamen's strike that is now going on brings in business, of course, because lots of seafaring men want to be tattooed, and the strike gives them time to have it done."

When Millie was telling me about her unusual profession, she was seated in her booth in the rear of a barbershop. Her equipment consists of half a dozen electric needles, pots of red, blue, yellow, green, and black paint, a pot of vaseline, and bottles of antiseptic. Scores of designs in color hang on the wall from which customers can make their choice.

EACH pattern is known as a "piece," and the more shading it has, the more difficult it is for the operator. Prices vary from twenty-five cents to two dollars, and some big, showy pieces, such as the head of a Red Cross nurse, with rosy cheeks and a red cross on her cap, are much less difficult than a green wreath, with each leaf shaded and all sorts of tints in the sunset scene inside the wreath.

"I get quite a few women customers, and usually they want some heart design, with maybe their sweetheart's name," explained Millie. "It's queer, but nearly all people have a heart pattern as their first piece of tattooing. Sailors like pieces showing sailor girls, or other women, or patriotic pieces with flags and anchors, or daggers and snakes. Italian boys often choose religious pieces—a cross, a sacred heart, the Holy Family, and the like. And lots of people like a heart pattern, with the word 'Mother.' The mother piece is very popular with both men and women."

She was putting the fin
business partner, Thomas
designs which had alread
ing masterpiece, being co
orate designs in dark blu
red lace underwear. On
on his back a large design
Family. Only his face, n
Millie herself has been
tattoos the women custom
a man's work. "Just like
man give them a haircut

"Yes, I get some reque
then," she said in answer
notions some people ha
tattooed on his back, and
and a notary public. The
his back. Then they laid
outlined their signatures.

"Another fellow broug
be tattooed on various pa
to trace the Yiddish lette
a piece of celluloid, so fin
in English. What do you
is guilty of my death.' H
would be questioned if
about it afterward. Mayb
ting to kill him, and may
to be afraid of her. You c

"Another man wanted
Some want their name an

"No, it isn't specially
pared to having your tee
the pricks feels about li
healed up in ten days. B
going to hurt, and someti
feel their arms going cold
best not to eat any greasy
avoid beer and cheese. Th

"Women are less nerv
only had one woman back
every once in a while a m

FOR each piece, the ta
celluloid. The pattern
tattooed. The outlining n
and goes one-eighth of an
in the celluloid which ar
apart. The shading is lat
needle, which has severa
gether. This needle does
skin. Black is the easiest
and causes less irritation.

Some people cannot tak
stain the skin properly a
skins resist red. Some skin
Women's skin, being thinn

The arms and back are
to be tattooed. The chest
where the flesh is thin and
the most painful spots. Th
the work is being done. W
on the chest, another per
It may have to be pulled
taut.

The tattooist works wit
to staunch the blood, rub
and then covers it with vas
line should be washed off

"Then you can just for
But just try to forget t
life!

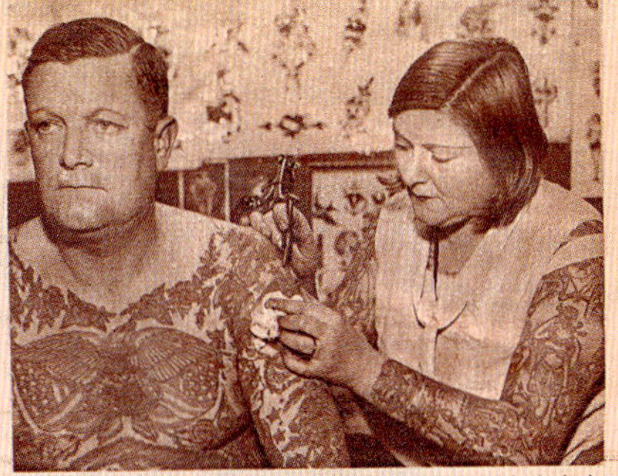

Thomas Lee, Millie's partner and tattooing masterpiece, might justly be called a marked man. The best he can do now is escape with his neck

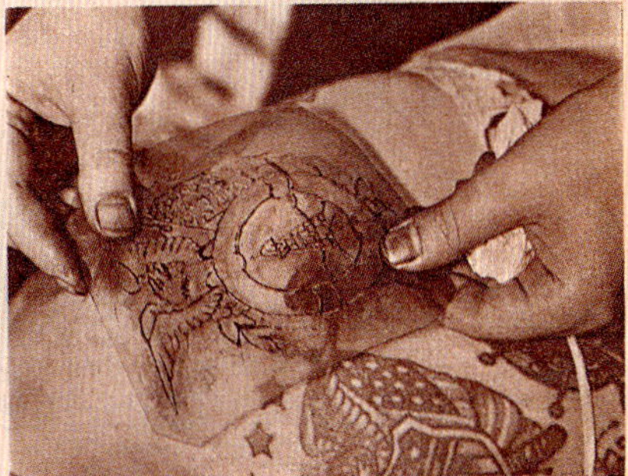

One step in exterior decoration: The pattern, outlined by tiny holes in celluloid, is put over the spot to be tattooed. Next, the outlining needle

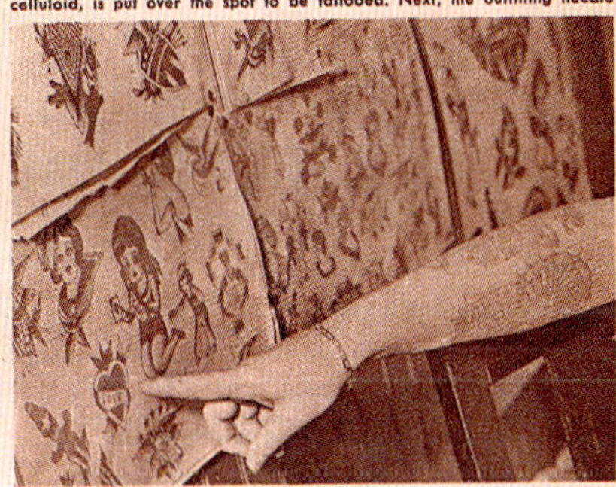

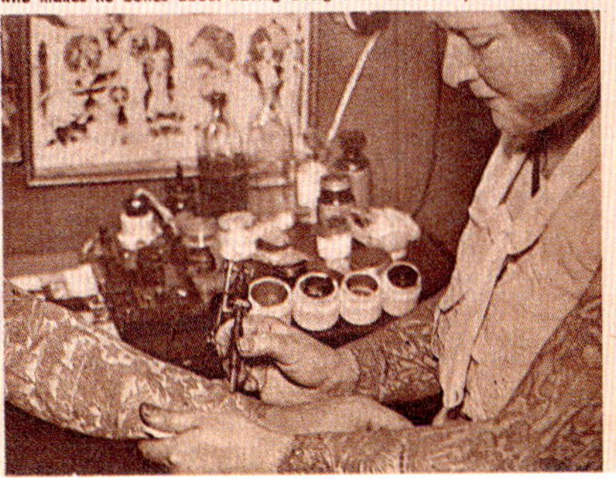

Heart patterns are most popular. (Below) Millie at work. She's one woman who makes no bones about having designs on most every man she meets

a design on her
d, shading a few
He is her tattoo-
to foot in elab-
suit of blue and
American eagle,
instep the Holy
are not tattooed.
ed by Lee. Lee
y seem to prefer
ld rather have a
observes Millie.
designs now and
'And what crazy
wanted his will
g two witnesses
mes in pencil on
e needle while I
legal.
ng in Yiddish to
I couldn't seem
experimented on
to let me write it
t said, 'My wife
ke sure his wife
ously. I worried
ed she was plot-
d a good reason

tattooed on him.

tooed—not com-
nstance. Each of
bite. They're all
ervous, think it's
excitement. I can
ing on them. It's
're tattooed, and
you sick.
Millie says. "I've
was started, but
e."

attern traced on
the spot to be
as a single point
ces through holes
ghth of an inch
nd with another
ints working to-
rely piercing the
"takes" the best

, the dye does not
disappear. Other
attoo than others.
attoo than men's.
l spots on which
any other places
r the surface are
e stretched while
esign is being put
stretch the skin.
ections to keep it

of cloth in hand
the pierced skin,
e hour, this vase-
water.
," says Millie.
've got *them* for

The *Family Circle* cover, 1936

Millie Hull graced the cover of popular American news weekly *Family Circle* in 1936. In the article—in which she is mistakenly referred to as Millie Hall—she explains how, like other New York tattooers at the time, she made a good living tattooing sailors stationed out of the city's naval yards, as well as their sweethearts.

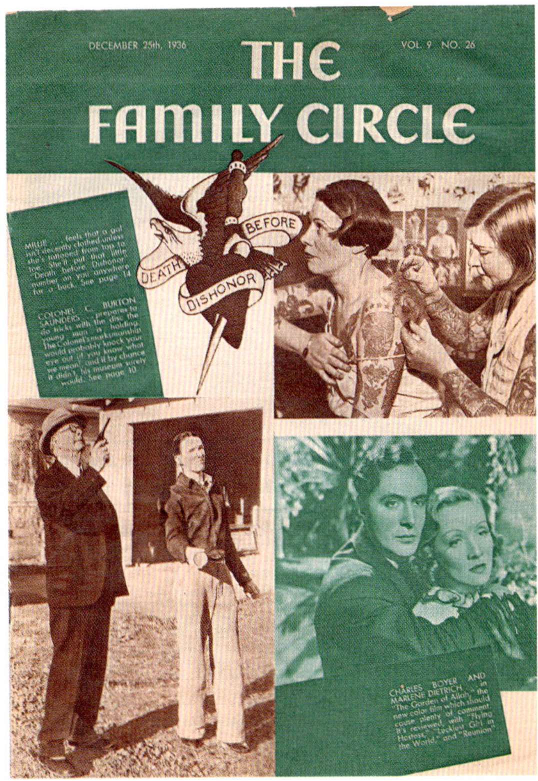

Chapter Six

Tattooing's Winter

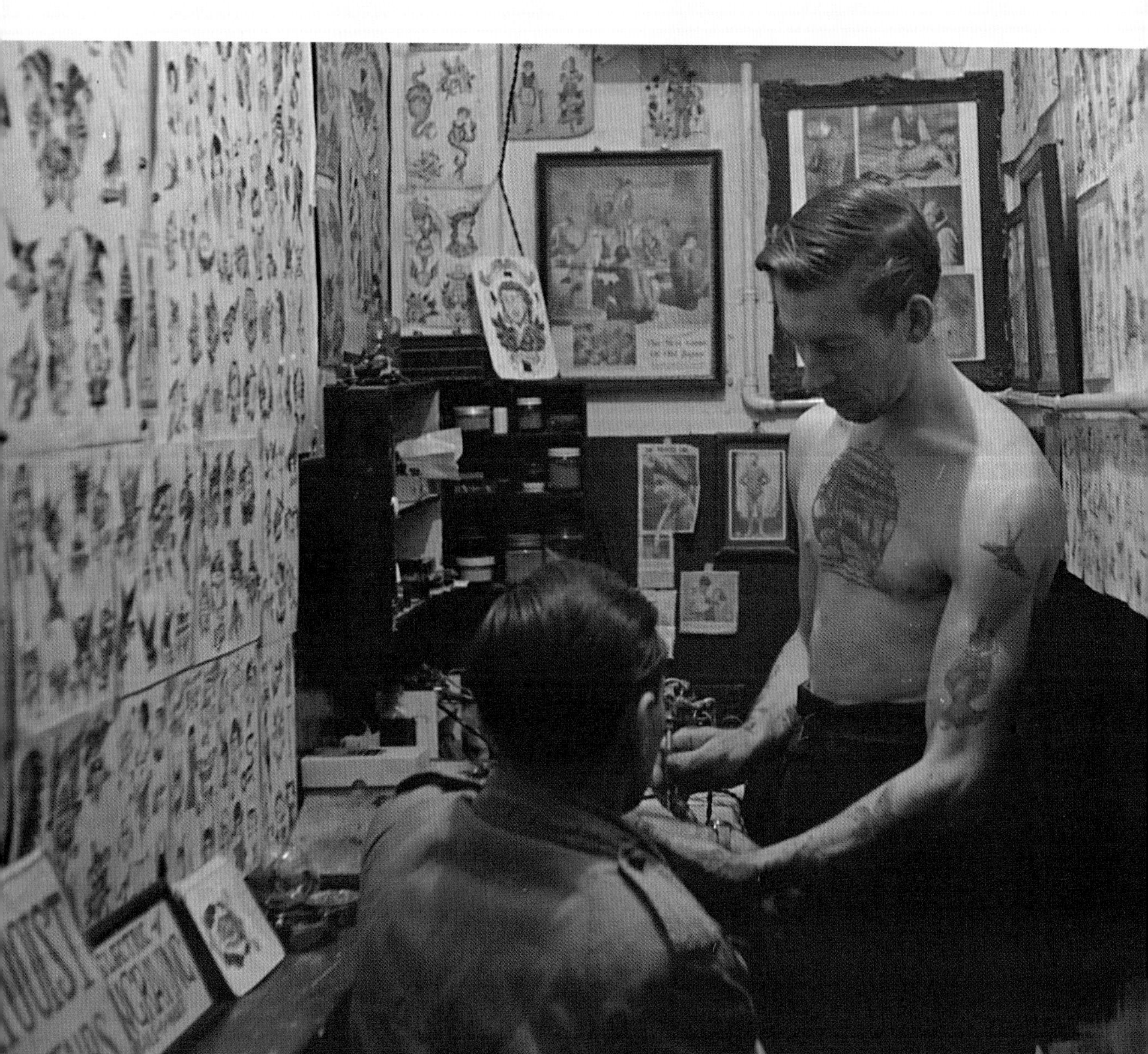

"It may be that I have rediscovered the 'Lost Art of Tattooing'—or has it never been lost?"

Leon Martinetti, 1931

At the circus In the aftermath of World War II, tattooing became a much less profitable trade than it had been previously, and was much more strongly associated with working-class men. Charlie "Cash" Cooper—pictured here surrounded by designs in a cramped tattooing booth off Piccadilly Circus in the center of London in 1951—was inspired to form a professional association in the image of the Tokyo Tattoo Club, clippings about which hang on the wall behind him.

The idea for a club of British tattoo artists had first been mooted in the correspondence pages of traveling show trade publication *World's Fair* in November 1931. A somewhat ill-tempered and nostalgic missive had been written in the journal a few months earlier, ruing the fact that Britain had few remaining tattooers of note, save for a list of increasingly elderly men whom the pseudonymous author "P. A. T." deemed praiseworthy. Though Britain had boasted a veritable panoply of world-class tattooers in the previous decades, the author argued, few young artists were entering the profession and there were barely any of repute left who could be relied upon to work booths at the traveling fairgrounds. Even scarcer, apparently, were heavily tattooed women needed to play the iconic sideshow role of the Tattooed Lady. The letter prompted a flurry of indignant responses over the issues raised, from furious younger artists demanding to be taken seriously, and from heavily tattooed men recommending a whole new generation of upstart tattooers, working beyond the horizon of the cynical old veteran.

Reluctantly, Pat—suspected by those in the trade to have been Joe Kilbride, a traveling tattooer from Bradford who'd worked around the United Kingdom, in the United States, and in Ireland since the late nineteenth century, and who was by this time in his seventies—eventually apologized in print, cowed by the enthusiasm of the correspondence he had received and by the chastisement of fellow industry grandee Joseph Hartley of Bristol. Hartley agreed with Pat that the "young 'uns" had it easier than them in their early days, given the wealth of information and equipment now made available by suppliers such as himself. Hartley reminded him, though, that there were at least a few talented and creative professionals left of whom they should take notice. And in any event, he said, "as to making comparisons between the older men and the young 'uns, this is neither sense nor justice."

Most persuasive of all was a correspondent called Leon Martinetti, a trapeze artist and trained dancer who had made a late career move into the fairground circuit with ambitions to become "the highest classical tattooed human being" with the "finest and most artistic designs ever executed in the country." Boasting about the global quality of tattooing and in disagreement about a generalized decline, Martinetti told Pat and the readers of *World's Fair* about a reputed "Grand Lodge of Tattooers" in the Marquesas Islands, a guild of experts of such legendary quality and talent that any claims to a paucity of tattooing talent must be simply a British problem, if it were a problem at all. This, in turn, caused Pat to wonder whether, if a similar organization "could be formed in these isles, plenty of subjects would come forward to present themselves."

None did so. At least not immediately.

In a further response, Martinetti lyrically imagined something anticipating modern tattoo conventions: a club with regular meetings, competitions, prizes, and press releases; professionals sharing tips and equipment, and enthusiasts coming together to bond over a shared love of tattooing. He even proposed a system of categories, and a judging system which accounted for neatness, originality, speed, and composition, pre-empting televised tattoo competition show *Ink Master* by almost a century. Despite offering to donate a silver cup himself should something be arranged for the following year, no such club would materialize for over two decades. Fittingly, though, the creator of Britain's first tattoo club was a man who had once been a young pupil of Joseph Hartley, that Bristol tattooer who was so eagerly waiting for the next generation to teach the industry new tricks.

An In-and-Out Business

Les Skuse had wandered into Hartley's shop on Blackfields in Bristol, UK, in 1928, barely fifteen years old at the time. After two abortive attempts brought on by nervousness, Skuse finally allowed Hartley to tattoo a bird on his arm, and the pair struck up a quick friendship. Over the following years, Skuse morphed slowly from customer to apprentice, first by drawing designs and mixing inks, and then eventually covering for the old-timer while Hartley took boozy lunch breaks at one of two nearby pubs. Skuse's nascent career under the guidance of the storied master must certainly have been one of the reference points for Hartley's cautiously optimistic assessment of the industry at the time of his letters to *World's Fair*. But little could he have realized that that particular "young 'un" would become the central nexus of a network of tattoo artists that would connect tattooing across the Western world, become the foundation and inspiration for the transformation of the global tattoo industry, and buoy a broken and depleted industry through perhaps its darkest period since its inception.

After World War II, the European and American tattoo industry was in disarray. By 1955, just a decade after the war's end, some major port cities, such as Portland, Oregon, which had been important hubs for the practice when they were thronging with sailors, no longer had any working tattooers at all. "Tattooing," *The Oregonian* wrote punningly that year, is "inherently an in-and-out business."

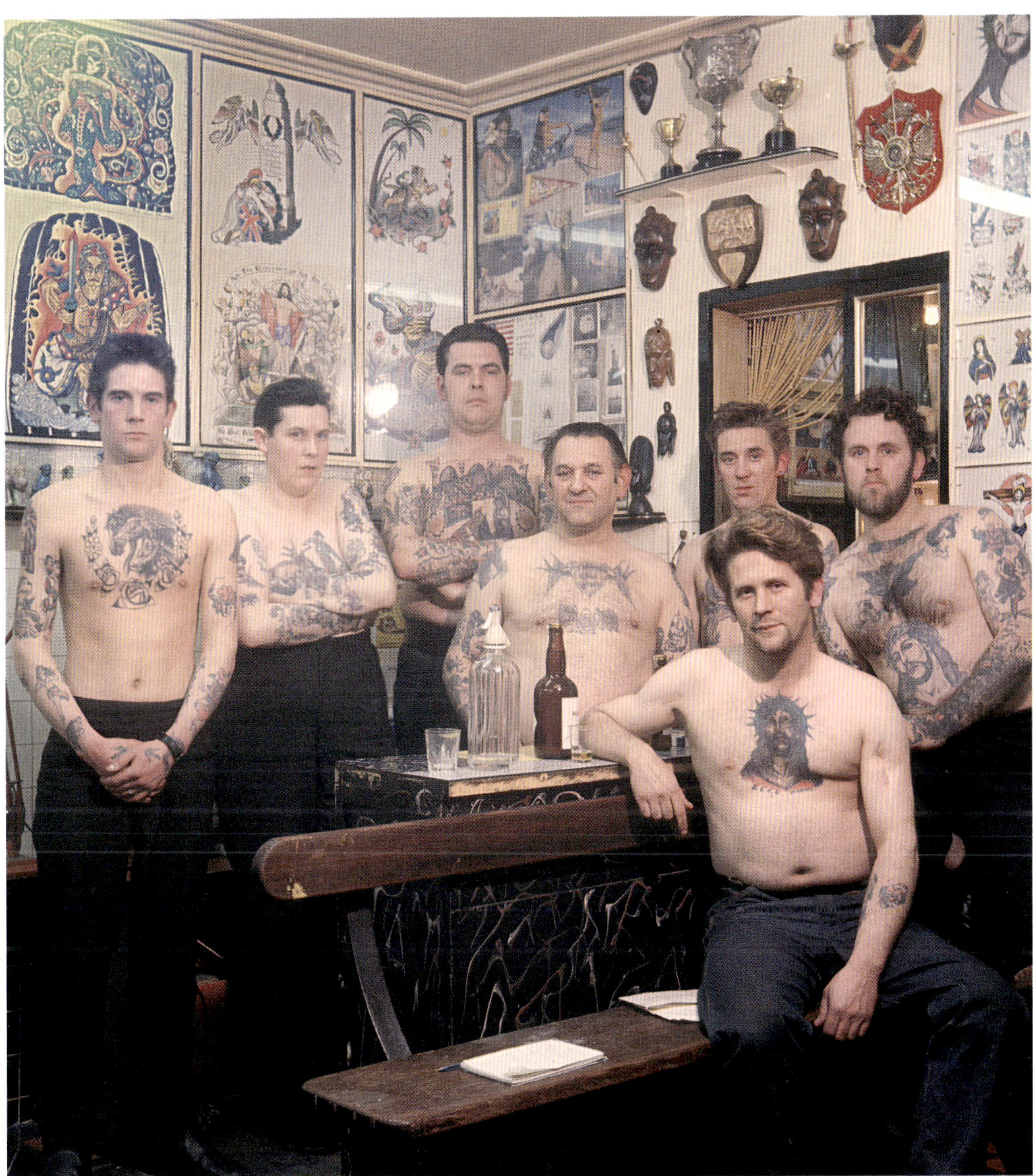

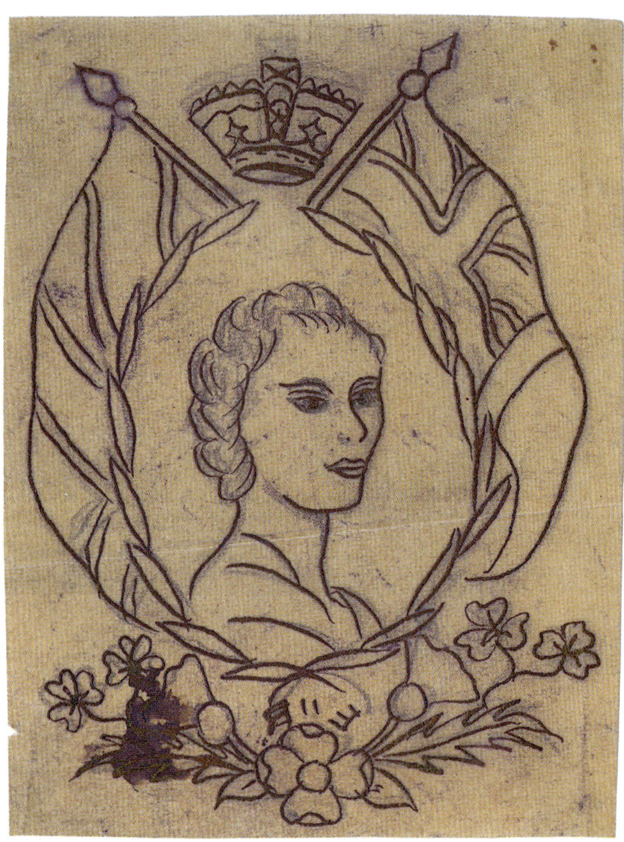

Coronation special (*left*) This design by George Burchett was for a commemorative tattoo on the occasion of Queen Elizabeth II's coronation in 1953. Burchett died a month before the actual coronation, and so it is unknown if he completed the tattoo, or if it was carried out by his son Leslie. Coronation tattoos had proven popular for previous monarchs—Burchett had even tattooed a portrait of Edward VI on a man's bald head.

Changing tastes (*right*) Fine-lined designs like these, by George Burchett, were becoming old-fashioned by the end of World War II. This design language had dominated Western tattooing since the late 19th century, but tastes had changed.

In the immediate aftermath of the war, tattooing's image had been desperately tainted through association with the sadistic infliction of identificatory numbers onto the arms of victims of the Holocaust at Auschwitz, and through the inscription of blood type tattooing on Nazi SS officers. Article after article revealing the horrors of the Nazi camps to the general public made mention of the forcible, dehumanizing tattooing on Jews and other men, women, and children detained there. And even as British tattooers like George Burchett made headlines for helping cover or remove these marks, the practice as a whole took on a sense of stigma as a result.

Moreover, and paradoxically in some senses, the racial science of European eugenics that had underpinned fascism had also slowly gained intellectual respectability in Britain and America since the 1880s, and by the 1950s, though waning in overt influence, had morphed into a more publicly palatable form, which its proponents claimed was specifically different from Nazi ideology. In the perverse logic of eugenics, inherited from nineteenth-century criminology, tattooing was indicative of atavism and primitive "savagery"—and as we saw in the previous chapter, the war had allowed tattooing to once again become seen as "exotic" and strange to white Euro-American eyes. Tattooing was even condemned as "savage" by the Union of Writers in Soviet Russia, which had explicitly rejected the social-scientific work of European criminologists and anthropologists.

Most significantly, perhaps, the entire landscape of contemporary visual culture had by the 1950s radically shifted from the decorative, fussy styles of the Victorian, Edwardian, and Art Nouveau periods to something resolutely more sleek, minimalist, and monochrome. Buildings, furniture, print, industrial design, and

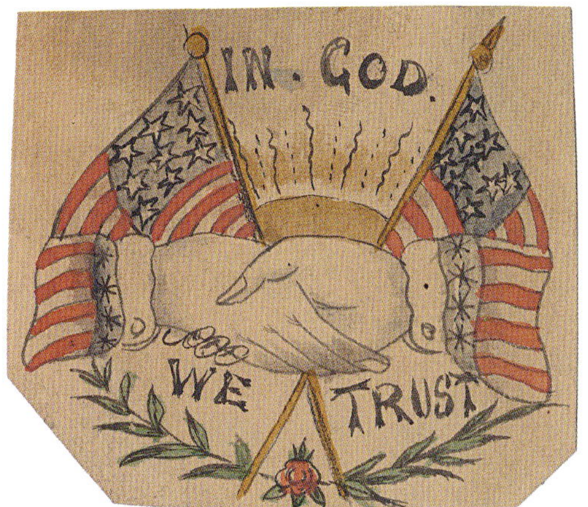

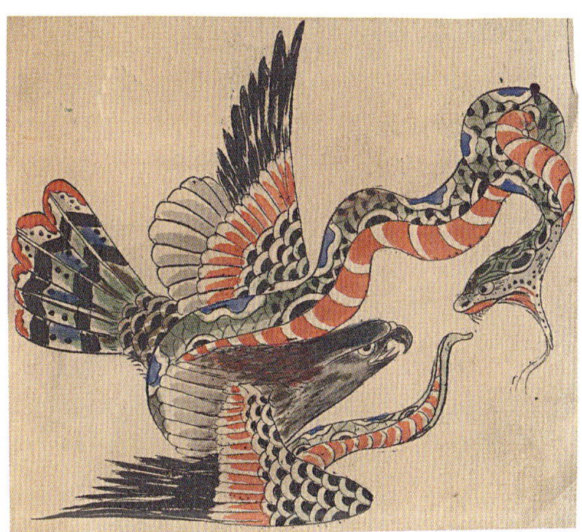

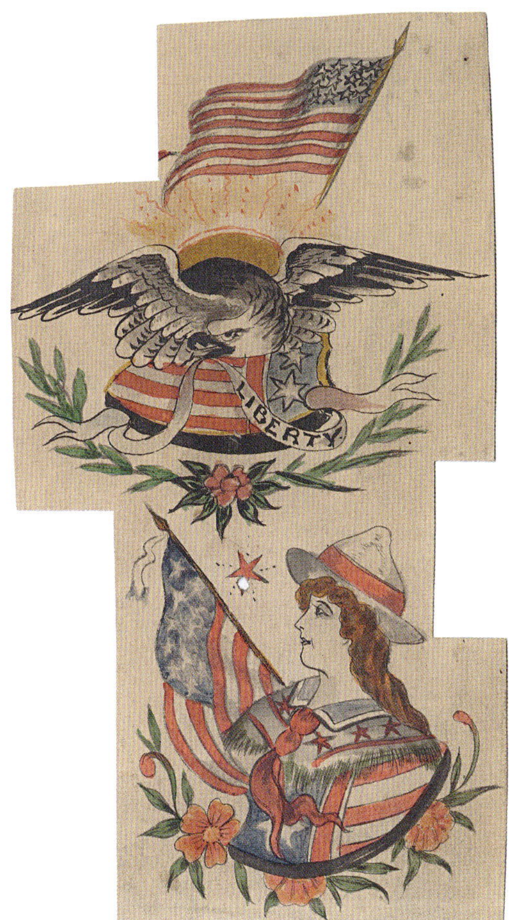

fashion embraced styles which explicitly rejected the previous two or three generations of stylistic cues. Some academics have argued that this visual shift has intellectual underpinnings in eugenicist thought, which prioritized progress, efficiency, and hygiene, but in any case, the dominant modernism of mainstream postwar visual culture did not tessellate well with the eclectic tattooing styles of the professional period, which had begun in the late nineteenth century and tracked dominant trends ever since.

As tattooing fell from fashion, innumerable men and women who had been tattooed during the war in moments of camaraderie and youthful folly wrote to magazines seeking tips on tattoo removal. Given the widespread popularity of tattooing during the war and the inefficiency of removal methods, by the 1950s there was a whole generation of kids with tattooed parents, grandparents, aunts, and uncles, many of whom regretted their inkings. Tattooing was no longer a youthful fad, but the habit of tragically unfashionable elders.

Even among the tattooers who were still working, several were grumpily unimpressed—as their own forebears had been—with the design choices of young people. Just as tattooers in the 1920s mourned the passing of the extensive Orientalist works of the Victorian and Edwardian periods, in turn tattooers in the 1950s looked nostalgically to those same 1920s. Texas military tattooer Bob Shaw recalled a postwar conversation with his colleague, "Painless" Jack Tyron, in which Tyron gestured wistfully at "stuff with blue outlines and brown outlines, oil-painted stuff . . . he had cowgirls, and girls standing on globes with big fat butts and flags draped around them . . . real old time."

"Who's gonna pick something like that?" Shaw said. "Not an eighteen-year-old boy in the Air Force."

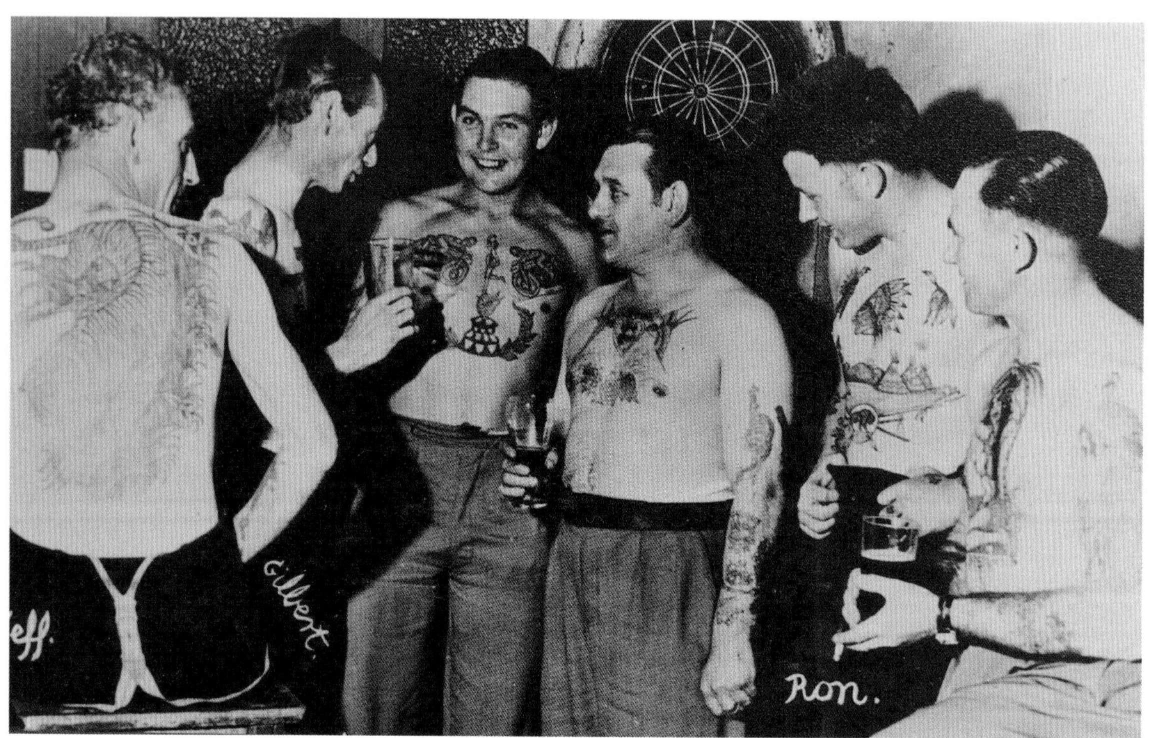
eff.
Gilbert.
Ron.

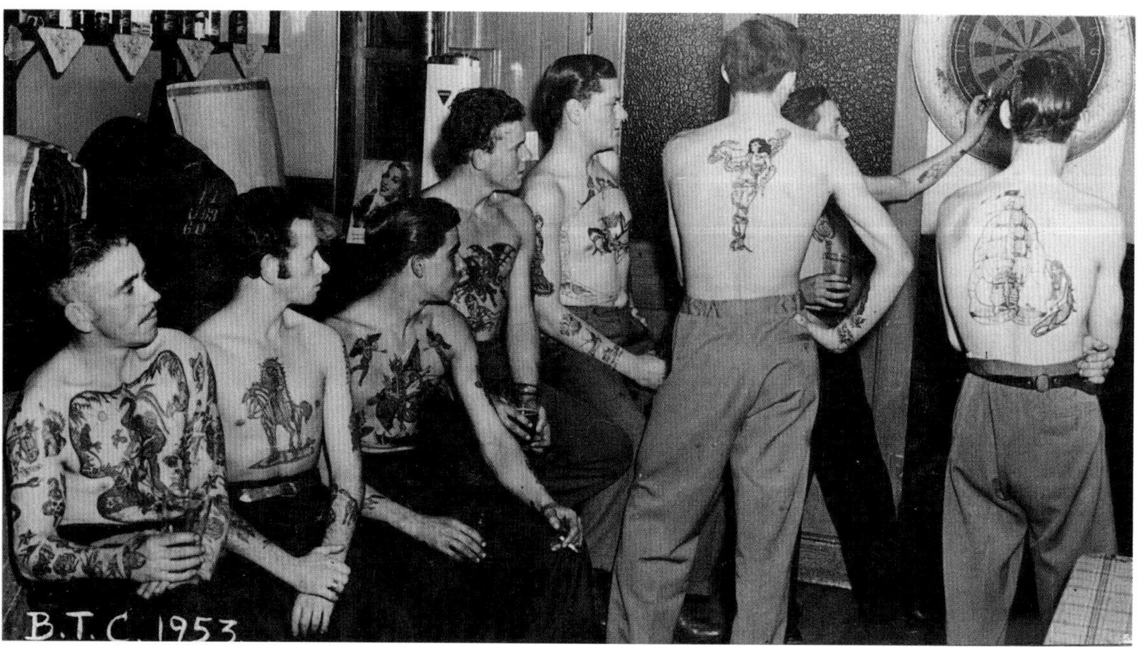
B.T.C. 1953

Drinking buddies Members of the Bristol Tattoo Club met, often shirtless, in pubs around town. These occasions allowed artists and clients to share their ideas and expertise, and to advocate for an art form that had become increasingly stigmatized.

Les Skuse didn't care that tattooing was no longer at the cutting edge of fashion. He loved tattooing deeply. By 1953, he had been tattooing for over twenty years but was barely in his forties, long enough in the tooth to have earned respect and connections in the industry, but still young enough to have the energy and vision to take the woes of Euro-American tattooing onto his shoulders. George Burchett had died in April 1953, and his death came to mark the passing of that generation of tattooers who had basically created the industry from scratch. The gap Burchett left both within the industry and in the wider societal perception of tattooing would have to be filled by those who loved tattooing and could steel themselves against the impending cultural opprobrium of the baby boomers, born into a world overtly hostile to the practice.

Clubbing Together

In 1948, articles and photographs were published around the world of Edo Chōyūkai, the Tokyo Tattoo Club, a longstanding association of heavily tattooed people whose regular gatherings had been interrupted by the war. The so-called "Hard Skin Club" of men (and a few women) had been extant since the time of the Meiji Restoration, and operated as a way for tattooed people to gather in public parks or bathhouses to show off their collections and to participate in competitions. These meetings inevitably involved drinking copious quantities of rice wine, such that the first meeting had to abandon the competitive elements as the competitors couldn't stand still long enough to be adequately judged!

At these gatherings, Professor Masaichi Fukushi from the Nippon Medical School in Tokyo often gave lectures on the history of Japanese tattooing and on the extraordinary collection of preserved tattooed skins he had amassed since the 1920s—a set of circumstances that became the basis for Akimitsu Takagi's 1948 mystery novel *The Tattoo Murder*.

These tales of Japanese tattoo conventions were the direct inspiration for Skuse to found the Bristol Tattoo Club (BTC) in 1953, noted in its early years as "the only club of its kind in the world outside of Japan." In an interview with a local Bristol tabloid in 1954, Skuse complained that such were the dire straits facing tattooing that there were only about eight tattooers left in the country. If there were more, he hoped "We could organise friendly competitions, and it would help to raise the standard of the profession, one of the oldest in the world."

The journalist wrote admiringly of Les Skuse, saying he was a perfectionist and humble. He quoted Skuse as saying, "I never have been, and never will be satisfied with techniques and equipments, nor with my own ability and my own designs."

"Many people think tattooing is common and degrading, only being patronised by people of low mentality," Skuse reflected. "This impression is only due to ignorance and lack of understanding, and the Bristol Tattoo Club has been able to promote a more fair and proper appraisal of tattoo work among the general public."

Immediately, the profession took notice. The BTC held initial meetings of about a dozen members—artists and clients together—at the White Horse pub in Bristol, but moved to the Cornish Mount Club in 1954, drawing almost sixty members in its first year. Members were tattooed with the club logo—a small black bat—

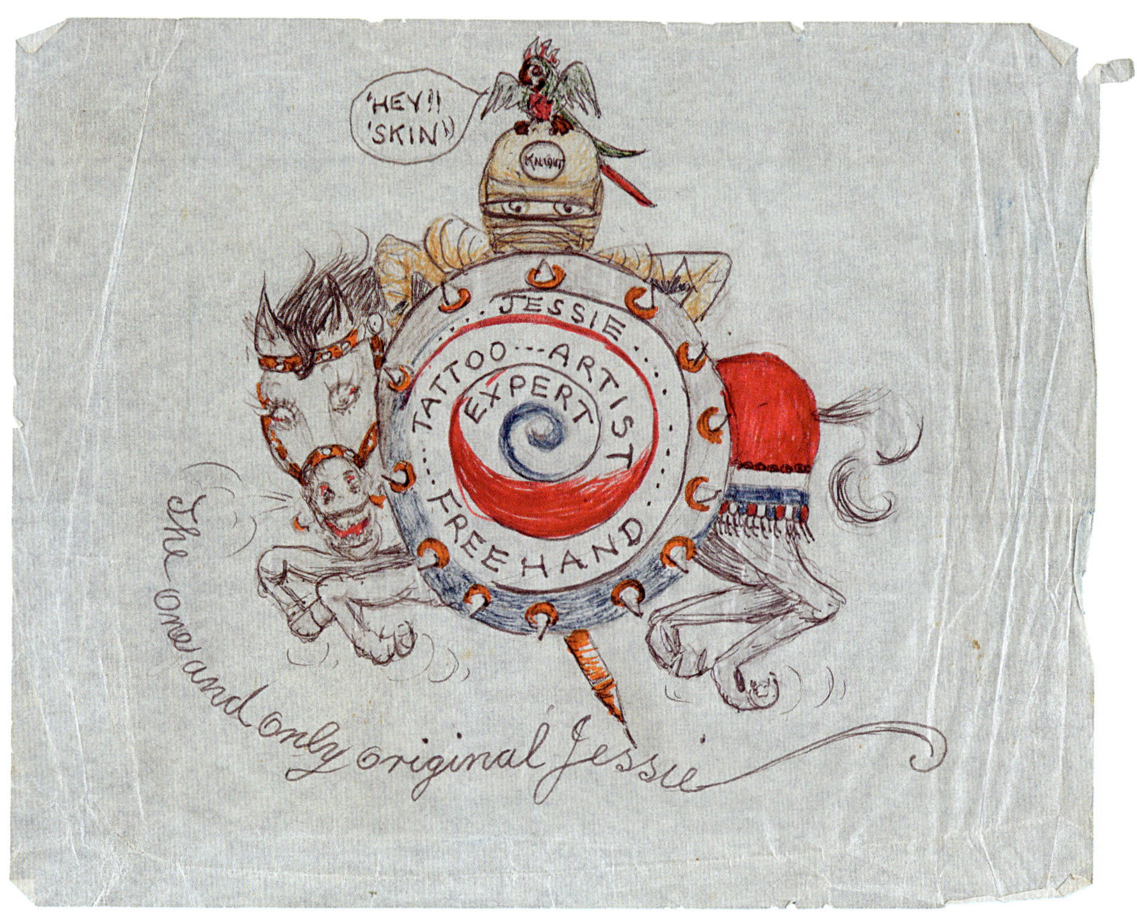

in return for their membership dues, and the club quickly attracted not just national but global attention through frequent press and television appearances. An affiliated London club run by roguish tattooer Charles "Cash" Cooper sprang up almost immediately, as did the North West Club in Rhyl, Wales. Skuse also began corresponding with a tattoo artist in America, Al Schiefley of Sandusky, Ohio, who made a trip to England in 1955, inspiring Schiefley to establish his own international tattoo club by 1958.

Skuse credited Schiefley with the introduction of American tattooing methods, machines, and colors into Britain. Quickly, the network of artists centered around the BTC became the incubator for the revival of the Euro-American tattoo industry, and though previous academic work has claimed the 1970s as the decade that hailed the "Renaissance of Tattooing," that title was used for a segment on British television in 1958,

where Cash Cooper was interviewed as an upstart successor to the late George Burchett.

Jessie Knight, Lady Tattooist

As we shall see also in the next chapter, the opportunities provided by the Bristol Tattoo Club and its offshoots for collaboration, knowledge exchange, and camaraderie inspired and characterized the development of tattooing for the following decades, at least until Skuse's death in 1973. A core group of young artists established themselves at the center of the industry, and were ever-present at gatherings and in the press—Skuse himself, Cash Cooper, Londoners Jack Zeek and Rich Mingins, Frank "Len Lone Wolf" Horsler in Luton, Al Schiefley from a distance in Ohio—and one more.

Though there were many female clients and partners at the clubs' gatherings, there was only one female tattoo artist: Jessie Knight.

Knight on horseback (*left*) In this sketch from c.1960, perhaps intended to be pinned on the wall of her studio, Jessie Knight presents herself as a knight in golden armor, inured to the slings and arrows she often faced as the lone prominent woman in British tattooing. Rendered with characteristic humor, she imagines leaving her competitors in the dust as she gallops past them, unaffected by their insults.

Female clientele (*right*) Jessie Knight tattoos an unknown client in c.1960. At one stage in her career, surviving shop signs suggest that Knight refused to tattoo women, given the social taboos, though she clearly made exceptions on occasion.

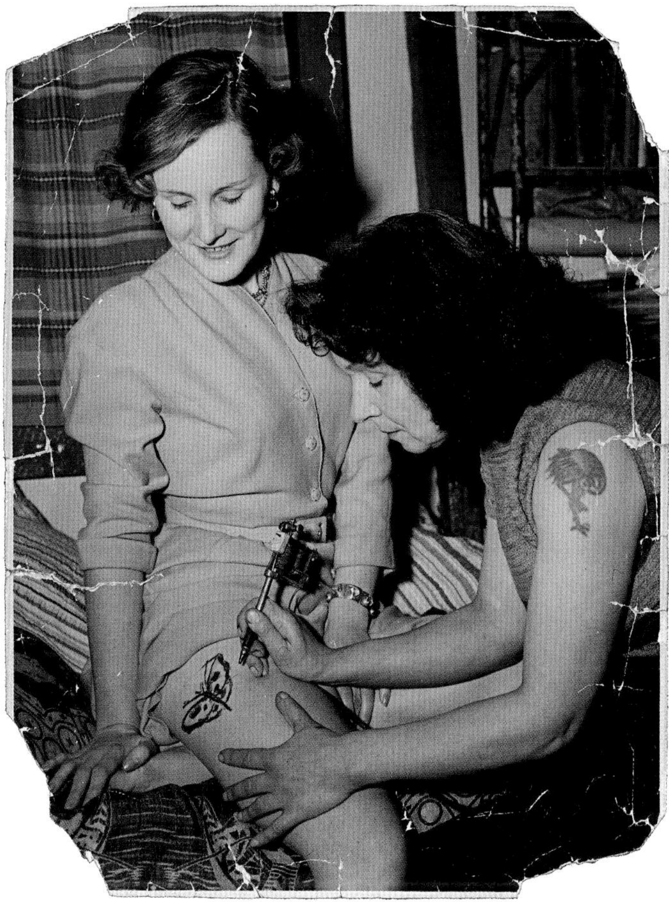

On May 5, 1955, Jessie attended the second meeting of the London Tattoo Society at the Horseshoe pub in Clerkenwell, London. Schiefley was over from America, and Skuse had come into the capital from Bristol. Photos from the event show the group of Skuse, Schiefley, Mingins, and Knight arm in arm, sharing pints and closely examining their friends' and rivals' work on skin. In collaboration with the BTC, the event hosted the first ever "Champion Tattooer of All England" competition, to be judged by writers from the *Sunday Pictorial* and *Sunday Dispatch*, some twenty-five years after the idea was first mused upon by the old-timers. Skuse won the competition, of course, but Jessie Knight, the best and probably only female tattooer working in the country at the time, came runner-up with a full backpiece design of a Highland fling, proudly cementing her place among this pantheon of the most influential tattooers in the world at the time.

Though women had been working in Britain and America as tattoo artists for decades, it was usually alongside their husbands or fathers, who generally overshadowed them in reputation if not ability. Jessie, by contrast, became a huge name in her own right, forging a formidable reputation in Kent and then later in Aldershot and Portsmouth. Even though her father had been a tattooer, it is Jessie's reputation and legacy that overshadows his, rather than the other way around.

Jessie worked in Charlie Bell's shop during the 1940s, perhaps alongside Grace Bell, who we encountered in the previous chapter. Jessie had come to know Charlie Bell through her father, Leonard, who was known professionally as Charlie, Sailor Knight, and, on occasion, as "Two-Gun Rix." As well as being a tattoo artist, Charlie Knight had forged a career as a performer in circuses and sideshows, telling an elaborate legend of having emigrated to the United

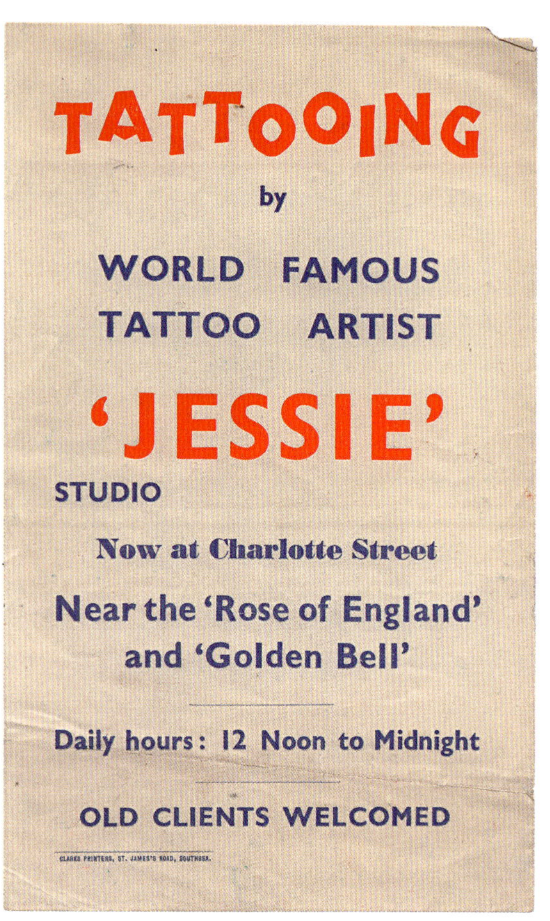

Gone to the pub (*left*) Jessie Knight's advertising flyers, such as this one from c.1960 promoting her Portsmouth shop, often oriented potential customers to her location by noting its proximity to two nearby pubs, useful for some "Dutch courage" before the tattoo or a celebration afterward. Knight's shop signs did warn in blank verse, though, that if anyone was "over the eight"—too drunk—they were "too late."

Hell for "lether" (*right*) Knight's father Charlie had learned cowboy skills, including sharpshooting and rope tricks, in the US, and made a good living working as a performing cowboy under the name Two-Gun Rix. Her brother worked as a cowboy act in the music halls and circuses for decades, and her sister Ella married another famous cowboy performer, Hal Denver. While the circus was not for her, Jessie clearly loved the thrill and freedom which the Wild West symbolized, as evidenced in this charming design.

States from Croydon after running away to sea from a respectable job as a clerk in the City of London. In America, he said, he had worked as a Texas Ranger, learning sharpshooting and lasso rope tricks, as well as how to tattoo.

On his return, Charlie Knight began to work as a tattoo artist in Southampton, with "Princess Cristina," the future wife of Charlie Bell, being his most famous customer. In the 1920s, Knight moved his family to Barry, a seaport in Wales, and on the 1921 census, young Jessie—then only seventeen years old—was listed as assisting her father in his tattooing business. When he returned to sea in 1927, she took sole charge of the tattoo shop. She also briefly took a role in Charlie Knight's cowboy act, though clearly preferred tattooing. (Her sister, Ella, stuck with the circus, and survived her dad accidentally shooting her through the head during a "William Tell" act!)

From her correspondence with Skuse and her proximity to the BTC, it is clear that Jessie was taken very seriously as an artist. She owned a machine custom-built for her by Cash Cooper, and letters and photographs from her survive in the archives of Rich Mingins and the wider BTC-centered network. But being a small, slight woman in such a hyper-masculine industry was clearly tough for her, and writing, poems, and ephemera reveal a robust and humorous approach to her profession, coupled with a soft, reflective, and meditative side.

Jessie's great-grandmother had been a commercial poet in the Victorian era, and Jessie embraced her blank verse style for everything from shop signs to song lyrics. "Please Note," one sign said, "When tattoos are on a lady, folks are apt to think she's shady. But as this is not always true, tattoos for ladies is taboo." Another warned customers that if they were "one over the eight"

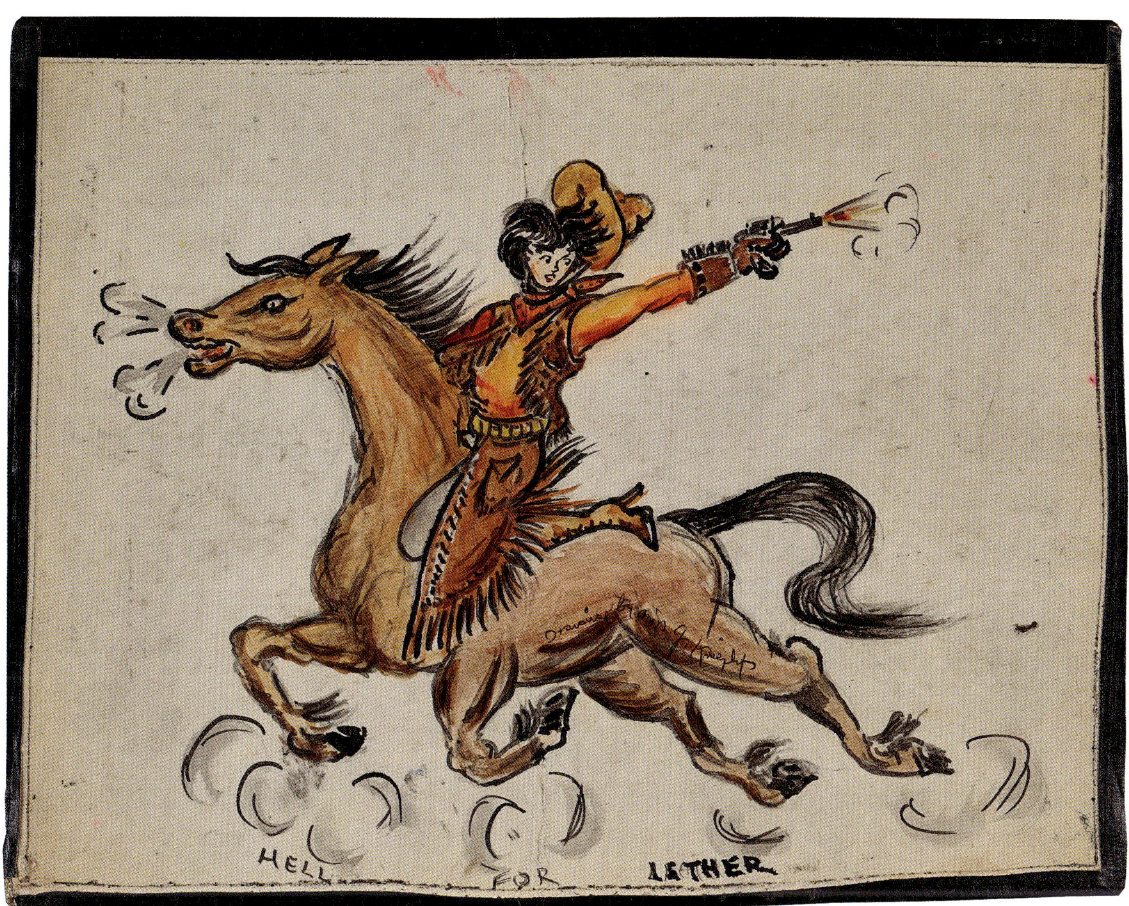

they were "too late"; another admonished, "I don't like dirty jokes, so keep it clean, will you blokes!?" Of her surviving lyric sheets, perhaps the most revealing as to her sense of her own place in the industry is "Squint Eye the Tattooed Witch," an autobiographical remixing of "Popeye the Sailor Man" to tell her own tale of being called a bitch by "scratch artists" trying to "steal her pitch." While she had earned the respect of the industry's gatekeepers, still plenty of lesser artists needed reminding that she was not to be messed with. After all, she had once borrowed a gun from a regimental customer and used it to shoot her estranged husband in the leg.

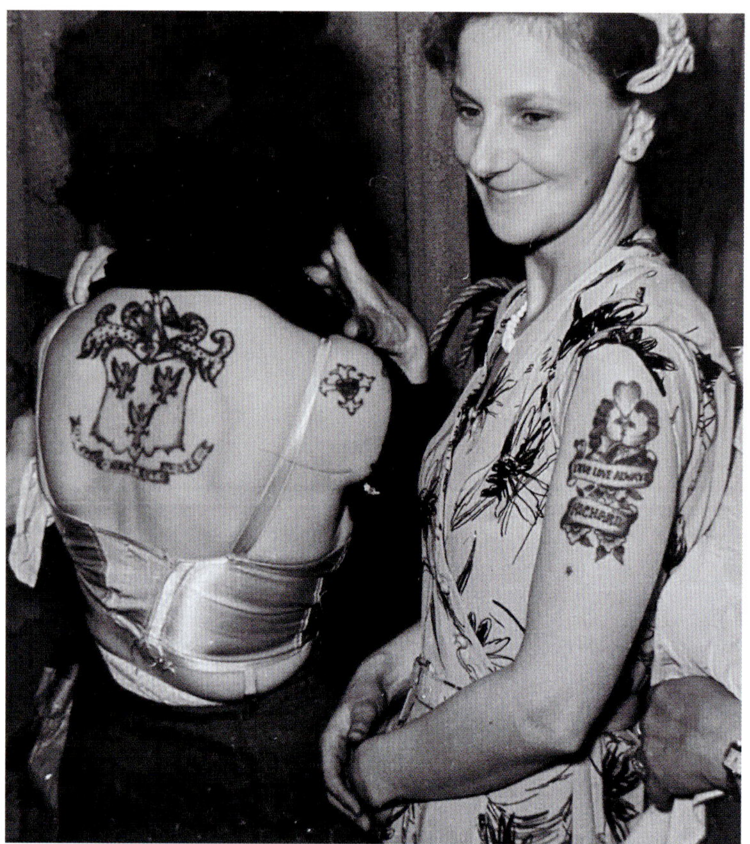

Jessie Knight with friend, 1950s

Knight's backpiece design—her family crest—was fittingly tattooed by her father Sailor Charlie. Though Jessie was not the first or only woman to wield a tattoo machine in the UK, she was by a long way the most prominent, visible, and respected. Next to her is Margaret Mingins, Rich Mingins' wife.

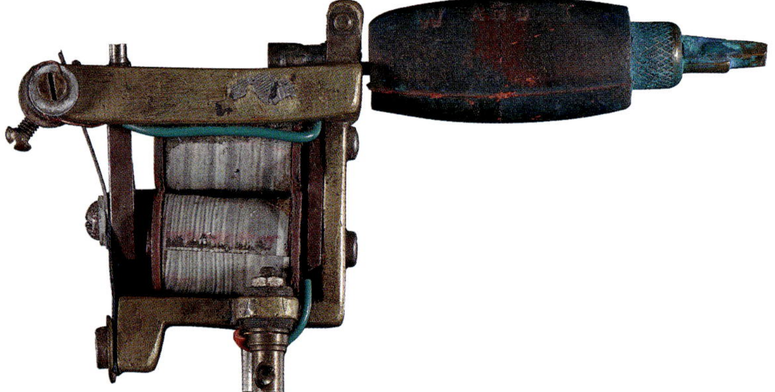

Tattoo machine made by Cash Cooper for Jessie Knight, 1950s

As evidence of her esteem in the industry, Knight's collection is packed full of letters, photos, design sheets, and tools sent to her by her peers. This machine was custom-built for her by her friend Cash Cooper, who modified the standard form of the tattoo machine to better fit Jessie's diminutive hands. Though fierce, she was tiny, reportedly standing at under 5 ft (1.5 m) tall.

"Highland Fling" tattoo by Jessie Knight, 1955

This decorative backpiece depicting bagpipers and a dancer jigging in the Scottish Highlands earned Jessie Knight runner-up in the Champion Tattooer of All England competition in 1955, and the long-term respect of the titans of her industry. Despite her talents and popularity, she was plagued with jealous and sexist barbs from rival male tattooers throughout her career—a topic about which she penned several poems.

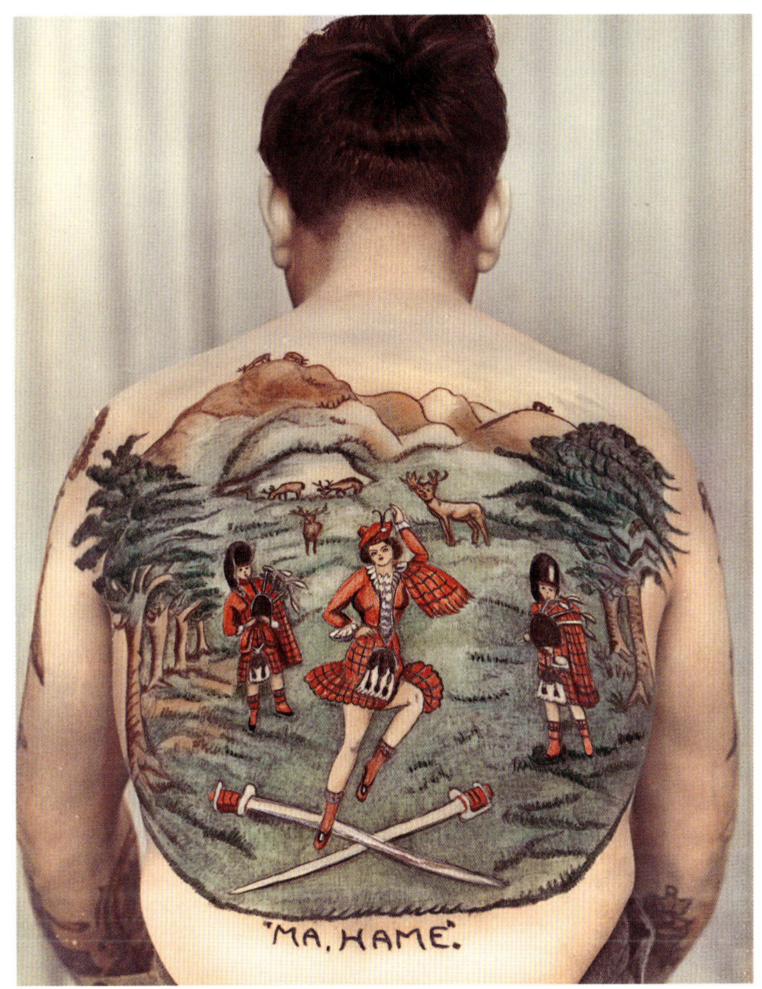

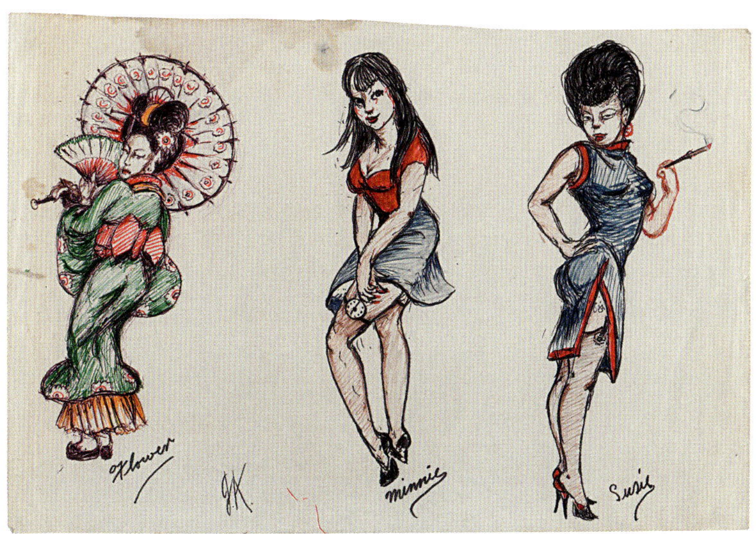

Tattoo designs by Jessie Knight, c.1960

Knight was perhaps not the most naturally gifted draftsperson of her era, but her drawings exhibit a sharply observed edge untypical of her male colleagues. Rendered in biro and cheap felt-tip pen, Knight turns stereotypical, coquettish pinups into slyly observed portraits of real, human women, each of which bears a smirk, a snarl, and in the case of the woman on the left, a stare approaching contempt.

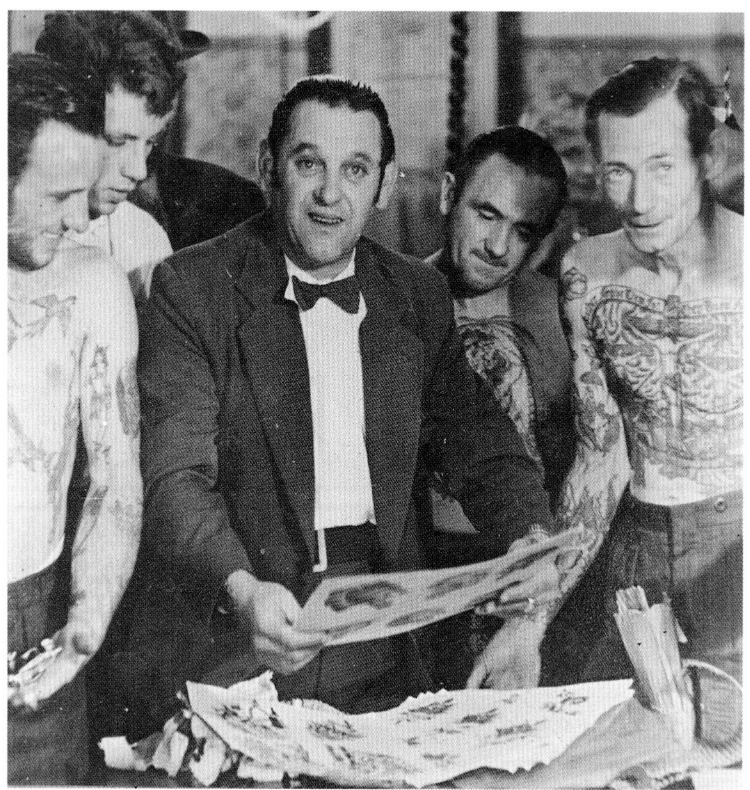

Bristol Tattoo Club members, c.1955 (*left and below*)

Bristol Tattoo Club members with Les Skuse, pictured at the 1955 London Tattoo Society competition.

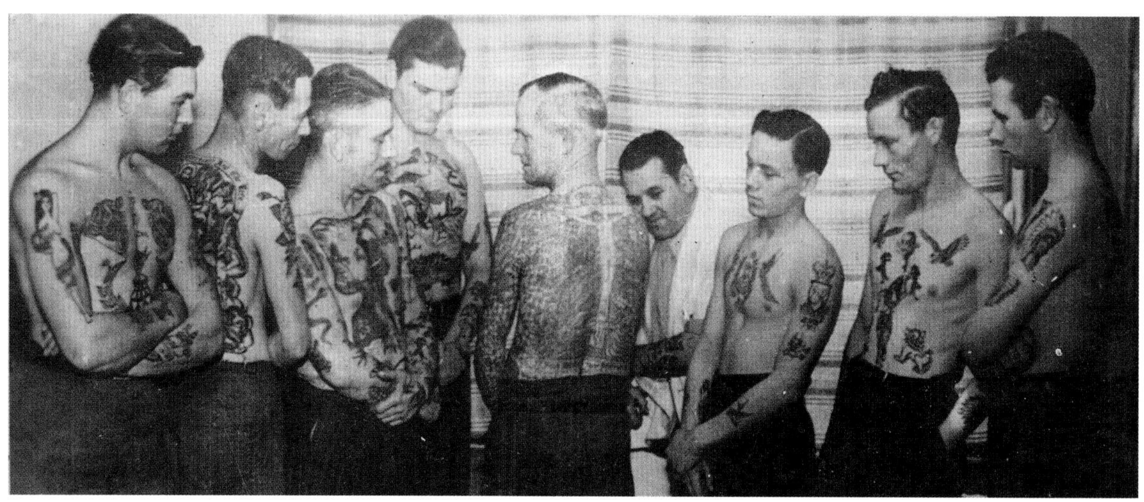

Bristol Tattoo Club members playing cards at the White Swan pub in Bristol, 1954 (*right*)

Members Terry Heal (*top left*), Len Williams (*top right)*, Gilbert Milsom (*bottom left*), and Phil Marshall (*bottom right*) show off work by Les Skuse in a publicity photograph for a Bristol Tattoo Club event.

Gathering of the London Tattoo Society at the Horseshoe pub in Clerkenwell, May 1955 (*below*)

Gathered attendees at the London Tattoo Society meeting in Clerkenwell. Those pictured include (*from right*) Frank "Len Lone Wolf" Horsler, Jessie Knight, Les Skuse, and Rich Mingins, as well as Cash Cooper (*center*).

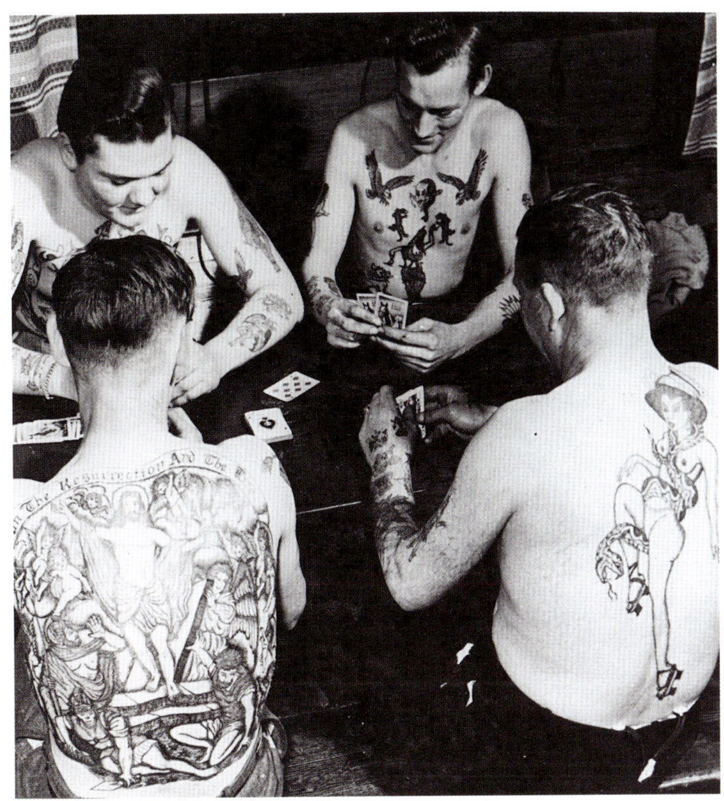

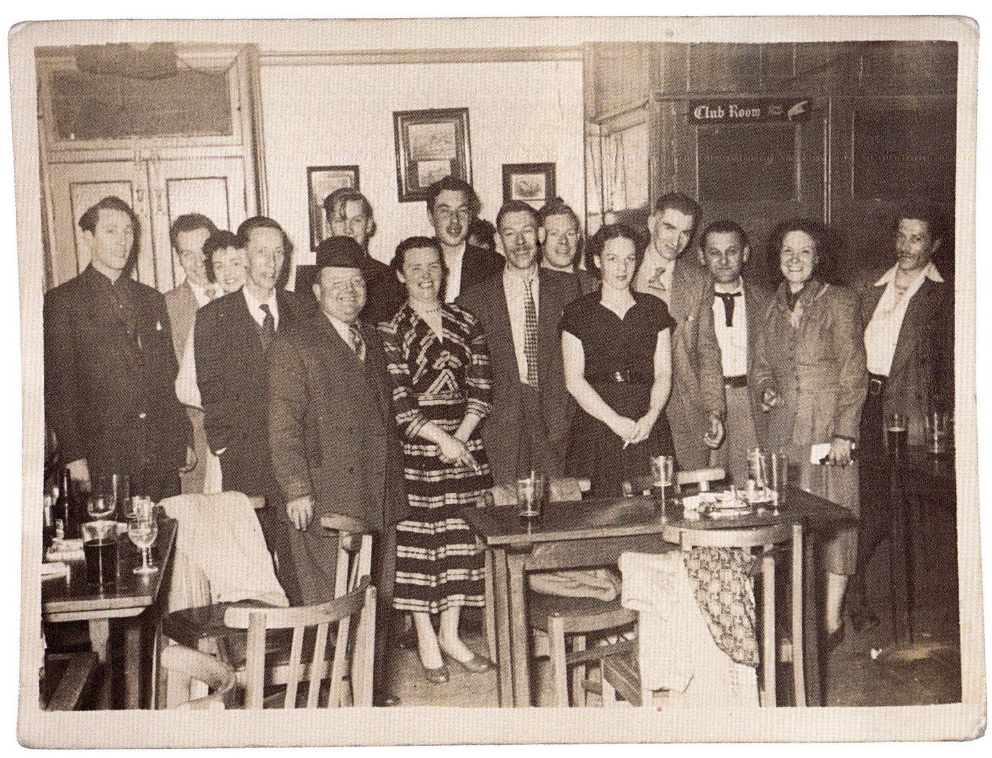

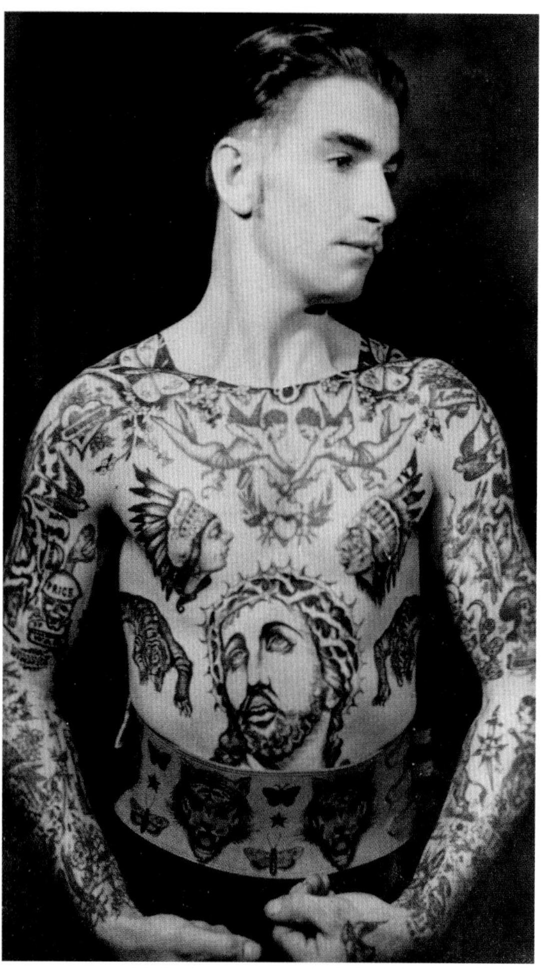

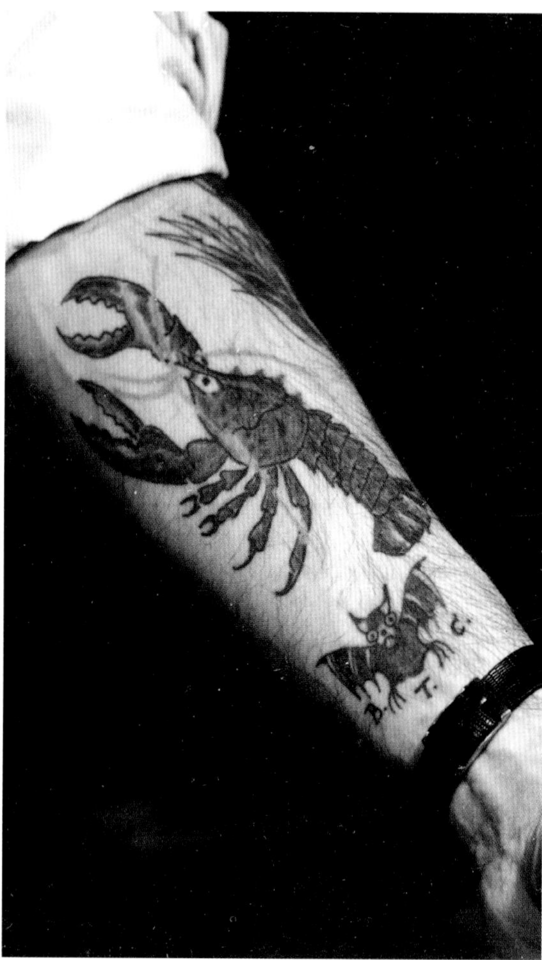

Rich Mingins, c.1955

Rich Mingins was a tidy, fastidious, and quiet man who did not court publicity and was not prominent in newspapers and magazines in the way Les Skuse or Burchett were. He was, however, an incredibly talented tattooer, and had a vast pool of knowledge about the history of tattooing, amassing an enormous archive of photographs, news clippings, and cartoons about tattooing from around the world. With Les Skuse and Cash Cooper, he was central to the interconnected British tattoo scenes of the 1950s and 60s. Born in 1916 in Cumberland in the north of England, he tattooed unassumedly in a room in his house in Harlesden, North London, through to his death in 1968.

Bristol Tattoo Club membership tattoo, c.1955

Members of the Bristol Tattoo Club were marked with the club's emblem: a bat. The logo and the lobster here were likely tattooed by Les Skuse.

Charles "Cash" Cooper, photographed by Rudi Inhelder, c.1960 (*right*)

Cash Cooper was a brash and bombastic tattooer who learned to tattoo in the Royal Navy. Following the war, he tattooed in central London, before moving to Manchester in the 1960s. Unlike the quiet and reserved Rich Mingins, Cooper was an inveterate showman—he briefly had a pet hawk in his studio and once tattooed a mustache on his face to try and win a "most unusual tattoo" competition. Sadly for Cooper, and much to his annoyance, the prize was only a box of chocolates.

Ron Ackers tattooing a client, 1960s (*below*)

Ackers worked in Portsmouth from 1966 after periods tattooing in Chester in the North West, and Rhyl in Wales, on the coast of the Irish Sea. He was an excellent networker, making correspondence connections with tattooers in the United States such as Lyle Tuttle, and importing American machines into England.

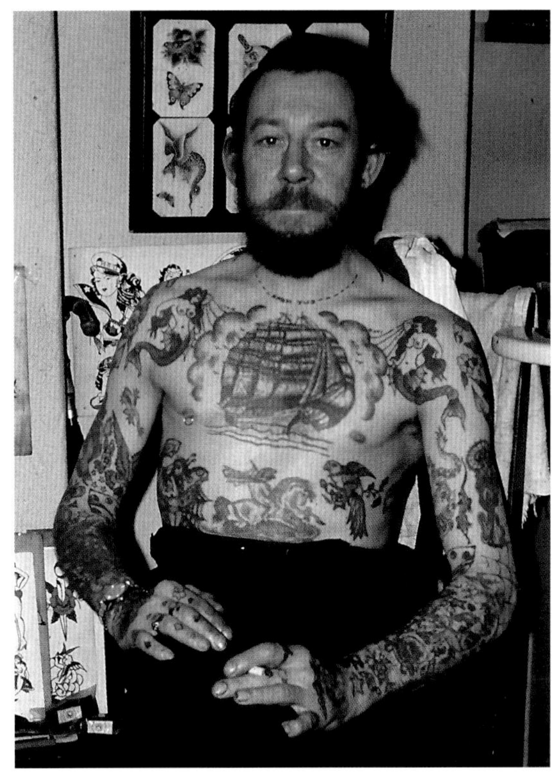

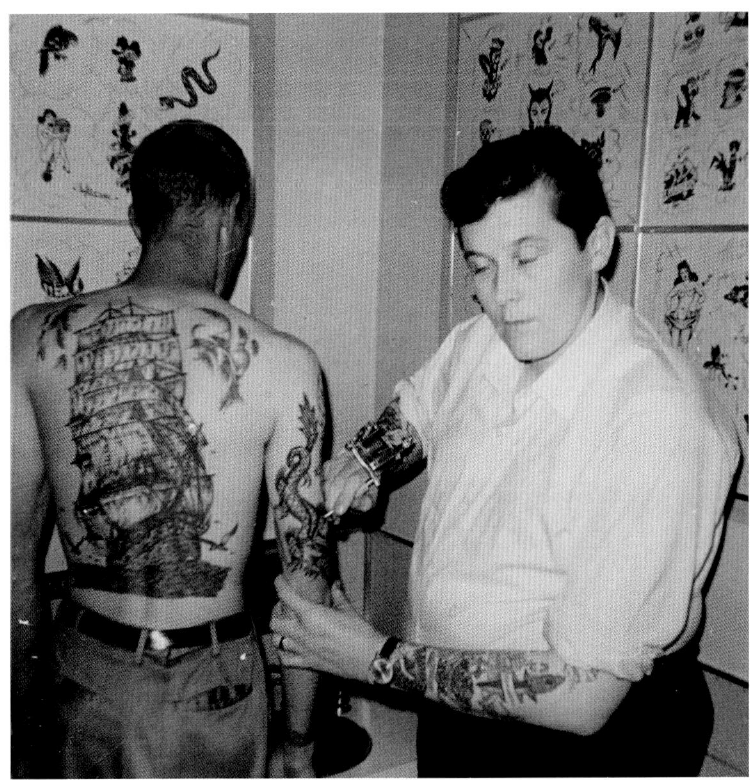

A Fragile Coalition

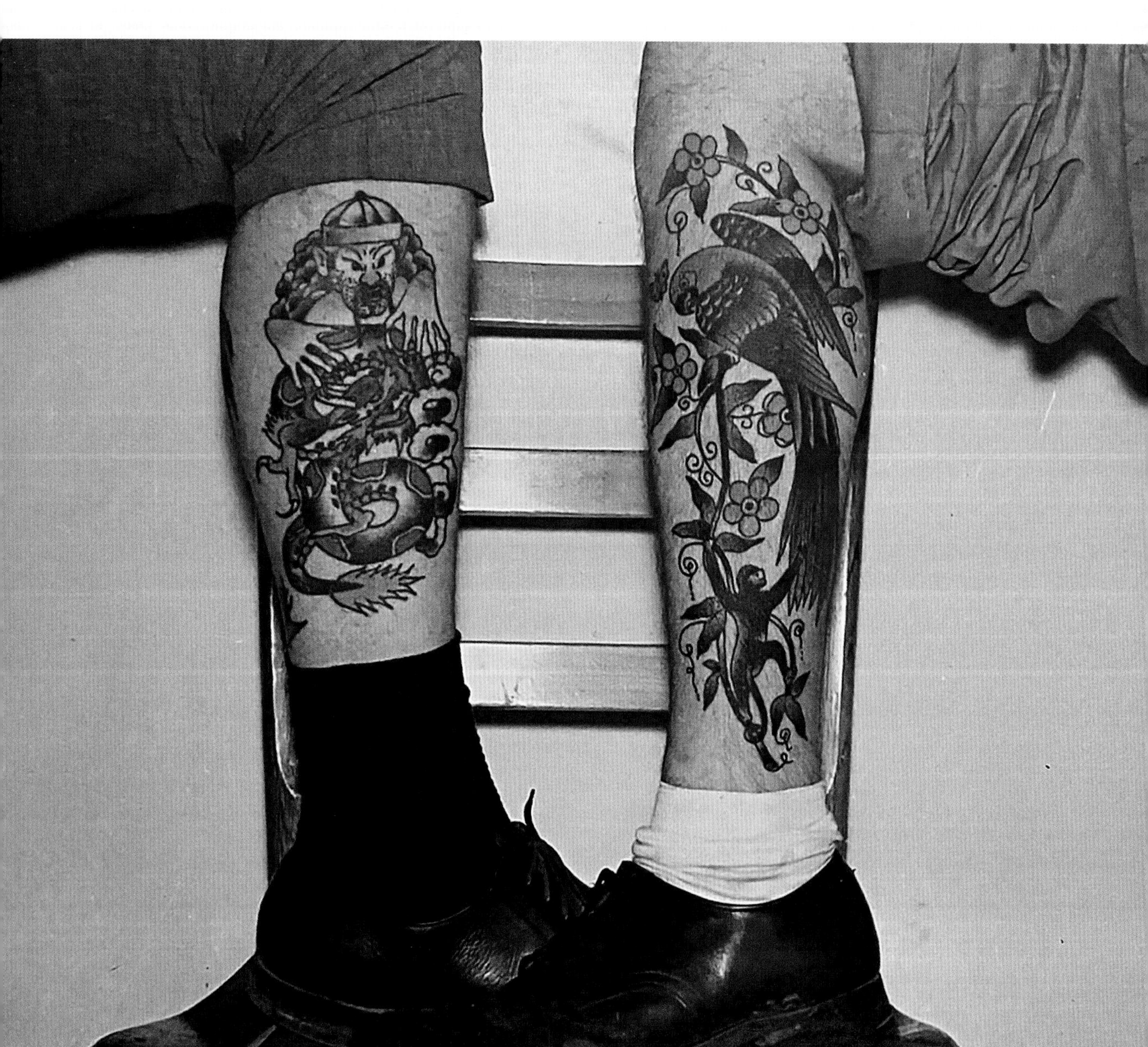

> "Tattooing is how you look at it. The concept falls somewhere between Ray Bradbury weird and a sleazy carnival kickback to Uncle Bernie's first glorious navy drunk in Hong Kong. But it wasn't always that way."
>
> *Rolling Stone*, 1970

Lasting connections This photo of calf tattoos by Huck Spaulding from 1963 was collected by Les Skuse as part of a longstanding and important friendship between the two, which spanned the Atlantic Ocean.

Another attendee at the 1955 Horseshoe pub meeting was a young Swiss man in his mid-twenties named Hans Rudolf (Rudi) Inhelder, who was on a pilgrimage of sorts. Inhelder had become fascinated by tattooing after reading a book called *Pierced Hearts and True Love*, a vivid but rather unreliable history of Western tattooing published in 1954, and had contacted the book's author Hanns Ebensten (a man who claimed on the dust jacket to not really like tattooing at all) in search of more information. Ebensten (born Ebenstein) in turn suggested that he might best contact London tattooer Rich Mingins, who had been instrumental in helping collate material for the book. When Inhelder wrote to Mingins, revealing an interest in photography, the tattooer offered him the chance to take pictures of their upcoming event in London. It was auspicious timing. Inhelder's trip to London just a year after the BTC had been formed, and his subsequent friendship with Mingins, would prove pivotal for the Western tattoo industry in ways which are only now becoming clear. In short, though he was not himself a tattoo artist, Inhelder would become a connective node between European, British, and American tattooing, and would also help to foment friendships and working relationships between mainstream and rather conservative tattooers and a diverse group of subcultural tattoo and body-piercing enthusiasts. These links undergird not only the particular directions Western tattooing would take over the 1960s, 70s, and 80s, but also the interconnections between tattooing and the emergent body-piercing industry.

Inhelder found the networks of the London and Bristol Tattoo Clubs intoxicating. In particular, he was obsessed with Mingins' painstakingly acquired collection of contemporary and historical photography and newspaper clippings, which documented

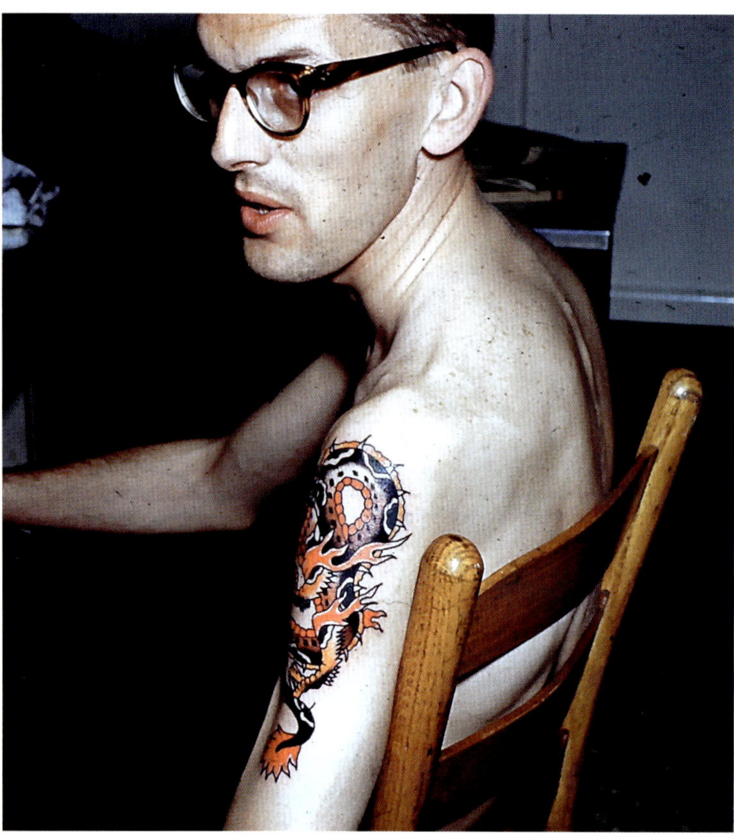

Collaborative effort (*left*) Rudi Inhelder, pictured here in the early the late 1950s or early 1960s, sporting a dragon tattooed by Paul Rogers and Sailor Eddie Evans in Camden, New Jersey.

A sincere enthusiast (*right*) Tattoo clubs offered members certificates which could be displayed on shop walls, and printed magazines to disseminate information. On the left is the *National Tattoo Club of the World*, the membership newsletter of what became the National Tattoo Association (NTAA). On the right is the membership certificate of Rudi Inhelder and Paul "Scotty" MacNaughton's Tattoo Club of America. The certificate is unnamed, but the allocated number was given to Rich Mingins in London, UK.

professional tattooing since its inception in the late nineteenth century. One of the reasons that Mingins was so useful to Ebensten was that, over his career, Mingins had assembled two voluminous scrapbooks of tattoo material—one of photos he had taken, bought, been sent, or traded, and another of newspaper and magazine articles received through a decades-long subscription to a newswire—both of which are now invaluable archives of the industry's earliest years.

Inhelder clearly saw in Mingins something of a kindred spirit. Directly inspired by Mingins, Inhelder went on to amass an enormous amount of material on tattooing over his lifetime, collecting business cards from artists, magazines, and books, and a vast trove of photos from correspondents and dealers across the world, though sadly much of his collection (perhaps at one point the largest in Europe by his own estimation) was destroyed after his death. Buying,

selling, and trading photographs was a key feature of tattoo networks through the postwar period, and the acquisition and transmission of images played an important role in the establishment of connections among this nascent community.

In addition, Inhelder was a gay man. While Mingins was not, there's a charge of homoeroticism and homosociality in much of Mingins' photo collection, given the volume of images of barely clad young men showing off their tattoos. Mingins himself poses in some photos in ways that are reminiscent of Greek statuary, clearly unperturbed by a presumed male gaze for the resultant images.

Rudi Inhelder Can't Fail

In 1957, Inhelder moved to New York for work. He was a physicist, specializing in optics, and proved particularly useful in the Cold War defense industry.

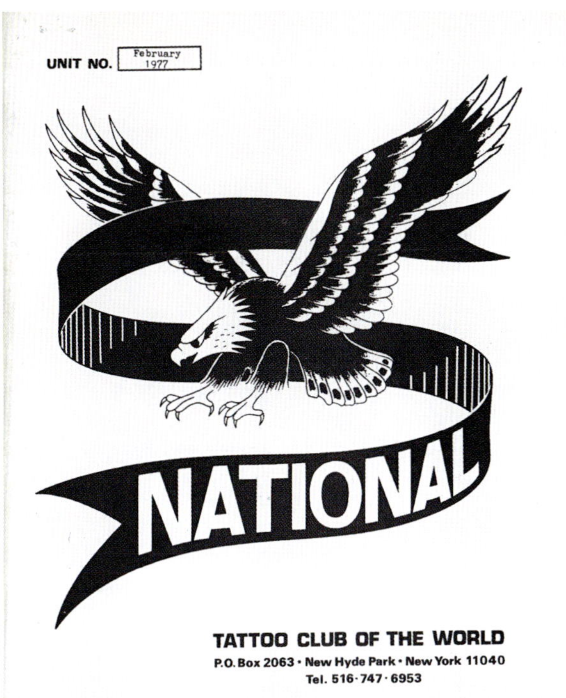

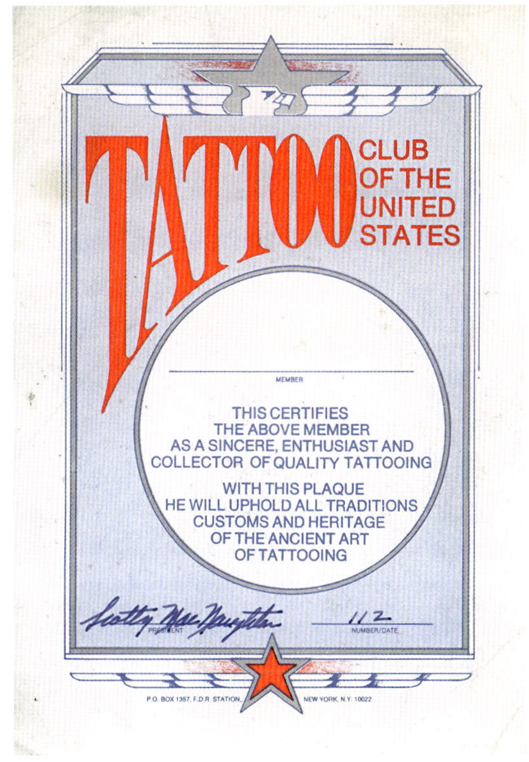

While in America, he found himself longing for the camaraderie, connection, and companionship of tattooers and tattooed people that he had found in London a few years earlier. He had begun to get tattooed once he had arrived in America, eagerly seeking out some of the most prestigious artists in the eastern United States, including Paul Rogers in New Jersey and "Crazy" Eddie Funk in Philadelphia. By his own account, however, he "had difficulties meeting others of the same interest," frustrated in part by the outright banning of tattooing in New York City in 1961 following a hepatitis outbreak. "Therefore," he told a magazine interviewer some decades later, "some friends and I in New York decided to do something about it."

Rudi Inhelder founded the Tattoo Club of America (TCA) in 1963 with his friend Paul "Scotty" MacNaughton, explicitly conceiving it as a way to replicate the membership network of artists and enthusiasts which had arisen from Skuse's BTC back in Bristol. In the mid-1950s, Al Schiefley had established the Sandusky Tattoo Club in Ohio, and Milton Zeis had founded another BTC-inspired organization—the International Tattoo Club (ITC)—as an offshoot of his supply business. But perhaps due to their focus on the tattoo profession, rather than a wider community which included clients as well as artists, or perhaps simply due to their geographic remoteness, neither drew a particularly diverse or active community of members in the United States. The TCA, however, grew quickly to around 250 members by December 1964, buoyed by Inhelder's direct solicitation of members from across the country, as well as Canada and his existing contacts in the UK and Germany. Members in 1964 were on average thirty-four years old, with only 6 percent women. Only around 30 percent were tattooers themselves, while 24 percent

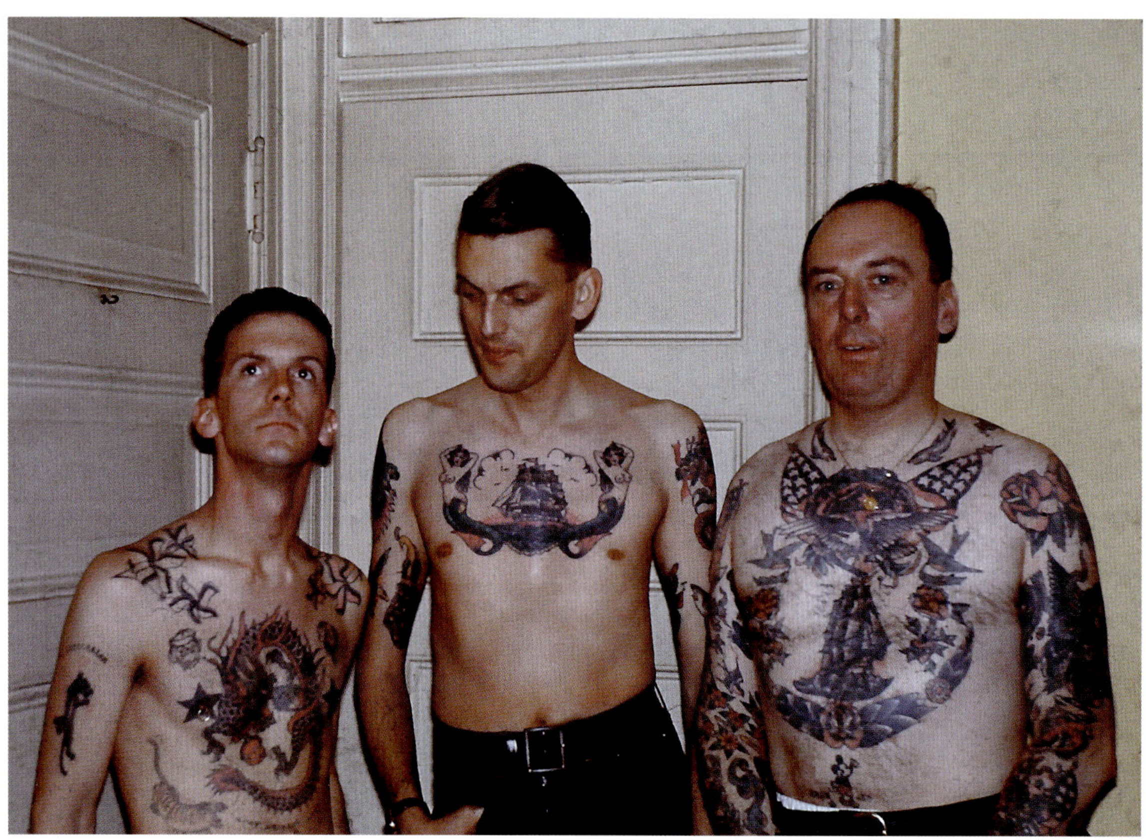

were professionals, and 56 percent white collar workers. As such, the sharing of detailed trade secrets and techniques proved rather controversial for the life of the club, with working tattooers often keen to hold insider knowledge close to their chests.

In establishing the TCA, Inhelder crafted a membership form which he mailed to artists and friends and included an extensive personal questionnaire, alongside an explicit request for suggestions of artists who should be invited to the club. "Dear Tattoo Friend," the invitation letter read, "We know of your interest in tattooing . . . The TCA is a non-profit organisation having the purpose of spreading the knowledge of tattooing and making it more generally accepted." The club also published a member's newsletter, *Tattoo News*, promising to collate "information on new studios opened, extraordinary work done, new equipment available and personal news from artists and members . . . It will direct to sources of supply for tattoo photographs, to new books and magazine articles, and to news from tattoo clubs overseas." As a broad-spectrum information sheet, *Tattoo News* was perhaps the first ever periodical focussed solely on the practice (though Zeis's club had published a newsletter of sorts, *Tattooing the World Over*, a few years earlier).

The questionnaire itself was expertly designed to allow Inhelder to extract a kind of demographic survey of the membership, and in particular to identify those with whom he felt a particular compatibility. The form asked respondents to indicate if they were interested in meeting others, in exchanging or buying photos, or in reading about various topics including history and professional techniques. Members were asked to list their tattoos, and also, even before any visible body-piercing industry or scene came into being, if

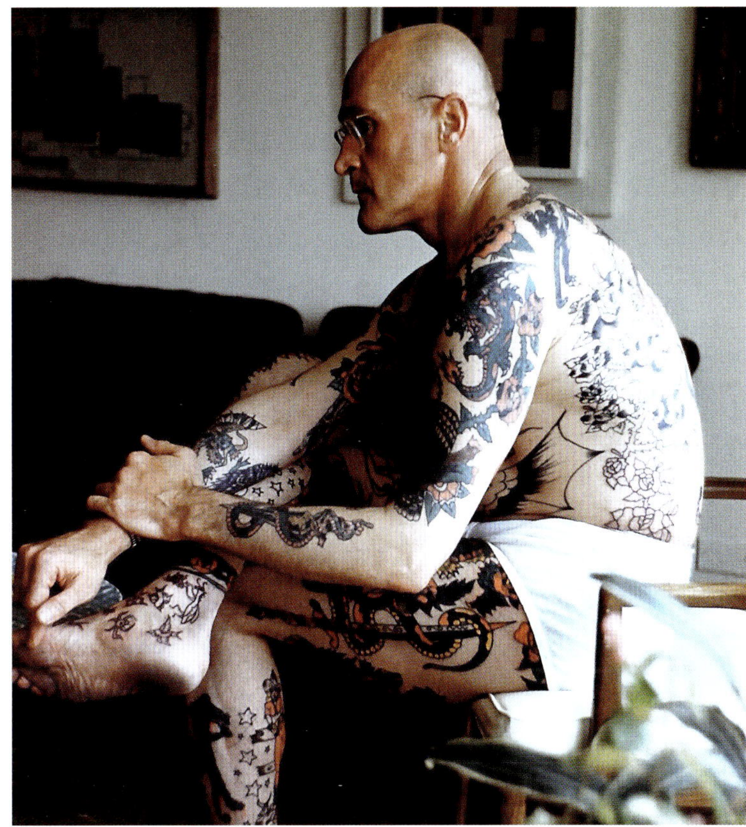

they had any piercings. And by ticking "Interested,"
"Indifferent," or "Not Interested," not only could
Inhelder hone the offering of the club, but he could
also begin to develop a sense of who he would be most
interested in striking up personal correspondences
with, and which of his members he might suggest
get in touch with each other. If, for example, a new
member indicated that they were "Interested" in photo
exchange, but "Not Interested" in tattooed women, he
might surmise that the respondent was interested in
men, and was perhaps even homosexual.

During the Cold War, in the years before the
Stonewall Riots, particularly for men like Inhelder in
the defense industry, being openly gay was virtually
impossible. Coming out as gay risked ending a career,
given McCarthyite fears of shamed homosexuals being
particularly susceptible to Communist thought or
targeted blackmail. This kind of innocently presented

networking thus provided a way through which queer
men who wanted to make contact with likeminded
others could do so at greater reach than their local
environs in relative safety.

This recruitment strategy allowed Inhelder to build
a fragile, short-lived network that encompassed the
whole spectrum of the industry. Members spanned
conservative, battle-hardened military tattooers through
to radical and queer experimenters with tattooing,
young and old. A 1965 membership list includes, for
example, veteran Brits Les Skuse and Rich Mingins,
photo traders Bernard Kobel and Bill Skuse (Les's son),
key figures from the respective tattoo scenes in France
(Bruno Cuzzicoli), Germany (Herbert Hoffmann,
Horst "Tattoo Samy" Streckenbach), Denmark (Ole
Hansen), Canada (Doc Forbes), Hong Kong (Pinky
Yun), and Australia (Jon Entwistle, Cindy Ray); tattoo
enthusiasts who would go on to make major impacts

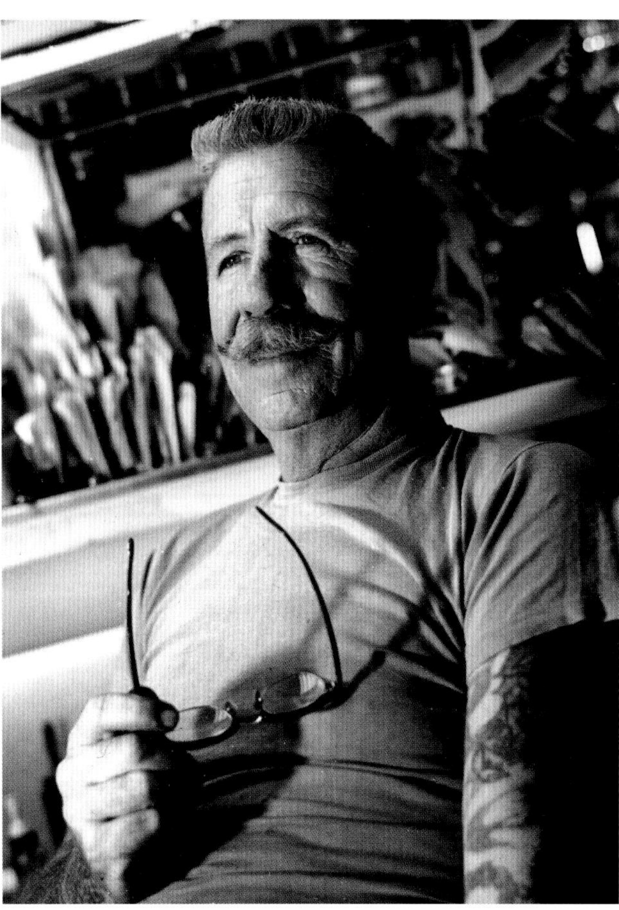

Hori Smoku (*left*) Norman "Sailor Jerry" Collins in his Hawaii shop during the 1960s or 70s. While heavily influenced by Japanese tattooing, Jerry was often contemptuous and dismissive of Japanese people. Inspired by the tradition of Japanese artists to assume a professional moniker—where the honorific "Hori" [carver] denotes a master tattooer—Jerry dubbed himself "Hori Smoku," mockingly punning on the exasperated exclamation "Holy Smokes!"

Night and day (*right*) Pinups became a recognizable staple of Sailor Jerry's flash. Named for the centerfolds of magazines and calendars which lonely servicemen could affix to the walls of their bunks, such voluptuous women were a common feature of vernacular military art during World War II and the Cold War, featuring not only as tattoos, but also painted on the nose cones of airplanes, and onto leather jackets.

themselves, such as Albrecht Becker in Hamburg, Roland Loomis (a.k.a. Fakir Musafar) in California; and individuals who would become notorious through later publications for their pioneering interests in body piercing, such as Tom "Til of Cardiff" Fothergill and Bud "Viking Navaro" Housen. Each member's postal address was listed, facilitating the continuation of the club's correspondence networks even beyond its own limited existence.

"Sailor Jerry": Pride, Pettiness, Pinups, and Purple Ink

Among the American artists, the contrast between two in particular is illustrative of the sheer breadth of personalities and attitudes that were held within the TCA's orbit, but also as to what brought the tattoo club together in the first place.

Legendary naval tattooer Norman "Sailor Jerry" Collins was club member #133. *Tattoo News* of July

1964 reports favorably on Jerry's studio in Honolulu, describing among various other modern and hygienic fittings a particularly progressive "white noise" machine, supposedly used by dentists to relax customers and reduce the sensation of pain. Jerry was clearly fond of the club in turn, designing its membership certificate and proudly advertising his affiliation to the club through a notice posted prominently in his shop. Despite his affable and clubbable engagement with the TCA, and though his writings and drawings are suffused with humor, Jerry was otherwise a notoriously prickly character, known for extended and petty competitive squabbles with industry rivals he considered to be bringing the profession down. Even his nickname, Sailor Jerry, was apparently borrowed from a "particularly stubborn mule his father owned," such were the similarities between the young Norman and the obstinate beast.

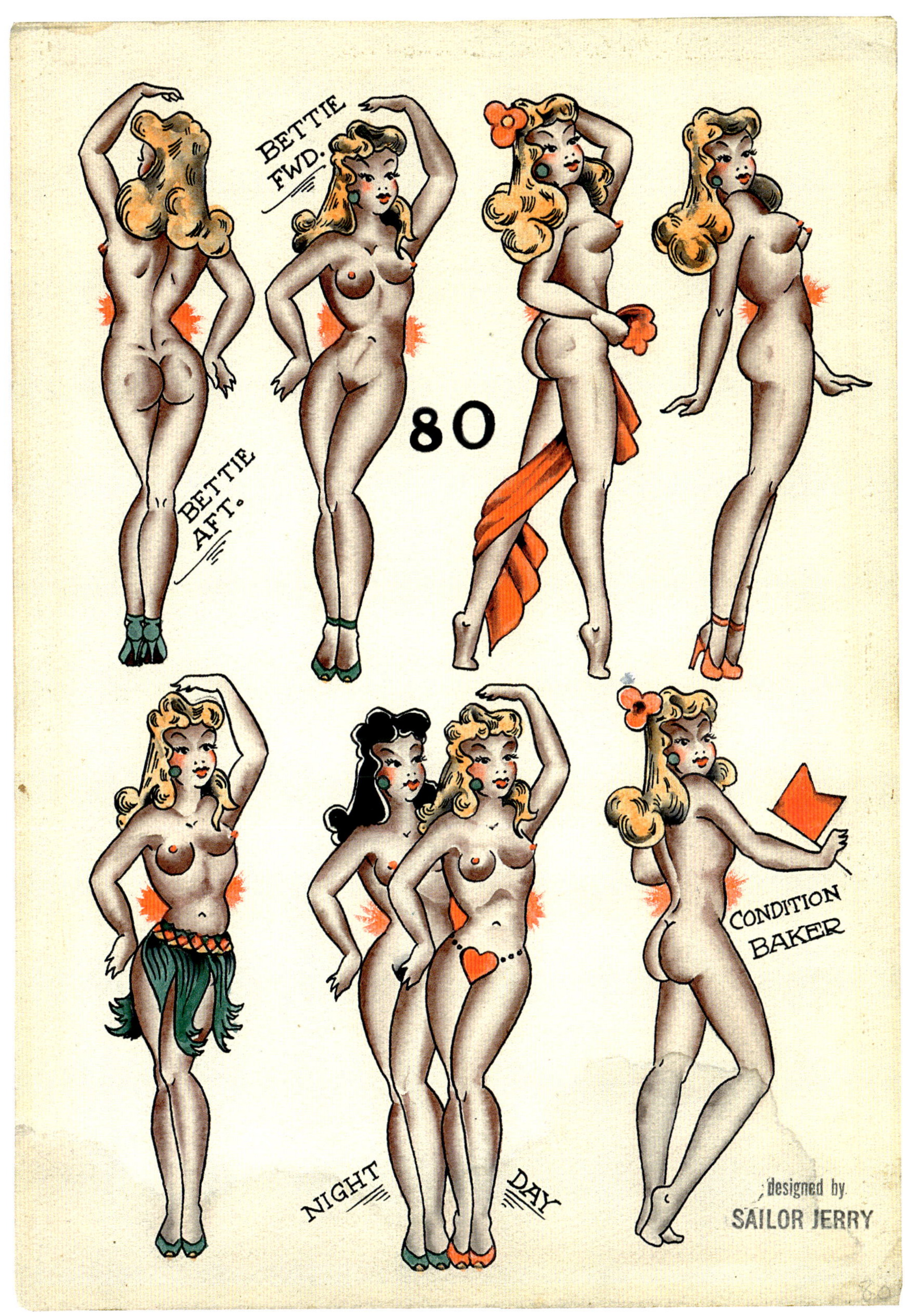
BETTIE
FWD.
BETTIE
AFT.
80
NIGHT
DAY
CONDITION
BAKER
designed by
SAILOR JERRY

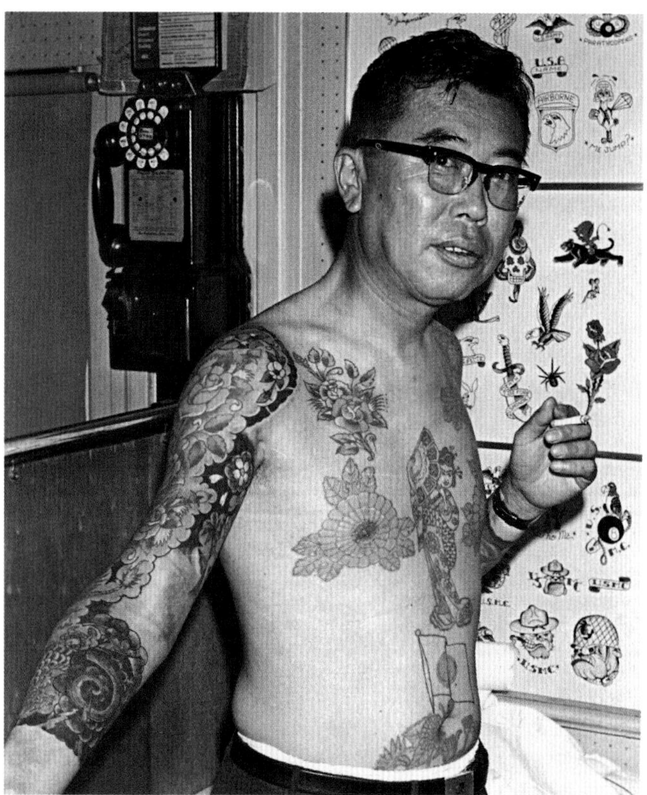

Mystery man (*left*) Mr Yasutaro Kita is a little-known but important figure in the post-war connections between the United States and Japan. Kita (also referred to as "Kida" and "Ikeda" in the sparse surviving records) is pictured here in Lyle Tuttle's shop in California, having also met with Fakir Musafar and Davy Jones. Note his Western-style tattoos.

Master of his art (*right*) This extensive tattooing on customer John Breem is by Norman "Sailor Jerry" Collins. While most of Jerry's customers got small flash pieces, he also worked at scale, emulating the bodysuits of traditional Japanese Irezumi.

Born in Reno, Nevada, in 1911 and raised in Northern California, Jerry credits Chicago tattooer Gibs "Tatts" Thomas as his first teacher in the art of tattooing. By the time of the establishment of Inhelder's club, he had been working in the industry for thirty-eight years, moving to Hawaii around 1929. He was able to cut his teeth during one of the busiest periods for American tattooing, working at a time when tens of thousands of sailors thronged the busy Hotel Street in Downtown Honolulu, killing time on shore leave. By one estimate, there were thirty-three artists in the town's eight licensed shops, tattooing a total of 500 people per day and netting something in the region of $60,000 per shop per year—a veritable fortune.

Jerry's ideology was deeply patriotic and individualistic, and characterized by a strong libertarianism and distrust of government. Later in his life, that worldview had—according to a close confidante—developed into an extremely conservative, "virulently anticommunist, racist outlook that verged on the paranoid." Nevertheless, he was possessed of both great technical intelligence and a deep and abiding love for tattooing in all its romance and diversity. Over his career, and particularly by the mid-1960s, he had come to think of himself as something of a custodian of the practice, always working to maintain traditions while at the same time constantly seeking refinements and improvements in design, technology, and technique. Through the TCA, he directly donated money to try (unsuccessfully) to overturn New York's tattoo ban, for example, and he was deeply scornful of youngsters who thought themselves "hot shit," unwilling to take the time and practice patiently to become a truly great tattooer. He was also a remarkable draftsman, and his designs are rightly hailed today as the greatest exemplars of the

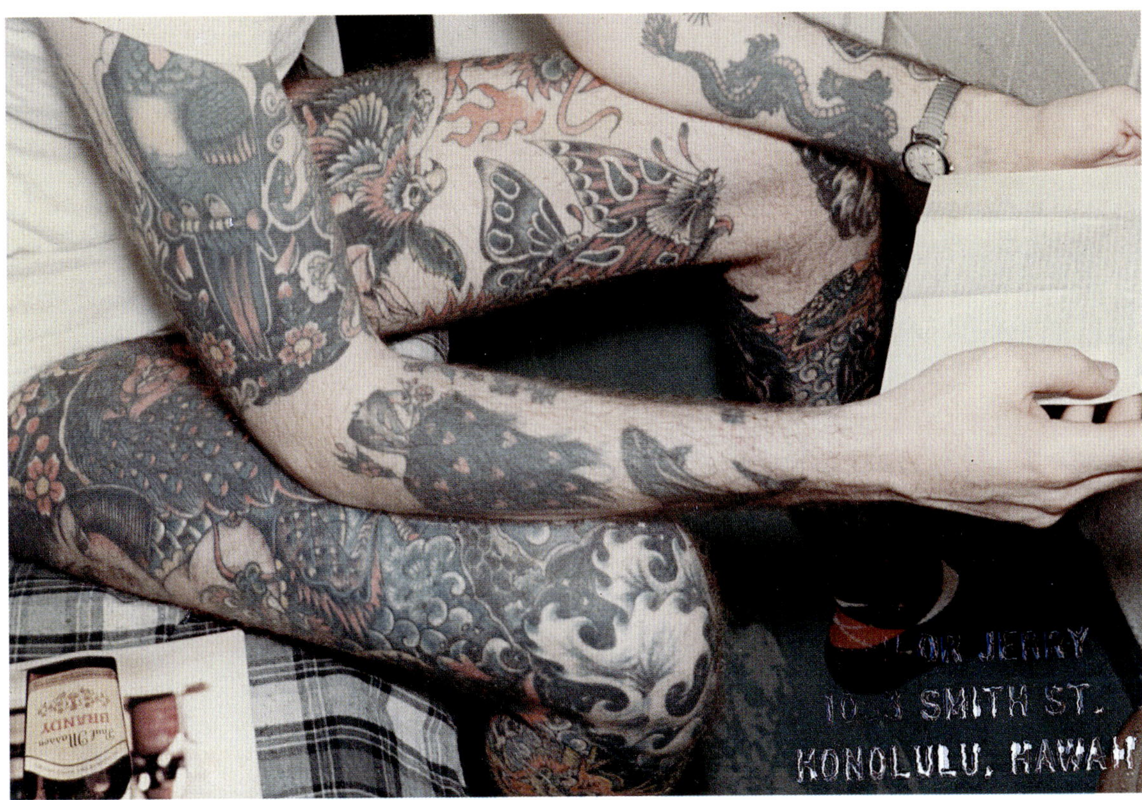

mid-century American style, characterized by bold military iconography, clear and solid black line work, and a soft but durable shading he apparently learned from an Australian naval tattooer called "Long Andy Libarry" (born John Andrew Ellicott). Though much of his design book is rooted in the work of predecessors like "Brooklyn" Joe Lieber, Bert Grimm, and Cap Coleman, his precision and care distilled these histories into something recognizably his own.

Though he didn't often share wisdom with anyone he didn't respect—"I just won't give what I've sweated for to these wise scratchers"—he was generous and enthusiastic with those he considered peers. And though thoroughly suspicious of the Japanese following the war, and possessed of a generalized racism toward "Orientals," a term he used indiscriminately, he struck up correspondences with tattooers Horiyoshi II (Tamotsu Kuronuma) in Tokyo, Horihide (Kazuo Oguri) in Gifu, near Nagoya, and Pinky Yun (Yun Bing Kwan) in Hong Kong, as well as with a mysterious Japanese man called Yasutaro Kita. Perhaps Kita dabbled in tattooing himself, and from surviving photos it is clear that he sported both Japanese and Western designs. He visited San Francisco tattooer Lyle Tuttle in the 1960s, met Tattoo Samy at some point, and appears to have been an important link between the United States and Japan in the 1960s, as it was he who initially introduced Jerry to Oguri. Little is known about him, even in Japan.

Jerry was profoundly inspired by East Asian tattooing and, through a bilateral exchange of design language, and pigment, revivified the use of Orientalist designs in Western tattoo practice, transforming the traditional forms of the Japanese tattoo lexicon into snappier, more popularized forms for an American client base. His flash sheets hum with dragons and geisha girl pinups, which translate the same Japanese source material that had so inspired Victorian and Edwardian tattooers into comic-book-style, fat-lined decals which could be put on quickly, confidently, and clearly. In surviving letters he frequently suggests, however, that Americans are likely inherently superior tattooers than the Japanese, and that their design traditions and exceptional black and gray inks were somewhat wasted given what he racistly perceived to be their lack of talent. And when inviting Japanese artists to Hawaii, he would drive them to the Pearl Harbor Memorial on his way back from the airport before even taking them home to unpack.

Jerry's technical legacy is also remarkable. His friend Bob Palm had studied chemistry at Columbia University before becoming a tattooer, and Palm and Jerry worked together from the late 1950s onward to create new pigment recipes to ensure colors would be bold and durable in the skin, and therefore able to do justice to the graphic style Jerry was refining. In particular, Jerry was known for having the first good purple ink, his secret weapon, which he happily shared with Horiyoshi and Horihide, and which, in private, he mocked his competitors for failing to discover. "I brought out purple," he wrote to Ed Hardy, "and so far, dam few have it, and that's the way it should be. Anybody can get good color, but dam few can get it in . . . just put on work that makes the blind customer realize he's been fucked over but good." Other artists wrote letters to each other every time they thought they'd discovered one of his secrets—"this is top, triple secret information," one said; "the purple that Jerry Collins used and gave to a select few is doxime carbazole [sic. the chemical is actually called carbazole dioxazine] from Sun Chemical, Staten Island, New York."

Such was the impact of Jerry's colored inks in Japan that Horihide was dubbed "Horihide Purple" by his contemporaries in Tokyo. In return, Oguri taught Jerry how to perfect gradated gray-wash shading which had long been a hallmark of the best Japanese tattooing, but was little understood in America.

Phil Sparrow: Scholar, Lover, Tattooer

By contrast, compare Jerry to TCA's Member #199, Phil Sparrow. Both men made the TCA's top ten list of the best tattoo artists in the world in 1965—a list that also featured Les Skuse and Rich Mingins, of course. The same issue of *Tattoo News* that discussed Jerry's shop also announced that Sparrow was moving out of Illinois, as the state had increased the minimum age to be tattooed to twenty-one, rendering his shop unsustainable. The two men were roughly the same age, with Sparrow the elder by about three years. Like Jerry, Sparrow had been tattooed by Tatts Thomas in Chicago. He ultimately sought out the tutelage of Amund Dietzel in Milwaukee as he sought to become a professional tattoo artist, after having initially tried to learn from Zeis's correspondence course in the early 1950s. "I purchased a correspondence course in tattooing from some con artist in Rockford, Illinois," Sparrow wrote in his autobiography, "and learned next to nothing from its pages. Becoming a tattoo artist was like trying to learn to swim from a book in your living room." Also like Jerry, Sparrow was rapaciously intelligent, keen to learn everything he could about tattooing, and dismissive of those he considered beneath him in terms of ability. Unlike Jerry, though, who had

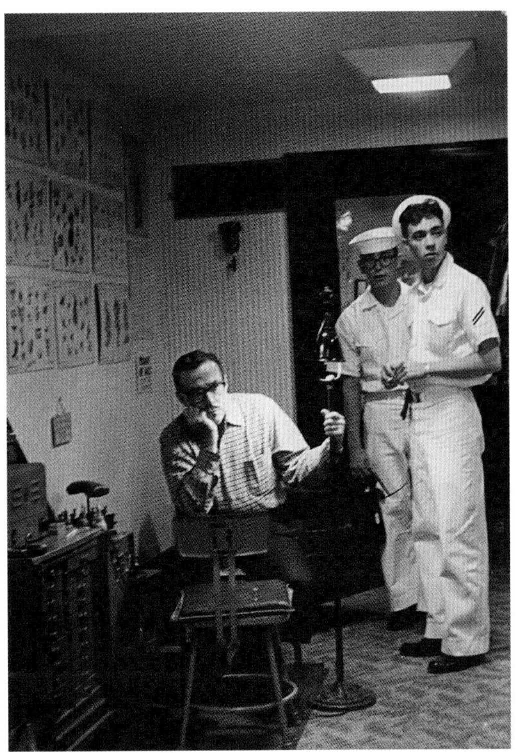
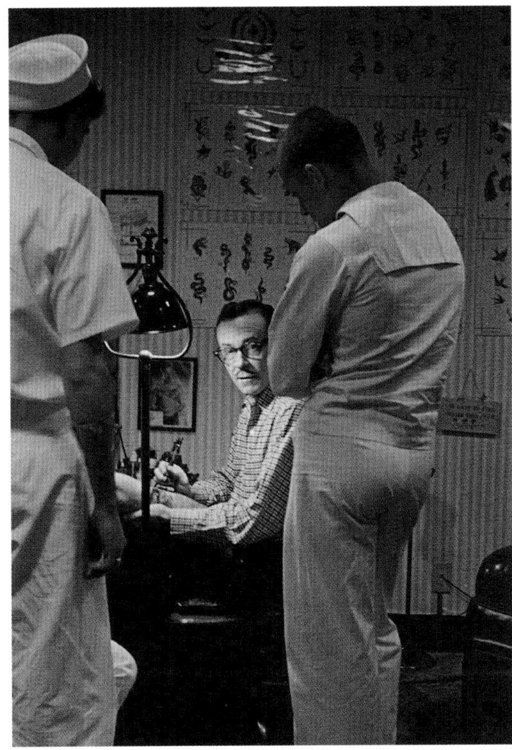
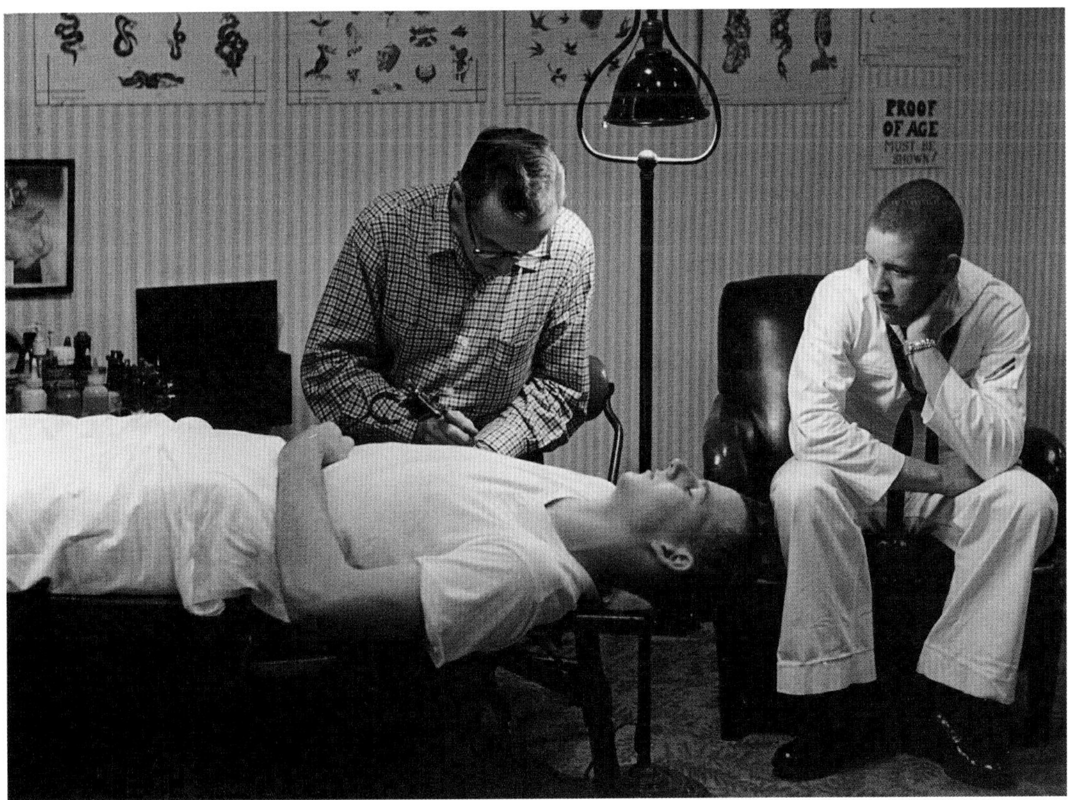

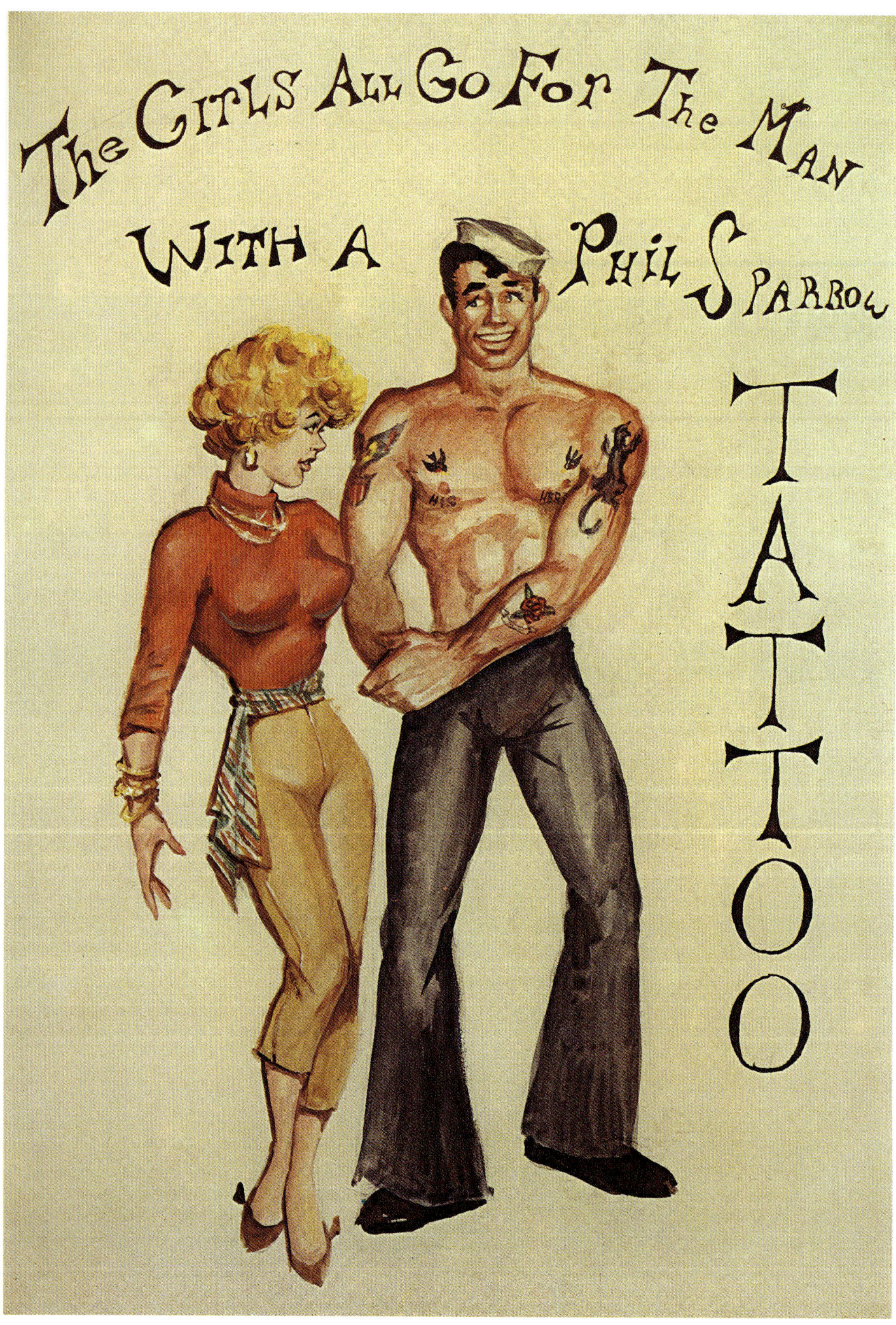
THE GIRLS ALL GO FOR THE MAN
WITH A
PHIL SPARROW
TATTOO

Girls all go for the man This advertising flyer is deeply comic, given Sparrow's rapacious homosexual desires. Sparrow wrote at length in his book *Bad Boys & Tough Tattoos* about what he saw as the primarily sexual roots of tattooing, suggesting that "decoration is a questionably 'pure' motive, in certain instances decidedly sexual with the purpose of attracting the opposite sex —or perhaps even the same sex."

spent his youth riding trains before enlisting in the navy, Sparrow held a PhD in English literature and had, at one point, been hailed in the New York Times as a budding literary talent reminiscent of Henry James.

Sparrow—born Samuel Steward—had worked from 1934 onward as a professor of literature in Montana, Washington State, and then ultimately in Chicago, serving stints at Loyola and DePaul. His debut novel, *Angels on the Bough,* was sufficiently well-hailed to connect him to a lifelong friendship with Gertrude Stein and Alice B. Toklas in Paris, but its salacious storytelling about a suite of sexually promiscuous characters proved so shocking to the president of the State College of Washington that he was fired instantly. The remainder of his academic career was beset with a deep-rooted anger at capricious authoritarian bureaucrats in the academy, and a growing disgust at his colleagues and students who he increasingly felt were lazy, stupid, "cowed, clannish and conformist."

Ultimately, as much as a glowing resentment of academic life, Sparrow was enticed into tattooing by sexuality. He was gay at a time when to be so was illegal, but lived dangerously close to the curtain of public visibility, painting homoerotic murals on the wall of his Chicago apartment, working extensively with Alfred Kinsey on the follow-up to *Sexual Behavior in the Human Male,* and making barely coded allusions to homosexual promiscuity in a column he implausibly wrote for the *Illinois Dental Journal.*

Possessed of a grand sexual appetite, and with a particular taste for naval men, Sparrow spent much of his time outside of teaching writing, thinking about, and having, sex. Over the course of his life, he extensively documented his thousands of sexual

encounters in a self-declared Stud File, which listed the specific details of each and every man with whom he had had relations. He even tattooed a handy series of measurement marks on his forearm in order to accurately record the particular prowess of each of his partners for posterity. And yet, as he got older, he found it increasingly difficult to meet the kind of men to whom he was attracted. By the age of forty-four, he even found himself sidelined at orgies he himself was hosting, and was longing for a more interesting and fulfilling existence. "Hie me to a seaport town," he wrote lyrically to a friend, "rent a shack and hang out a shingle, and spend my golden twilight years putting lovely designs on strong young brown arms and shoulders—and thighs and buttocks and phalli if the request arises"; "I wanted freedom," he described later; "[tattooing] was a grand new way to feast the eyes on male beauty, that one could now touch the skin which you could only look at in the classroom—the arms, the legs, the chest—and there would be no one to raise an eyebrow, and even that you could in the right instances take a young man to the cot in the back room."

Taking the pseudonym Phil Sparrow from an obscure sixteenth-century poem, he opened his small Chicago booth in 1954 among arcades and flophouses, initially in the evenings, on weekends, and during summer breaks between teaching. When his double life was discovered, however, he was fired. Insulted at first, he quickly realized that he could make as much money in a week as a tattooer as he did in a month as a literature professor, and ultimately took to his ejection from academia with some exuberance.

Sparrow tattooed in Chicago, Milwaukee, and Oakland, California, where he became the official tattooer of the Hells Angels. While working for the Angels, he was once disturbed by a telephone call urging him to come back to his shop, where he was met by a gang of bikers who had abducted a young man who had foolishly been tattooed with the Angels' emblem despite not being a member. Shocked, the gang asked him to black out the imposter's tattoo, and they held him down while Sparrow completed the job—a rather surprising career turn for a gay literature professor!

Sparrow took a certain pride in having replaced the authority he had held in the lecture halls with power in tattoo studios, and though he was not the seismic force in tattoo design Sailor Jerry had been, he was a very expressive draftsman in his own right, producing tender and occasionally filthy homoerotic takes on the classic American flash book. Like Jerry, though to a lesser degree, he was also a technical innovator, developing the use of plastic tubing which could be safely sterilized. And his natural curiosity led him to a desire to share the discoveries of others, including his distribution across America of a new tattooing machine design made by his friend in Germany, Horst "Tattoo Samy" Streckenbach.

His principal contribution to the TCA network, and to tattooing more fundamentally, though, was his scholarly attention to tattooing's history, artistic contexts, and sociological and psychological features. Jerry had created connections with artists in Japan, but Sparrow acquired a library of books on the topic, including academic work on the history of Japanese tattooing, which he would go on to share with a young Ed Hardy. In the pages of *Tattoo News*, he shared bibliographic details of a collection of research articles, and he would later go on to publish *Bad Boys and Tough Tattoos*, a memoir-cum-sociological study of tattooing based on data collected for Kinsey, in which he concludes—naturally for him—that tattooing is fundamentally about sex. That book also includes an extensive review of extant literature on tattooing, which thoroughly dismisses nearly every book on the subject thus written! As a rapacious scholar, collector, and gay man, he also found a great friend and client in Rudi Inhelder, who he would go on to tattoo extensively.

Jerry and Sparrow came together in the Tattoo Club of America because they loved tattooing. Sparrow spoke highly of Jerry, recommending him to Ed Hardy as the finest exponent of Orientalist tattooing working in America. Their careers, though Sparrow started much later, carved out a space for joyous, glorious tattooing during the postwar decades, where business was increasingly tough and hard-bitten at times. They both, in their own ways, loved the romance and the danger and the sheer *humanity* of tattooing. More so, they wanted it to be better, and both men—fiercely intelligent, arrogant, inquisitive, and driven—found the networks provided by Inhelder could stoke their egos and fuel their desires to both learn more and to advocate for their professions. Their vocations. But the tattoo industry—indeed, the tattoo community— could not straightforwardly contain queer academics, conservative political reactionaries, and their bookish clients for much longer, at least not openly.

The Beginning of the End of the Beginning

The TCA hosted the United States' first true tattoo convention on October 5, 1964, but it only formally existed for about two years, as the demands of Inhelder's job left much less time for organization and

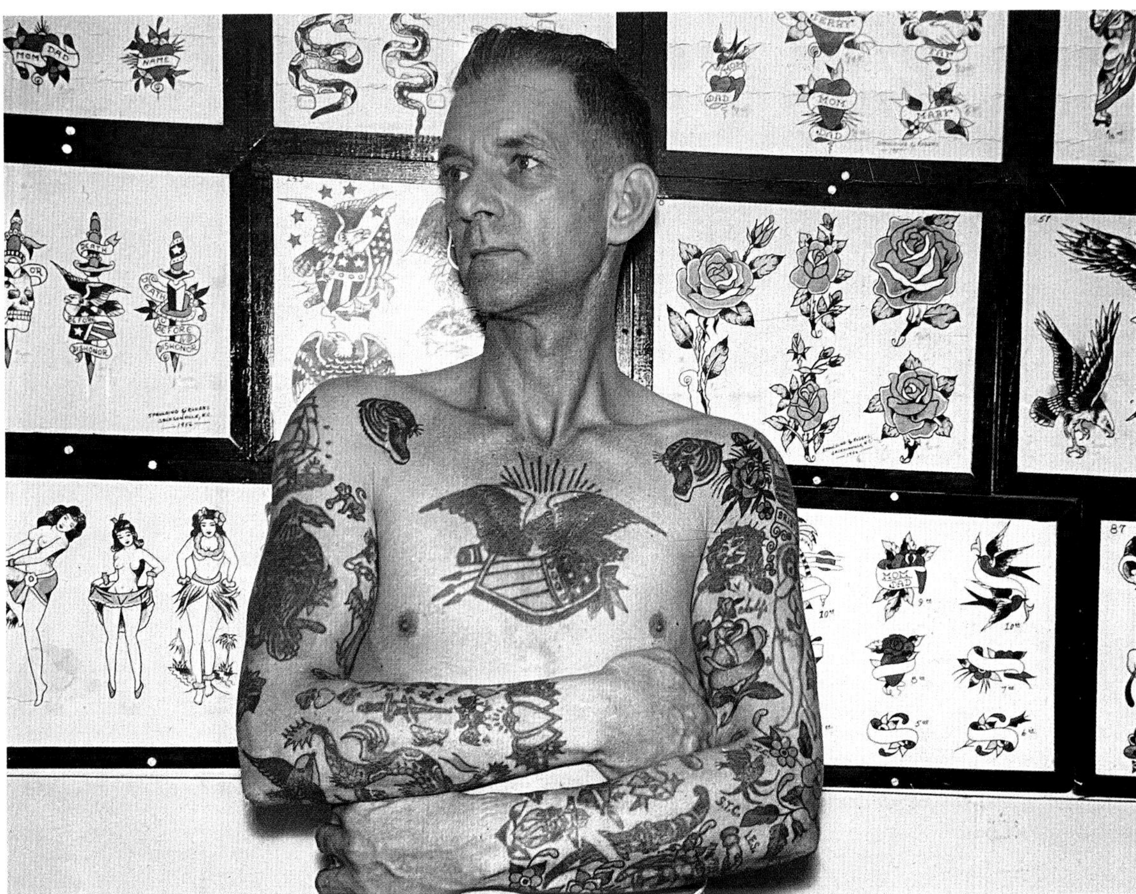

publication. "As you know," he wrote to his members in 1966, "the whole burden falls on the shoulders of Rudi Inhelder." The final issue of *Tattoo News* features an article by Les Skuse, describing his own career as well as the lineages that connect his club in Bristol with the networks now extant in America due to the TCA. "I would like to end by paying tribute to some of my many tattooing friends," Skuse wrote. "Al Schiefley, Paul Rogers, Huck Spaulding, Doc Forbes, Charles Harding, Paul MacNaughton and Rudi Inhelder. With men like these in the profession, the art will never die."

The period up to the publication of the last issues of *Tattoo News* was the final time in the history of the Euro-American tattoo industry that everyone with any reputation could belong to the same organization. Indeed, for the first and only time in the history of the industry, there were enough people involved and interested to sustain a membership organization at some scale, while at the same time being few enough potential members that a single club could contain the tattoo community in all its multitudes.

As the industry continued to grow, it was destined, for a time, to fracture.

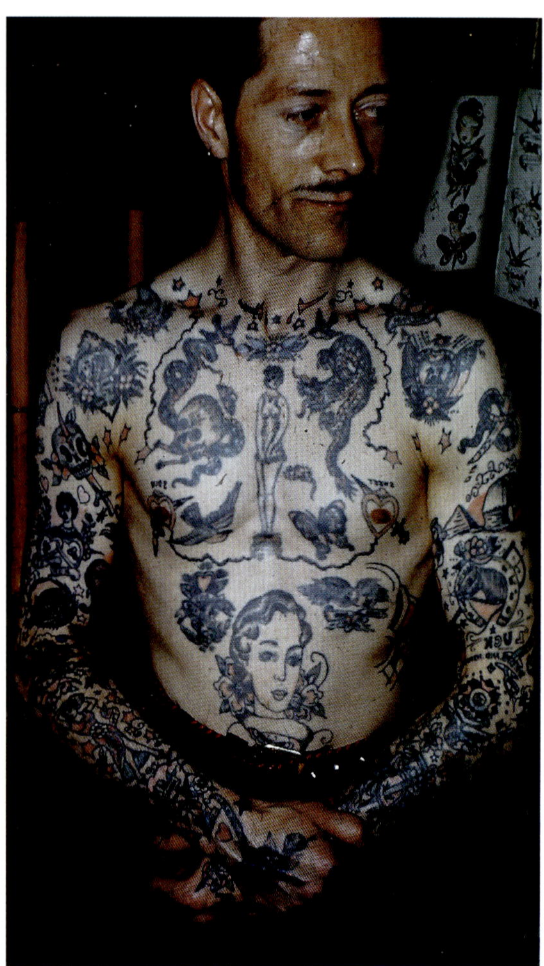

Dick Hyland (b. Bernard Wrottenberg), the "Human Autograph," photographed by Rudi Inhelder, 1960s (*right*)

Hyland had been a performing tattooed man on the Bowery in New York through the 1940s, working for Ripley's "Believe It or Not" show. Wrottenberg took on the name "Dick Hyland" in emulation of a boxer from California, initially perhaps as a way to evade attention from law enforcement who sought him in connection with reckless driving charges, but stuck with it for the rest of his career. His body was eventually covered in tattoos—by Charlie Wagner, Willy, Walter, and Stan Moskowitz, and others—which emulated the signatures of over 1,000 of his favorite celebrities, primarily boxers, as well as names of friends and former shipmates in the merchant navy.

Frank "Len Lone Wolf" Horsler, photographed by Rudi Inhelder, 1950s (*left*)

Frank Horsler, here photographed by Rudi Inhelder, was a core member of Cash Cooper's London Tattoo Club. Dashingly handsome, Horsler tattooed in Luton, north of London, and was first tattooed by George Burchett, aged fourteen, and subsequently by George Bigmore.

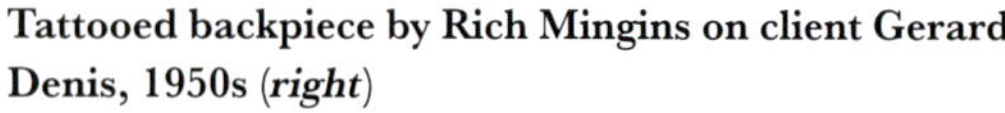

Tattooed backpiece by Rich Mingins on client Gerard Denis, 1950s (*right*)

Mingins's ambitious, large scale tattooing—such as this crawling tiger tattooed on client Gerard Denis—is indicative of the sheer quality of the work undertaken by the influential circles of the British tattoo clubs of the 1950s and 1960s. As photographs circulated globally among eager tattoo aficionados, attribution of individual work could often be lost. Mingins's solution here, learned from the practice of certain Victorian-era tattooers, was to sign his work permanently on the skin. Incidents of tattooers signing their work have been rare, and the "RM" signature here is unusually large even among extant examples.

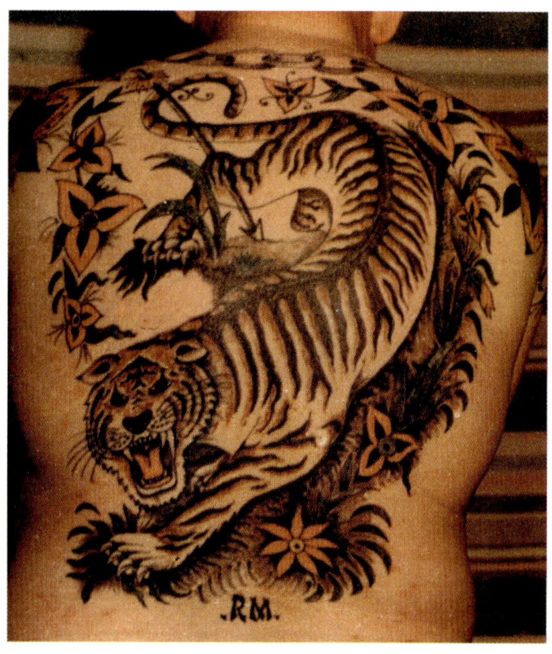

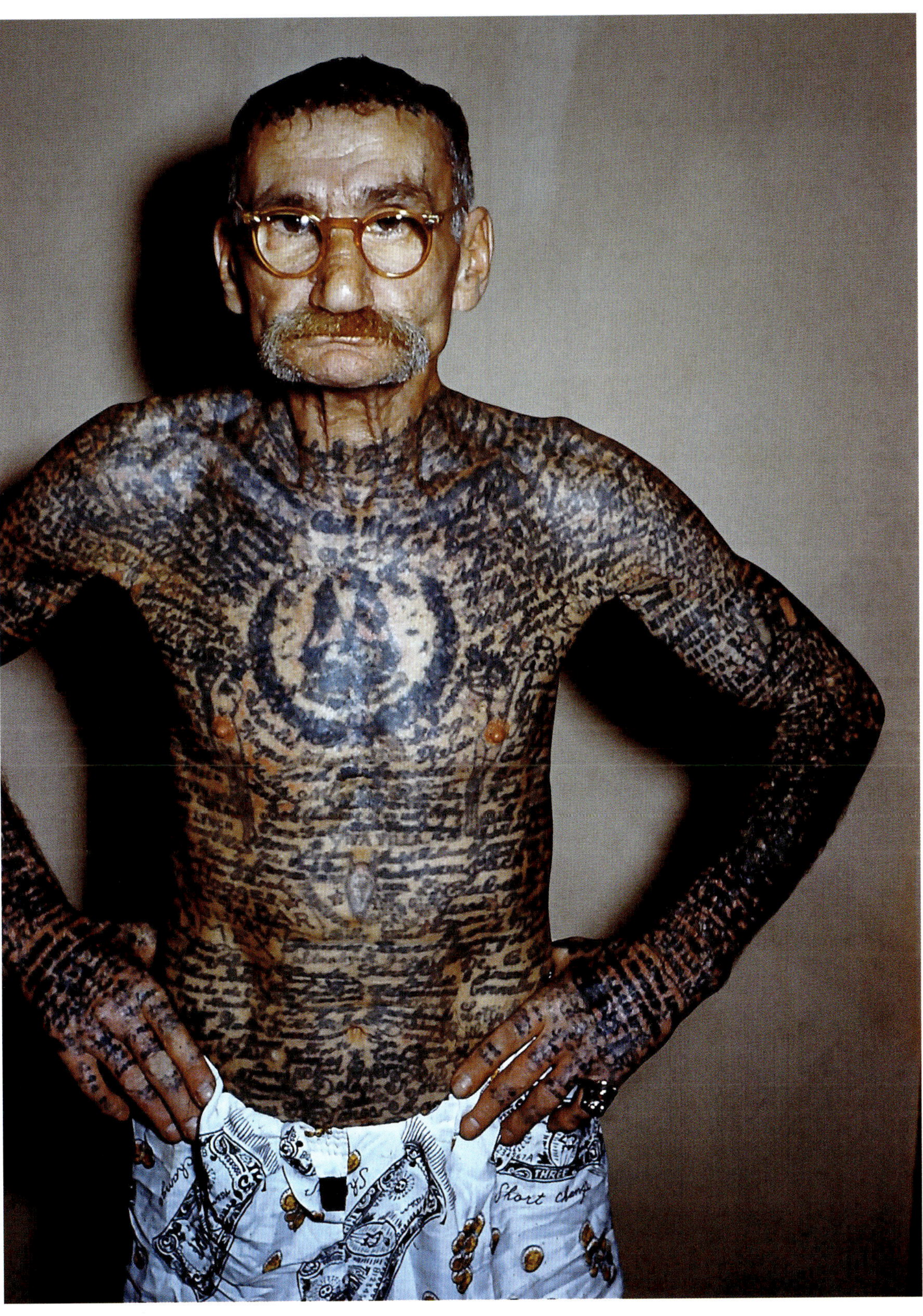

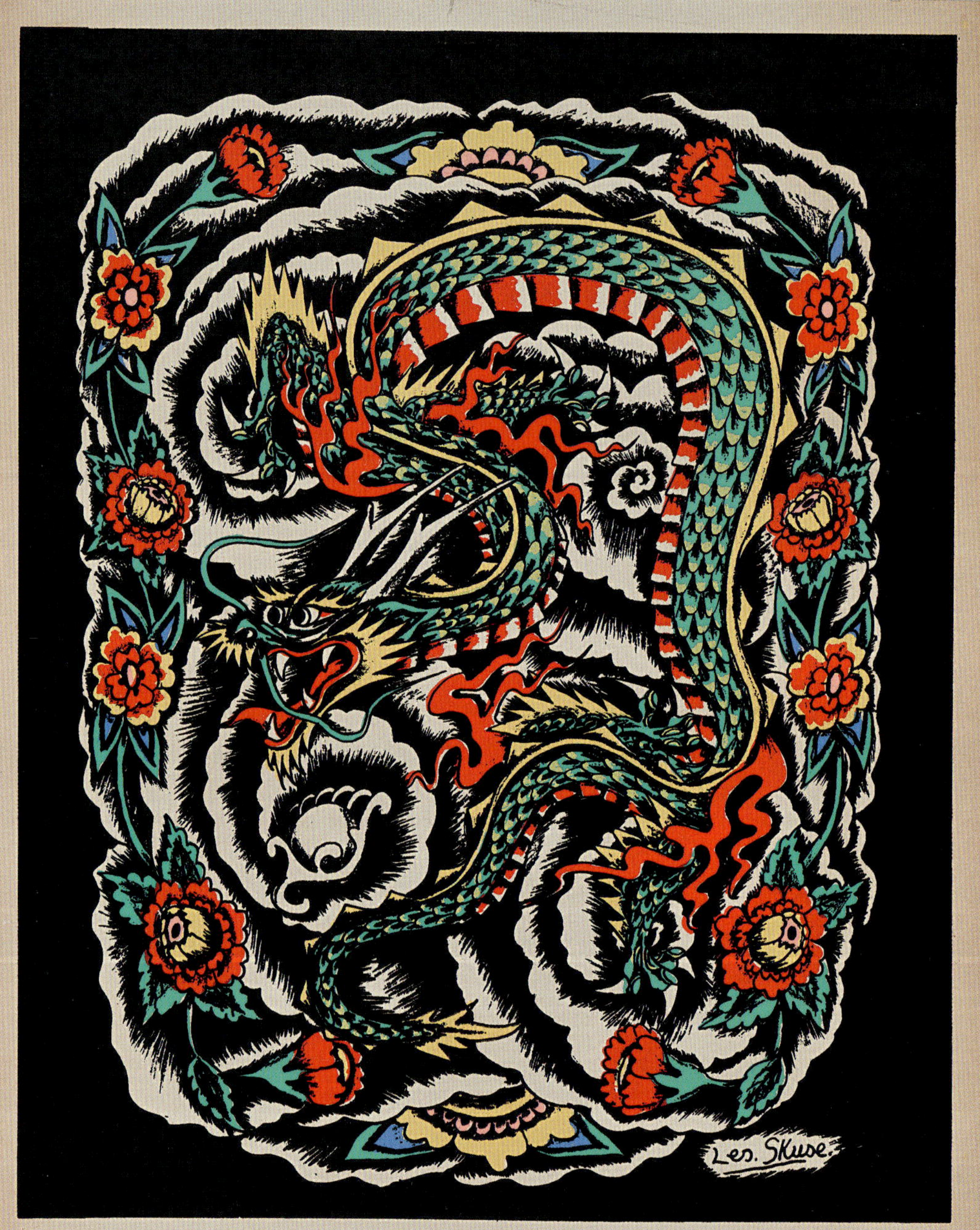

LES SKUSE, The Champion Tattoo Artist of All England

A retrospective exhibition at the CAMDEN ARTS CENTRE, Arkwright Rd., London NW3.   Feb 13th–March 5th
Tues–Fri 11–8, Sat 11–6, Sun 2–6, Admission free. Mr. Skuse will be available for tattooing   Feb 13th – Feb 20th
After these dates please telephone the Centre 01 435 2643/5224 for an appointment.

ORIGINAL DESIGNS   PRINTS   PHOTOGRAPHS

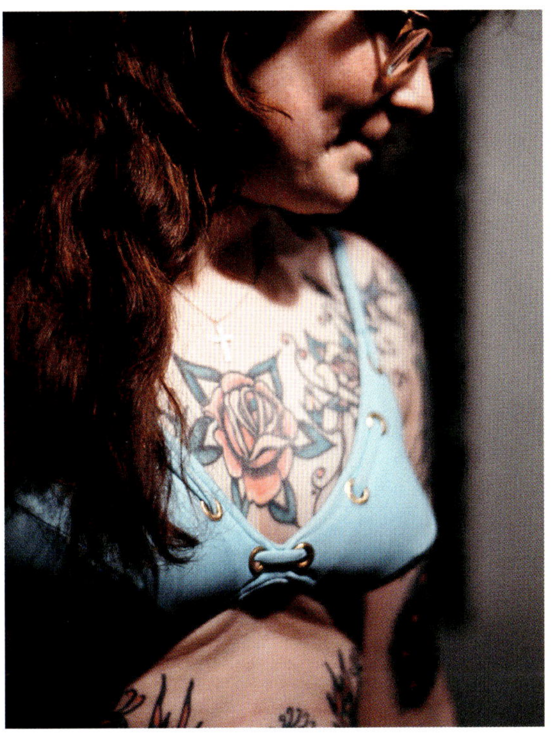

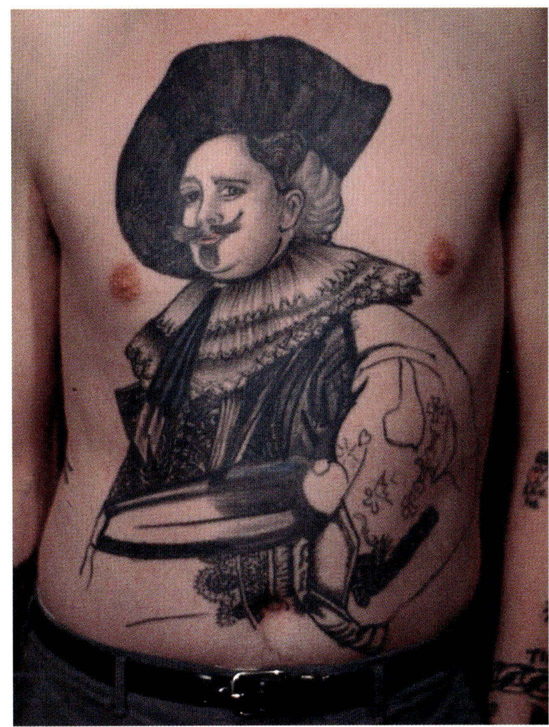

Les Skuse exhibition poster, 1972 (*left*)

Les Skuse was invited to offer guest lectures to students at Bristol Arts College, and he also staged the first art exhibition by a tattooer in the UK, held at the Camden Arts Centre, London, in 1972.

Les Skuse exhibition, photography by Professor Adrian Forty, 1972 (*above and right*)

Alongside photos and drawings hung on the gallery's walls, the event's opening night featured many of Skuse's best canvases parading as living art objects in the gallery. Pictured above are Marion Hollier—whose tattoos featured on the cover of Supertramp's *Indelibly Stamped* album—and her husband Ivor, whose front was tattooed with a large copy of Frans Hals' *Laughing Cavalier*. At bottom right is Bristol Tattoo Club member Ron Cook.

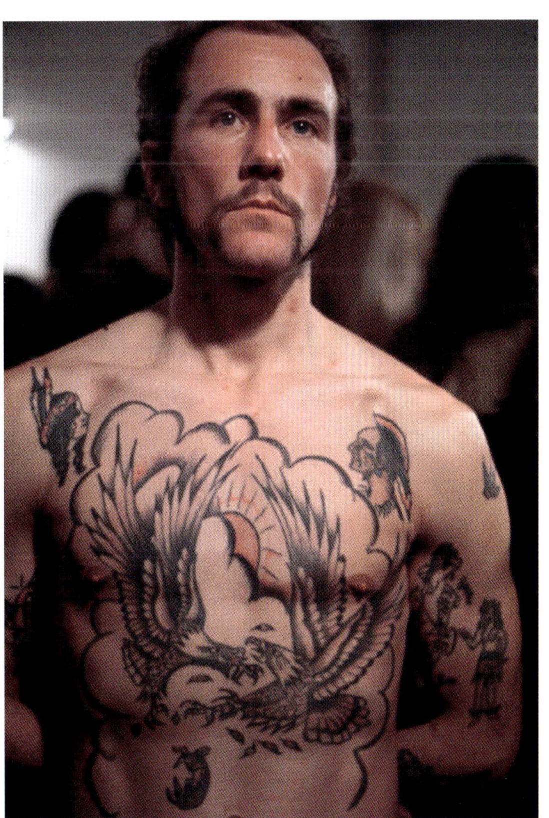

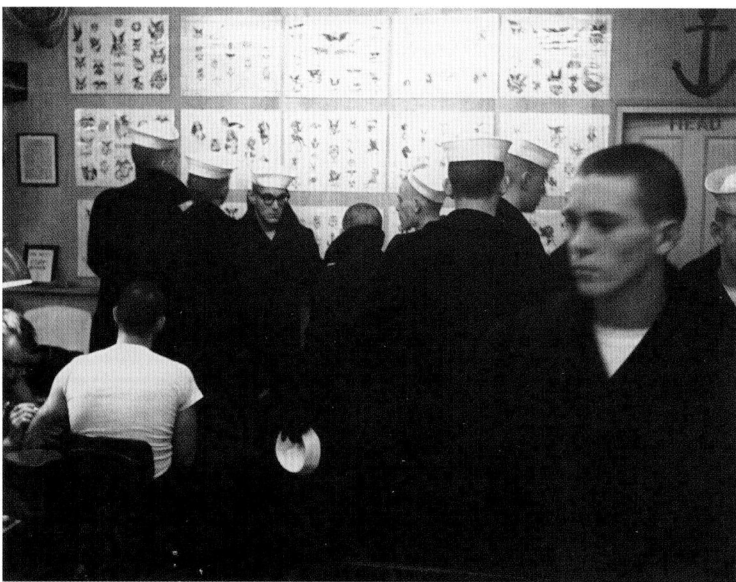

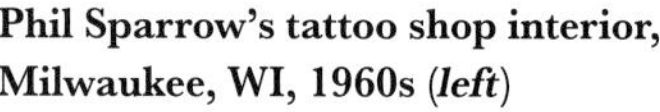

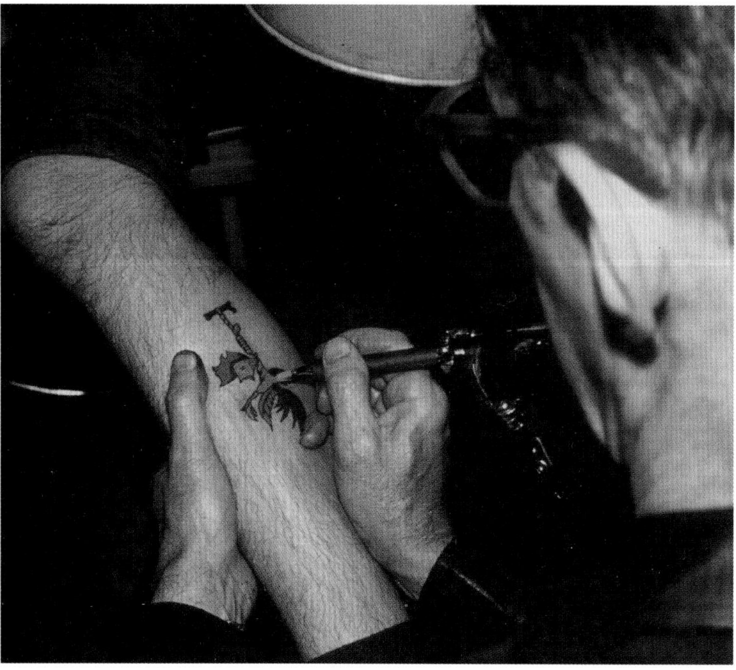

Phil Sparrow's tattoo shop interior, Milwaukee, WI, 1960s (*left*)

In 1965, following a brief spell in Wisconsin, Sparrow moved to Oakland, where he was forced to quit tattooing altogether in March 1970 as violence and social disorder swelled. The increasing visibility of tattooing made the business more onerous, with frequent visits from cops and health inspectors, as well as gangsters. Far from seeing the late 1960s and early 1970s as a "renaissance" of tattooing, Sparrow saw this period as marking its endpoint, a decline from its great heights as a fashionable art in the early decades of the twentieth century.

Phil Sparrow tattoos a customer in his Anchor Tattoo studio in Oakland, c.1970 (*left*)

The "choking chicken" design is a bawdy visual pun perhaps expected of young men away from home for the first time. However, the design also has a folkloric significance: sailors joked that as chickens could not swim, having one tattooed on your feet or lower legs would keep you safe from drowning.

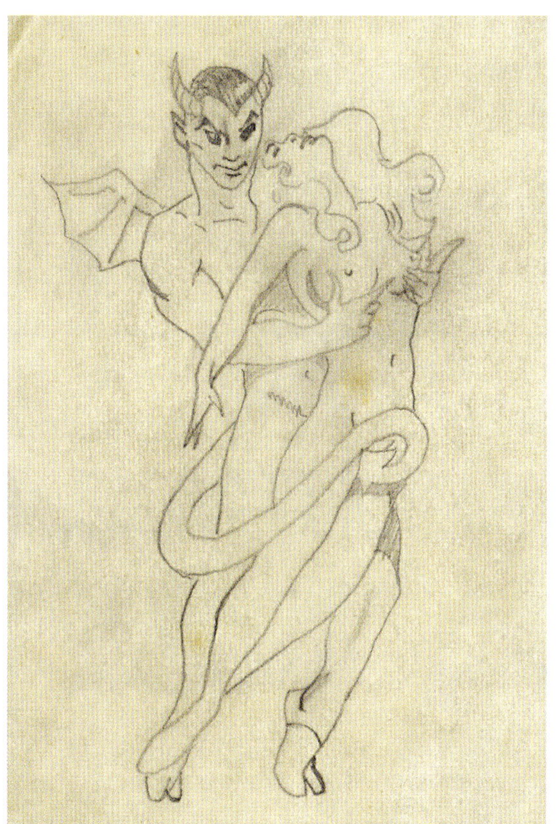 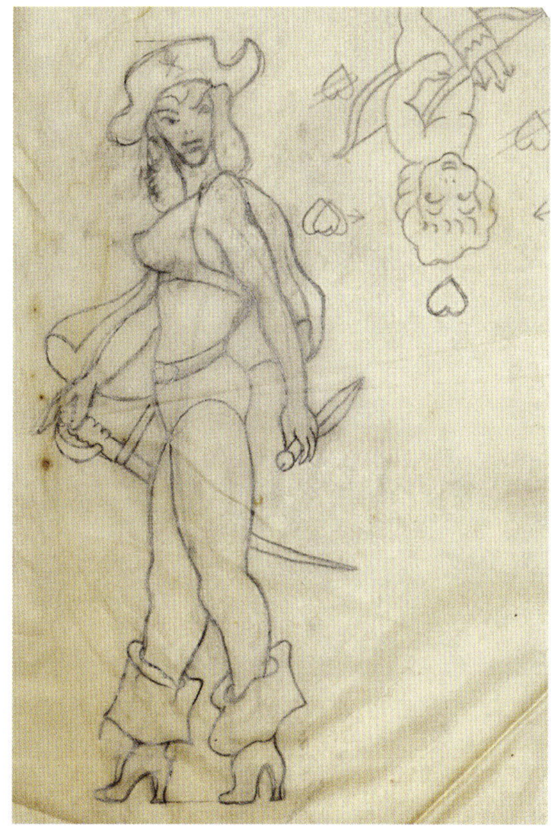

Stencils by Phil Sparrow, 1960s

When he quit teaching English in universities, Sparrow dedicated himself to learning
how to tattoo, and became a proficient draftsman. His flash has not been widely seen,
but it reveals a studied appreciation of the popular tropes of American tattoo designs
of the period.

The First Good Look

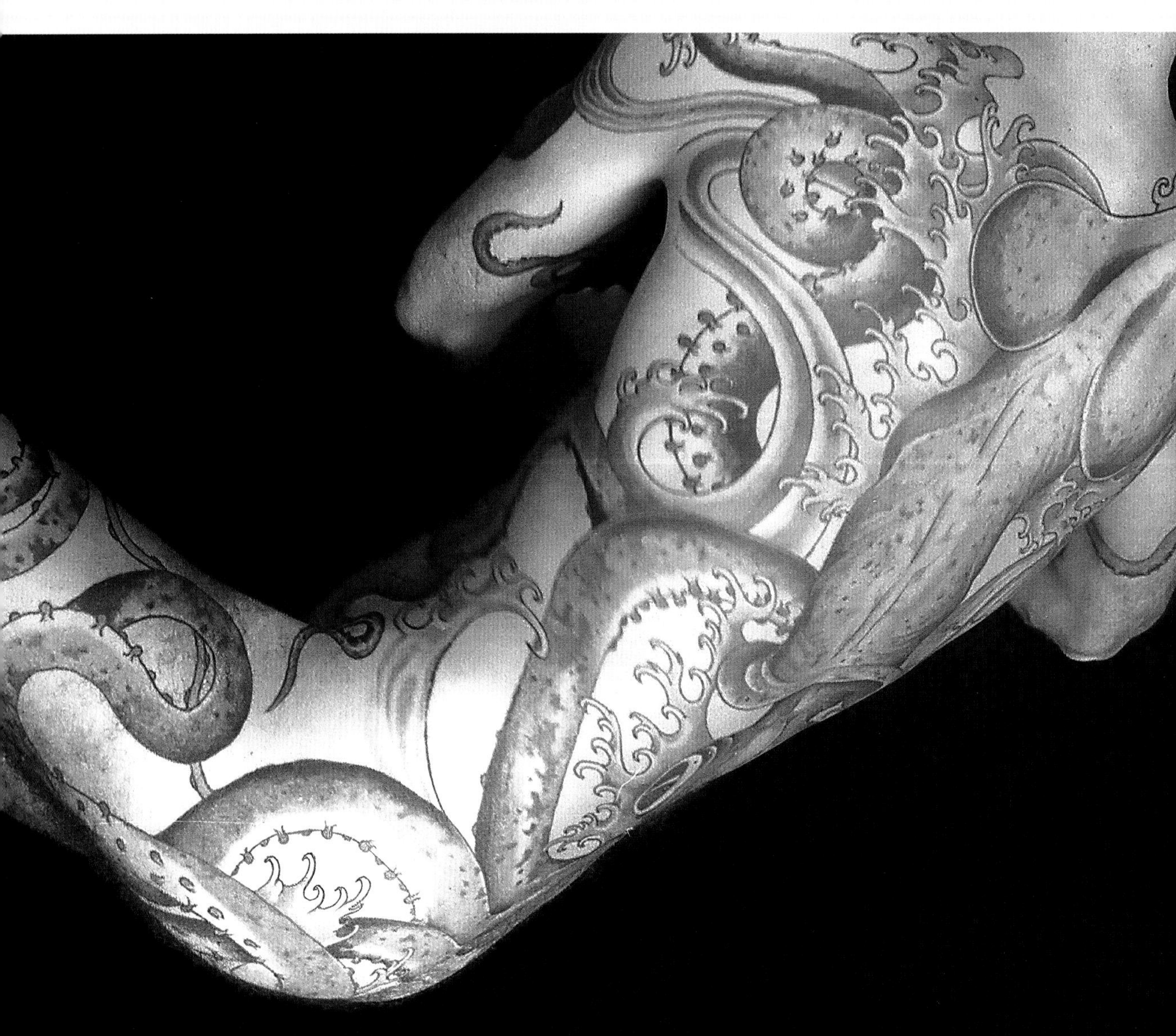

Influential figures This large octopus backpiece by Ed Hardy on Dr. Andrew Lemes, completed c.1976, was an iconic piece of work and featured on the cover of Albert Morse's book, *The Tattooists* (1977). Lemes exploited his relationship with Hardy to learn trade secrets, which he published to the world in a controversial book in the early 1980s. Hardy later called him a "big prick" in a letter he wrote to a friend.

The fragile coalition which Inhelder had assembled in the mid-1960s became increasingly dispersed through the latter part of the decade and into the 1970s. After Inhelder had ceased to be able to manage the TCA, it was briefly resurrected—or perhaps more accurately, recreated—in 1975 by New York tattooer Spider Webb (born Joseph Patrick O'Sullivan), who had become a torch-bearer for the stranger and more avant-garde side of the industry. Webb had an MFA, and was particularly interested in pushing the conceptual limits of tattooing as an artistic practice, with projects including singular tattoos which spanned multiple bodies, and tattoos of arbitrary time stamps designed to sever the link between tattooing and the straightforward articulation of didactic meaning: "people carry the time markers wherever they go," he wrote, "carry the marking of an arbitrary point in time. Its significance is to illustrate the meaninglessness of time when it is conceived of numbers in a void." Collaborator and friend Annie Sprinkle—rather grandiosely—called him "one of the all-time greatest artists and philosophers."

Forced to work in Mount Vernon, due to New York City's ongoing ban on tattooing, Webb undertook a long crusade against the prohibition. In 1976, in defiance of Section 181.15 of the New York Health Code, he set up an impromptu tattoo studio in front of the Museum of Modern Art. During the performance/protest, he tattooed a female tattoo artist called Shadow, irritating local police officers (many of whom, he remarked, were tattooed themselves) but delighting an assembled throng of journalists and reporters.

Webb sought to articulate that tattooing was *art*—not because it was beautiful, necessarily, but because it shared formal features of production with more conventional media. This was a gamble, and one that could perhaps only ever have worked within the

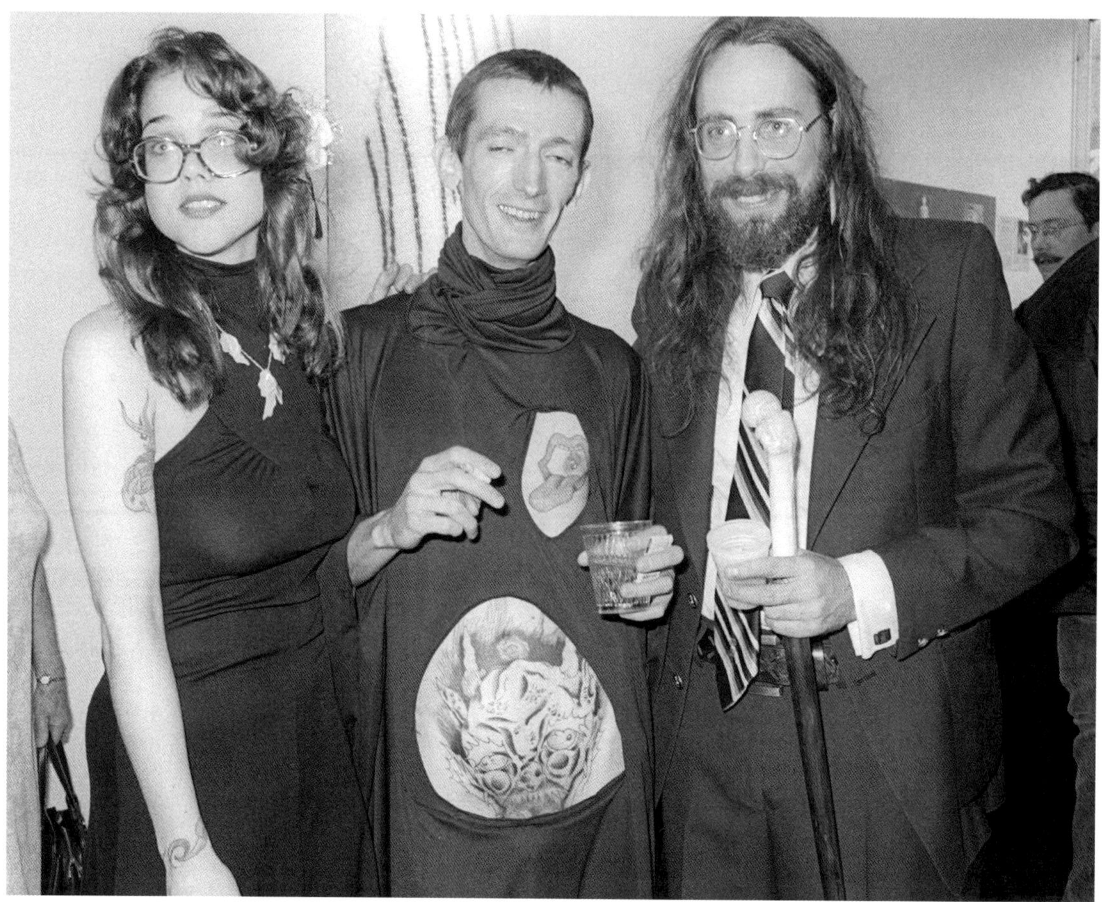

cultural context of 1960s and 70s New York, which at the time was the global epicenter of art-world conversations about the expanding definition of art based on a particular account of practice rather than form or aesthetics. George Maciunas's 1963 *Fluxus Manifesto* is perhaps the most obvious illustration of this theoretical zeitgeist, calling for—among other things—"living art, anti-art." And while Maciunas was not initially thinking about tattooing in the context of his new movement, he did release a boxed set of temporary *Fluxtattoos* in 1967, which mixed designs from classic American flash with conceptually wry lifts from sources including Egyptian hieroglyphics, hardware and interior décor catalogs, military medals, surrealist photography, and psychedelic geometry.

Ultimately, Webb was arrested following the 1976 protest, as planned, but his subsequent challenge to overturn the prohibition in the courts, alleging its unconstitutionality in light of the First Amendment, was a failure. Though his argument was conceptually sophisticated, the New York legal system was not yet ready to judge the artistic nature of tattooing on the basis of analogy to other forms of constitutionally protected creative practice. The State Supreme Court was firm in its judgment that, in their view, tattooing was "a barbaric survival, often associated with morbid or abnormal personality." The Lawyers for Artists organization also spurned his request for representation, stating bluntly that "tattooing is not an art."

This was a particularly frustrating defeat, as just a few years earlier, in 1971, tattooing had been featured in a major exhibition at New York's American Folk Art Museum. The authorities were apparently initially concerned that the exhibition was a cover for the application of illegal tattoos, but the show nevertheless

Cultural acceptance (*left*) Spider Webb, shown on the right of the photograph, and frequent collaborator Shadow, shown on the left, are pictured here with a client at an exhibition Webb held at the Chuck Levitan Gallery in New York, 1976. The exhibition was staged as part of Webb's ongoing campaign to get the city authorities to accept tattooing as an art form rather than a health risk.

A winning smile *(right)* Pioneer Lyle Tuttle at his Houston convention, 1976. Tuttle began tattooing at age seventeen in 1948, and opened his first shop in 1957. He was criticized by some older tattooers for his relentless self-promotion, but he earned a place at the very center of the industry, becoming the figurehead of tattooing's increasing mainstream visibility. Life magazine dubbed him "chief exhibit of the art" in 1972. He was also an important custodian of tattoo history, saving key collections from disposal and dispersal, and becoming, per one of his business cards, "a walking illustrated encyclopedia of tattoo history, lore, and social significance."

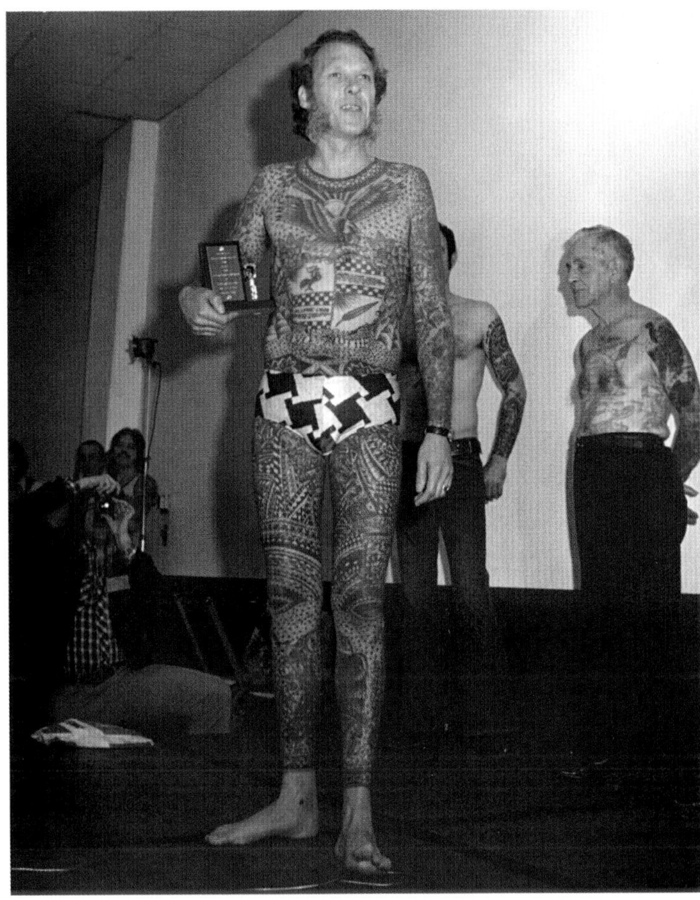

received a warm review in the *New York Times* and seemed to signal a further step toward tattooing's broad cultural acceptance. The show, simply called *TATTOO!*, featured works by Sailor Jerry, and a diorama staged by Ed Hardy, Mike Malone, and Kate Hellenbrand, explicitly anchoring American tattooing in a serious and institutional art-anthropological context for the first time.

In England, this was paralleled the following year by Les Skuse's presentation of his work on both paper and skin. While George Burchett's work had featured in the Whitechapel Gallery's 1951 exhibition of English folk art, *Black Eyes and Lemonade*, it had not resulted in a great insurgence into the museum world. By 1972, though, Les Skuse was also able to present his work in both fine- and decorative art contexts: firstly, at London's Camden Arts Centre, with live models parading through the opening reception with large

back- and chestpieces on display, and then again later that year at Brighton's Design Museum, as part of an exhibition entitled *Vanity*. Skuse had also become a fairly regular guest lecturer at Bristol's art college, sharing his professional knowledge with students at the invitation of art historian Adrian Forty.

The Renaissance that Wasn't

By the 1970s, then, the tattoo industry was in something of a bind, as its public perception was riven with contradictions. *Time* magazine, for example, spoke of tattooing's "Renaissance" in December 1970, making much of San Francisco tattooer Lyle Tuttle's recent appearance on the cover of *Rolling Stone*. Academic writing about tattoo history has also tended to accept *Time*'s framing of this period as the start of a designated "Renaissance." Tuttle had been tattooing since the late 1940s, and by the late 1960s had become a key organizer in the West Coast tattoo scene. He had been feted for tattooing celebrities such as Janis Joplin, and as such, for the first time since World War II, the industry was again beginning to find acceptance and visibility in conventional terms.

Counter to this framing, however, tattooing did remain stigmatized, as its refreshed proximity to polite society revivified old panics about hygiene, atavism, and the disfiguring follies of youth. Sailor Jerry, in particular, despised Tuttle's showmanship and his courting of a public profile, blaming him for tattooing changing too rapidly. Increased popularity had brought with it increased scrutiny, and Webb's failure to convince New York that tattoo was art thus signals something of the paradoxical problem with terming this moment a "Renaissance" at all.

On the one hand, recall that the term had already been used some decades earlier by a British television show from 1954—and even then signaled too hard a break between tattooing's past and its present. In this sense the term is too late; there was nothing that was truly being "reborn" at all.

On the other hand, there was still no broad-based cultural acceptance of tattooing in Europe or America, and deep-seated social and cultural obstacles remained to its full acceptance as a legitimate trade and an artistic practice in its own right. Moreover, moral and hygienic concerns were driving regulations which greatly impacted the working practices of many artists, not only in New York City, but in states such as Florida, South Carolina, Oklahoma, Indiana, and Massachusetts. Additionally, serial killer Richard Speck murdered eight nurses in Illinois in 1966, and his "Born to Raise Hell" tattoo ultimately led to his capture,

further cementing the connection in the American popular imagination between tattooing and depraved criminality. From this perspective, then, calling this a moment of "Renaissance" applies the term too soon.

Webb's theatrical, obtuse, and intellectualized approach to both the professional practice of tattooing and the resistance of over-regulation did not enamor him to many of his fellow tattooers. Counter to Webb, the more conventional strata of the industry sought a path to mainstream acceptance through strategic acquiescence to dominant cultural narratives about their subculture. The industry's self-appointed figureheads acknowledged, for example, that if tattooers wanted to operate as a recognized profession and avoid heavy regulation or outright prohibition, they would need to present themselves in a way which polite society could more easily tolerate. As a result, by the mid-1970s, many in the industry had come to see some parts of the broad coalition of artists and collectors who had come together a decade earlier as inconvenient ballast to be cast aside.

Don't Mess with Texas

Thus, a moment of profound schism came at the close of the second ever international tattoo convention, which was held at a Holiday Inn in Reno, Nevada, in January 1977—a moment Ed Hardy called "the first good look we got at how rapidly the tattoo movement was expanding."

There had been a small gathering of tattooers the previous year in Houston, Texas, organized by Lyle Tuttle and David Yurkew of the North America Tattoo Club (NATC), which had brought artists together to talk shop and show off their craft to the wider world.

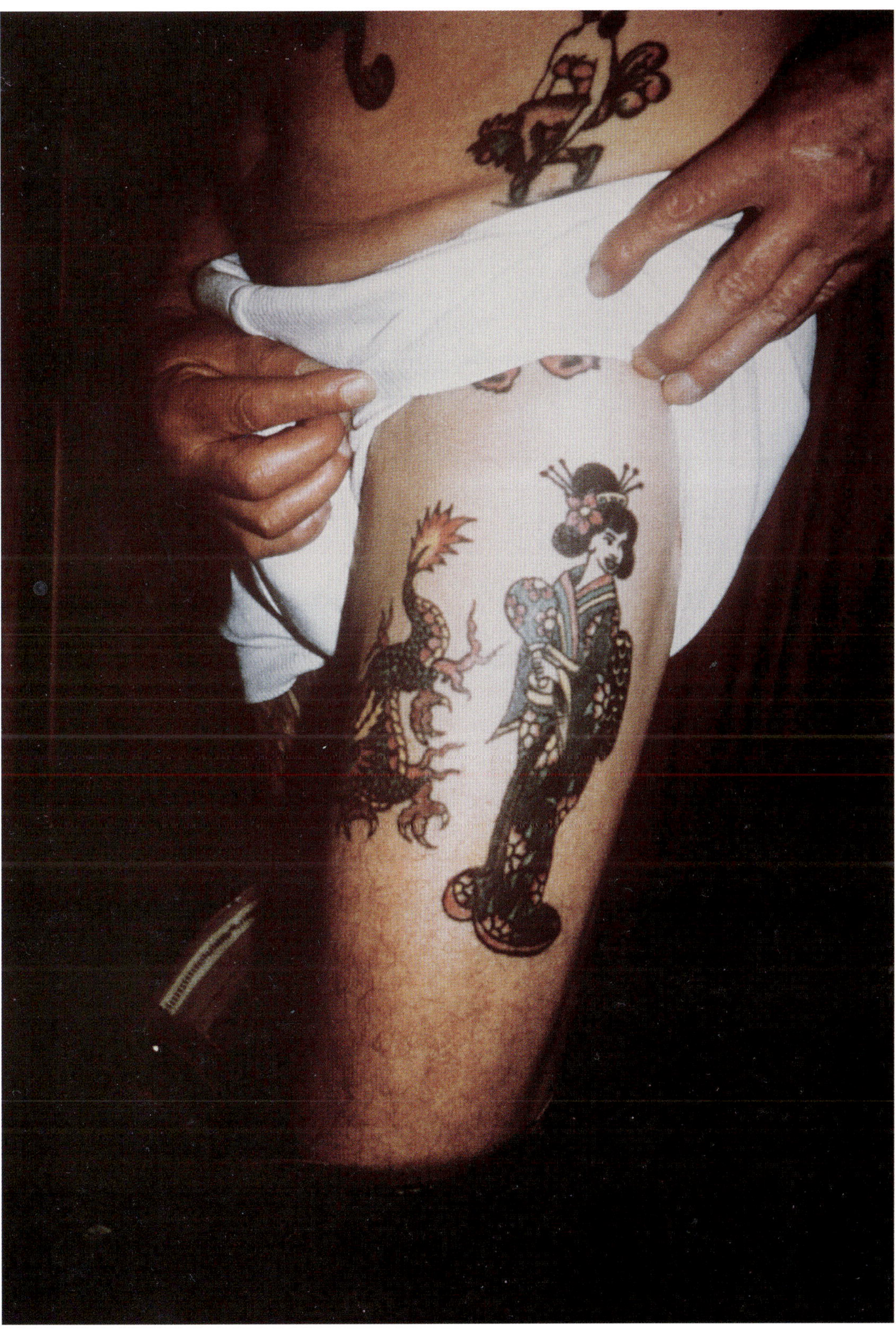

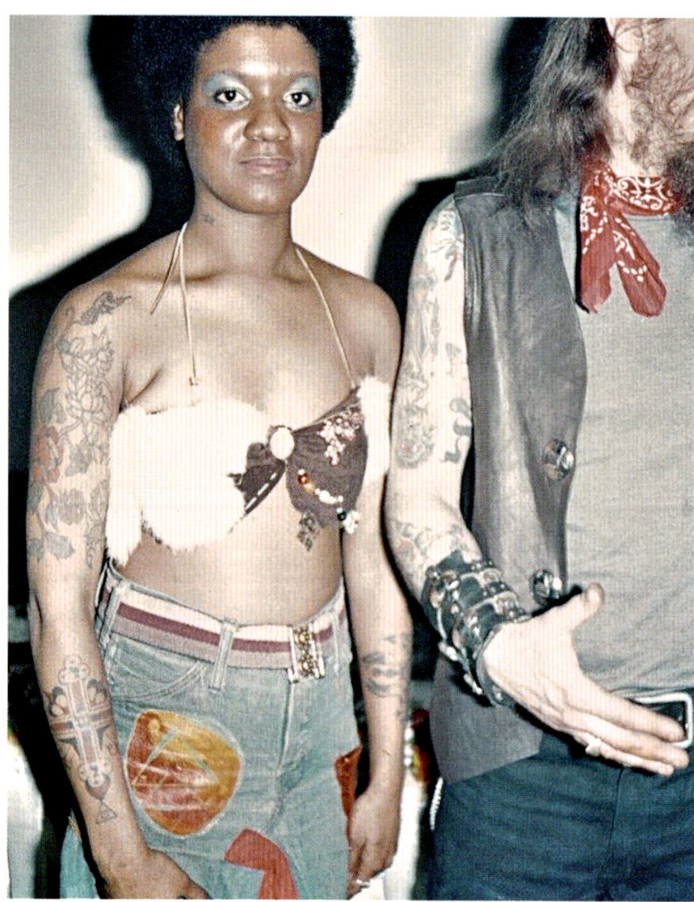

Changing the narrative Valeria Watson Doost, a fine artist from Denver, Colorado, was crowned Best Tattooed Female at the first international tattoo convention in Houston, 1976. African Americans have been under-represented in tattooing as both clients and artists, but Valeria is a clear example of the importance of Black people to the history of modern tattooing, as well as an illustration of the intersection between tattooing's emergence into mainstream visibility and the changing social and civil rights landscape of 1960s and 1970s America.

"We wanted to get rid of the drunken sailor image," Yurkew said. This event is typically hailed as the first international tattoo convention, which is true only in a limited sense—Al Schiefley had, of course, attended the 1950s Bristol and London meetings from the United States, as had Rudi Inhelder from Switzerland. Schiefley hosted Les Skuse in return in 1956, at a small gathering in Ohio, and it is likely that there were international guests at Inhelder's convention in 1964.

Recollections differ as to whether 50 or 150 people showed up in Houston: "bikers galore, big, beefy killer types with their backs and arms covered with skulls, panthers, and gross obscenities which would make the average housewife blush," the *Chicago Tribune* reported. "But there were plenty of housewives, and they didn't blush." Female customers dominated the event's final day, and African-American fine art student Valeria Watson Doost was crowned "Best

Tattooed Woman," featuring alongside Tuttle in a major splash in *Esquire* magazine. Indeed, the visible presence of so many women was one of the most politically prescient features of the convention, as though while conservative lawmakers were trying to harden their crackdowns on tattooing around the country, the burgeoning women's movement pushed in the other direction, with increasing numbers of female customers seeking out tattooing as part of an ebullient moment of cultural change. In the context of campaigns including support for the constitutional Equal Rights Amendment, and that driving the landmark 1973 abortion rights case *Roe v Wade*, bodily autonomy, gender norms and patriarchal beauty standards became key battlegrounds for feminist organizers of the period. As such, the increasingly visible uptake of tattooing among American women took on a particularly pointed air.

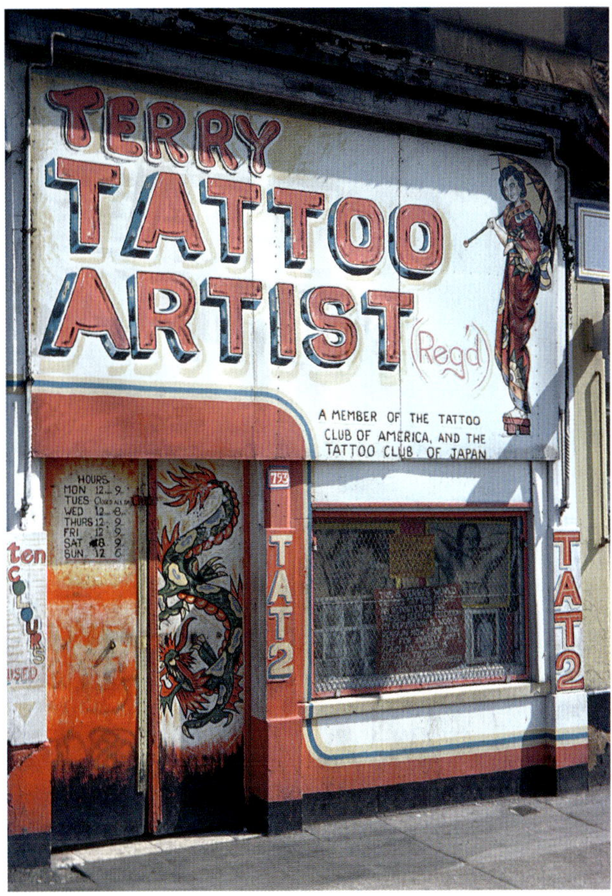

Registered As head of the International Tattoo Artists' Association, Terry Wrigley, whose tattoo shop in Glasgow, Scotland, is pictured here, drove advances in professionalism in the UK, helping others in the tattooing industry to navigate a changing regulatory environment.

Despite the gathering's press coverage—one attendee, Horst "Tattoo Samy" Streckenbach, would later denounce it as rather introspective—it provided a successful test run for the following year's event, to be hosted jointly with the International Tattoo Artists Association (ITAA) in order to boost reach and legitimacy. At the very least, the event had proven that tattoo conventions were viable as a format to bring the community together, and to display some of the diversity of tattooing at the time.

It must be noted, of course, that this diversity was rather bounded. As we have seen, women and people of color had been involved in the industry since its founding as both customers and artists, and the growth of tattooing following these early conventions created a wake in which a more robustly diverse industry would emerge through the late 1970s and into the 1980s and beyond. Nevertheless, the group of people which made up the core of the tattoo industry as organizers and influencers at this time were largely men, and more-or-less exclusively white or Japanese.

"An Association to Protect Ourselves"

The ITAA was formed in the UK in 1975 by art-school-trained tattooer Terry Wrigley, whom Tuttle had listed among the top twenty tattoo artists in the world a few years earlier. Founded as an artists-only club, it quickly boasted members across the United States, as well as in western Europe, Australia, and Japan. Wrigley was a key member of the global tattoo network of overlapping, acronymic clubs in this period, and had been a member of both the BTC and Inhelder's TCA. But unlike both iterations of the TCA, which sought to bring together anyone who enjoyed tattooing and its culture, Wrigley's ITAA explicitly stated a mission to work in service of those employed

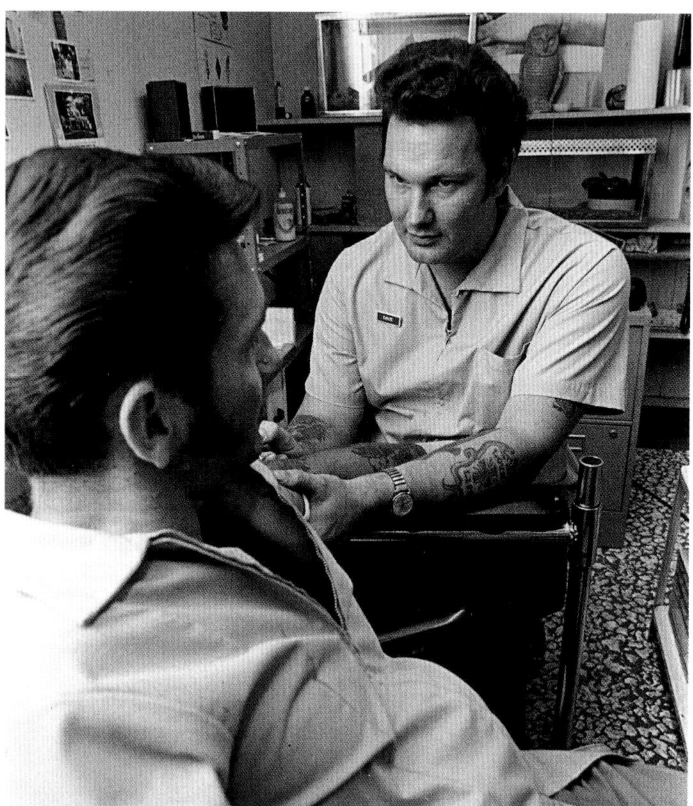

Call me Dave (*left*) David Yurkew, pictured here tattooing a customer in the mid-1970s, was the head of the North America Tattoo Club and the principal organizer (with Lyle Tuttle) of the first full-scale international tattoo conventions that took place in Houston and Reno. In 1980, he unsuccessfully sued the Minneapolis State Fair Association for refusing to grant him a license to work at state fairs in Minnesota.

Young Bones (*right*) London tattooer George Bones was one of a handful of British artists who attended the seminal Reno convention. Bones spread the word of the astonishing scale and quality of work he saw there to customers and colleagues back home. Pictured here with a client in 1977, Bones is still working as of 2024. He began tattooing in his parents' back bedroom in the 1960s, and was for a long while Britain's most tattooed man.

in the industry by improving its reputation and lobbying on its behalf. Growing visibility and reach had led to something of a backlash in the UK too, and as had happened in the United States, regulators began to take notice.

In England, tattooing had been banned for under-eighteens in 1969, following a moral panic and the difficult 1966 prosecution of an artist who had tattooed twelve- and thirteen-year-old boys. The ruling left the British tattoo industry in something of a predicament, as it ruled that tattooing could, in certain circumstances, be a crime, while offering no clarity for professionals as to where the line between legal and illegal conduct was drawn. And while most of the prominent professionals had long been extremely serious about hygienic technique, for example, several tattooers in London apparently still only changed their needles once a month!

For industry leaders like Wrigley, the solution was to get serious about self-regulation before such regulations were enforced upon the industry from the outside. Tattooers had long been protective of their craft, denouncing amateurs and even competitors as dangerous scratchers and jaggers. Since the earliest days of the Victorian cradle of the profession, cleanliness and a generally cautious approach had been hallmarks of the most visible and influential artists. Even Phil Sparrow made the victim of the Hells Angels reprisal tattooing sign a release form!

The American press had also taken notice of what was happening in England—a medical columnist in California called the British ban a "reasonable" measure to protect the "maladjusted"—and thus it had become increasingly urgent that the industry came together as a united international profession. As Wrigley wrote in the club's first newsletter, in the run

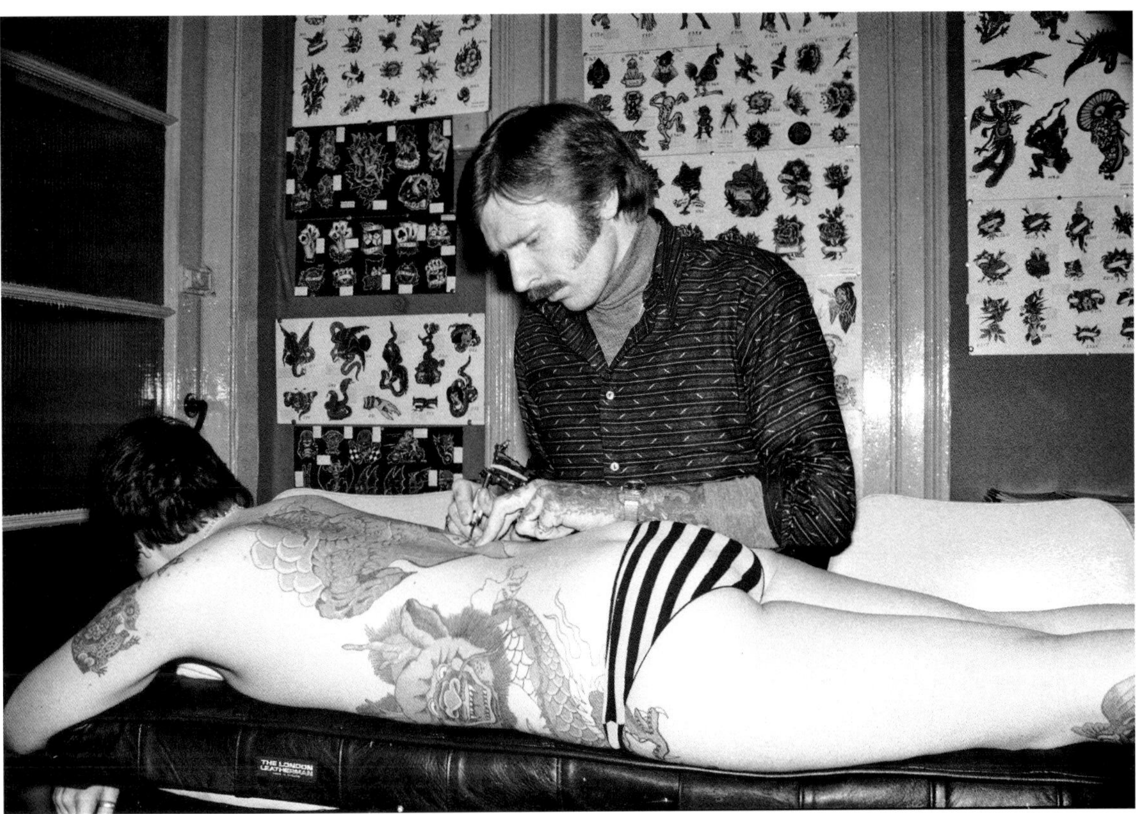

up to the Reno convention, "We need an association to protect ourselves. It's funny, but the British Hang Gliding Association was formed last month. After hang gliding being popular in the UK for only four years, if an association hadn't been formed, hang gliding would have been banned. But because the newly formed Hang Gliding Association was formed, and gave an assurance that it would police itself, hang gliding is allowed to stay in the UK. At a time when more and more local authorities want to ban tattooing, it would seem to be a good idea that ITAA should police itself in regards to badly ran and dirty studios . . . How we can do this effectively," he foreshadowed, "can only come about by discussion at the Convention."

In a similar vein, convention organizer Mike LeCuyer told the *Nevada State Journal* that "We're trying to upgrade tattooing." Alongside LeCuyer at the helm again was NATC president David Yurkew, who would himself, like Webb, later attempt and fail to seek First Amendment protections for tattooing as an art form in the Minnesota State Courts.

Tattooed a Man in Reno

The convention, though again denounced by Tattoo Samy as timid in its public advocacy for tattooing as an artistic practice, was well attended, with figures such as George Bone from London and "Tattoo Ole" (born Ole Hansen) from Copenhagen taking booths. Over 1,000 members of the public attended. Artists from across the United States attended too, and new styles were made visible not only to the world at large, but to the artists themselves. Hardy, for example, recalls being blown away by the single-needle monochrome illustrative style—now known as "black and gray"— which had been pioneered by Los Angeles tattooers "Good Time" Charlie Cartwright and Jack Rudy.

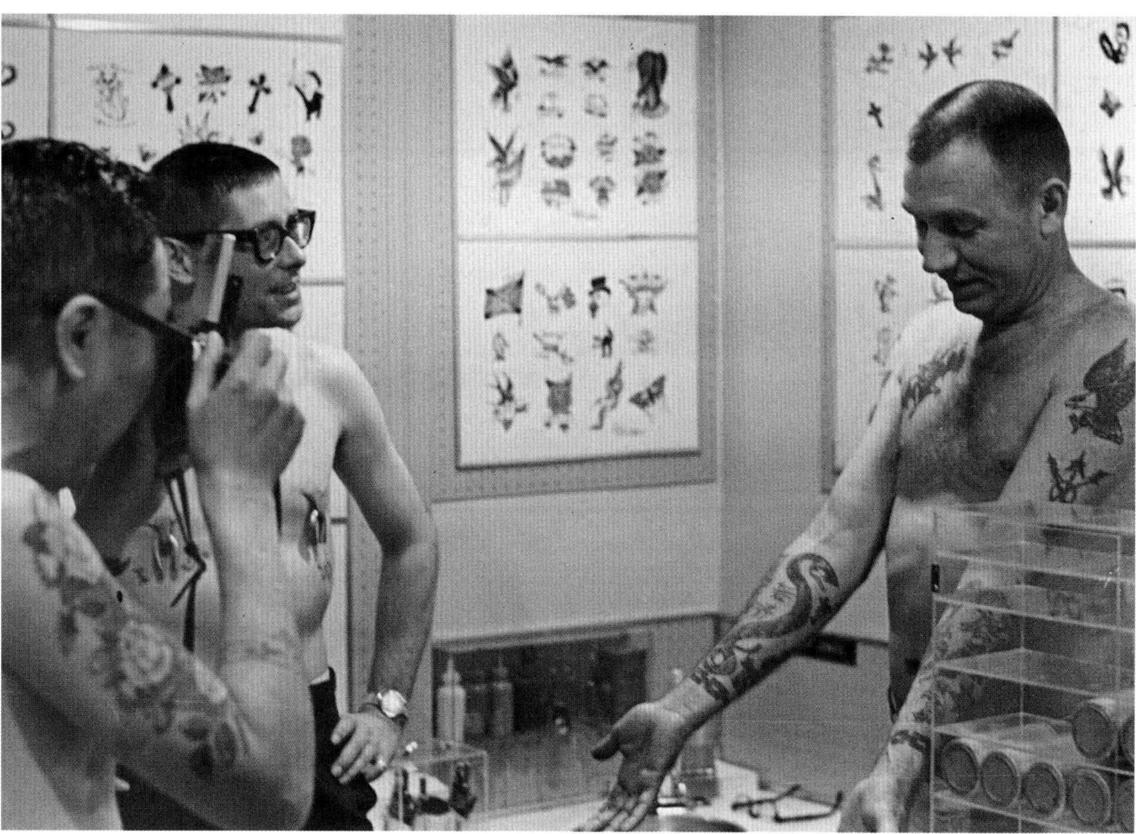

Hardy was less thrilled, however, by an event held on the final day of the convention. Born Donald Edward Talbott Hardy, and still occasionally referred to as "Don," Ed Hardy had first fallen in love with tattooing as a child in California. Hardy had initially pursued an art degree at the San Francisco Art Institute, soaking up referents including Goya, Dürer, and American structuralist Bruce Conner, before getting an offer to study at Yale. He had chosen to set a fine art career aside, however, to pursue the dream of becoming a tattooer, finding himself (via a recommendation from Milton Zeis) in Phil Sparrow's tattoo shop in Oakland, and then shortly after in Sailor Jerry's in Hawaii.

Hardy is, perhaps, artistically and professionally best understood as a synthesis of the most admirable qualities of both of these men—Sparrow's pride, erudition, and rough-hewn sensitivity; Jerry's perfectionism, creativity, and generationally defining penmanship—though without Sparrow's hubris, Jerry's racism, or both men's spiteful irascibility.

"When I got into tattooing," Hardy wrote in his autobiography, "I wanted to make it more like painting. Most tattooing was simple black outline, a solid color in each field. I was after blended colors, gradients, a more extended palette … I brought things to tattooing that no one else did."

This is self-mythologizing to some degree, of course. Nevertheless, through artistic talent, self-confidence, clever and sincere networking, and an abiding and deep love for tattooing, he was able to bring forth the tattoo world in which he wanted to live. The TCA network, and the other mid-century tattoo clubs, had already forged many of the connections with which Hardy was able to supercharge his own career, and the careers of those around and after him.

Meeting of minds (*left*) Davy Jones shows off his tattoos to Japanese visitor Mr Kita and Roland Loomis, aka Fakir Musafar, at Lyle Tuttle's shop in the early 1960s. In the 1960s and early 1970s, Loomis's experimental body play and the more traditional tattooing world, as exemplified by Tuttle, intersected to fertile and mutual benefit.

Bed of blades (*right*) Fakir Musafar gave a jaw-dropping performance at the close of the 1977 Reno convention, assisted by Sailor Sid Diller and an unidentified belly dancer. The performance drew numerous headlines, bringing attention to tattooing which some more traditionally minded artists found unwelcome.

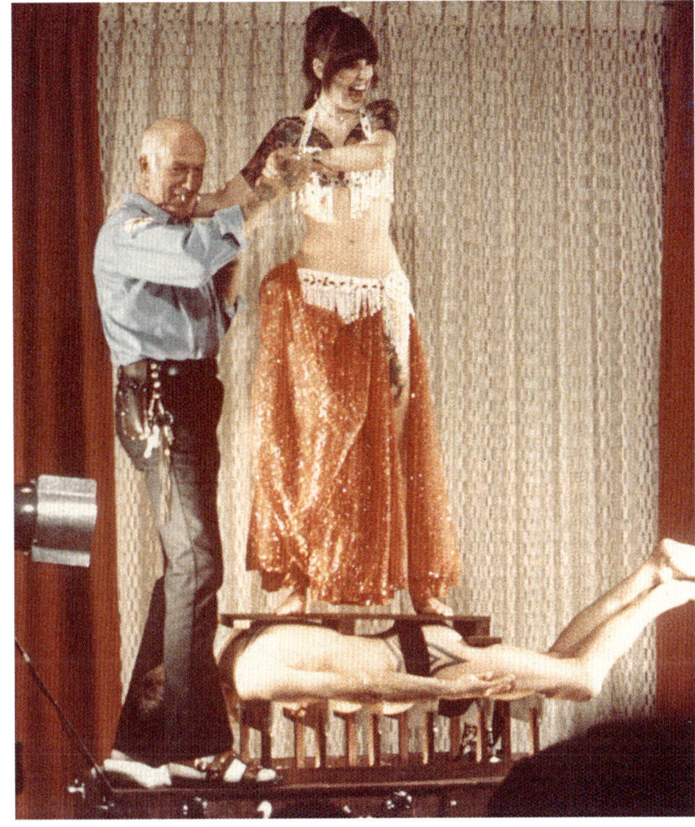

Quickly, he rose to become the brightest young star in America's tattoo firmament, voted best tattooer in the world by his peers several times over in the late 1970s. Hardy is an incredibly talented draftsman. He is a clever, innovative, and brave artist on the skin and off, with astonishingly sharp instincts for form, composition, and meaning. He has a scholarly grasp of art history (mostly stripped of Webb's fondness for conceptualism) and a deep knowledge of—and curiosity for—tattooing's history. He is a savvy businessman, a humble yet confident public speaker, and a phenomenally talented writer, particularly when expounding on tattooing which has particularly thrilled him. He has wit, wisdom, and zeal in immense quantities. He is essentially a funnel through which much of tattoo history has flowed in the decades since he began his career, and even by the Reno convention, he had assumed something of a leadership role within the industry.

"At the very end of the Convention," Yurkew wrote in his own newsletter following the event, "Ed Hardy asked to speak. Ed talked about piercing. He felt, as did the overwhelming majority of artists there, that it did not belong at a tattoo convention and should not be linked to tattooing." In Hardy's own recollection, he wrote that piercing "raised the sinister specter of S&M at a time when we were pushing to gain a little respectability for tattoos. Most of us pushing to expand the work didn't buy the argument that tattoo and piercing were on the same level . . . this was a coming out party for the new tattoo."

Hardy was specifically perturbed by a performance by Roland Loomis, an advertising copywriter from South Dakota who had been a TCA member himself. From his teenage years in the 1940s onward, Loomis had been experimenting with piercing and a suite of other practices he called "body play" in the privacy

"Tattoo Artist of the Year" Cliff Raven (b. Clifford Ingram)—pictured here in 1975—studied art at Indiana University and apprenticed under Phil Sparrow. He tattooed in Chicago and California through to the 1980s, and was hailed "Tattoo Artist of the Year" in 1978. Raven was key to the development of both blackwork and Orientalist tattooing in the early 1970s. As an openly gay man, his art and advertising was often powerfully homoerotic.

of his own home. Inspired by practices he had read about in *National Geographic* magazine, Loomis bound his waist, pierced his genitals, hung weights from his skin, recreated Mandan hook suspension rituals, was tattooed in ways which aped indigenous practices, and began to connect with other enthusiasts around the world. In Nevada, accompanied by his friend Jim Ward, who in 1975 had established Gauntlet, the world's first modern body-piercing studio, Loomis was to perform at the conference's closing dinner, under one of his on-stage personas, Fakir Musafar. During the performance, he presented feats including laying on a bed of nails and across blades, pulling a belly dancer in a cart using hooks pierced into his chest, and having wooden blocks broken over his back.

Loomis subsequently described this moment as "coming out" as Fakir. As the piercing and tattooing industries diverged, the performance has come to be seen as seminal for the subsequent development of body-piercing trends, and the aesthetic and philosophical trajectories of what Fakir called "modern primitivism," which would go on to define much of subcultural practice through the 1990s. Jim Ward, who had been undertaking piercing demonstrations throughout the event, felt enormously aggrieved at the hostility and hypocrisy of Yurkew and others, recalling years later that "the whole attitude left a bad taste in my mouth," and had soured him on tattoo conventions thenceforth.

Hardy's denunciation of piercing surprised many of his clients and colleagues. After all, piercing had been a part of the tattooing scene since the 1950s, and an integral part of Inhelder's TCA. Some of Hardy's best clients were members of piercing clubs, and one of his artistic collaborators, fellow Phil Sparrow apprentice

Cliff Raven, sported nipple piercings of his own. Even Wrigley, as co-organizer of the convention, had reminded readers of his newsletter that several English tattooers would be bringing their piercing equipment to Nevada. Tattoo Samy—himself a key figure in the links between tattooing and piercing, as the inventor of the piercing barbell jewelry and perhaps the first person to sport a tongue piercing—pointed out, in a flyer he distributed to attendees of the following year's convention in Amsterdam, that even Yurkew himself had been bolstering his tattoo income by doing the occasional body piercing.

Fakir's show dominated media coverage of the convention, however, and clearly did not provide the tone of respectability and caution that Hardy, Yurkew, and others felt was necessary. For Hardy, the decision was clearly pragmatic, and was paired with a further distaste for facial tattooing, which also projected the wrong image. For others, the distaste for piercing was doubtless driven as much by homophobia as it was for professional concerns: body piercing had really blossomed in the contexts of subcultural sadomasochism among gay men, and all the key pioneers were at the very least not straightforwardly straight.

The Stonewall Riots of 1969 ushered in a newly confident mood among American gay activists. Homosexuality was finally removed from the official *Diagnostic and Statistical Manual of Mental Disorders* (DSM) in 1974, and the decade saw many states decriminalize homosexuality for the first time. As we have seen, queer networks underpin the transition of the Euro-American tattooing in the postwar period, and openly gay men in particular had long been prominent in the industry. But even as America was

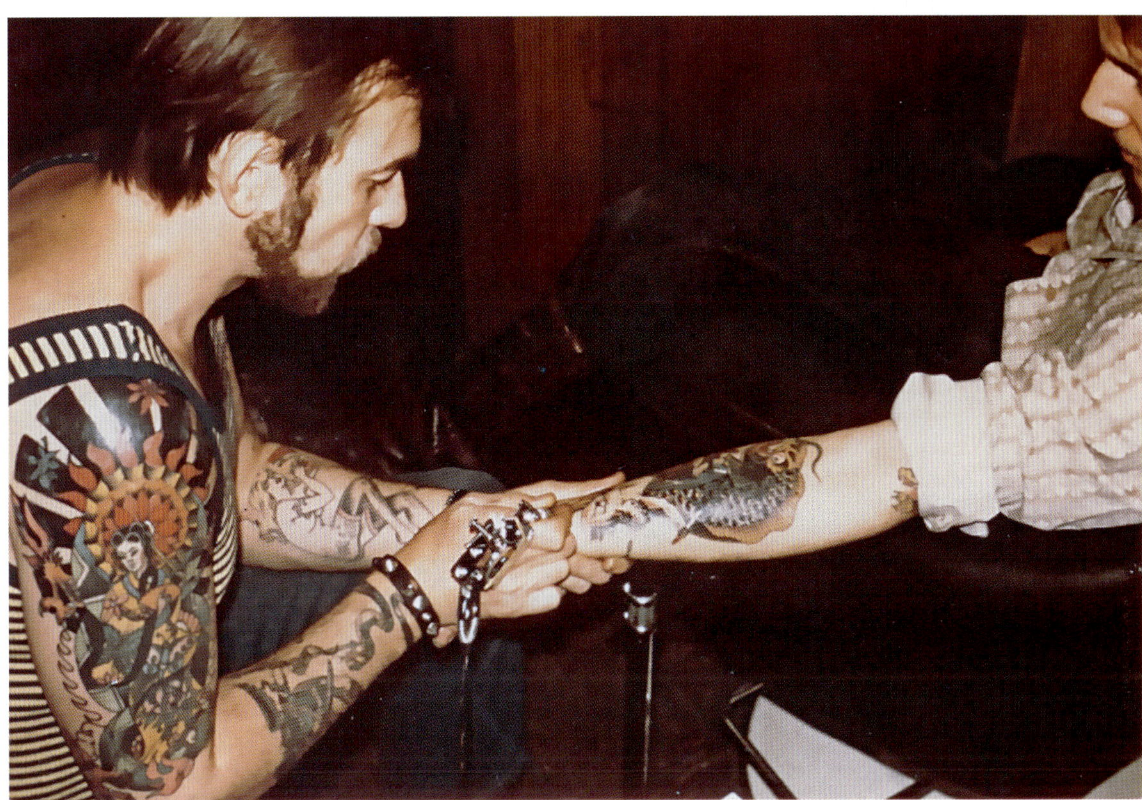

becoming slowly more tolerant of homosexuality, stigma remained. And for some tattooers, the new confidence that encouraged gay subcultures to emerge from the shadows presented a countervailing force to their own desire for cultural legitimacy.

It is generally unclear to what degree this desire to ostracize those with visible piercings was a desire to ostracize queerness, and to what degree it was a desire simply to ostracize strangeness in general. The most vocal figures in the industry, including Hardy in the US and the major trade magazines in the UK, were vocally supportive of gay members of their community, even as they vocalized extreme disdain for piercing. But for several years afterward, many tattoo conventions did explicitly ban visible piercings on attendees, or the practice of piercing on the convention floor. The next ITAA event, Amsterdam 1978, didn't do so explicitly—Tattoo Samy and the openly gay Cliff

Raven both won "Tattoo Artist of the Year," despite their piercings—but many piercers, including Jim Ward and Doug Molloy, received a frosty reception. What they found was, in their opinion, an event that had become more about self-congratulation and gatekeeping than an opportunity to fully promote even more mainstream tattooing to a wider set of audiences. Their friend and fellow piercer Sailor Sid Diller described the whole event as a "fuck up," the product of a "nothing organization"; "an hour and a quarter of nothing but presentation of some trophies and crap . . . a complete waste of time."

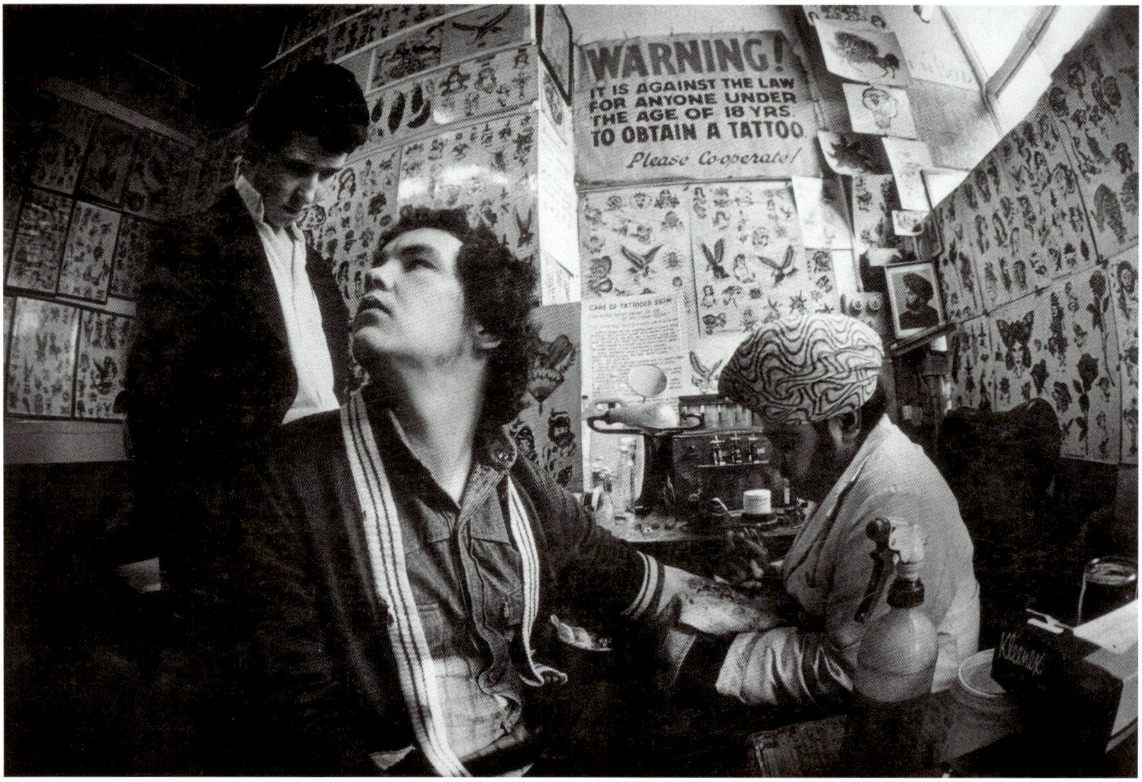

Dalbir "Sinbad" Singh tattooing in Middlesbrough, 1970s (*above*)

Dalbir Singh, known professionally as "Sinbad," was one of the first professional tattooers of color in the UK. Sinbad was a local legend in the North East of England, with his tattoos fondly remembered as "Sinbad Specials." He learned tattooing in his native India, and once in the UK, he worked tattooing men on the dockside, and in a longstanding permanent studio. Customers remember him as a particularly bad speller—one man ended up with "FARTER" instead of "FATHER"—and not a particularly strong draftsman. His eagles, some said, looked more like chickens, and his pinup girls sometimes had six toes.

Sign from Sinbad's shop, 1969 (*left*)

This sign appeared in Sinbad's shop, notifying customers of the impacts of the "Tattooing of Minors Act" of 1969, which made tattooing illegal in England for under eighteens.

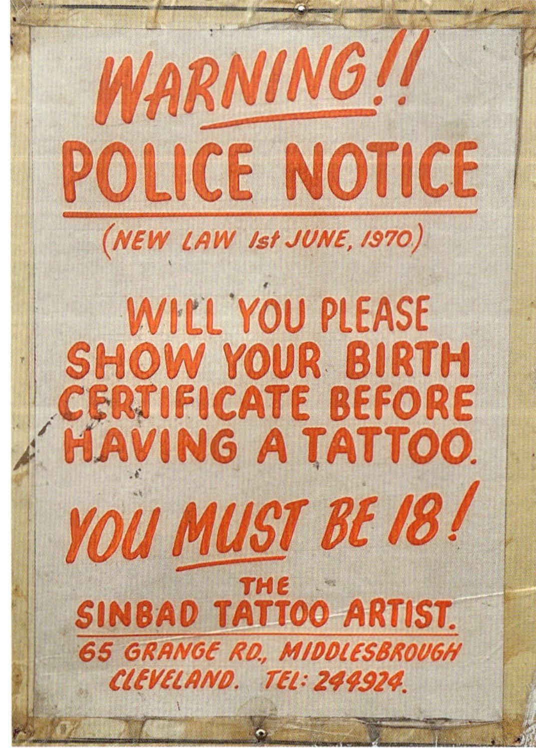

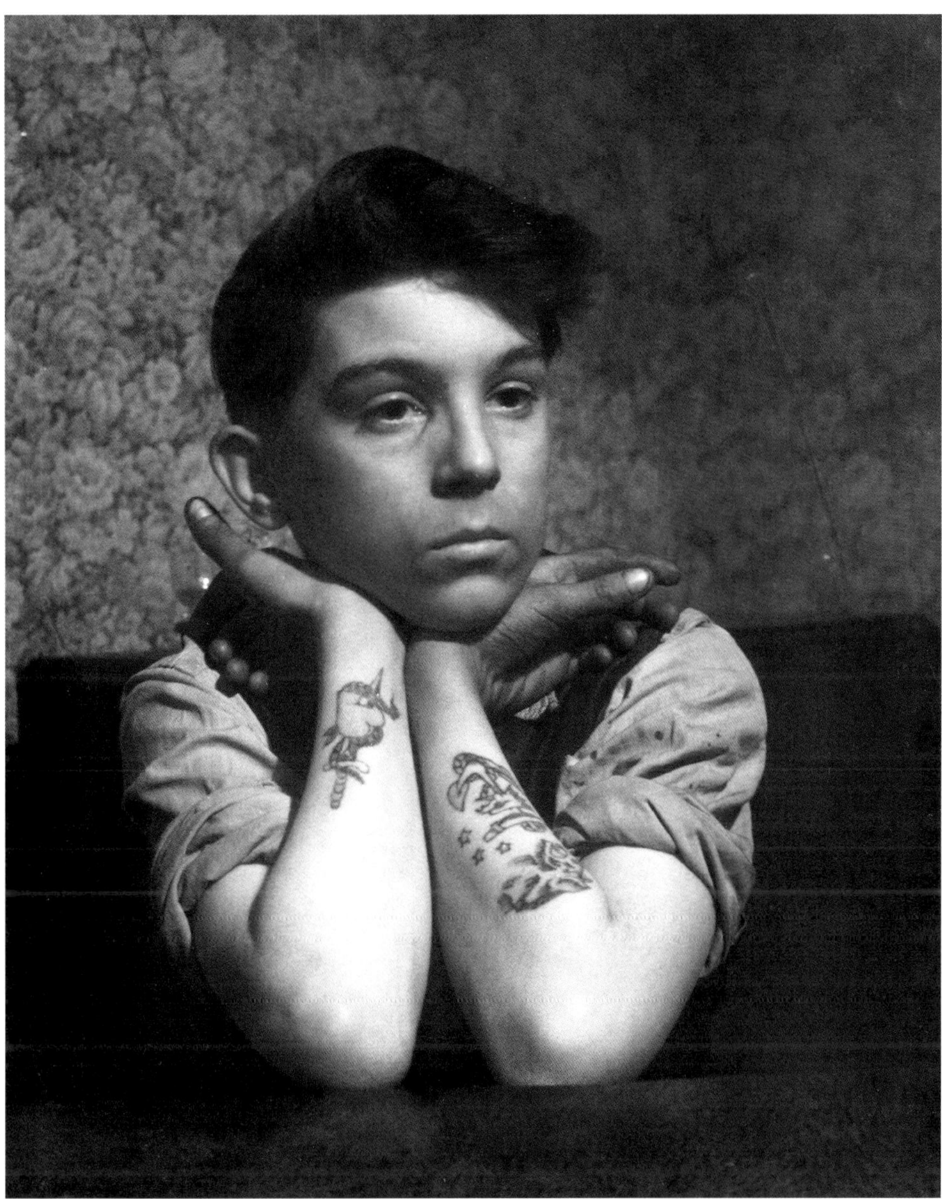

Schoolboy Arthur Waterworth, 1956

There were no laws in England which explicitly banned the tattooing of children until 1969. Regulations were brought in following the case of Burrell v Harmer (1966), in which a tattooer was convicted of assault for having tattooed two boys, aged twelve and thirteen. Before then, most self-respecting professionals would generally avoid tattooing children, simply for the sake of their reputations, but stories appeared regularly in the British and American press decrying the latest crazes in underage tattooing. Pictured here in a powerful representation of adolescence in postwar Britain is fourteen-year-old Arthur Waterworth from the North West of England, showing off his striking designs.

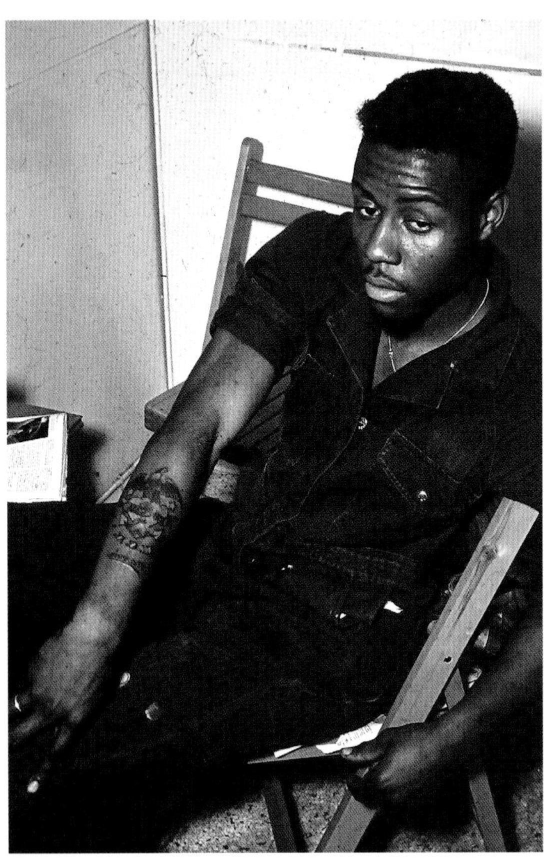

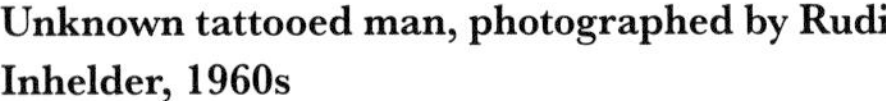

Unknown tattooed man, photographed by Rudi Inhelder, 1960s

Black clients have been part of modern tattooing for over a century, showing up in sailor description books, for example, and in intimate photographs such as this one, depicting a friend of Rudi Inhelder's in the 1960s. Nevertheless, prominent groundswells of African American tattoo collectors and artists did not become central to American tattooing until the 1990s, when Black artists and celebrities such as Dennis Rodman and Janet Jackson drove trends for tattooing amongst Black youth.

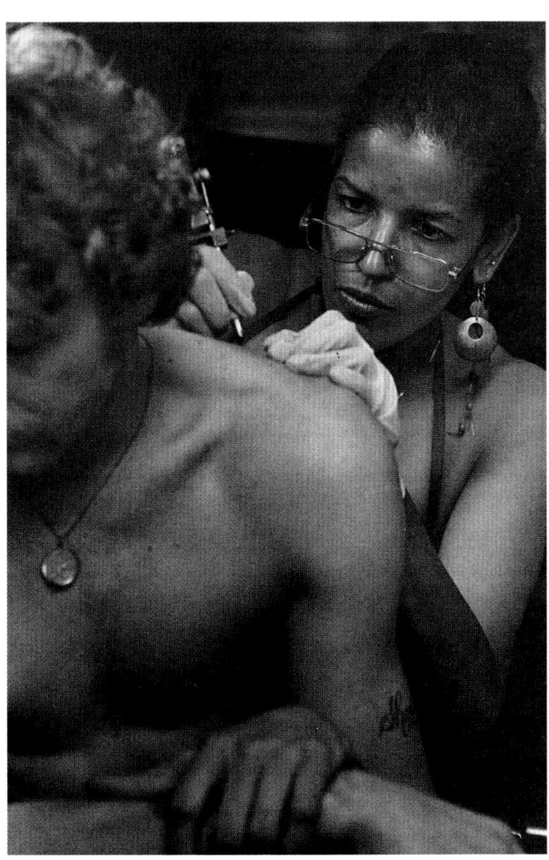

Jacci Gresham tattooing a client, c.1980s

Jacci Gresham was laid off from a job working at General Motors in Detroit in 1976, and thus decided to move to the sunny city of New Orleans to take up tattooing. African Americans had been vastly underrepresented as both artists and customers in modern tattooing, and Gresham was a pioneer—the first Black woman to tattoo professionally in the United States, and, by her own reckoning, perhaps the only one for almost two decades. Though she faced racism and sexism in the white, male-dominated industry, she also found champions and friends, hosting the New Orleans tattoo convention as guest of honor in 1978.

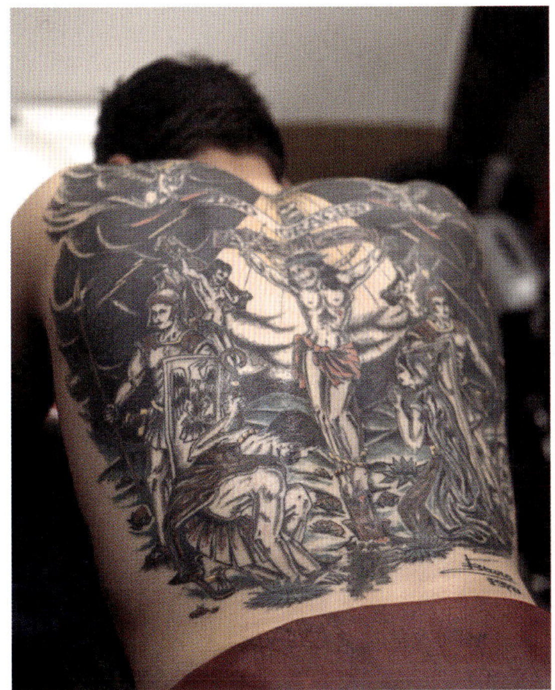

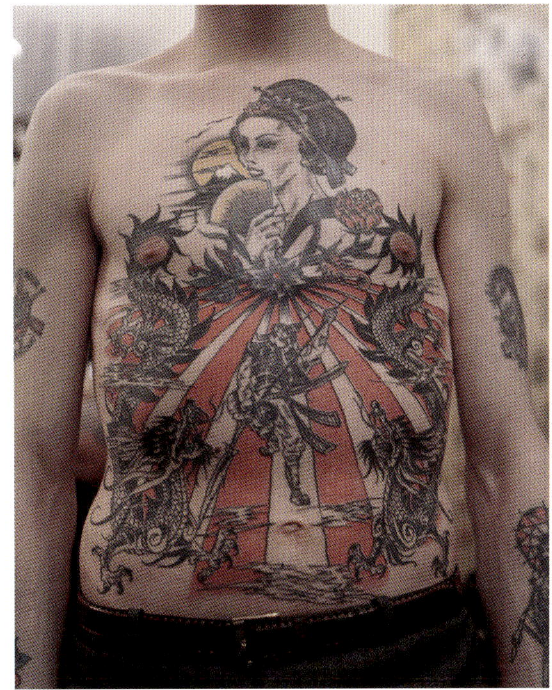

Tattooing by Parisian artist Bruno Cuzzicoli, 1972

Known mononymically, Bruno was the most famous tattooer
in France in the 1960s, 70s, and 80s, and the French tattoo
world's strongest connection to the networks rooted in the UK
and the United States. Tattooing had long been stigmatized
in France, and was subsequently much less visible there than
in the Anglosphere. There were no professional tattoo studios
in France, but having initially tattooed itinerantly in a van,
Bruno successfully applied for a license to open his studio in
October 1962.

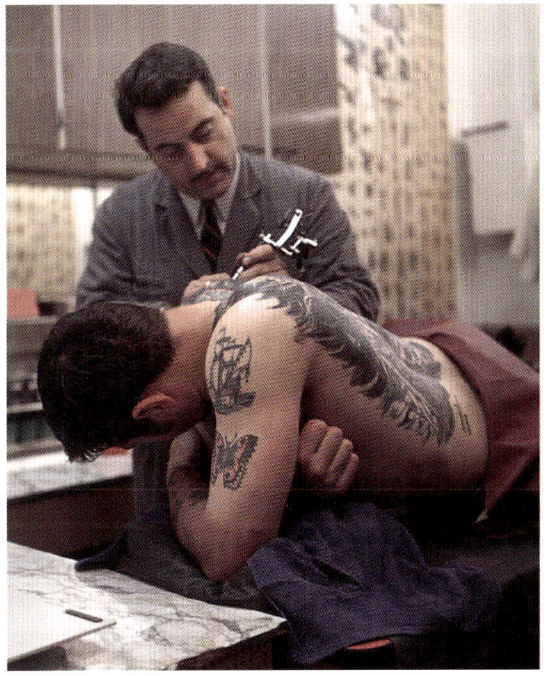

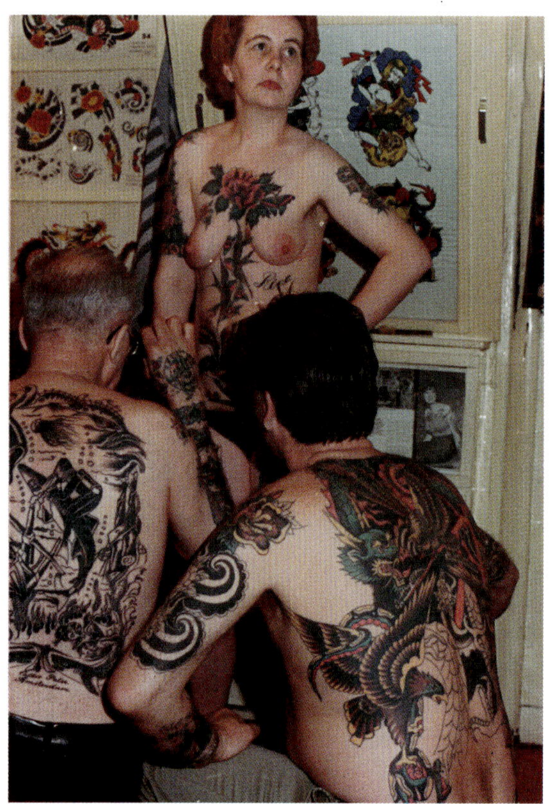

Tattoo Peter with clients in Amsterdam, 1960s/70s

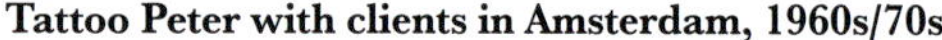

Pier "Tattoo Peter" de Haan (*left*) opened his tattoo studio
in Amsterdam in 1955, having lost his leg during World
War II. As in similar environs all over Europe, Dutch ports
remained reliable places for tattooers to ply their trade, even
as wider society increasingly frowned upon it. Tattoo Peter
became a prominent member of the Bristol Tattoo Club and
Inhelder's Tattoo Club of America, and provided inspiration
to a younger generation of influential Dutch tattooers, most
famous of whom is Henk "Hanky Panky" Schiffmacher. At
the 1978 convention in Amsterdam, which was cut short after
drunken attendees infuriated venue security, Tattoo Peter was
awarded a prize for "doing the most for tattooing."

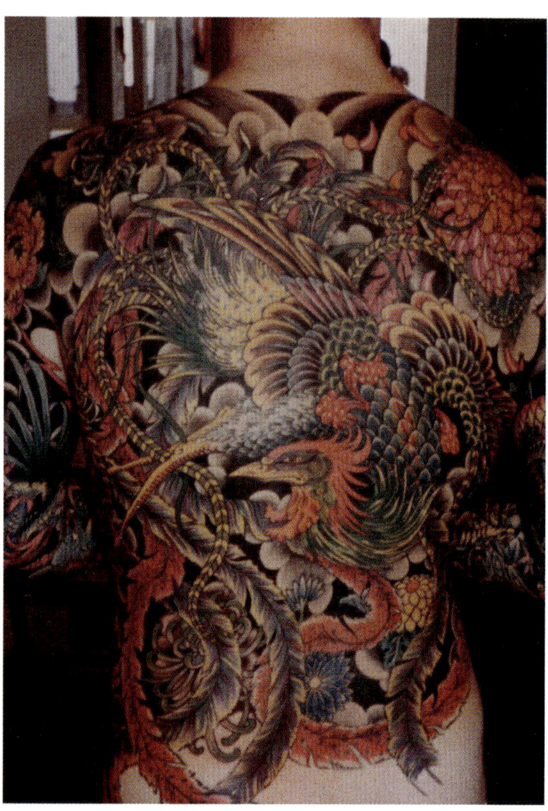

**Tattoo by Ed Hardy on Jack Preston, photographed by
Tattoo Samy at the Reno Tattoo Convention, 1977**

Hardy had embraced Japanese tattooing aesthetics after
being introduced to them by Phil Sparrow, and made strong
connections with artists in Japan, including Kazuo Oguri,
aka Horihide. This piece takes cues from traditional Japanese
designs, but updates them in confident, multicolored graphic
style. Hardy's work draws upon studied reverence for tattooing's
time-honored traditions but transforms them in novel, syncretic
ways. Artists and attendees at Reno were flabbergasted at the
ambition, execution, and power of his work.

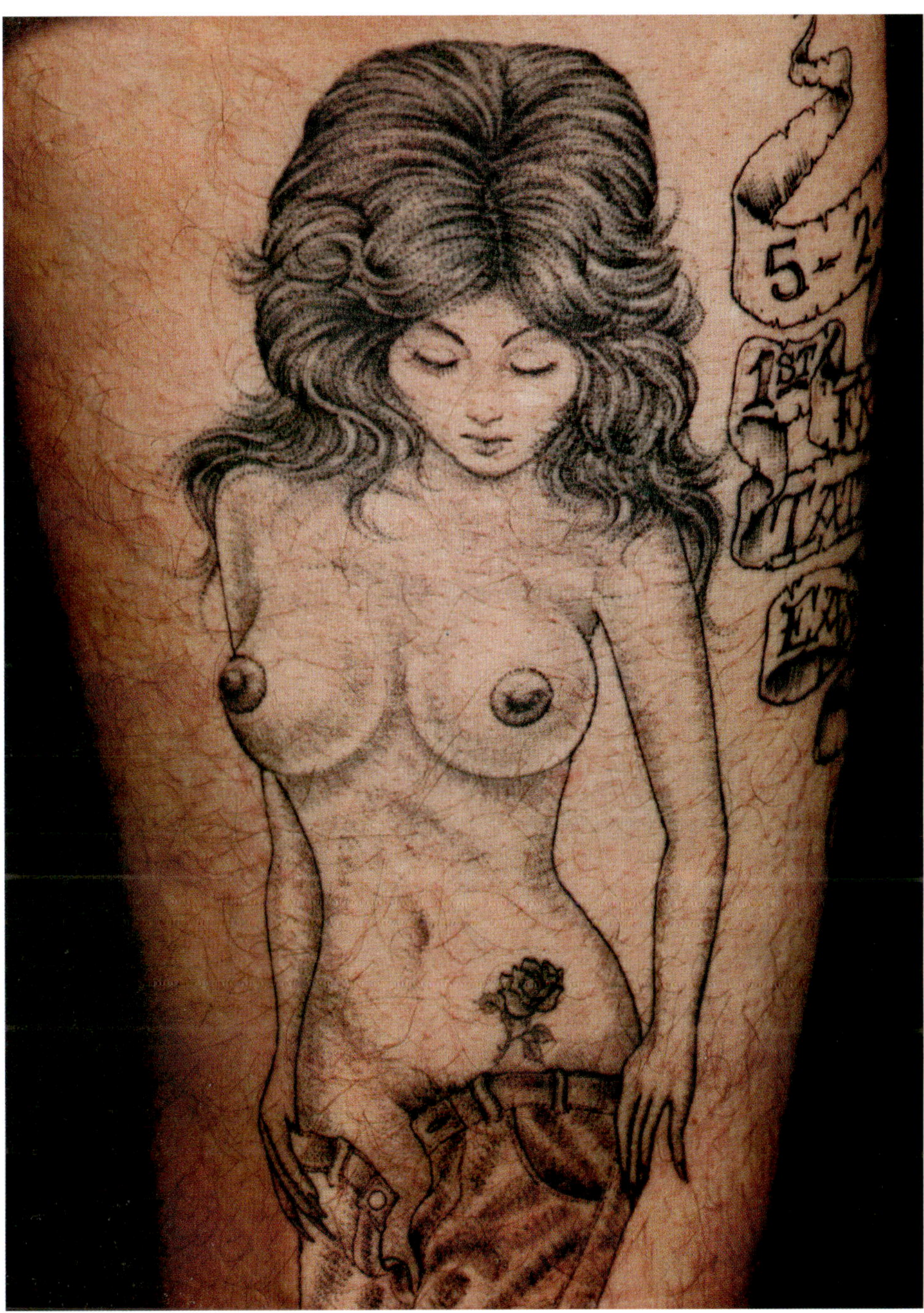

Tattoo by Jack Rudy on unknown client, c.1979

The revelation of Jack Rudy's fine-line black and gray work to the wider tattoo scene in 1977 was a key pillar in the transformation of modern tattooing into the stylistically diverse visual practice it is today. Rudy, along with mentor Charlie Cartwright, drew inspiration from their customers from the Chicano culture of East Los Angeles.

TattooTime to Modern Primitives

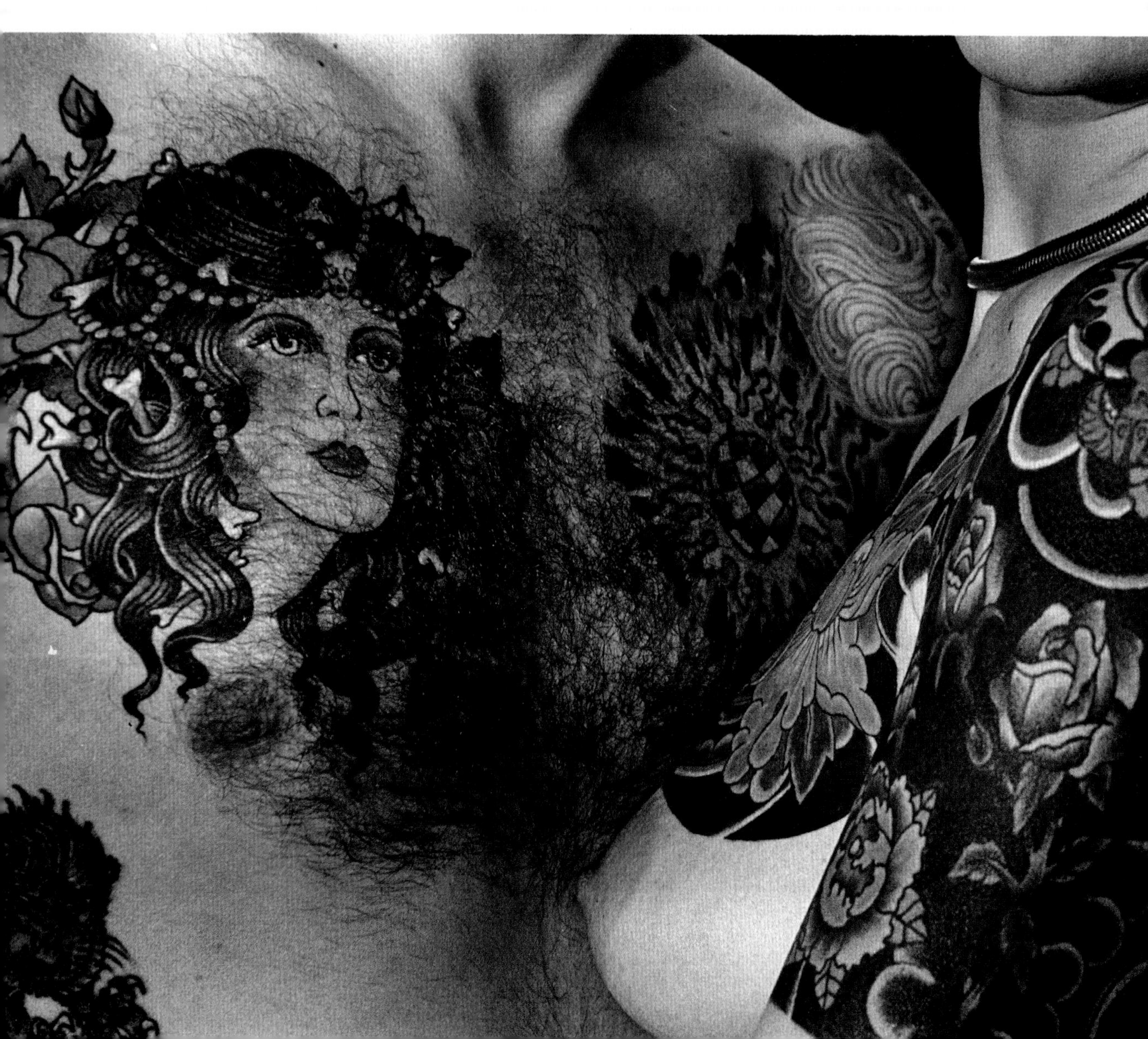

A synthesis of styles These tattoos by Ed Hardy were used as the poster image for Tattoo, an exhibition of tattoo art and photography at the Oakland Museum in 1977. Hardy's work in this period is emblematic of a rapid stylistic synthesis, combining design cues from American Traditional tattooing, "pre-technological" blackwork, and Japanese Irezumi.

nhelder had brought a group of enthusiasts together in the 1960s, but the political and practical demands of the 1970s meant that, for a while at least, the queerer side of the industry, populated by piercers and performers and body modifiers, could not easily coexist with the tattooers dragging tattooing back into the light. From this moment of divergence, both Musafar (Roland Loomis) and Hardy continued to develop their professional and artistic projects, until history would bring them back together again a decade later under another awkward and ill-fitting umbrella.

The 1980s were essentially bookended by two publications that well illustrate the paths tattooing took following the fallout in the aftermath of Reno. The first, published in 1982, was Ed Hardy's *TattooTime* periodical, in which tattooers and academics within Hardy's circle shared information about current and historical tendencies in tattooing. *TattooTime* advocated for innovation within the industry, but within a framework that sought legitimacy through engagement with anthropological research and artistic practice.

The second, published in 1989, was the generationally definitive *Modern Primitives* by V. Vale and Andrea Juno, which foregrounded Fakir Musafar's more esoteric and experimental engagement with tattooing within a broader array of other body-modification practices, including piercing. Although Vale had worked with Hardy as Assistant Editor on *TattooTime*, his own project would conceptualize this moment rather differently. The implosion of the hippie movement at the end of the 1960s had given way to a new kind of appropriative spiritualism, and California was the epicenter of so-called "New Age" movements, which blended a confusing panoply of non-Western and pseudo-mystic cultures and beliefs into a strange and volatile brew. Against this cultural background, Musafar coined the term from which the book took its title, and it has thus long been taken as something akin to Musafar's own manifesto. Many writers since have also falsely claimed that Musafar himself inspired an enormous movement of so-called "Modern Primitives"—people inspired to align themselves directly with his particular and esoteric blend of corporeally-focused and self-consciously atavistic spiritual "body play," and to take the term as an identity label.

But though Musafar is the book's first printed interviewee, Ed Hardy is its second. Moreover, very few of the other people featured are in line with its aesthetic, spiritual, or ideological approaches either. For example, "Good Time" Charlie Cartwright nods appreciatively when asked about Native American tattooing, and Lyle Tuttle obligingly connects his experience of being tattooed in Samoa with his own practice, but it's resolutely clear that neither would claim to be "primitive" themselves, in any sense. It is more accurate to say that while a small group of Musafar's acolytes did fully embrace "primitivism" as an identity, most of those whom academic anthropology has classed as "Modern Primitives" were really nothing of the sort. In short, not everyone with a "tribal" tattoo claimed an affiliation with novel spiritual practices. The book is instead better read as a snapshot of a wider set of intersecting visual strands in tattooing that define the 1980s, several of which had arisen entirely independently of Musafar's guiding ideas. If there was a "movement" of Modern Primitives, it was small, and directly aligned with Musafar's work; much of the culture of tattooing depicted and inspired by the book cannot simply be read in this way.

A more precise comparison between Musafar's and Hardy's practices during the 1980s is thus warranted.

Evangelizing for the New Tattoo

Buoyed by his emerging role as a spokesman for the industry in the wake of the 1977 Reno convention, Hardy had been inspired to open a new tattoo shop—Tattoo City—in San Francisco with his friend and collaborator Bob Roberts. Hardy and Roberts had been working in their private, appointment-only studio Realistic for several years, but this new venture afforded them the opportunity to spread their developing ethos of innovative, custom tattooing to a wider client base. Inspired by Charlie Cartwright's studio Good Time Charlie's in East LA, where a group of artistically aligned tattooers worked not just by appointment, but also on anyone who walked in, Hardy hired conceptually trained fine artist and sculptor Jamie Summers and then-rookie Chuck Eldridge to take the reins at Tattoo City while he and Roberts were at Realistic.

Summers is perhaps the best illustration of Hardy's approach at the time: she and her husband were, Hardy said, "the first people … who sensed the bigger picture behind my obsession." Hardy taught her to tattoo as she was looking to incorporate it into her wider artistic practice, though she was quickly persuaded that it was a powerful medium all of its own, producing striking, painterly pieces which flowed in abstracted swirls over her clients' bodies. She was perhaps the first tattooer to have her work featured in canonical art periodical *ArtForum*, and alongside her tattoo practice, had a solo show at the New Museum of Contemporary Art in New York at the time of her tragic death in a

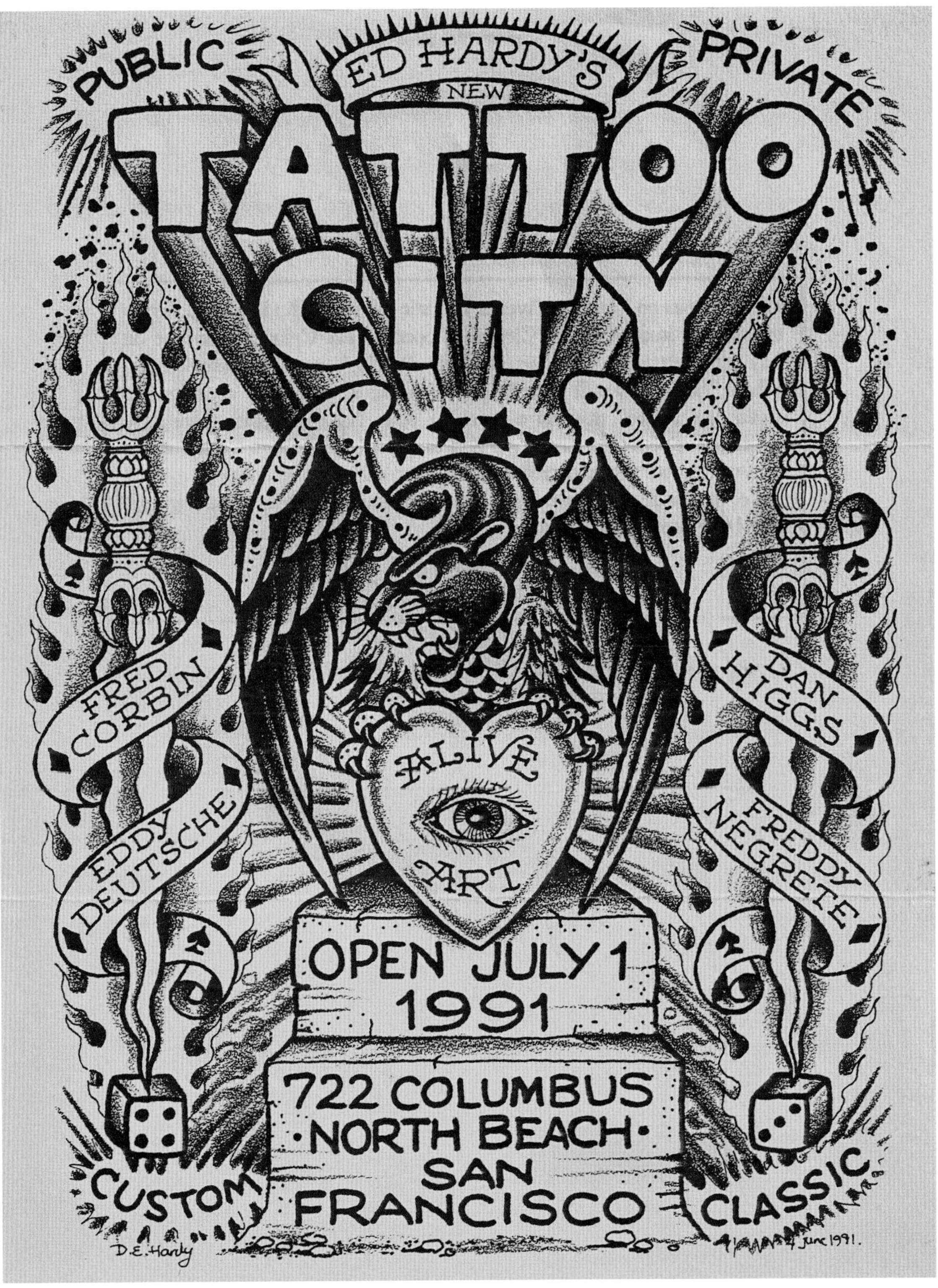
PUBLIC
PRIVATE
ED HARDY'S
NEW
TATTOO
CITY
FRED CORBIN
EDDY DEUTSCHE
DAN HIGGS
FREDDY NEGRETE
ALIVE ART
OPEN JULY 1
1991
722 COLUMBUS
· NORTH BEACH ·
SAN
FRANCISCO
CUSTOM
CLASSIC
D.E. Hardy
4 June 1991.

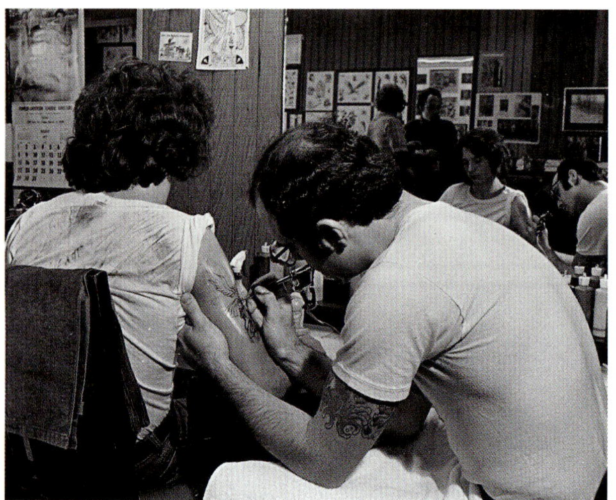

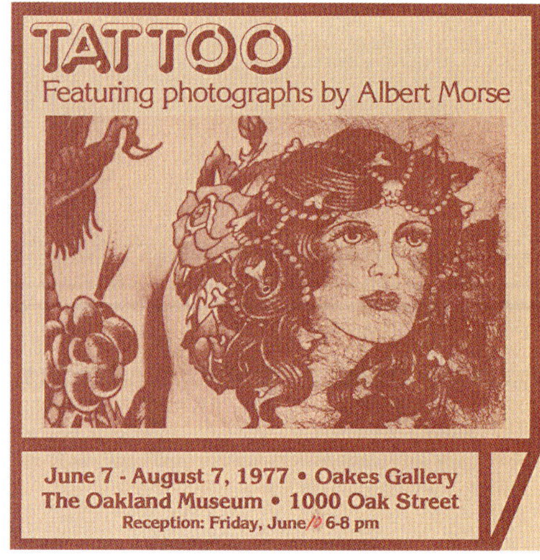

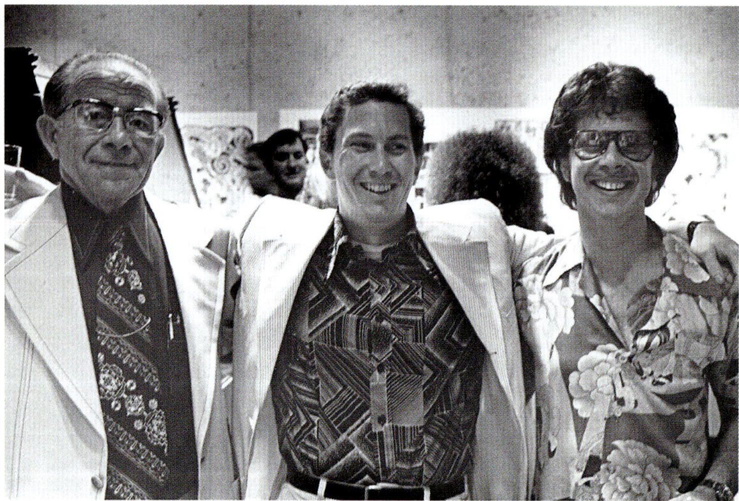

Oakland exhibition (*above and top left*) Curator Jeffrey Long, working with Ed Hardy, staged Tattoo, an exhibition of Californian tattooing and its influences, to coincide with the publication of *The Tattooists*, a lavish photobook by Albert Morse. Morse, a lawyer by profession, was a keen tattoo fan, and collected historic tattoo materials, as well as documenting contemporary work photographically. The exhibition featured objects from Morse's collection, as well as flash donated by Hardy's industry connections, including Phil Sparrow, Cliff Raven, and Jack Rudy. The photo of the tattooer, top left, was included in the press release for the exhibition.

Generation game (*bottom left*) Hardy, shown at the center, with tattooers Sailor Vern Ingemarson on the left and Steve Stone on the right, at the Oakland Tattoo exhibition in 1977. Both the veteran Ingemarson and the young Stone contributed flash to the exhibition, illustrating Hardy's desire to connect Californian tattooing across generations.

motorcycle accident in 1983. The catalog essay for the show explains, hauntingly, that "in her practice, Summers emphasizes the ritualistic aspect in which the tattoo acts as a talisman, providing a 'shock point to the psyche'."

Tattoo City thus became something of a beacon for a newly energized community of tattooists, and the open shopfront allowed any client who chose to stumble in off the street to walk away with a piece of art from some of the greatest working tattooers in the world at the time. The model was a democratization of this new energy in tattooing, and ensured that the kind of creative, powerful tattooing Hardy so loved would spread confidently into the wider consciousness.

As briefly mentioned in the previous chapter, Good Time Charlie's had become the first professional shop in the world to specialize in single-needle black-and-gray tattooing. This innovation was born out of Cartwright's desire to ink portraits of his client's loved ones freehand, as well as his own stylistic preferences. Cartwright had taught himself to tattoo by hand-poking designs using handmade tools, and he thus adapted his machines to replicate that style as closely as possible, running the needle much more slowly than usual in order to create a precise, careful gradation of tone. This also signaled a backlash against the comic-book styles of the 1940s and 50s, and something of a return to the more delicate styles of Victorian and Edwardian tattooing, which early electric tattooers had sought to emulate. Jack Rudy, who worked with Cartwright at Good Time Charlie's, himself acknowledged precisely this lineage: "George Burchett was doing single-needle tattooing in England. I saw some of his flash from the old days, and I can't imagine doing that stuff except

single-needle. I don't know for a fact that anyone was doing it way before we did, but, if that's true, we reinvented it in 1976."

Rudy and a self-taught artist called Freddy Negrete, who also worked at Good Time Charlie's, further iterated Cartwright's practice. These two younger artists adored the delicate tattoo designs emerging from the Chicano gangs of LA's prison system, as well as the visual effects resulting from the technical limitations imposed by incarceration. The beautiful, often photorealistic work coming out of the Good Time Charlie's studio essentially offered a refinement of the kind of tattooing being done in jails, where it was necessary to use makeshift single needles made from guitar strings, to build clandestine tattooing machines from cassette motors and toothbrushes, and to fashion black ink from dust and shoe polish. In addition, the visual landscape of East LA further inspired new letterforms and script styles for textual tattoos, with Cartwright's crew riffing on the graffiti styles they saw around them in order to expand the stale, unchanged repertoire for tattooing names and slogans. "Ghetto art was in a traditional period of becoming respectable," Cartwright recalls. "It had a more refined look and took on a more serious tone in terms of art, and wasn't cartoony like the bright colored military or carny tattoo."

When Cartwright announced his retirement in order to more sincerely reconnect with his childhood Christian faith in 1977, Hardy saw an opportunity to preserve the incubator for this radical new fine-line technique. He hired the febrile pairing of Rudy and Negrete at his newly opened Tattooland studio in East LA, ensuring they could continue to invent what has

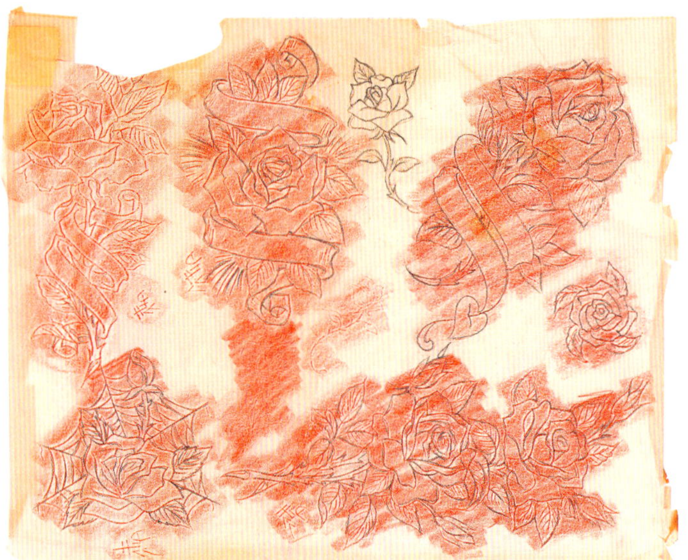

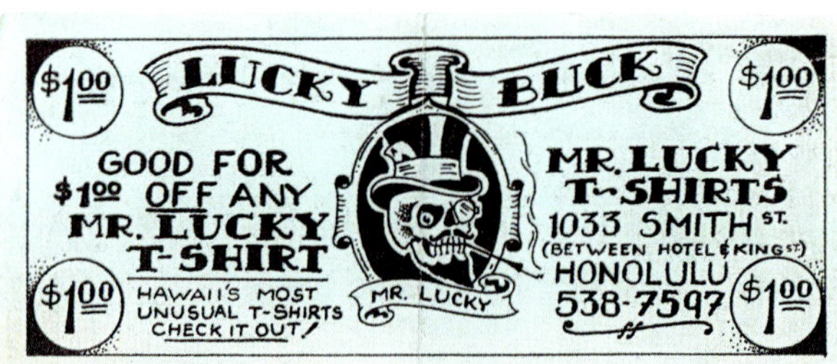

The flash that gets the cash (*left*) Mike "Rollo Banks" Malone's entrepreneurial instincts, combined with his gift for drawing and his deep love of traditional tattoo designs, led to the creation of several profitable and influential enterprises which capitalized upon—and helped to spur—the booming tattoo economy of the 1980s and 1990s. His acetate stencil rubbings can be seen here, above a discount voucher for his "Mr Lucky" T-shirt brand, an offshoot of his "Mr Flash" business.

Artistic legacy (*right*) Malone took on Sailor Jerry's studio in Honolulu in 1973, renaming it China Sea. Malone, along with Ed Hardy, ensured Jerry would become the familiar name he is today. The pair produced books of Jerry's flash, and licensed merchandise featuring his most popular designs.

Fury of the deep (*far right*) This backpiece by Mike Malone, c.1979, is a classic piece of stylistic hybridization of the period, combining elements of traditional American tattooing with compositional reflections of Japanese ukiyo-e prints, updated in a contemporary graphic style.

since become one of the most prolific styles in tattooing today. "I took it upon myself," he later wrote, "to save the great historic tattoo style these guys created."

A Californian Family Tree

In the summer following the Reno convention, Hardy sketched several drafts of a "family tree" of Californian tattooing for the curators of an exhibition to be held at the Oakland Museum. The genealogy he sketched is essentially the organizing logic of influence upon which much of the modern tattoo industry is built. Hardy, as we shall see, became such an important node for the future of tattooing that his network of predecessors and successors is, in some senses, a substantial branch of every working tattooer's professional ancestry.

Anthropologist Alan Govenar—who documented the emergence of this Californian focal point contemporaneously from a position of close proximity—

has long argued that this moment was in fact the "renaissance" of tattooing. As already discussed, though, it seems that the deep roots of Hardy's network speak to something of a continuation of an ever-present industry rather than the rebirth of anything that had truly ever disappeared. (The genealogies sketched during the preparation for the Oakland Museum show, for example, stretch back in an unbroken chain over half a century to include Edwardian artists such as Amund Dietzel [tattooing from 1913], Harry Lawson [from 1911], and "Brooklyn Joe" Lieber [from c.1900]).

Hardy's "parents," so to speak, are the aforementioned odd couple of Phil Sparrow and Sailor Jerry, with extra lines of input coming from Long Beach tattooer Bert Grimm, who Hardy had watched in awe in his youth; Kazuo Oguri (a.k.a. Horihide), with whom Hardy briefly worked in Japan; tattoo

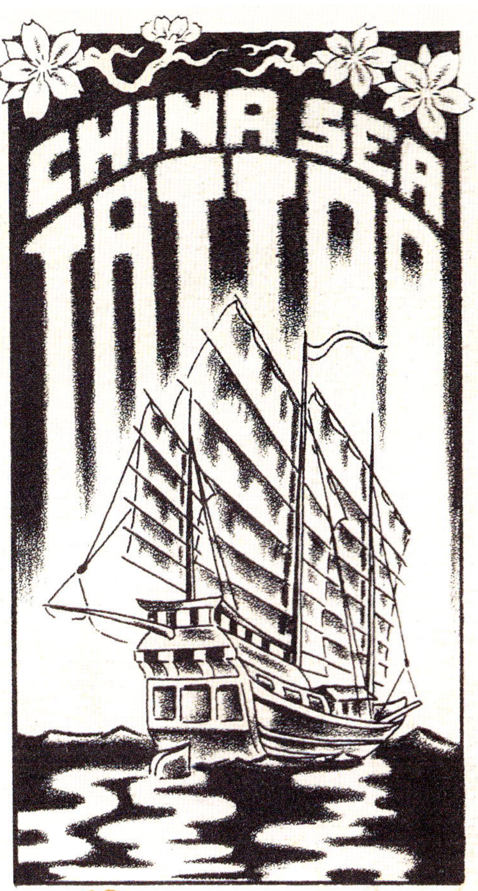

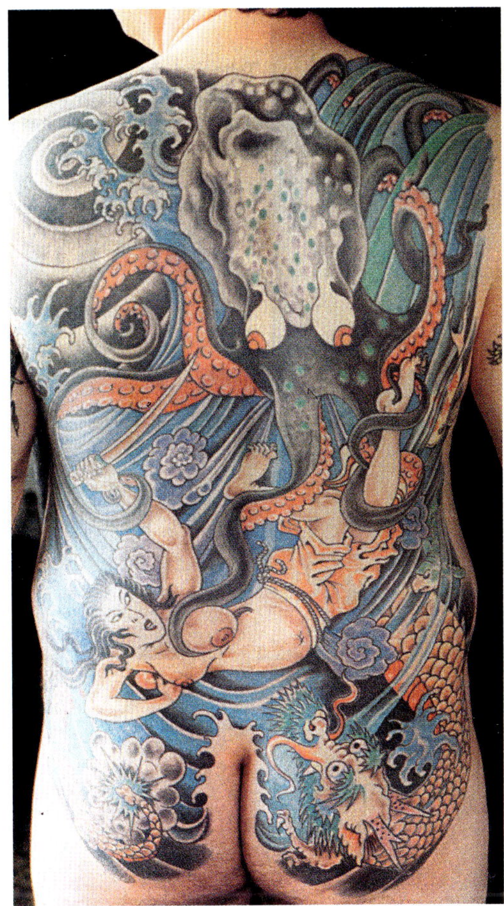

machine builder and supplier Paul Rogers; and several younger innovators, including Jack Rudy, who had broadened his sense of what was possible in tattooing. In something like the position of "sibling" sits Mike "Rollo Banks" Malone, one of Hardy's closest and most consistent collaborators.

Malone was a photographer and graphic artist from California, who, like Hardy, had engaged in some childhood experiments with tattooing using some shadily acquired equipment. When he moved to New York in the late 1960s, the prohibition on tattooing was in full swing, leading him as a customer into the makeshift home studio of Thom DeVita, a renegade jazz fan from Harlem who was the only even vaguely visible tattooer in the city. Malone had first met Hardy through his work on the Folk Art Museum *TATTOO!* show, and the two became firm friends, particularly as he was able to take bootleg photographs of hundreds of Kuniyoshi Utagawa prints held at the Museum of Fine Arts in Massachusetts—a rare commodity at the time. As Hardy remembered, "Duplicates of these were shared with Jerry, Zeke [Owen], DeVita and [Phil-Sparrow-protégé] Cliff Raven. They became the key reference base for us to transform Western tattooing."

In 1972, Malone and his then-partner "Shanghai" Kate Hellenbrand accompanied Hardy to Hawaii to meet Jerry and Oguri, and the couple stayed with the American old-timer for three weeks after Hardy had returned to California, soaking up as much knowledge as they could. Both Malone and Hellenbrand had worked for Hardy in San Diego for a while, but when Sailor Jerry passed away in 1973, Malone was able to strike a deal to take over the Hotel Street shop in Honolulu, saving its trove of contents from a bonfire, and becoming the guardian of Jerry's artistic and cultural legacy in the process.

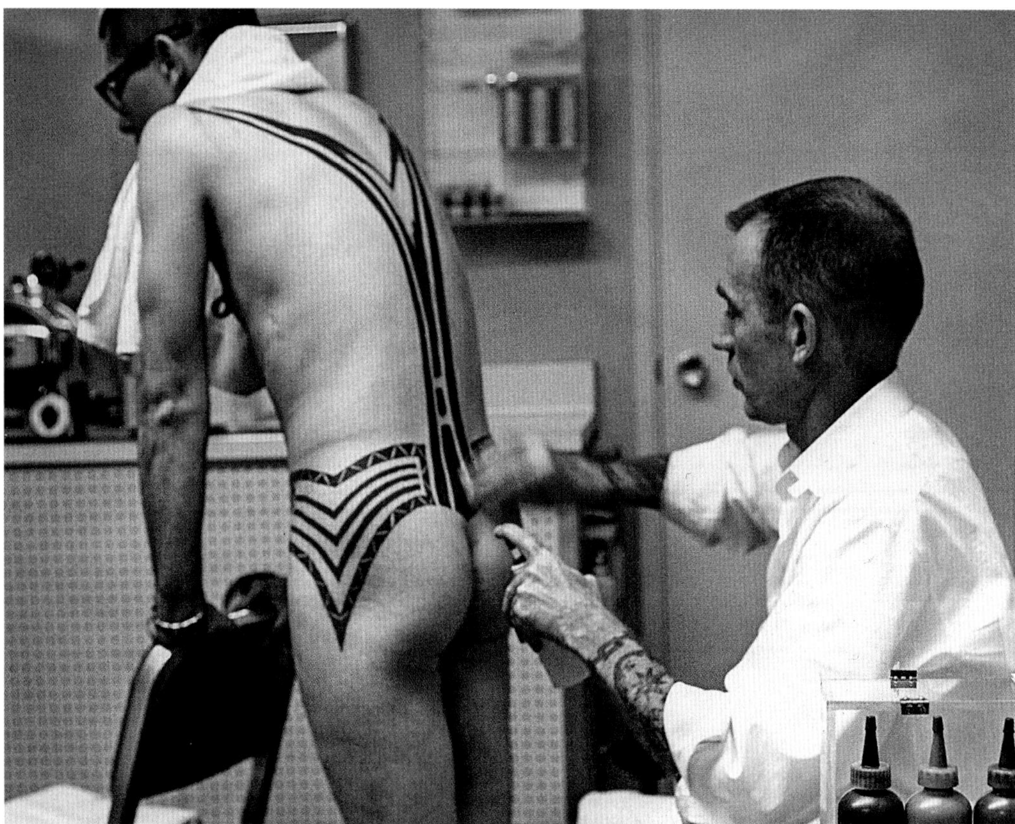

Malone renamed the studio "China Sea Tattoo Company," and for the following three decades he operated it as a base from which to develop a reputation both as an artist in his own right, and as a powerhouse of modern flash design, under the brand name "Mr. Flash." Malone was a visual magpie, devouring inspiration not only from Jerry, but from Japanese tattooing, traditional Hawaiian tattooing, art historical painting and sculpture, and contemporary pop culture, and through his drawing and distribution, much of the Californian energy of this period was permanently ensconced on tattoo shop walls throughout the globe.

Other branches of the genealogical tree—Hardy's tattooing cousins, perhaps—include his contemporaries Cliff Raven and Lyle Tuttle, as well as Tuttle's employee, one Davy Jones.

Davy Jones' Tattooing Locker

Hardy's own autobiography does not mention Jones at all. Jones is curiously also not mentioned in *Modern Primitives*, which is surprising given that he was one of the pioneers of the so-called "tribal" style of Western tattooing which exploded in the book's wake. He had begun tattooing in 1948, and served a stint in the merchant navy before setting himself up as a tattooer, but he is generally much less well known than most of the other names on the "family tree." In light of his later obscurity, it is interesting to note the Oakland exhibition's acknowledgment of Jones's place in the pantheon of West Coast tattooing, particularly given the fact that Jones' most famous tattoo played a central role in the Reno closing event which had so piqued Hardy's concern earlier that year.

It was Jones who had tattooed Fakir Musafar, then still plain Roland Loomis. The striking monochromatic

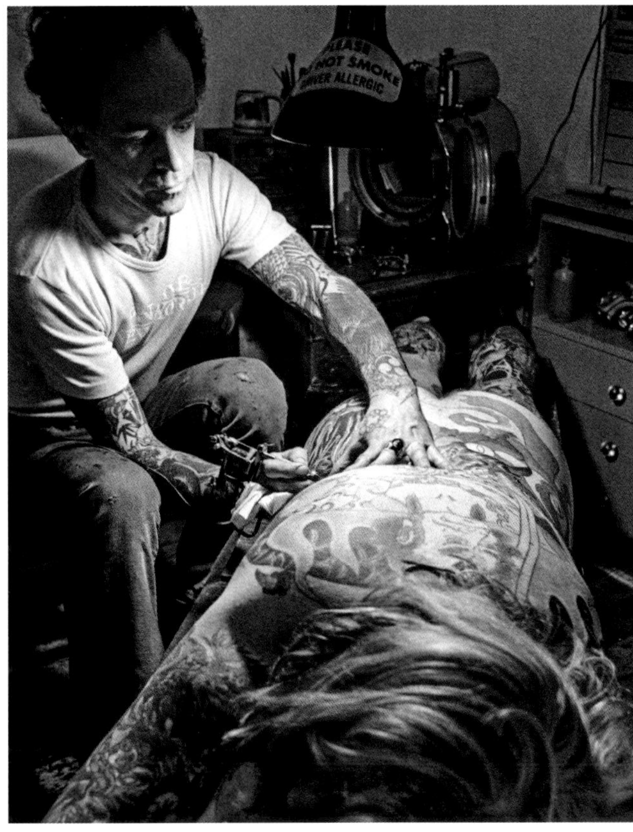

Flying V (*left*) Davy Jones wipes the backpiece he has just completed on Fakir Musafar. This radical blackwork tattooing, taking cues from ethnographic photography of Indigenous tattoo traditions, would explode into a global phenomenon through the 1980s and 1990s. Though Jones is the creator of one of the most iconic pieces of blackwork tattooing in the Western tradition, he is little remembered today.

Going underground (*right*) Thom DeVita tattooing in his secretive studio on New York's 8th Street. One of the only tattooers in New York City working during the practice's prohibition, DeVita was inspired by abstract expressionists, collage artists, and jazz musicians, producing tattoos that frequently strayed from the rigors of predetermined flash designs through the additions of flourishes and crude embellishments.

design, applied around 1964, formed what Musafar called a "flame from the earth": an enormous inverted "V" across his entire back, and would become emblematic of a newly emerging zeitgeist in Euro-American tattooing, which would draw upon—and often even totally appropriate—indigenous tattoo traditions from around the world. Musafar suggested that Jones had picked up South Pacific-style tattooing while "living amongst tribal people [sic] in the Pacific" and had been "ritually tattooed in Western Samoa," which obviously enamored him to Musafar, even as the veracity or extent of these connections cannot be verified. The two men had been members of Inhelder's TCA, though Musafar was first referred to Jones by Lyle Tuttle, for whom Jones was working. Nevertheless, their collaboration became an important milestone on the way to Musafar's public emergence into the world. "I had a vision for years and years that I would only be

me if I had a certain tattoo on my back," Musafar later told an interviewer. "It's a Native American design and depicts flames coming out of the earth. I made a large photograph of my back and I took what I saw in my vision and sketched it on tissue-paper. I started going around to various tattoo artists and they'd look at this and laugh. They'd say, 'You want that on your back? How about a nice panther, how about a rose, how about a dagger with "Mom" in it?' Finally, after a lot of searching, I found a man called Davy Jones who was receptive. He was the official tattoo artist for the Hells Angels. He saw my tattoo and instantly connected with it. As far as I know that was the first blackwork that was ever done in this country."

Aside from Musafar's piercings and carnivalesque performances, it was his blackwork tattooing that really underscored the aesthetic gulf between him and many of the other attendees at the Reno convention. He was

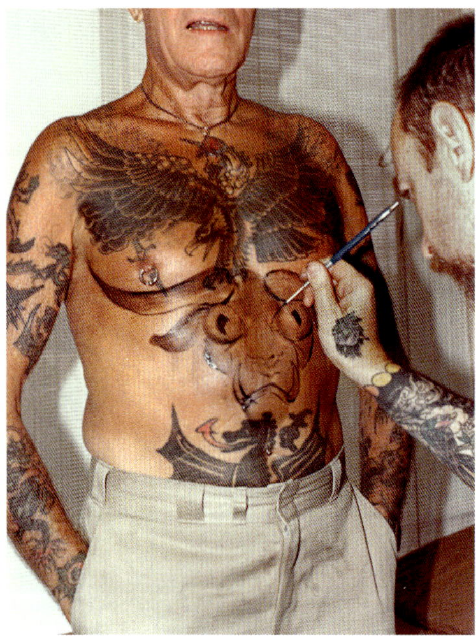

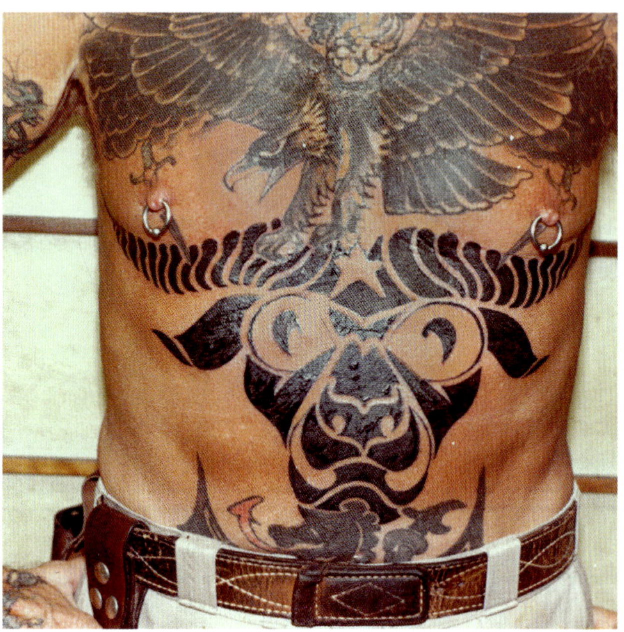

not the first white man to appropriate and approximate indigenous tattoo styles: Sutherland Macdonald had copied geometric frieze patterns from the Moorish Alhambra as part of a backpiece in the 1890s; George Burchett had inscribed pseudo-atavistic designs onto the face and body of performing tattooed man The Great Omi (Horace Ridler) back in the 1920s; while Omi's schtick was itself reproducing motifs first established during exoticized performances of the late eighteenth and early nineteenth centuries, where tattooed "transculturites" such as John Rutherford and Captain George Costentenus would regale audiences with tall tales of having been tattooed in captivity in various far-flung lands. Within the industry, it is DeVita who is commonly held as the first tattooer in America to produce work in a blackwork, "tribal" style, and had recently been experimenting with hard-edged, geometric black tattoos, which drew upon indigenous

influences as well as the graphic modes of postwar American artists such as Franz Kline. Other tattooers, including Cliff Raven, had also been working in this mode since the 1960s—Raven apparently preferred the term "pre-technological" over "tribal" to describe this style, and though he claimed to have developed the idea with his own clients, independently of Jones, he did acknowledge receiving a letter from him featuring photos, and credited him as an early influence. Despite these other examples, and though (as discussed in the introduction), their *Primitive Urge* book was not ultimately published, Jones's tattooing on Musafar's back would nevertheless become the largest and most widely publicized tattoo in this style in its earliest days. From these stuttering and murky beginnings, the incorporation of graphic blackwork drawing upon indigenous tattoo traditions would go on to spawn another new strand of contemporary tattoo aesthetics.

Raging bull (*left*) This heavy blackwork bull design by Cliff Raven was tattooed on Sailor Sid Diller. Raven called his version of "tribal" tattooing "pre-technological," and it was for him a primarily aesthetic move, rather than one that was encoded with deep metaphysical import. It was, he said, "based on a conviction as to the inherent validity of this style." Nevertheless, he admitted that the style "may be attractive to some as a way to plug into their own past."

Invention of a movement (*right*)
Ed Hardy published the first issue of *Tattootime* in 1982. The cover features tattoos by Hardy on a client called Ron Postman, drawing upon Samoan, Japanese, and contemporary graphic influences. Postman is credited with the overall concept for the composition, and Hardy gave the piece a name, as a painter might title a work on canvas: *The Beginning and End of All Things*.

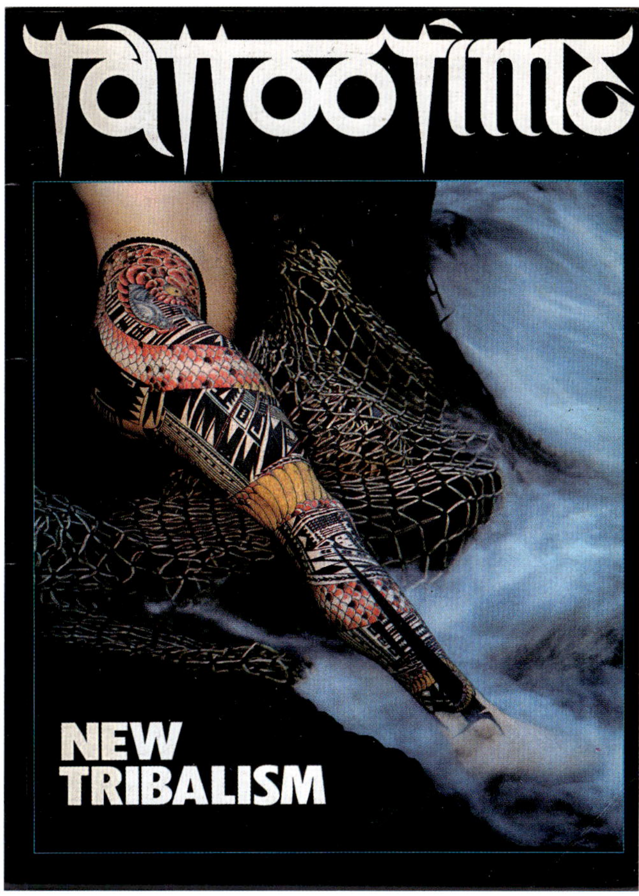

TattooTime

Hardy had begun publishing a journal of tattoo history and culture called *TattooTime* in 1982, and its first issue was called "The New Tribalism." The cover sported a photo of a man's leg, fully covered in a geometric black design, which certainly referenced the kinds of patterns that occur frequently in Samoan pe'a tattooing, for example, but which did not directly claim any "authentic" lineage with them. Layered over the blackwork is an enormous, luminous purple snake coiling menacingly up the outstretched limb. This is a truly postmodern piece of tattoo art, synthesizing Japanese and American Traditional notes, and running them through a filter of 1980s neon Californian pop.

The principal difference in approach is evident in the labels chosen by Hardy and Musafar for their projects. Musafar's "Modern Primitivism" implicitly brings the past into the present, looking backward. By contrast, "New Tribalism" is rather more prospective, creating something novel. In practice, Jones had worked with a Native American design to help augment Musafar's spiritual quest, within which experimentation with traditional indigenous tattooing played a key role.

Musafar, perhaps quixotically, sought a kind of "authenticity." His was a sincere, if often clumsy, engagement with corporeal practices not his own, exploring foreign cultures through magazines in secret. Against the backdrop of the cultural climate of the 1950s, this is understandable. Conversely, Hardy had learned from DeVita and Raven that heavy blackwork was a visually striking move on its own terms, and which, rather than fashioning a direct connection to the past, actually forged a new path into the future.

Many of Hardy's friends and collaborators were certainly inspired by tattooing in places such as Hawaii, Borneo, New Zealand, and Samoa, both through

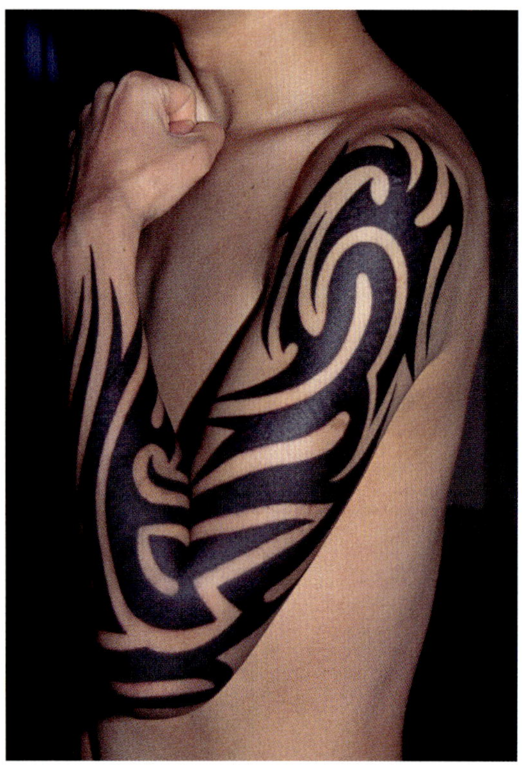

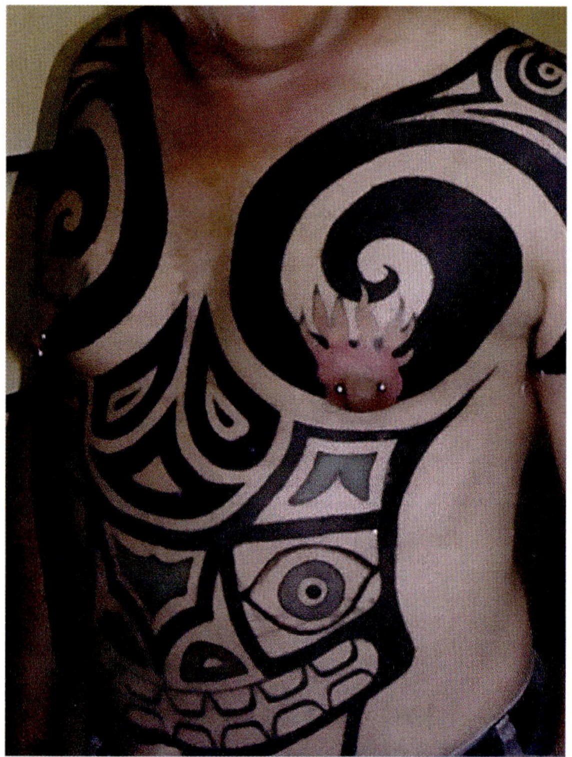

books and magazines, through correspondence and exchange with artists abroad, and through traveling to be tattooed themselves. Lyle Tuttle, for example, traveled to Samoa in 1972 to be tattooed, and Leo Zulueta, another central figure in the popularization of "New Tribalist" designs, grew up in Hawaii to Filipino parents, aware of (and inspired by) traditional indigenous practices from across the Pacific and Southeast Asia. Kandi Everett, who Mike Malone met in Hawaii in 1977, also innovated the style by drawing some influence from local traditions. But crucially, and with a naive enthusiasm that is in some senses the inverse of Musafar's, they were primarily drawn to the visual power of this design language more than any strongly metaphysical features of the cultures from which these designs were inspired.

Indeed, their fascination was with the beauty of the abstract tattoos, which accentuate and ameliorate the body they adorn, not with a particular philosophical narrative they are assumed to represent or even facilitate. In "The New Tribalism," Cliff Raven does acknowledge some interest in what he calls a "back to nature approach," but stresses primarily this interest in tattooing as a decorative art and describes his interest in indigenous tattooing as a "treasure trove of form." Hardy has described this style as a "powerful option for the repertoire of contemporary creative tattooing."

Hardy was messianic, proselytizing these new and re-energized takes on tattooing as loudly as possible, excitedly sharing the work which so thrilled him from the past and the present with almost anyone who was interested. He would regularly send Polaroids and flyers with his letters to friends around the world and, before tattoo magazines or the easy sharing of images over the internet, these missives from across the sea were a constant source of inspiration and thrill.

New tribes (*left*) Far left is a blackwork sleeve tattooed by Leo Zulueta on Ryoichi "Keroppy" Maeda from Japan in 1999. Note the continuity of the design, even while Maeda's arm is bent. The blackwork frontpiece directly to the left was completed by Cliff Raven on client Bob Houle in the early 1980s.

Hands across the sea (*right*) This painting by Ed Hardy for Ron Ackers was gifted on Hardy's first visit to work in England, in August 1979. The rear of this piece is inscribed with "I greatly appreciate the opportunity you've given me to return to the land of my roots, and hope this opens a new era of imagination and idea exchange for British and American tattooing."

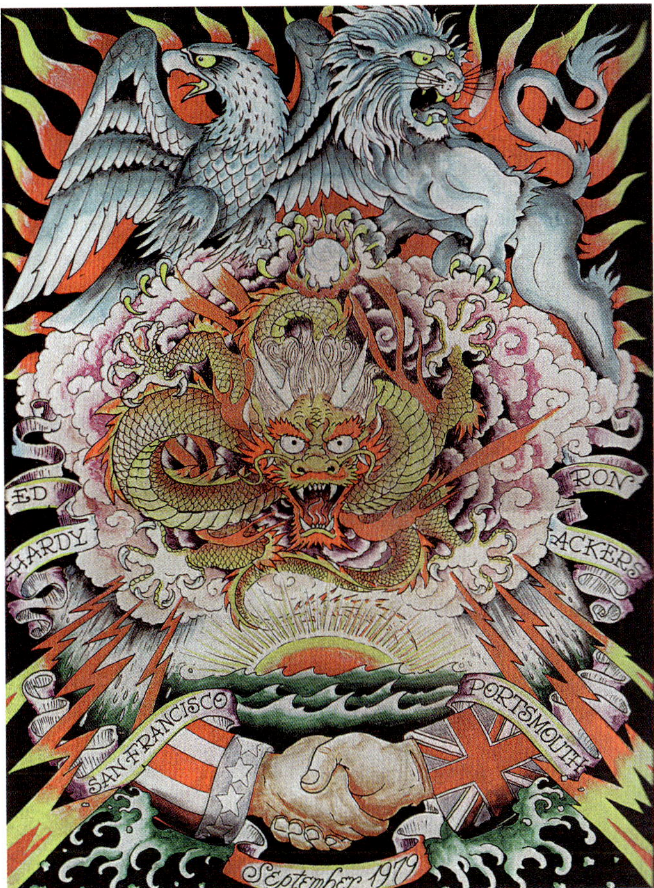

One incredible picture sent to a tattooer in London features a tantalizing close-up detail of the huge purple snake legpiece that would become the iconic cover of *TattooTime*, inscribed underneath with the teasing caption "The next big thing?" And it was: almost instantly, blackwork "tribal" became a staple at tattoo conventions everywhere. As he remembers telling his friend and collaborator Leo Zulueta: "We've invented an art movement!"

Hands Across the Sea

Hardy had numerous correspondents in England, and traveled to London for work on several occasions over the course of the late 1970s and early 1980s. He even sometimes wrote to British trade magazine *Tattoo International*, telling readers on one occasion that though they'd all recently seen pictures of Leo Zulueta's groundbreaking "bolder pattern tattoo work, if not downright tribal in flavor," they should not be directly copying his designs without attribution. "We all influence each other," he wrote, "but I am a bit of a fanatic for ORIGINAL, INNOVATIVE people getting their just recognition. Too often, whether intentional or not, imitators and plagiavists [sic] receive credit when it is not really due."

Ron Ackers, an old Bristol Tattoo Club stalwart and colleague of Les Skuse and Jessie Knight, who was by this period based in Portsmouth, first invited him across the Atlantic in 1979, and Hardy thus coupled his buoyant, fizzing new approach to tattooing with the deep-rooted hierarchy of tattooing in Britain, and as a result in Europe too. Following that visit, *Tattoo International* featured a battery of testimonials to Hardy's work which explicitly compared him in stature to the great Sutherland Macdonald, hailing him variously as "exceptional"; "one of the world's

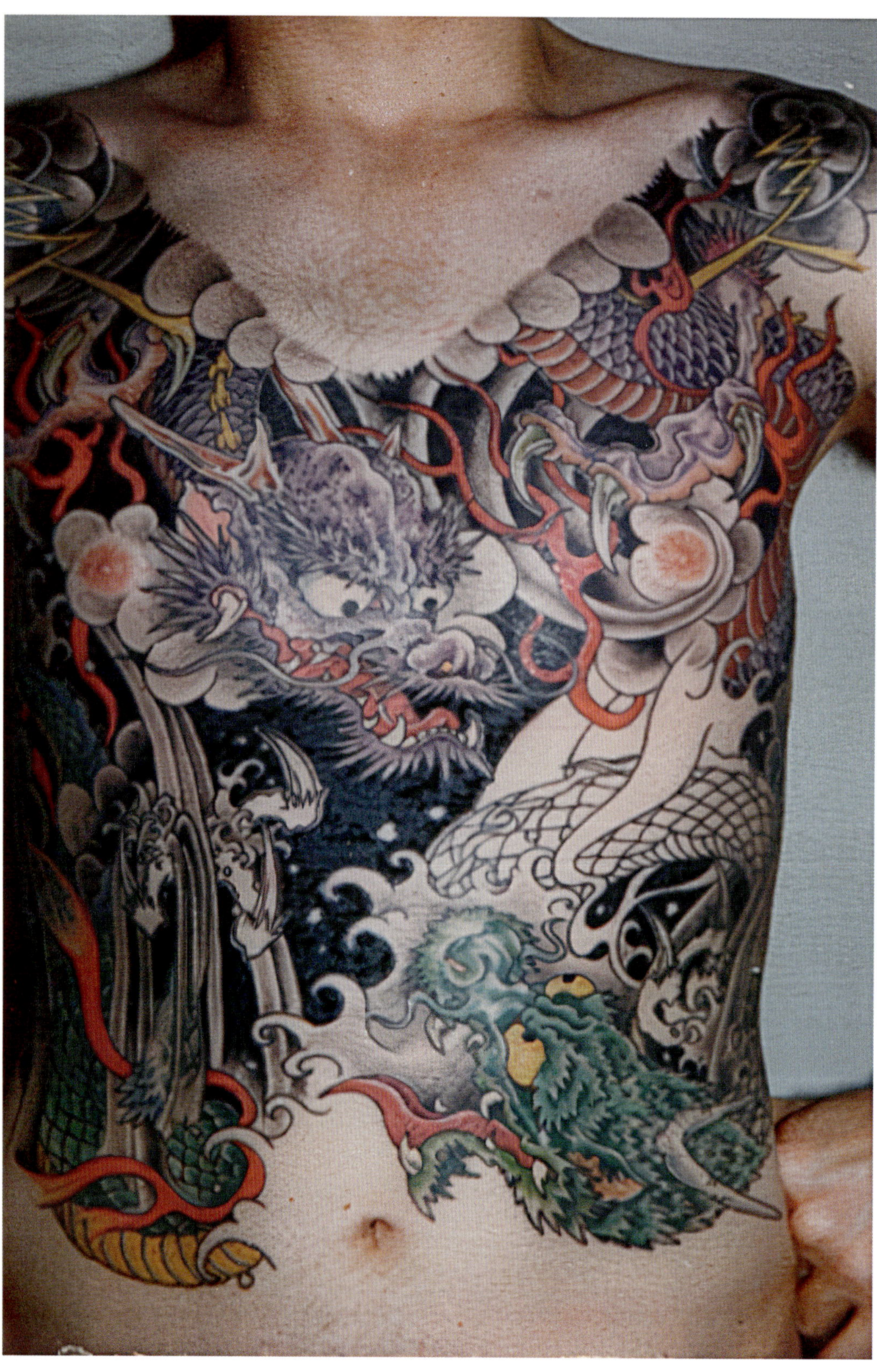

Purple haze A fighting dragons frontpiece on London tattooer Dennis Cockell, tattooed by Ed Hardy. Cockell was one of the first British artists to travel to America to be worked on by Hardy, and news of the scale and quality of the tattooing spread rapidly among Cockell's friends and peers.

top tattoo artists"; and "an artist of outstanding quality." One old-timer explained that "he has a way of capturing exactly what you want and giving you a little bit extra"; another gushed that "there is no limit to this man's capabilities."

Ackers had worked for a long period of his career in a seaside resort, and thus over the quiet winter months drove a van almost aimlessly around the European continent in search of customers, cash, and comradeship. He was one of the only people tattooing in Spain during Franco's dictatorship, for example, often taking his camper van to Spanish resorts where tattooing was technically banned. He also made strong connections in Ireland, from where he could more easily and cheaply import American equipment, as well as in Germany, Holland, Denmark, and Italy. He even spent a short time working with Lyle Tuttle and Davy Jones in San Francisco in 1958, before having to return home due to being unable to secure a work permit.

Ackers was thus perfectly placed to understand just what a hit Hardy would be in London. Hardy had in fact already tattooed some other English tattooers while they were in America, including Dennis Cockell—at that point perhaps the most famous tattooer in London, given his work on celebrity clients including the Sex Pistols, Bananarama, and rockabilly band the Stray Cats. Cockell made several trips to the American West Coast to acquire from Hardy a torso filled with nine dragons, and would offer teasing glimpses of this astonishing piece to friends and customers who had not seen anything like it in their lives. In terms of its stylistic and technical evolution at the time, the British scene was less obviously progressive than its Californian counterpart. But there were a number of artists who

were producing incredibly proficient work—Ian of Reading, George Bone, and Derek Campbell, to name just a few—and the London punk scene provided the city with a particular energy, which Hardy of course found intoxicating.

In 1980, a young punk tattooer called Lal Hardy (no relation, though Lal would long refer to the elder tattooer teasingly as "Uncle Ed") spotted a man having lunch in a café on Finchley Road. Peeking out of the collar of the man's shirt was a neck tattoo of a large black and gray hawk—something uncommon back then, even though some London punks had begun to sport visible tattoos. Lal did a double-take. It was, of course, Ed Hardy, taking time out from tattooing at Cockell's to grab a bowl of pasta.

Lal's work, which drew upon the cut-up and collage styles of punk 'zines, gave Hardy another stylistic thrill. Lal's pinups were edgier than Sailor Jerry's, raw and hard, forged in rain-swept Britain rather than tropical Hawaii, and dressed like real women on the punk scene rather than Jerry's girl-next-door fantasies. In a letter, Hardy praised: "I like your mohican designs and think you have hit on a really original thing, being able to express the wild youth design contingent so ably ... The force you have coming across in the designs for the most part is great." In another, he wrote, "There will be lots of interesting work in England inspired by the music, and people like you understand." So impressed was Hardy with Lal's "new wave" of punk tattooing (a moniker, incidentally, that Lal would take as the name for his shop) that he included one of Lal's tattoos in the first issue of *TattooTime*.

In 1982, Ed extended Lal an invite to work at the Queen Mary convention in Long Beach, alongside

Quality Irons Born in Philadelphia, Greg Irons forged a long but precarious career as an illustrator before being drawn to tattooing in the late 1970s. He quickly became one of the hottest talents in the industry, working for Hardy at Realistic and bringing his graphic, illustrative style—as seen on the flash sheets and flyer here—to skin. Tragically, he was hit by a bus in Thailand in 1984 and died aged just thirty-seven years old.

Cockell. Ed had gathered together a pantheon of tattooers, including Greg Irons, Leo Zulueta, Bob Roberts, Mike Malone, and Jack Rudy, among many, many more, to put on a convention that Lal recalls as "mind-blowing" and "inspirational." After the convention, Lal headed up to Hardy's studio; coming from London, where tattoo business could be slow and walk-ins were the bread-and-butter of any shop, Lal was astonished to see Hardy humbly and graciously redirect a customer who was seeking an entire backpiece to Irons, because he thought Greg's style would better suit the piece.

In 1984, Ed worked his first UK tattoo convention in Buxton, Derbyshire, tattooing and selling copies of *TattooTime*, noting in his Christmas message to Lal that year that "the quality of brilliant British and European work was inspiring." That year, he had also invited Lal to contribute a whole article to *TattooTime*'s third issue. It's evident that Ed held British tattooing in high regard, and even began ordering needles from Lal's supply company. Their correspondence continued throughout the 1980s and 90s, with a stream of back-and-forth letters eagerly sharing the newest developments in their art, swapping gossip, and doing business with each other.

Presciently, a letter from Hardy to Lal dated March 5, 1990, reads: "I would like to get together and visit next time I'm in England. I'm very keen on the old time stuff as you know, and a few of the current artists. I do think the new old style is what will be happening in the 90s, mixed in with the stuff that's been popular over the last 20 years. I will be featuring quite a lot of this stuff—what one guy calls 'American Psychotic'—in the next *TattooTime*."

Trends and Connections

In light of *TattooTime*'s oppositional account of many of the same people and practices documented in *Modern Primitives*, it is clear that Vale and Juno's book is not a document of a coherent group of people who all sought to use tattooing, body piercing, and other ritual practices to separate themselves from the modern world. Rather, it is the presentation of at least two interrelated groups of people who, by 1989, had been working in close geographic proximity for a decade using similar aesthetics and technological processes for often entirely oppositional ends. But both Musafar and Hardy must then jointly share the credit as popularizers for bringing the blackwork "tribal" style from its brave experimental beginnings into the cultural mainstream.

Trends come and go, but there are essentially four pillars of the modern Euro-American tattoo industry: Traditional (or "old-school"), Orientalist, black and gray, and blackwork. Each of these is defined by a combination of design and technique, and all other styles are arguably subcategories, iterations, combinations, or variations of these primary genres. During the 1980s, Hardy revived, canonized, and popularized the first two, and incubated the second two through patronage and publication. It's Hardy's world, and we just live in it.

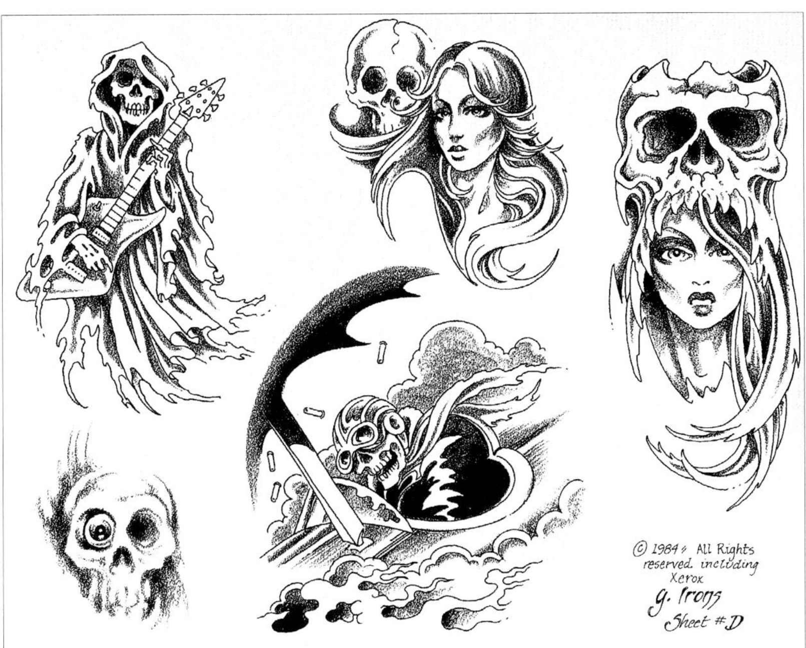
© 1984 ♦ All Rights
reserved, including
Xerox
G. Irons
Sheet #D

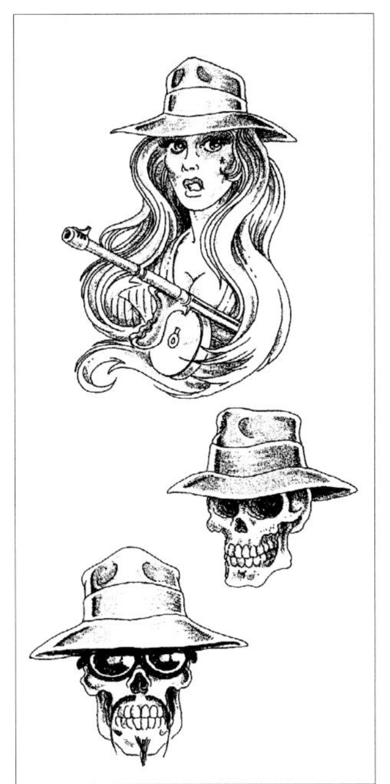

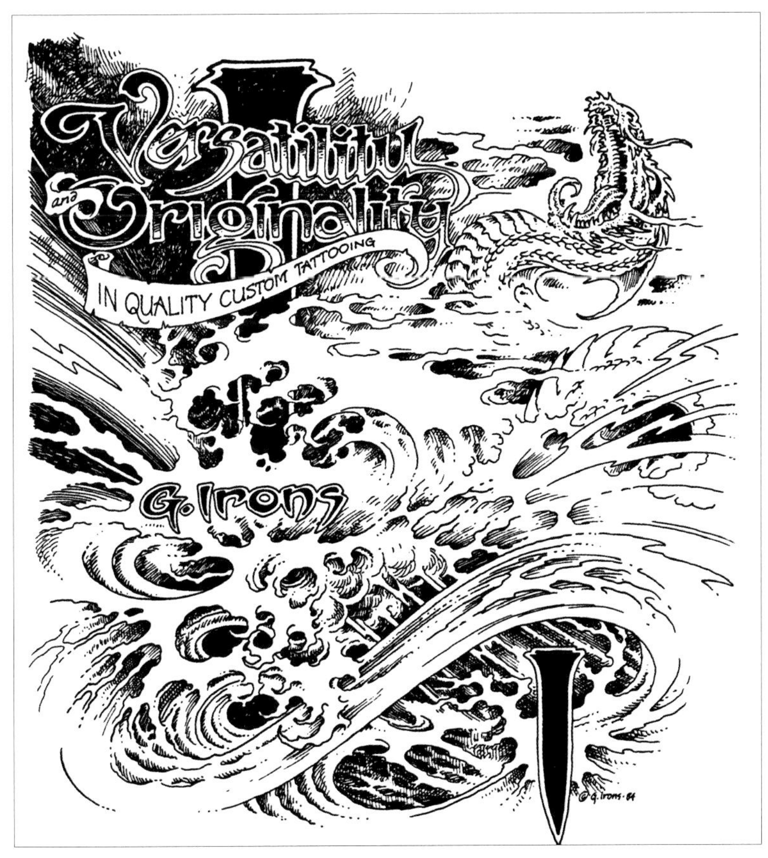
Versatility
and Originality
IN QUALITY CUSTOM TATTOOING
G. Irons

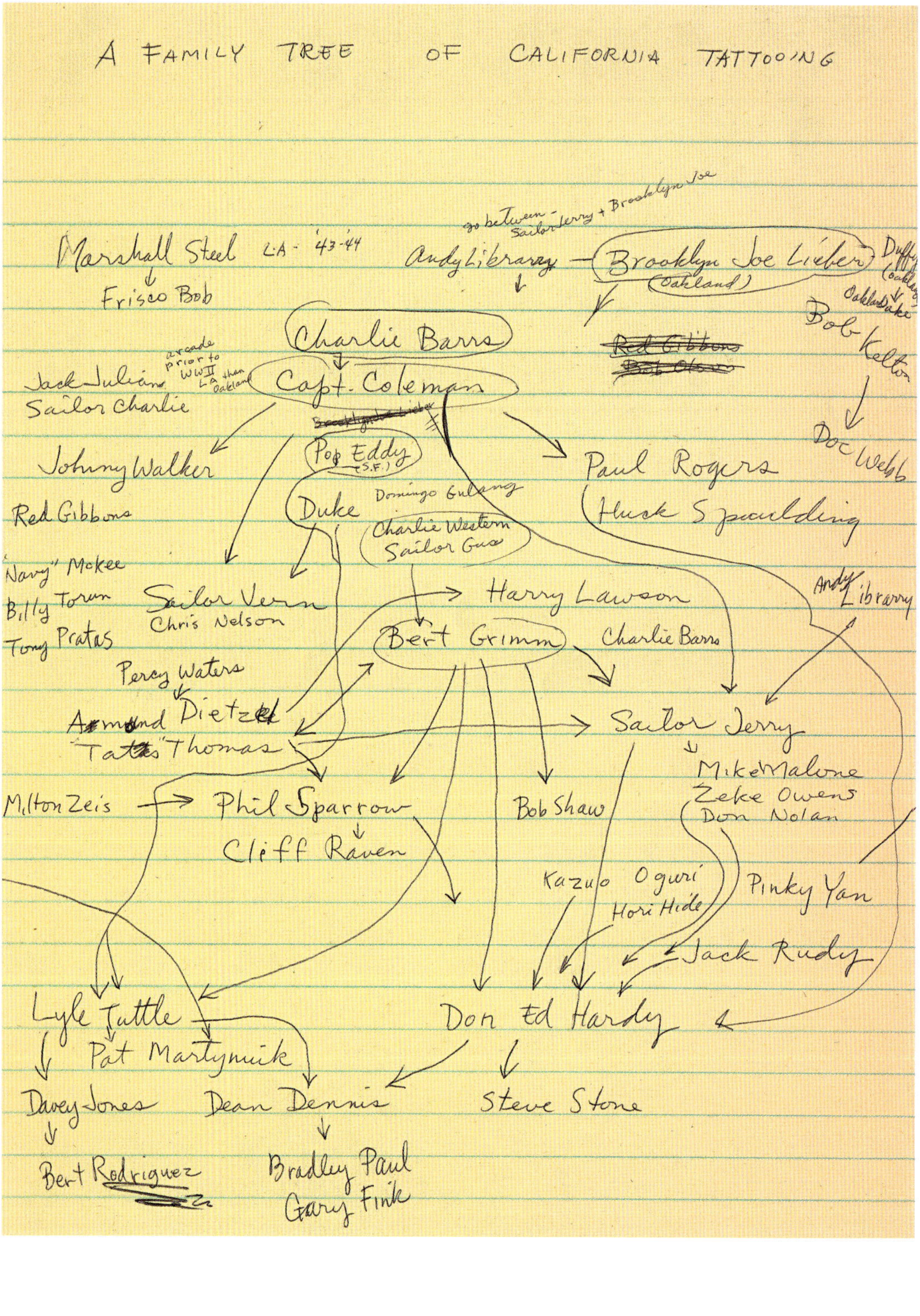

A FAMILY TREE OF CALIFORNIA TATTOOING

Marshall Steel LA - '43-'44
↓
Frisco Bob

go between -
Sailor Jerry + Brooklyn Joe
Andy Librarry — Brooklyn Joe Lieber
(Oakland)
Duffy
(Oakland)
Oakland Lake
Bob Kelton
↓
Doc Webb

Charlie Barrs
↓
arcade prior to WWII then LA then Oakland
Jack Julian
Sailor Charlie
Capt. Coleman
Brooklyn Lieber
Red Gibbons
Bert Olson

Pop Eddy
(S.F.)
Johnny Walker
Red Gibbons
Duke
Domingo Gulang
Charlie Western
Sailor Gus
Paul Rogers
Husk Spaulding

"Navy" McKee
Billy Torun
Tony Pratas
Sailor Vern
Chris Nelson
Harry Lawson
Andy Librarry

Bert Grimm
Charlie Barrs

Percy Waters
↓
Armand Dietzel
"Tattes" Thomas
Sailor Jerry
Mike Malone
Zeke Owens
Don Nolan

Milton Zeis →
Phil Sparrow
Cliff Raven
Bob Shaw

Kazuo Oguri
Hori Hide
Pinky Yan
Jack Rudy

Lyle Tuttle
↓
Pat Martynuik
↓
Davey Jones
↓
Bert Rodriguez
Dean Dennis
↓
Bradley Paul
Gary Fink
Don Ed Hardy
↓
Steve Stone

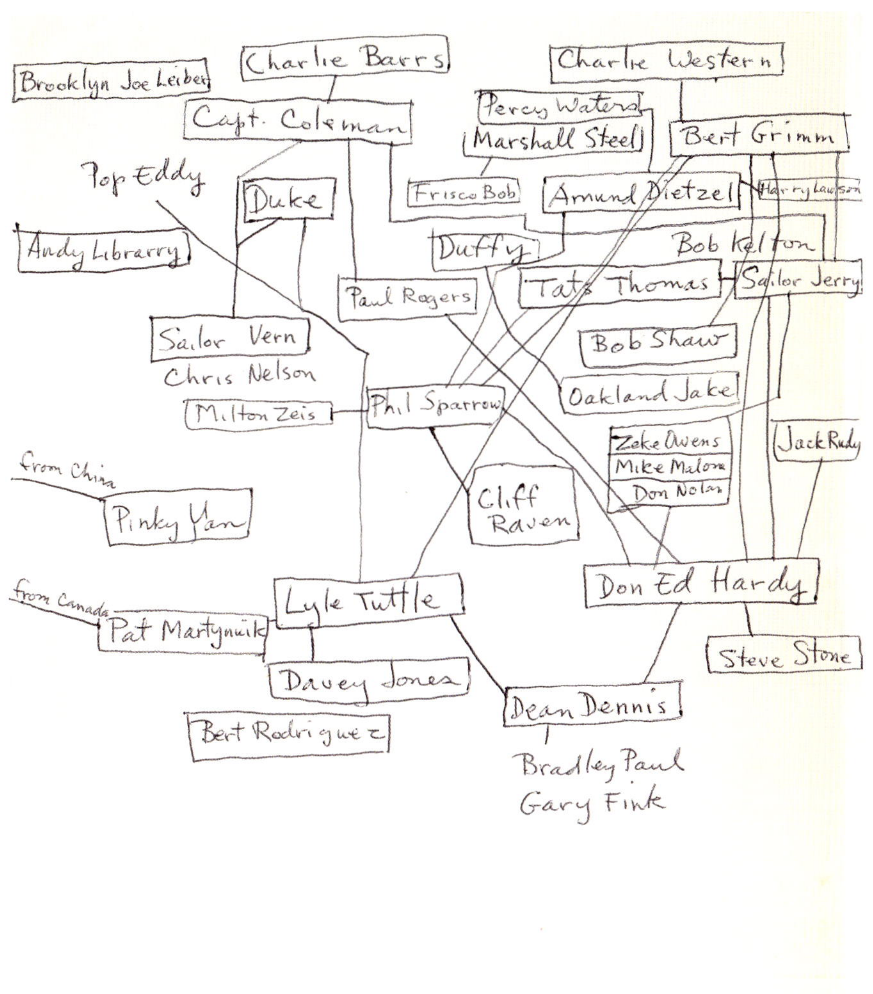

Family Trees of California Tattooing (production notes for Tattoo [exh.], Oakland Museum of California, June 7–August 7, 1977), *left* **attributed to Ed Hardy;** *above,* **author unknown**

These "family trees" (two of three produced) are archived with materials collected for the Tattoo exhibition in Oakland. Resembling (perhaps deliberately) Alfred Barr's famous 1936 diagram of the roots of modernist art, they are clearly intended to help the curatorial team, led by Jeffrey Long, understand the depth of influences that undergirded the contemporary tattoo scene in California. They were produced in discussions with Ed Hardy, and root the vibrant community of artists in the 1970s back to the early 20th century.

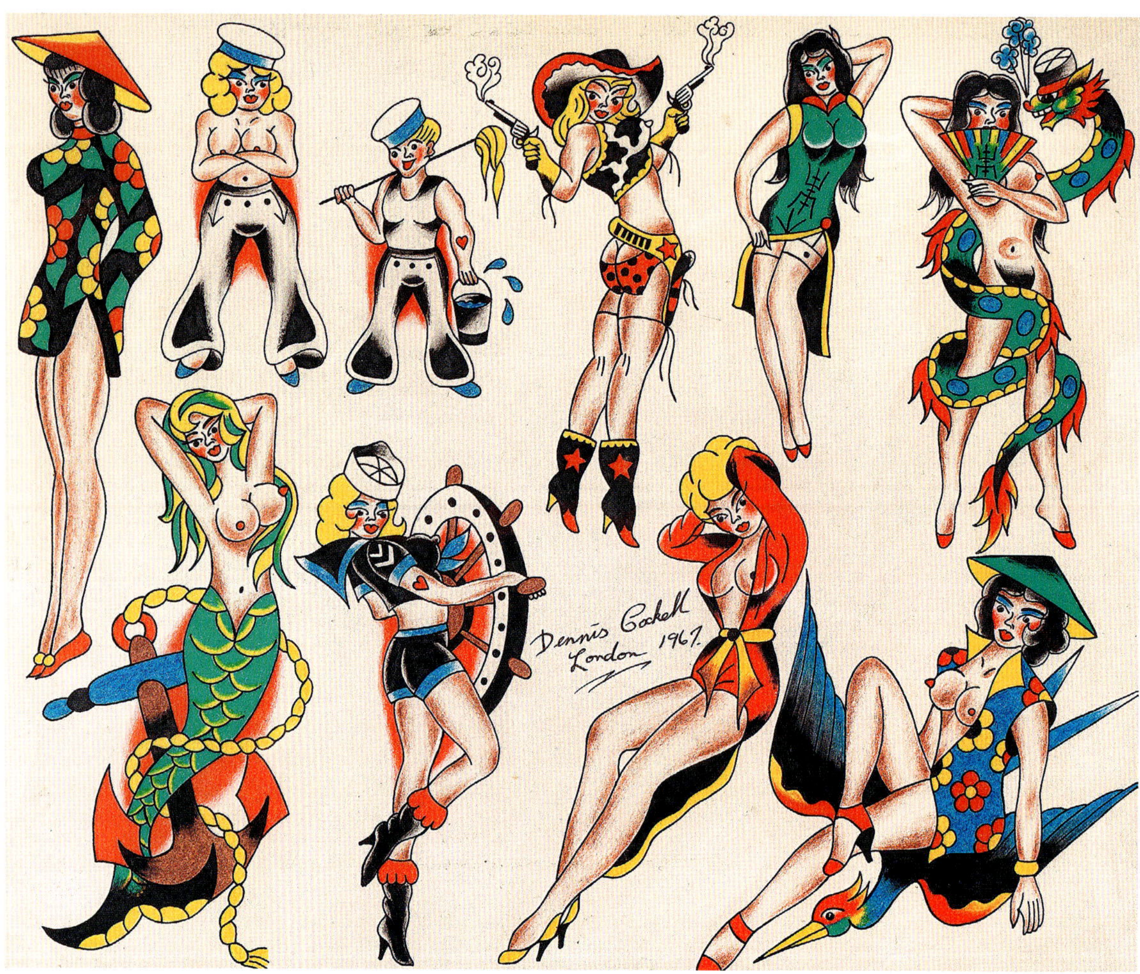

Pinups, flash by Dennis Cockell, 1967 (*above*)

Cockell's flash from the 1960s is stylistically informed by American tattoo traditions as distributed through supply companies such as Zeis, Spaulding and Rogers, and Chicago Tattoo Supply. Once the British scene was intimately connected with the trends and developments in the United States, British artists like Cockell inevitably worked in the same fashionable vernacular. Note the limited colors used here—green, red, yellow, and blue—indicative of the narrow range of pigments affordably and usefully available for tattooing in the period.

Fighting dragons, flash by Dennis Cockell, 1985 (*right*)

Following his encounters with him, Cockell's work shows huge and direct influence from Ed Hardy. Cockell here renders traditional Chinese ink-scroll dragons in an acidic color-palette which Hardy had popularized.

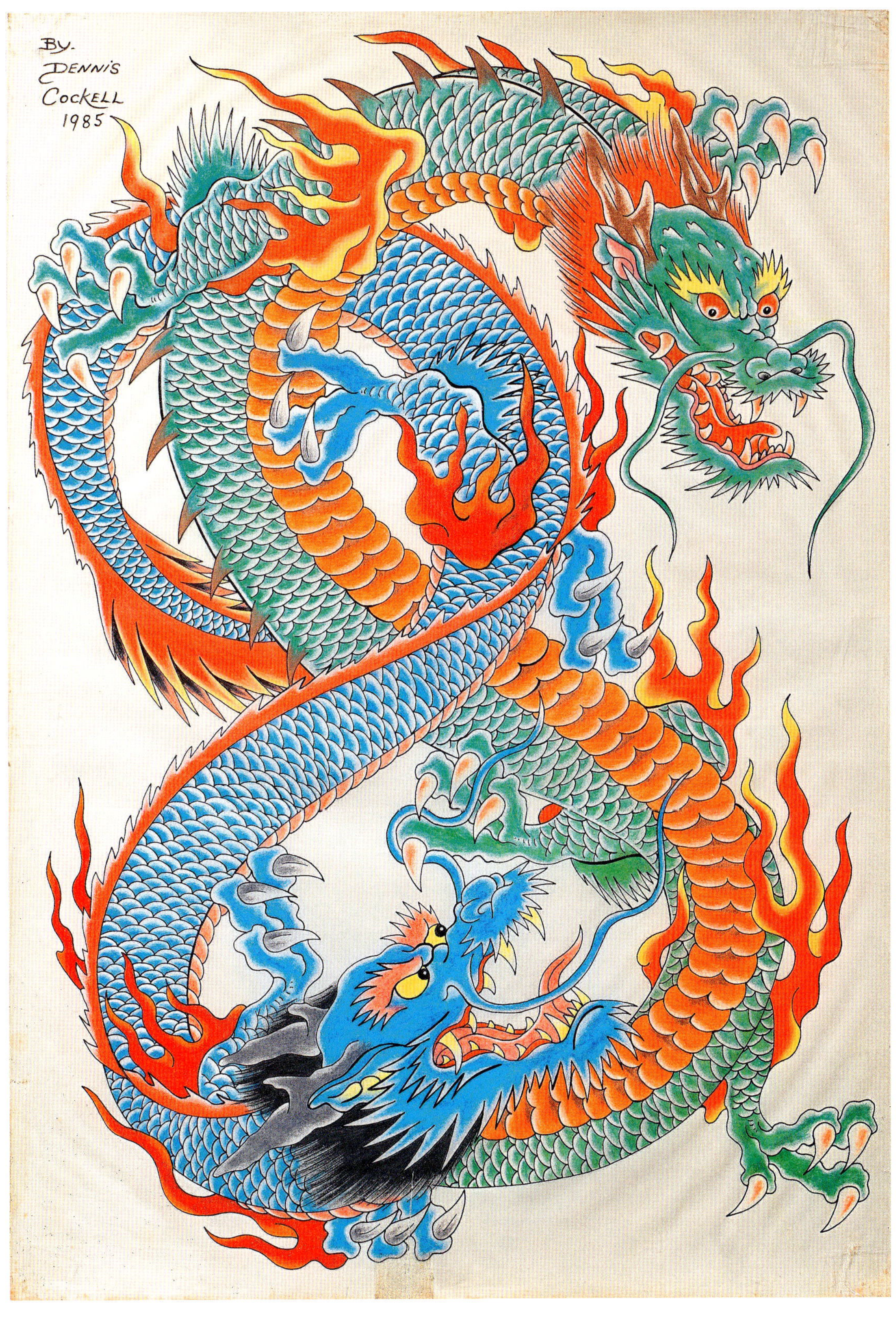
BY.
DENNIS
COCKELL
1985

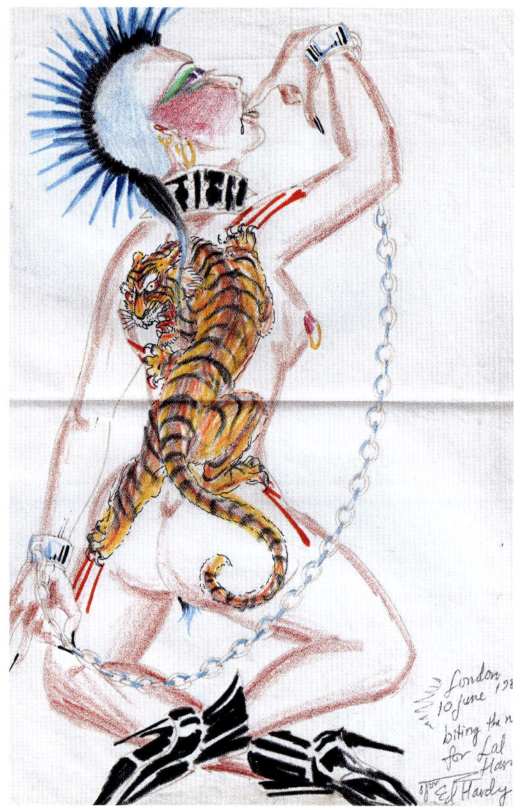

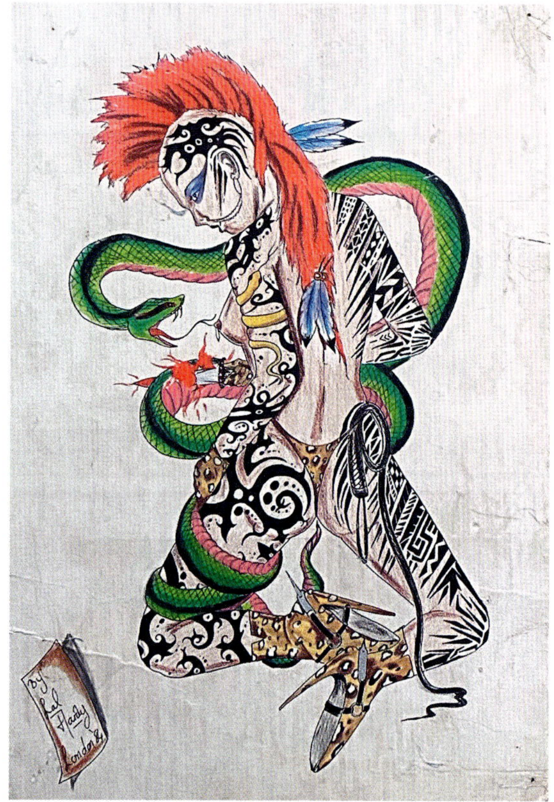

Tattooed pin-up by Ed Hardy, design for Lal Hardy, 1984 (*above left*); Tattooed pinup by Lal Hardy (based on a print source by Olivia Bernadini), 1984 (*above right*)

Ed Hardy's fertile period of discovery and adaptation in the late 1970s brought him to England to work alongside tattooers such as Ron Ackers and Dennis Cockell. The primary visual impact on his style in the period was from London's thronging punk scene: its fashion, its collage, and, of course, its tattooing. This design for a tattoo by Ed on London tattooer Lal Hardy's thigh (no relation) draws influence from Lal's own work, which Ed spread to a wide audience in the third edition of his *TattooTime* journal (1984).

Lal Hardy, photographer unknown, 1980s (*right*)

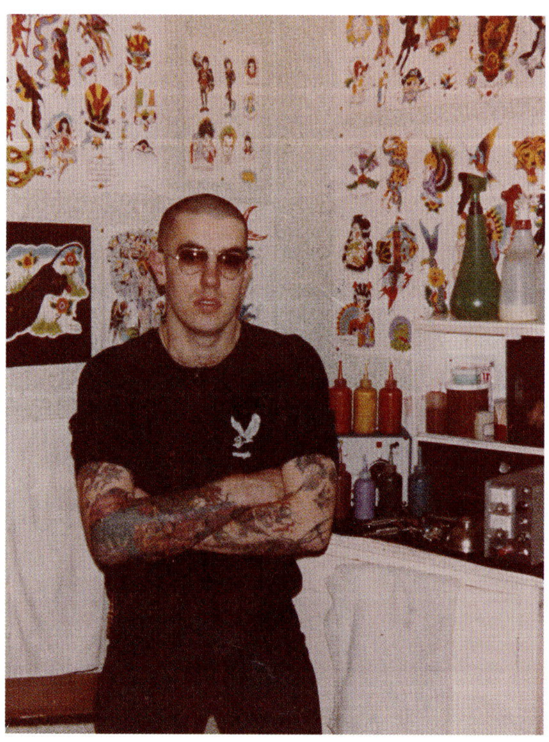

In *TattooTime 3*, Lal explains that "As with so many movements that are threatening to the status quo, the most shocking examples of tattooing were brought to the public eye and exaggerated. So although punk has added interesting influences to art, it has also helped reinforce the public's fear that tattooing is an underground and deviant practice as far as general taste and knowledge are concerned." This is, again, the central paradox of the so-called "tattoo renaissance," where increased visibility brought increased criticism.

**Flame from the Earth tattoo by
Davy Jones on Fakir Musafar,
c.1964**

Musafar drew inspiration for this
pioneering design from Native
American cultures he saw around him
growing up in South Dakota, and in
magazines like *National Geographic*.
By his own account, it depicts flame
coming from the earth. "I made a
large photograph of my back," he once
explained, "and I took what I saw in
my vision and sketched it on tissue-
paper. I started going around to various
tattoo artists and they'd look at this and
laugh. They'd say, 'You want that on
your back? How about a nice panther,
how about a rose, how about a dagger
with "Mom" in it?'"

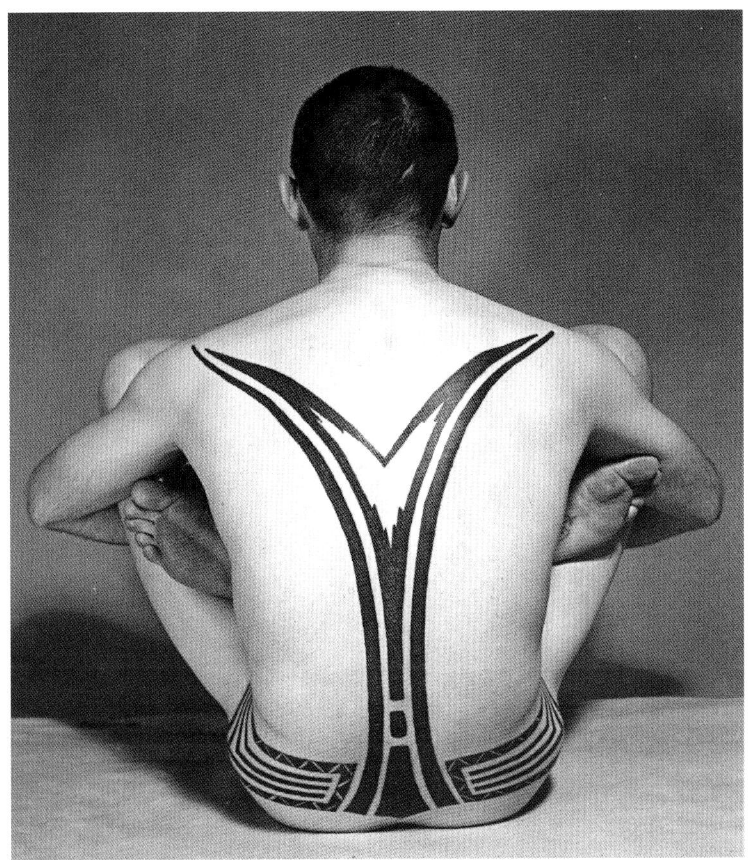

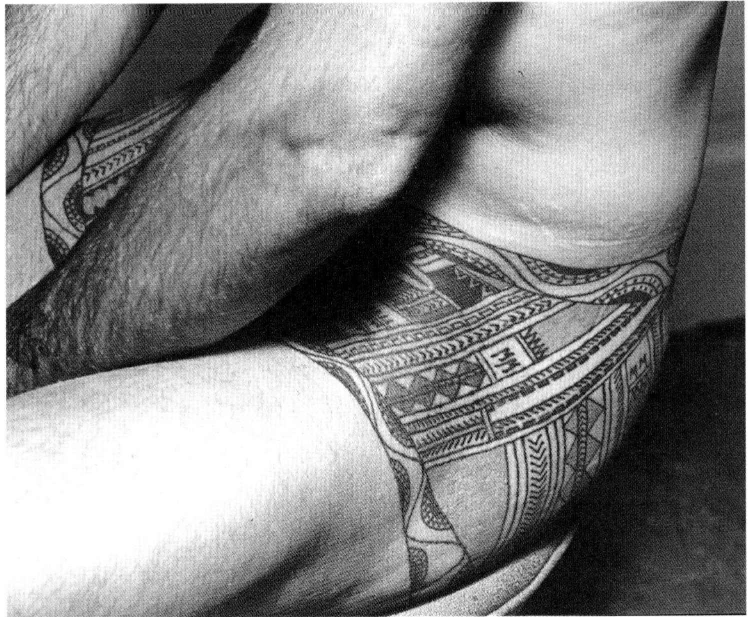

**Tattoos attributed to Davy Jones,
customer unknown, c. 1964**

This photo was one of a spread sent to
prospective publishers of Davy Jones
and Fakir Musafar's abortive book
project, *Tattooing: The Primitive Urge*
(c.1967). Presumably by Jones, these
intricately tattooed shorts take stylistic
cues from the Indigenous tattooing
practices of various peoples across
Micronesia in the Western Pacific.
Innocent and earnest, and undertaken
two decades before "tribal" tattooing
became a fully-fledged trend in Euro-
American tattooing, it is fascinating
to imagine just how much the visual
language of modern tattooing may
have changed, had these images been
published in the 1960s.

Chapter Ten

As Ancient as Time, as Postmodern as Tomorrow

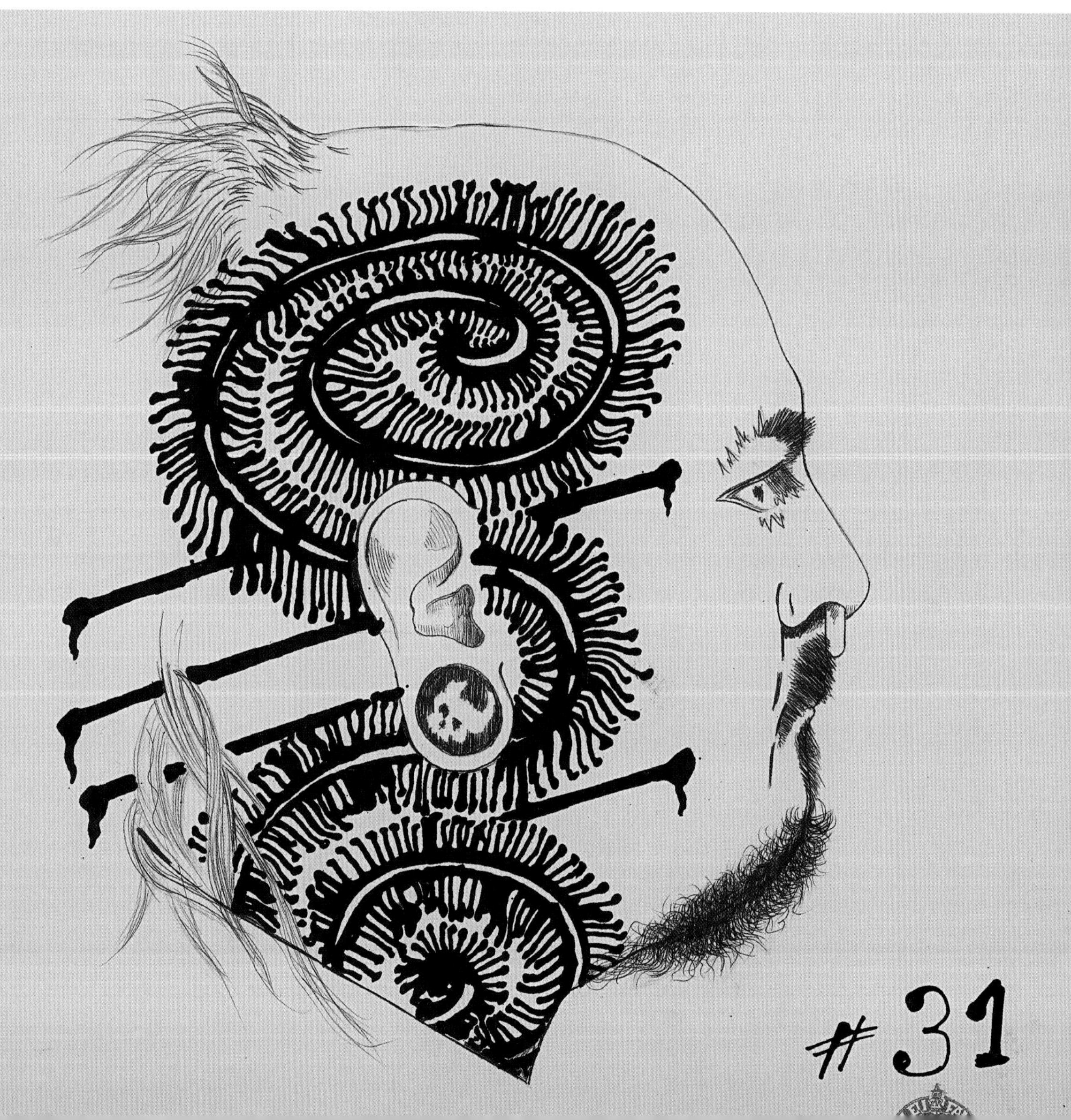

31

"Tattooing, once the exclusive and downmarket domain of sailors, soldiers and bikers, is to become a permanent feature at Selfridges, the favourite home of London's fashionistas."

Financial Times, 2003

A mark of the age This graphic facial tattoo was designed by Felix "Don Feliz" Leu for American tattooer Paul Booth in 2001, and tattooed by Filip Leu. The Leus' facial tattoo on Booth has become one of the most iconic tattoos of the early twentieth century. Felix worked up over forty ideas for the piece, inspired by expressive, abstract work on paper in Indian ink. As he had retired from tattooing, the final tattoo was executed by his son Filip.

After the fall of the Berlin Wall and the cultural complacency born by the end of the Cold War, the 1990s were—for middle-class urbanites in western Europe and America at least—a dull decade characterized by a popular culture generally riven by ennui and ironic detachment. Tattooing turned out to be something of an antidote to that bland homogeneity.

What followed the publication of *Modern Primitives* and the concurrent explosion of tattooing wrought by Hardy's patronage and dissemination was essentially the solidification of a recognizably contemporary tattoo industry. The connections between London, New York, Los Angeles, and San Francisco continued to be prominent ley lines for the most influential artists and shops in the industry, but the decade leading up to the new millennium marked the end of narrow, successive trend-cycles. In their place, in the 1990s tattoo world, anything was possible.

Tattooing in the 1990s felt so different from what preceded it, because, for the first time, the designs available to customers were so stylistically diverse. Professional tattooing in Europe and America had undergone a series of huge developments since its foundation as a proper trade, but (with few exceptions) these changes had been more or less serial: the small, religious woodblock stamps of the pilgrim tattooer became the hand-pricked handicraft icons of the Georgian sailor tattooer, which became the Japonesque reproductions of engravings in the early electric era, which became the smaller, scratchy military designs of World War I, which morphed into the bold, graphic cartoons of the mid-century, culminating eventually in the experimental diversity of the 1980s.

All of a sudden, several styles—black and gray, blackwork, Orientalist, and their hybridizations—existed everywhere all at once.

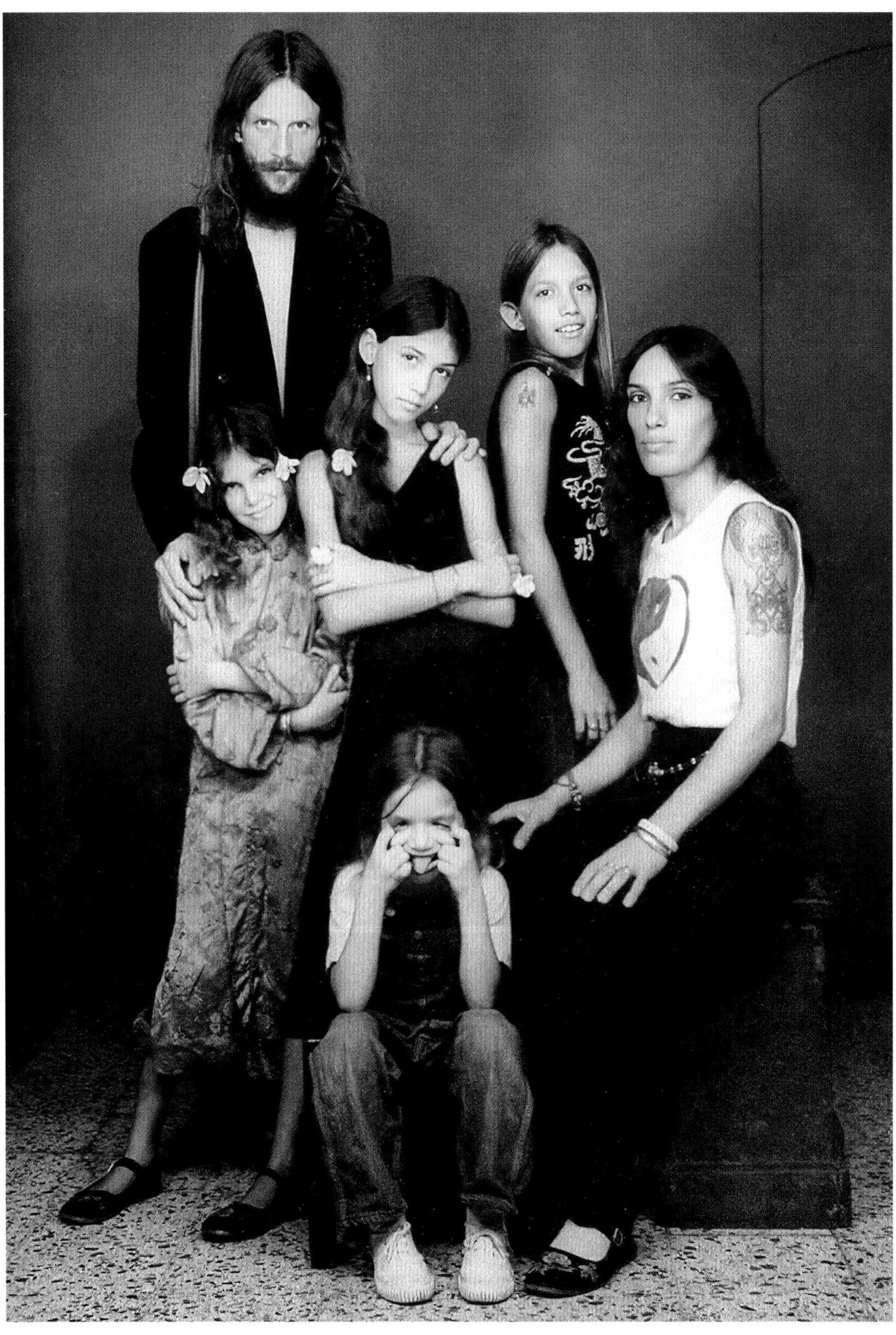

A family affair (*left*) Felix and Loretta
Leu with their children in Bombay, India,
in 1981. Aia, Ama, and Filip stand, while
Ajja sits playfully in front. The Leu family
stayed in Bombay for six months, working
with Jangoo Kohiyar, who was both a
tattooer and certified psychiatrist. Kohiyar
had long been a correspondent of tattoo
magazines in England, and was well-
connected to the Anglo-American scene.
He gifted Felix a copy of John Lemes's
controversial *Trade Secrets* booklet,
which Felix made sure to copy and share
with others.

Base of operations (*right*) The Leus
settled in Switzerland in 1981. Tattooing
was illegal in many Swiss cantons,
though it was permitted in Vaud, where
their chosen home of Lausanne is
located. Like Felix, Loretta, pictured here
tattooing in c.1982, was a trained artist,
having studied at the Brooklyn Museum
Art School, and the couple received joint
acclaim for their tattooing in this period.

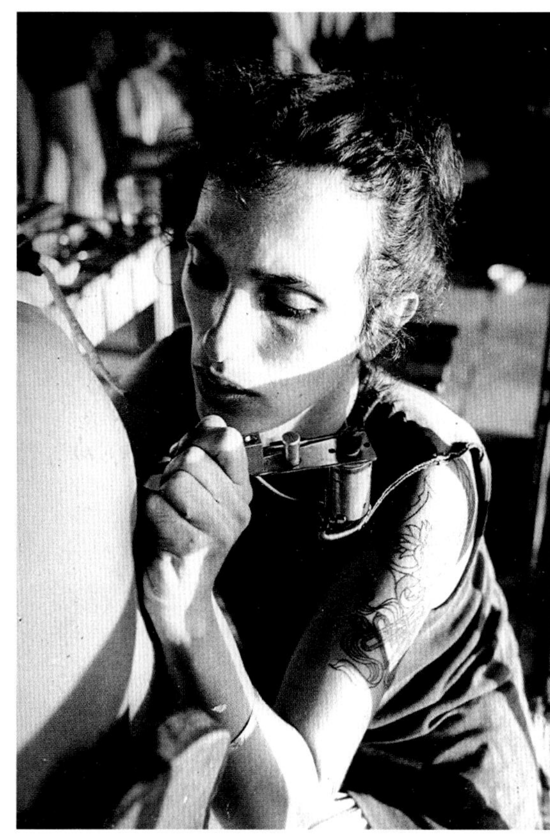

At the same time, the increasing visibility and circulation of tattooing's historical material flattened the visual lineages of Euro-American tattooing into a palimpsest, easily appropriated, revivified, and remixed into new forms. Through publications such as *TattooTime*, Lyle Tuttle's *Tattoo Historian*, and Shotsie Gorman's *Tattoo Advocate* artists and clients could learn about tattoo history and find inspiration for their next projects. Moreover, the building of collections of historic material by artists and enthusiasts such as Chuck Eldridge in the US, the Netherlands' Henk "Hanky Panky" Schiffmacher, and Paul Ramsbottom, Paul Sayce, Willy Robinson, and Lionel Titchener in Britain, saw the careful preservation of such material for the future, albeit beyond the embrace of institutional collections for the time being.

Increased ease of global travel and communication around the world further accelerated the emergence of creative, postmodern fusion styles, as artists interacted with diverse tattoo cultures, rendering the already magpie practice more porous than ever. Emblematic of this facet of the industry are Swiss tattooers Felix and Loretta Leu, their son Filip, and their wider Family Iron tattoo dynasty, which had begun in London in 1978. As travelers, hosts, and advocates for tattooing, the family have assumed a mantle of wise and inspirational leadership from their base near Lausanne.

Felix Leu was the son of Swiss artist Eva Aeppli and stepson to seminal kenetic artist Jean Tinguely. He had studied art at prestigious schools in America, and briefly worked with Tinguely and his new partner Niki de St Phalle in New York, but became disillusioned with the fine art scene and with urban American life. With Loretta, Felix went on to travel as a self-described free spirit, living a bohemian lifestyle, though often struggling for money. Fortuitously for the world of

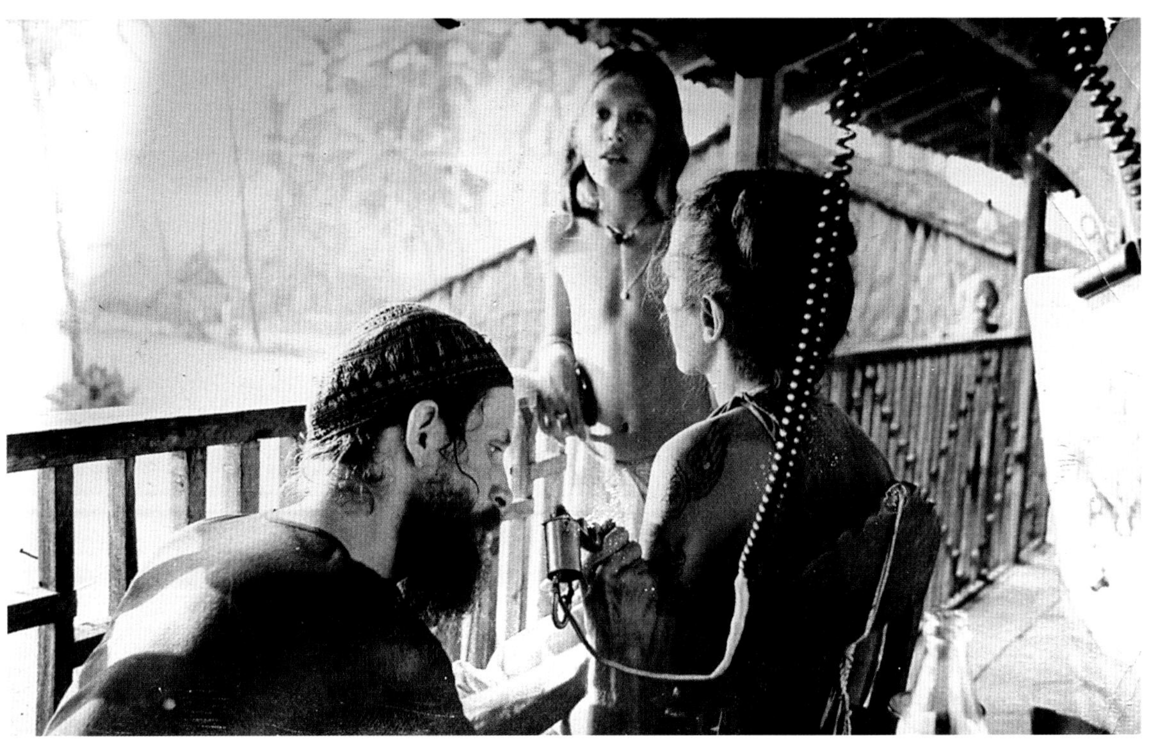

tattooing, while traveling in Kosovo in search of carpets that he could import to England, a number of local children approached him, waving handfuls of cash. Felix determined that the kids had incorrectly deduced that he and his tattooed traveling companion were perhaps itinerant tattooers, and wanted to engage their services. Though he could not oblige them, of course, he realized that tattooing might be a way to use his artistic talents to pay his bills and support his family, while still leaving him free to explore the world.

Felix was taught to tattoo by Jock Liddell, an old-school tattoo artist working out of a small, insalubrious booth near London's Kings Cross Station. Serendipitously, Lal Hardy was also learning his craft there at the same time. Squeezed together, the three men tattooed a rough set of clients, including skinheads and Hells Angels, all while Felix's young son Filip watched on, aged only about eleven years

old. After leaving London, the Leus tattooed in hippie destination Goa, India, then in Bombay, before ultimately returning to Switzerland, establishing their base of operations in Lausanne around 1981. Filip took time to study Japanese tattooing, taking inspiration from Horiyoshi III in Yokohama, and had (inevitably) also briefly worked for Ed Hardy in America. By the 1990s, the family had become standard-bearers for the new hybrid style, able to draw upon fine art, spit-and-sawdust tattoo traditions, and their closely observed knowledge of visual culture from across Southern Asia.

Filip's career output in particular has been prolific, characterized by innumerable, jaw-dropping Japonesque bodysuits which combine traditional motifs with a painterly and even often psychedelic style such that the finished tattoos are at once deeply resonant with tradition, while still being utterly recognizable as signature pieces.

Keeping it in the family (*left*) Felix Leu tattoos Loretta in India in 1979, as Filip observes. The design being produced here is Loretta's first large-scale tattoo— an intricate and meaningful composition of symbols of love, freedom, spirituality, hope, and friendship. Felix tattooed locals and visiting hippies on a veranda, sheltering under an umbrella during heavy monsoon rains.

Top billing (*right*) This 1981 advertising flyer for the Leu's first shop in Lausanne, Switzerland, shows both Felix and Loretta billed equally. In a sleepy Swiss town, the sprawling, tattooed, multilingual family of glorious hippies were exotic indeed, but their warmth and openness quickly enamored them to the locals.

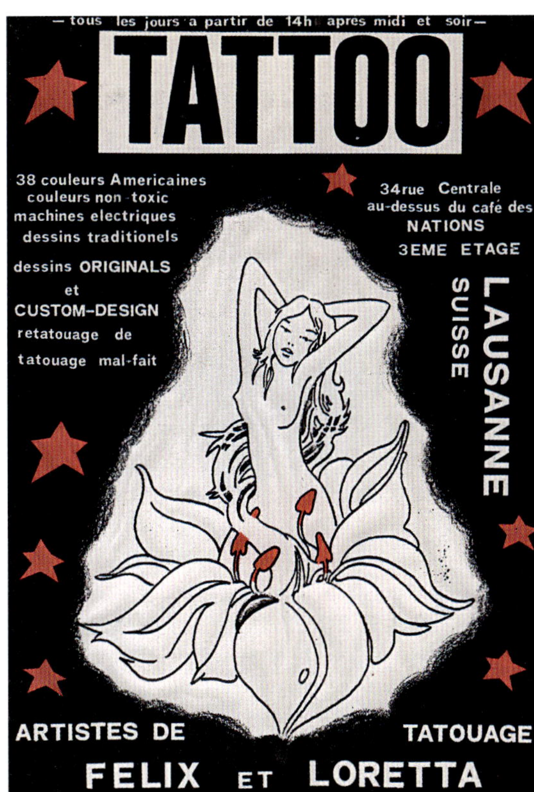

The Postmodern Tattoo

For some cultural critics of the period, the 1990s produced a hollowed-out, insincere popular culture which was, as philosopher Terry Eagleton summarized, "depthless, styleless, [and] dehistoricized," incapable of authenticity and driven only by ironic consumption. Indeed, many critics of *Modern Primitives* read the book—and the movement they imagined it represented— in precisely such terms, because its interviewees made shallow reference to an enormously wide range of cultural traditions from across human history.

But while Musafar's postmodern body play was certainly dehistoricized, it was not styleless. And while Hardy's postmodern championing of "new old styles" was styleless, insofar as it did not cleave closely to a single aesthetic, it could certainly not be described as depthless or dehistoricized. Euro-American tattooing had been denied a coherent account of its own historical depth due to a stubbornly persistent amnesia of its continuous presence in the Western world. As a result, the compacting of history in this postmodern moment, encouraged by publications like *TattooTime*, was precisely what enabled the tattoo industry to become anchored to its own distant pasts, and for new and revivified styles to catch fire.

Perhaps paradoxically then, both Hardy's and Musafar's visions of the future of tattooing came true at the same time. Conservative self-regulation by the European and American industries certainly didn't make tattooing a conventional or respectable profession, and the most prominent and celebrated artists faced the same ambiguous relationship to mainstream culture as their Victorian and Edwardian forebears. As in the late nineteenth century, even while late-twentieth-century tattooing was hailed as the height of fashion and the favored hobby of fickle

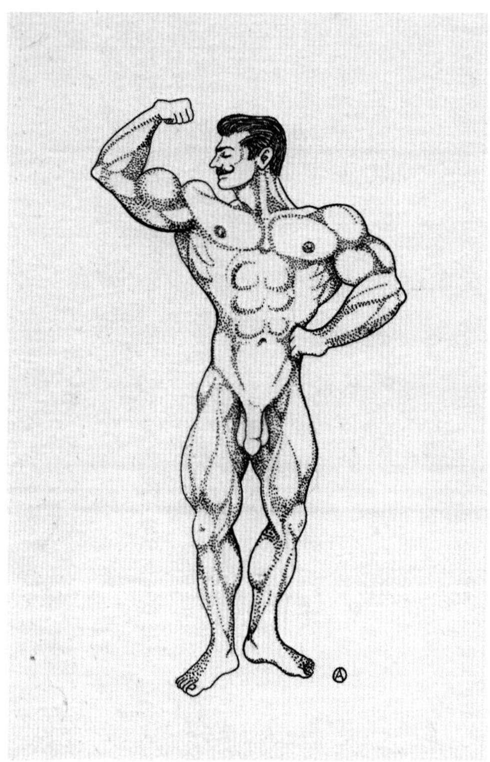

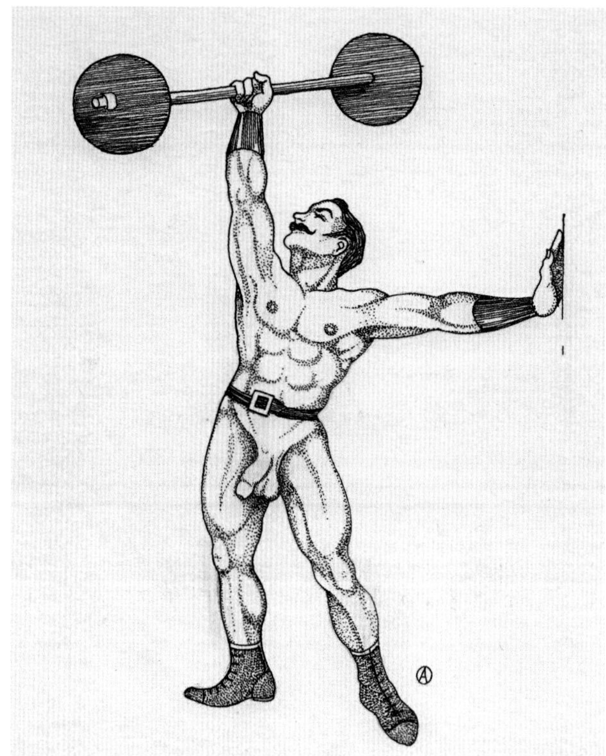

trendsetters, it remained strange, exotic, and confusing to most regular commentators. But a combination of improved hygiene techniques throughout the industry, an exponential increase in the quality and range of designs, and an influx of younger artists who had been directly inspired by both *TattooTime* and *Modern Primitives*, made tattooing increasingly attractive to a new generation of clients, without any diminishment of tattooing's edgy, antisocial appeal.

Mr. Sebastian

This interesting interplay between increased regulation on the one hand, and the revelation of the true strangeness and diversity of the industry, is also visible in how tattooing responded to the terrible scourge of the HIV/AIDs pandemic. Awareness of HIV had rapidly accelerated the standardization of sterilization and the use of disposable gloves for each tattoo

over the course of the 1980s, but it also forced the industry to confront its own homophobia, which led to a more open acknowledgment of the queer artists and customers who had been so instrumental in the forging of modern tattoo culture in the first place. In 1985, British industry trade-sheet *Tattoo Buzz*, for example, hosted a testy discussion about how best to respond to the perceived risks of HIV transmission during tattooing. The magazine fielded several letters from stubborn, homophobic artists who claimed they would refuse to tattoo any clients they imagined might be gay. The response from the magazine's editorial team was derisive mockery, openly chastizing the pearl-clutching correspondents and reminding them that, firstly, many tattooers were gay; secondly, it was not actually possible to determine sexuality by sight; and thirdly, tattooing was supposed to be a hard-edged, risky business. ("A puritanism has developed

Heavy lifting (*left*) Much of Mr. Sebastian's flash was very explicit, featuring beautifully-rendered illustrations of heavy sadomasochistic gay sex. These circus strongmen designs from c.1990 are among the least explicit drawings by him remaining.

Cock of the walk (*right*) Though he did work from flash, among Mr. Sebastian's most famous work was custom designs for his clients. He often tattooed on body parts that were not visible unless the client was completely naked—his portfolio was filled with photographs of intimate tattoos on an almost entirely male customer base. This photo, of a cockerel design by Mr. Sebastian on customer and lover "Bryan the Dog," was among those seized by British police during Operation Spanner.

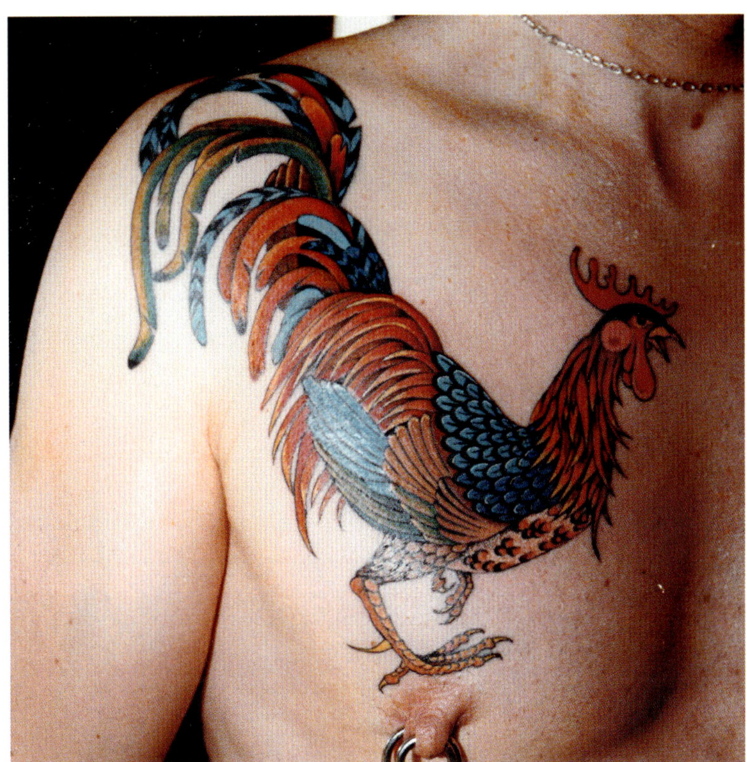

in this business," the editorial sighed, "which holds its hands up in horror at anything deemed by some to be unhygienic or too-oo risky. I hope that I shall never fear a Tattoo Parlour, Shop, Grott Studio, Clinic, Surgery, Tabernacle or whatever.")

The most high-profile gay tattooer in Britain was Alan Oversby, working under the professional pseudonym Mr. Sebastian. Unlike Musafar, who had become enamored with piercing through a fascination with anthropological magazines, Oversby had first seen piercings in the context of needle-play at gay, sadomasochistic orgies. Though Musafar and Oversby were friendly with each other, the Englishman's approach to body modification in general was also not definable in "primitive" terms.

Oversby was art-school trained, had worked as an art teacher in Liverpool, and was the only living English tattoo artist whose work featured in *Modern Primitives*. He worked on a mainly gay male client base in London from the late 1970s onward—including Rudi Inhelder—and is also recognized as one of the primary innovators of body piercing as a professional, public-facing practice, opening the first body-piercing studio in Britain. Though clearly not close to the central hub of British tattooing, preferring to work quietly in a private studio, his contemporaries speak warmly of him, he features proudly and prominently in several documentaries about British tattooing in the period, and was a regular feature at conventions. He is also another important link between London and California, and between the queer pockets of the industry and the more visible creative orbit of Ed Hardy, having been tutored in tattooing by—among others—Cliff Raven. His career was briefly derailed in the late 1980s and early 90s when he was caught up in Operation Spanner, a police crackdown on homosexual

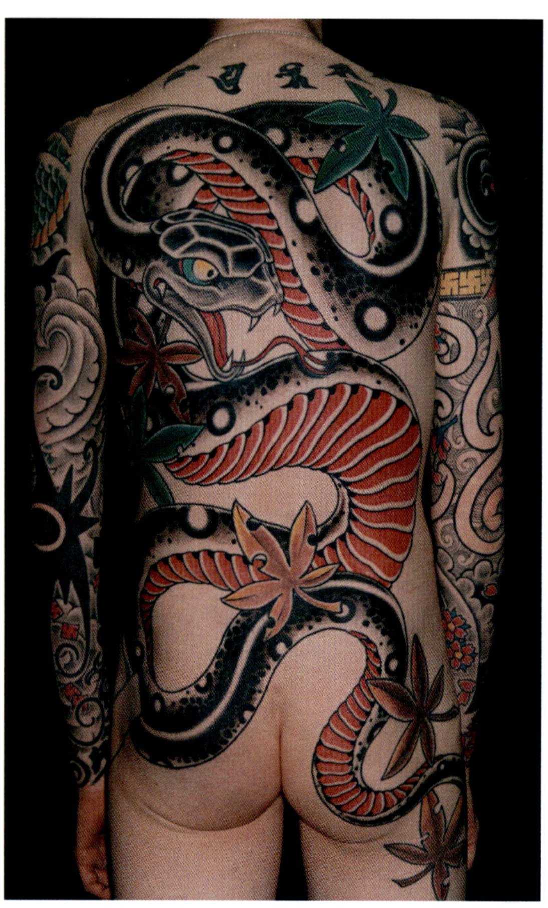

Something old, something new (*left*)
This syncretic work by Alex Binnie on his customer Desmond combines a graphic, negative-space take on "tribal" designs with a modern take on an Orientalist serpent. Binnie's tattooing is characterized by its powerful deployment of traditional motifs and styles, drawing upon the classic vernacular of tattooing's past while at the same time forging something resolutely modern.

Controversial scenes (*right*) Binnie first tattooed seminal performance artist Ron Athey, pictured, in Los Angeles, whilst working at Gauntlet in the early 1990s. Athey allowed Binnie to tattoo him extensively, including on the face, and the two became lifelong friends. Athey is infamous in art history as one of the most vilified faces of the so-called Culture Wars of the 1980s, as his controversial, bloody work on topics of AIDS and religion drew ire from conservative lawmakers in both America and the UK.

S&M, during which he received a suspended prison sentence for having carried out consensual genital piercing on a boyfriend. But as body piercing and tattooing increasingly became a mainstream fashion trend, he became very, very busy as his client base expanded far beyond the narrow bounds of the gay male community.

The strangeness and novelty of piercing, the air of risk cultivated by the meddling of the police, and the publicity that resulted from a failed attempt by London's Obscene Publications Squad to ban *Modern Primitives* certainly helped drive Oversby's business to some degree, while his genteel professionalism, art-school training, and scrupulous attention to hygiene practices made it possible for anxious style columnists to enter his tattoo studio, even as its walls were festooned with photographs of tattooed genitalia. "I don't mind being branded a fashion victim," wrote *The Independent*'s style columnist, who had made an appointment to have her navel pierced, "but an S&M victim I am not."

Oversby's edgy appeal also enamored him to younger tattoo collectors who felt alienated from the more conventional old-timers still working in London. Genesis P-Orridge of cult industrial band Throbbing Gristle proudly shows off his Mr. Sebastian tattoos in *Modern Primitives*, for example; and in a documentary called *Pigments of the Imagination*, first released in 1985, Oversby appears with a young, naked client whose nipples have been covered in heavy black Xs, and who sports an enormous backpiece of the Archangel Gabriel derived from a fifteenth-century German altarpiece.

This young client, Alex Binnie, would go on to form yet another link in the chain binding London and Californian tattooing. Binnie, born in 1959, had been obsessed with tattoos since childhood, and though he had acquired some small pieces at the end of the

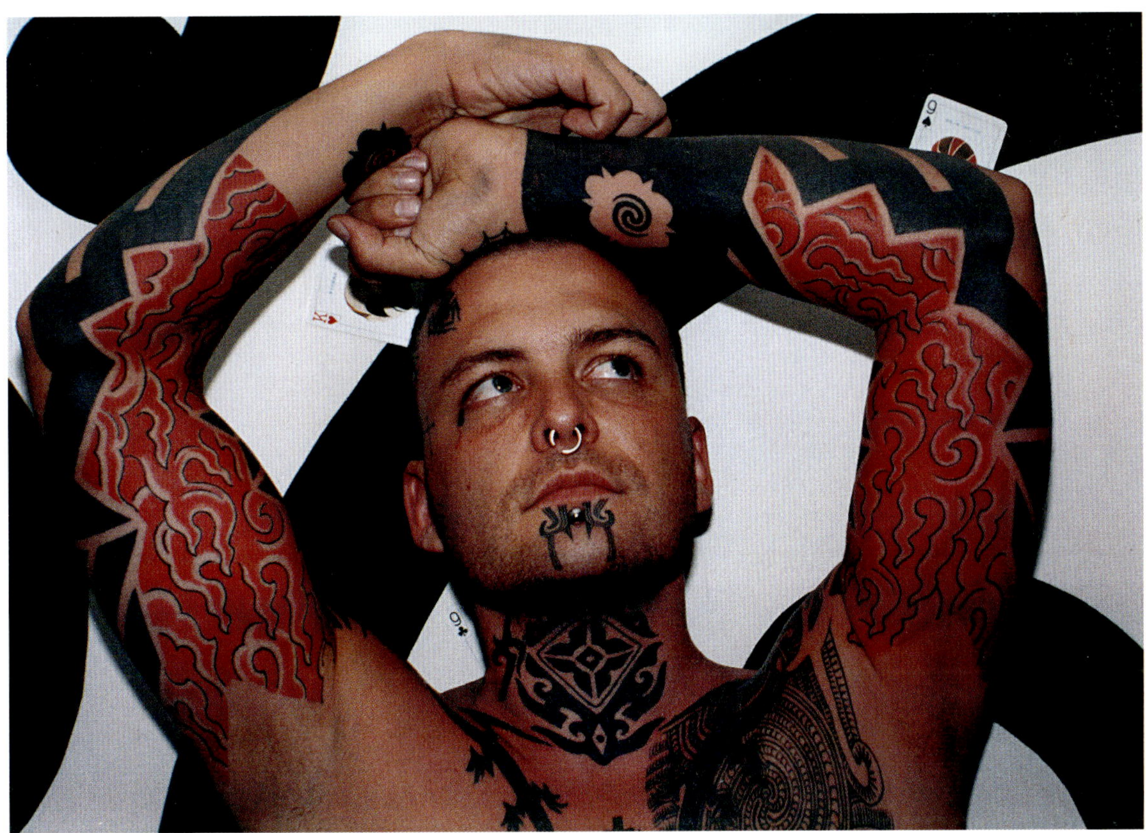

1970s—his first was done at the Great Gear Market on London's King's Road—he became increasingly uninterested in the type of work he saw being done in the UK at the time. After a period producing performance work at art school in Cardiff ("getting dirty and naked"), he returned to London with a vague but increasingly passionate interest in the possibilities of tattooing as an art-making process. *TattooTime* provided some inspiration, and as he became integrated with the postpunk and industrial scenes blossoming around London, he realized he could turn his hand to tattooing, at first working on his friends out of a squat just off Russell Square, London.

Though he had begun to make inroads into the tattoo scene, attending an early London convention at the Hammersmith Palais in 1987, and making sure to meet and learn from people like Lal Hardy and George Bone, it was clear that this upstart art-school kid

working out of a squat was not entirely welcomed with open arms by the old guard. Such was the opprobrium he generated that in 1989, *Tattoo Buzz* magazine called him "arrogant" and "worse than a scratcher," pondering "how anybody has ever taken [him or his] thoughts seriously."

That year Binnie attended the last Amsterdam convention held by Henk Schiffmacher at the Paradiso, meeting a host of American tattooers whose work he had long admired, including Ed Hardy, Freddy Corbin, and Chuck Eldridge. As well as this pantheon of tattooing superstars, he also met the woman he would go on to marry—Elayne Angel, piercer at the legendary Gauntlet in LA, early pioneer of the tongue piercing, and owner of one of the most iconic tattoos of the 1990s (a large pair of wings done by Bob Roberts, which was the first tattoo ever to receive trademark protection in the US)—and who would give Binnie his first job in a

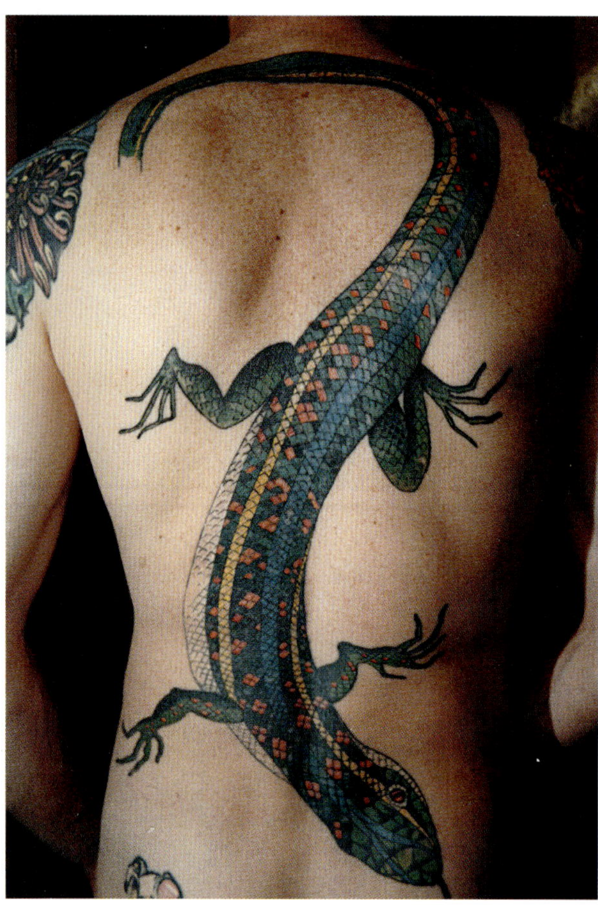

Varying techniques (*left*) Unlike most other tattooers, who would produce an outline first, shading second, and coloring third—over several sessions if necessary— Oversby completed this large salamander backpiece in fully completed sections, rendering a part of the finished design before moving on to the next.

It's alive! (*right*) Aaron Cain is one of the forerunners in the biomechanical style which emerged in the 1990s. This flash sheet adapts fashionable "tribal" designs into organic, ossified forms which resemble extraterrestrial weaponry and organs. Note, too, the eyeball at the upper right, which appears to be emerging from under a rippling alien skin.

tattoo shop. Following the convention, Binnie flew to America to be tattooed by Leo Zulueta, perhaps the most important early influence on his work after Mr. Sebastian, and immediately fell in love with Elayne, marrying her after what he fondly terms a "passionate love affair," and working out of a room at Gauntlet.

Gauntlet was a visionary space which brought body piercing out from the gay subcultures of Southern California and onto the high street, generating and making visible a specific and productive scene of people. Set up in 1975 by Jim Ward, a correspondent and friend of Mr. Sebastian's, Gauntlet's clientele were brave and exciting, and Binnie tattooed people who were bolder and more experimental than his clients in London had been, including performance artist Ron Athey. Binnie was almost immediately producing large, full-body blackwork, tattooing throats and hands, and generally able to push his own

boundaries and those of his customers into interesting new territories.

Such was the effect of his American trip on his reputation back home that four years to the month after having been called out in *Buzz*, the magazine (still under the same editor) gave him a full-page column to announce his triumphant return to the UK. By the time he arrived back in London in 1993, after brief stints working in Seattle and San Francisco (including a short stay at Hardy's Tattoo City), he knew he wanted to recreate some of that same culture back home—an American-style shop, with multiple artists working under one roof (a rarity in the UK at the time, when most tattooers worked alone in a small, cramped space). Moreover, he wanted a space that would be open to the public, like an American street shop, but producing only custom work. The shop, Into You, was initially set up by his friend and body-piercer

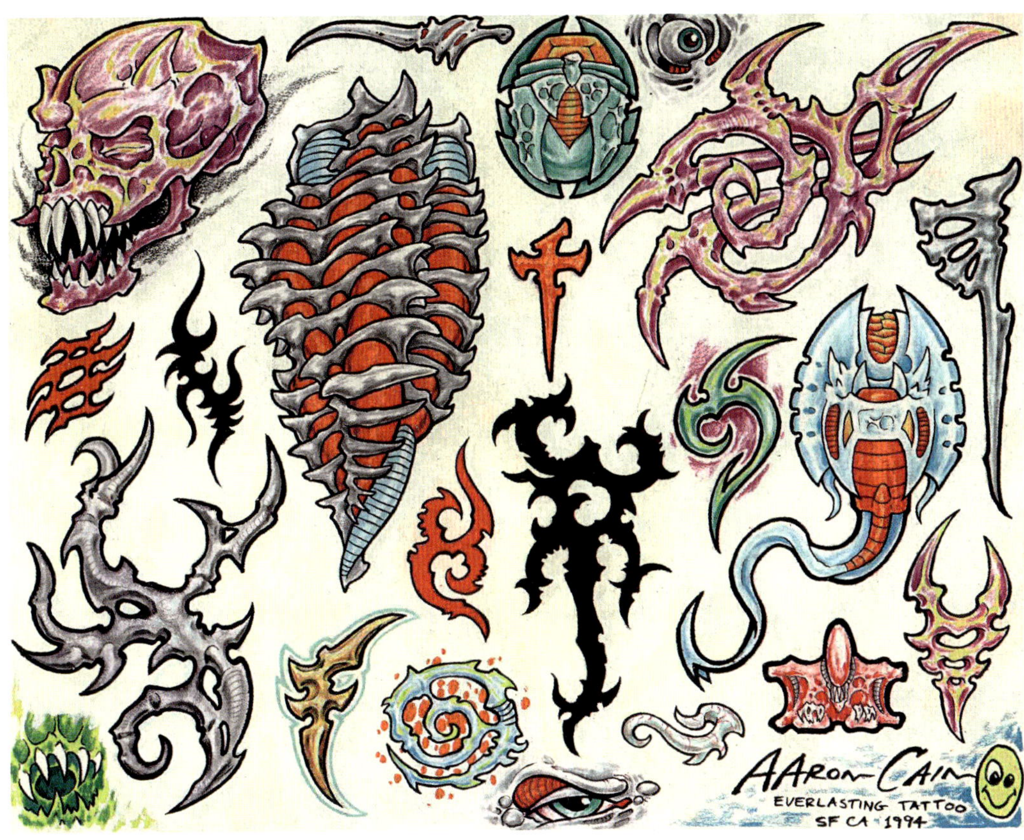

Teena-Marie, though Binnie "decided [he] wanted in," as "London really [was] behind other major cities abroad." The pair were soon joined by shop manager Blue, and another artist, Andreas "Curly" Moore. Uniquely for the time, there was no flash on the walls; instead, the spacious entrance room was used as gallery space for visual and creative artists. As Curly was also well known for large-scale blackwork tattooing with a "tribal" vibe, Into You became the primary driver of the introduction of that style into Britain, hosting many of the genre's key British innovators, including Xed LeHead, as well many other artists who would go on to legendary careers in their own right.

Tattooing for Cyborgs

The flip-side of the trend for blackwork tattooing in the 1990s was its visual and ideological antithesis: the biomechanical style, or biomech. Rather than drawing upon atavistic, appropriative styles approximating indigenous traditions, biomechanical tattooing imagines a cyborg human-machine fusion. Biomech tattooing usually works at large scale, aiming to create a trompe-l'oeil effect, which transforms the appearance of the fleshy, fragile human body into something resembling a scene from a David Cronenberg movie. The effect is of a skin-tear, revealing fractal layers of chimeric, machinic, and alien organs beneath.

Early experiments in the development of this style were made by Greg Kulz, who appears in *Modern Primitives*. While an art student in San Francisco, Kulz created a design of tubes and pipes for his arm, and asked Ed Hardy (who else?) to tattoo it. The primary innovator of the mature biomech style, however, was Chicago's Guy Aitchison. Inspired by artists including the Dadaists, who had played with trying to visualize the intersections of bodies and technologies during

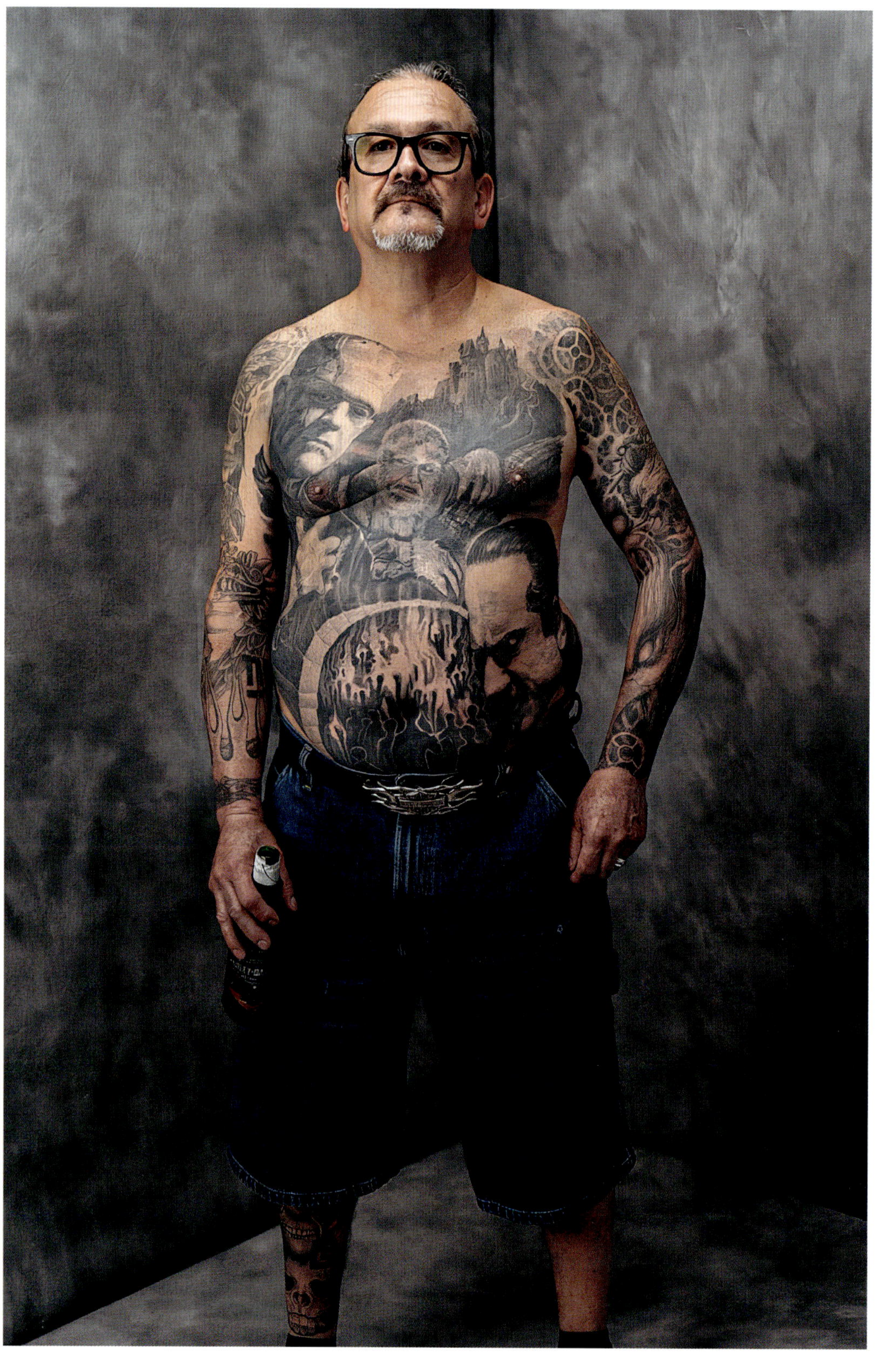

Full frontal horror (*left*) In this film design by Paul Booth on customer Michael Gallegos from 2009, Booth works exclusively in heavy, dark black and gray, achieving a signature realism reminiscent of drawing in ink or charcoal. Booth's version of this style built on the single-needle developments of the likes of Jack Rudy, but turned their delicate precision into saturated, deep and instantly readable monochromatic pieces.

Expanding possibilities (*right*) Guy Aitchison began his artistic career as a graphic illustrator, and took this approach into the expanded possibilities afforded by tattooing in the 1990s. As he explains, his tattoos "generally require a finely balanced yet maximalized approach, where all the tricks of depth and lighting are brought into play to bring out a highly dynamic visual experience. [My] favorite subject matter is abstract, but with a sense of realism applied so the viewer is transported into an alternate reality that they can truly immerse themselves in."

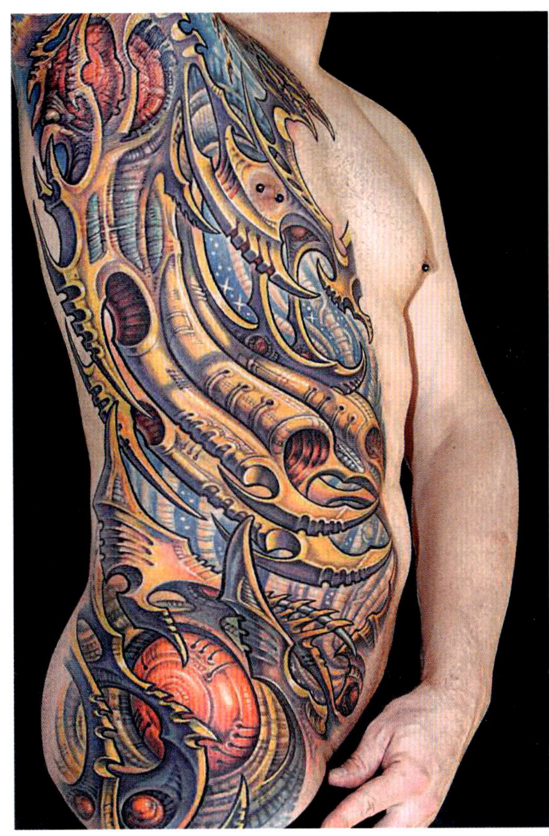

World War I, and by Swiss graphic artist and sculptor H.R. Giger, Aitchison was perhaps the first artist of the postmodern era to really create a new style of tattooing. His work of the period glows with a strange, discordant color palette of acid greens, purples, and oranges. The techniques he uses to produce detailed, illustrative, and dimensional designs were developed from those reinvented by the single-needle black-and-gray artists—Jack Rudy was an early supporter—but the visual forms are all his own: wild, unruly, and impossible to imagine in any prior era. As tattoo journalist Bob Baxter once wrote, "While other less adventurous tattooers have reputations, Aitchison has a mystique. No mere member of the earthbound tattoo community, Aitchison hovers above it like a spaceship."

Aitchison's work quickly made him a magnet for like-minded artists, with whom he could iterate the new landscape of biomechanical designs. He tattooed Kulz,

and also Californian artist Aaron Cain, who shared his childhood obsession with Giger. Since meeting Aitchison in 1991, Cain has risen in stature to be heralded almost as Aitchison's equal, with neon-toned renditions of monstrous fractal carapaces filling backs, arms, and chests.

Alongside Aitchison as a defining figure of 1990s tattooing is Paul Booth. In contrast to Aitchison, Booth works only in monochrome black and gray, but in doing so hews much more closely to the influence of H.R. Giger, from whose template Aitchison had begun to depart. Where Aitchison's work is brightly futuristic and sci-fi, Booth's is horrific. Where he does use biomechanical motifs, like Giger they come packaged with gothic and noir references evoking artists such as Francisco Goya. Hardy called Booth "the epitome of that monochromatic, photorealistic style with a fantasy swing to it."

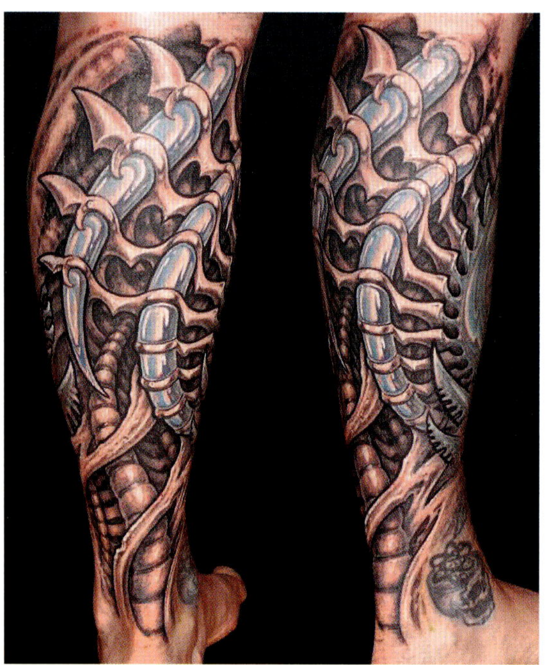

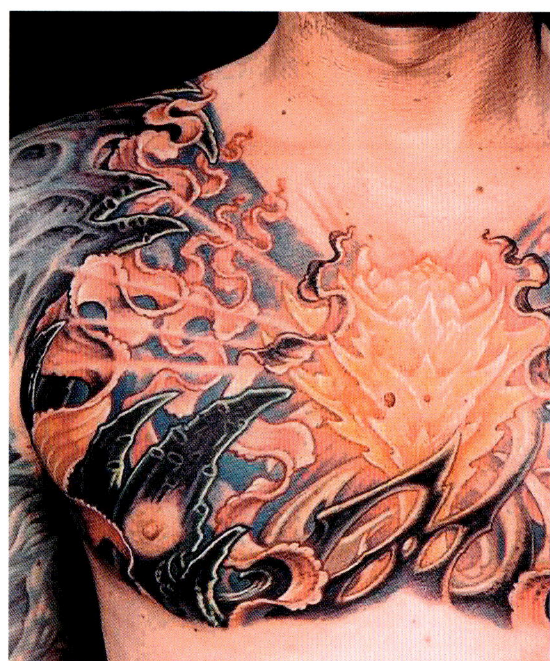

New Old Style

Asked in 2000 who his favorite tattooer then working was, Ed Hardy named Dan Higgs. Tattoo chronicler Shawn Porter says that, in his view, the 1990s is summarized tersely as "Guy Aitchison, Dan Higgs." And Higgs has been wildly influential, even though he withdrew from tattooing entirely so that he could focus on music and art.

Higgs learned to tattoo in the mid-1980s from an artist called Tux Farrar, a tattooer obsessed with old flash, and who had himself been inspired by the subterranean experimentation of Thom DeVita in New York. By 1991, he was working at Tattoo City, filling a vacancy left by the sudden death of Greg Irons in Thailand. His work featured in issue five of *TattooTime*, published that same year.

It's Higgs' work that must have been uppermost in Hardy's mind when he wrote about the "new old style"

to Lal in 1990, as Higgs is really the last piece of the postmodern tattoo puzzle that requires discussion here.

Much of Hardy's excitement through the 1970s was driven by a boredom with the standard, repetitious palette of American tattoo flash. Sailor Jerry and his forebears and contemporaries such as Owen Jensen, Percy Waters, and Joe Lieber had created the stark, functional design catalog of traditional American maritime tattooing, but it had ossified and become stale. Similarly, Good Time Charlie had pushed his own black-and-gray experiments in order to step away from that style, and DeVita is on record as saying, "I don't tattoo cartoons." So it is surprising, perhaps, to see Hardy praise a tattooer like Higgs, who worked in a style so directly connected to those old, bold lineages.

In Higgs' hands, the flash he had been immersed in through Farrar and Hardy's collecting became something like a spell-book: a Necronomicon of

Man versus machine Though "Tribal" tattooing came to represent tattooing in the public imagination in the late 1990s and early 2000s, for many aficionados, the surrealistic biomechanical creations of the likes of Guy Aitchison are just as iconic. The style is extraordinarily hard to execute well, as it must work convincingly with the body's musculature, creating trompe-l'oeil illusions of depth in color palettes that are unfamiliar to most conventional tattooers.

magical, powerful motifs, encoded with generations of accumulated meaning and formal refinement. In a rare interview, he recalls his enchantment with old sheets of designs. "Tux had some really old east coast stuff way up in the corner with spider webs and everything and it was real emblematic, head on symmetrical designs that had that cryptic look like they were saying something but you couldn't tell quite what, you know?"

Hardy calls Higgs' work "the rebirth of bold American classics," because it was in his hands that the oldest images in American tattooing could become new again. Instinctively, Higgs used heavier outlines in his designs than had been common over the previous decade, almost archeologically rediscovering the tried-and-true methods of people like Cap Coleman when they were aiming to replicate the visual cues of misregistered comic books. "I like things that have visual impact and then have a residual mental impact where there's something lingering that makes you think, and causes an emotional response." Higgs' tattooing perfectly captures this uncanny, durable power. His designs are familiar, somehow, as they refer in style and form to the most recognizable designs of the old, nicotine-stuffed shops: skulls, dice, hearts, daggers. But alongside them, Higgs sprinkles less straightforwardly comprehensible motifs: a mummy, a hooded monk, an arachnid clown.

This is not performative, ironic esotericism for its own sake. Higgs did not cultivate a deliberate, affected aura to impress those around him. Indeed, much of the drive for his complete withdrawal from tattooing seems to have been simply a desire to avoid being anything other than a tattoo artist—which, as his reputation grew, he could barely continue to be without

having to morph into a businessman, a celebrity, or a raconteur. In essence, Higgs stopped tattooing because, as its popularity boomed, it could no longer be what he needed it to be. Poignantly, too, Higgs was never possessed of an ego that would have allowed him to truly be comfortable sitting at the pinnacle of his industry. Like so many of those before him, he understood that he should, rightfully, only ever strive to serve tattooing. He was a waypoint, not a destination. "Traditional tattooing, or being traditional, doesn't mean staying stuck in the past," he told Ed Hardy in 1993. "It means nurturing something that came way before you because you deeply hope that it will continue way after you. It's about being in the middle, not being at the end. You're not initiating something, nor having the last word, you're just carrying it through, with the time you've got."

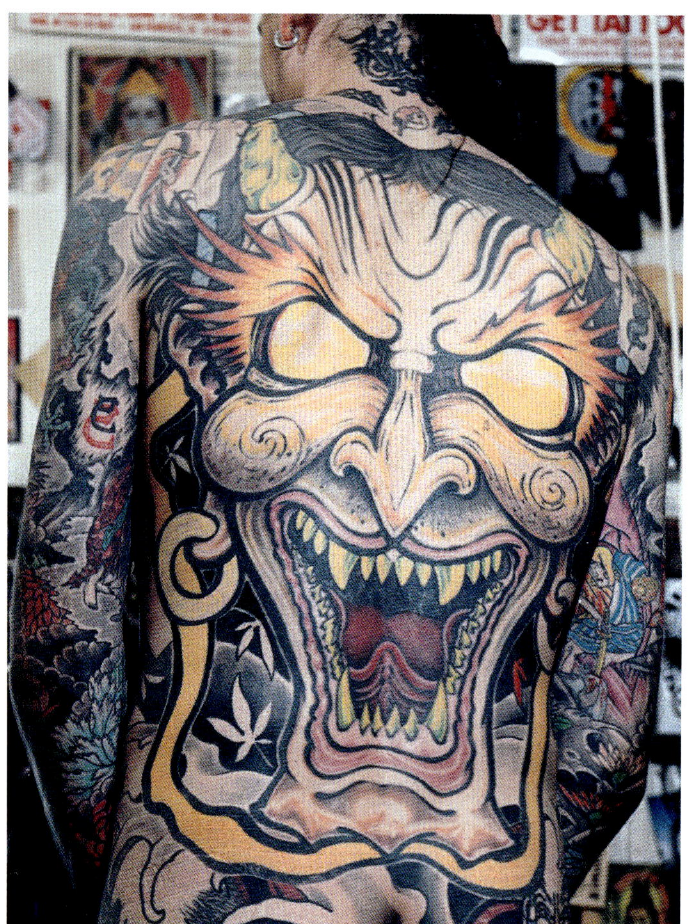

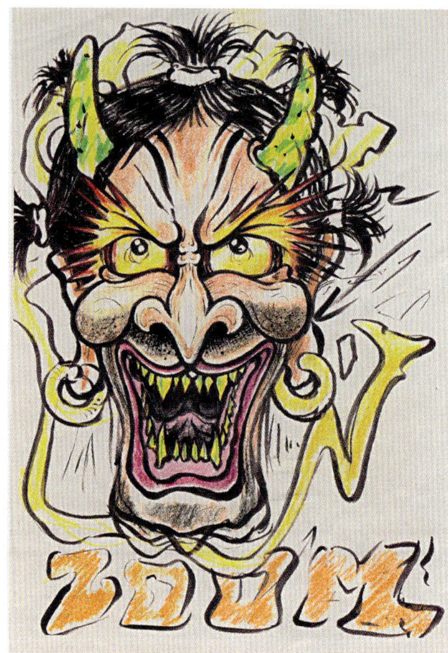

**Design and execution of Hanya backpiece, drawn by Felix
Leu and tattooed by Felix Leu, Filip Leu, and Loretta Leu on
customer "Mick", 1986**

Since the very beginning, the Leus' tattooing and creative businesses
have been a whole-family affair. This backpiece—a twisted, 1980s
take on a classic Japanese Hanya mask—was drawn by Felix but
tattooed by a collaborative team including Loretta and Filip.
Under the banner of the Leu Family Iron, they have built a multi-
generational dynasty of artists working across tattooing, painting,
drawing, sculpture, and digital art.

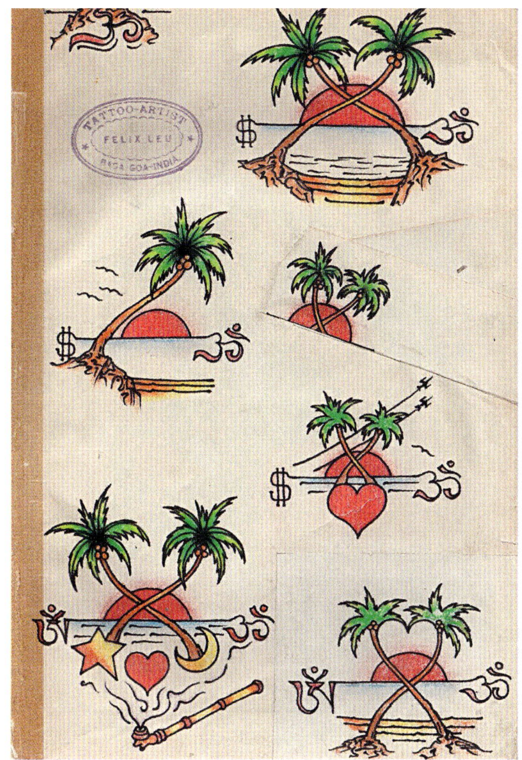

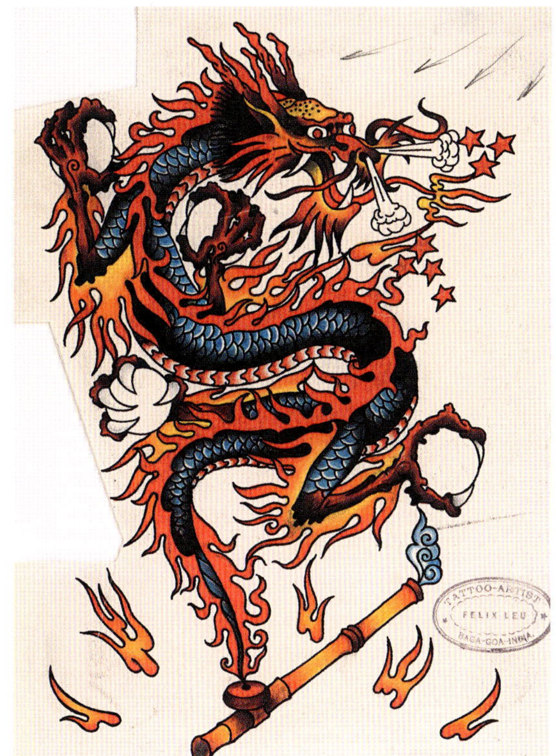

Flash and drawing by Felix Leu, 1977–79

Felix once described getting into tattooing as "a fun way to make money," but he was also drawn to its compelling majesty as an art form like no other: "I never tattooed for money . . . once I had established the price, I never thought about it again. I only worked for the glory, for respect—each and every tattoo I ever did." The flash sheets above were painted in Goa, India, just a year or so into his career, though they look like the work of a confident old hand. Right is a drawing by Felix from 1977, before he discovered tattooing. It seemed, perhaps, that tattooing was within him somehow, even if he hadn't yet realized it.

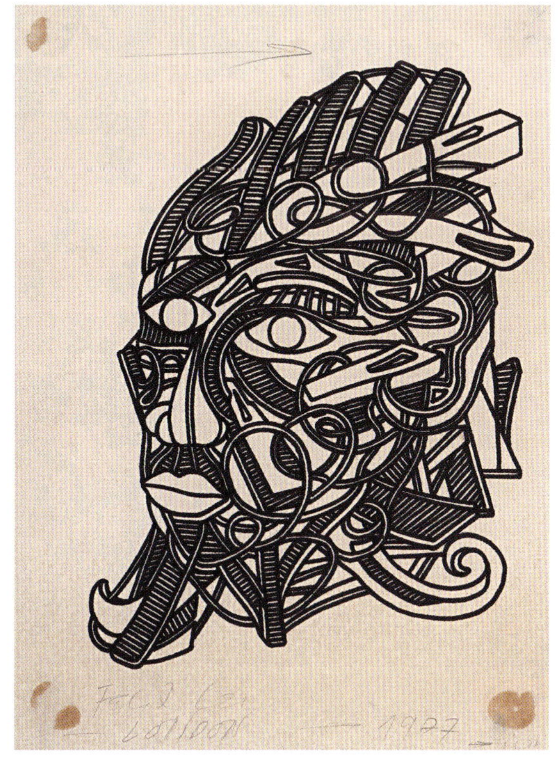

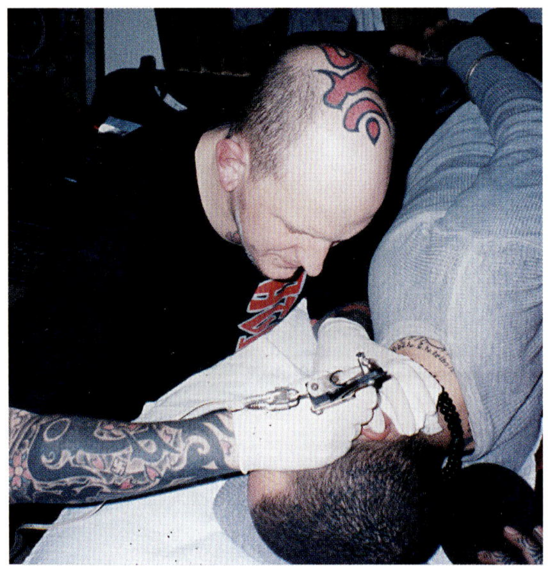

Alex Binnie tattooing a customer, c.1997

Alex Binnie operated his shop Into You in Clerkenwell, London, for twenty-three years—an auspicious period, given the importance of the number twenty-three in the parodic neoreligious movement Discordianism, popularized by countercultural groups in the 1960s and 70s and celebrated by such authors as Robert Anton Wilson and William Burroughs, as well as influential 1980s and 90s performance group KLF. The number twenty-three is also a key leitmotif in Genesis P-Orridge's interview in *Modern Primitives*, who describes receiving a tattoo of the number from Mr. Sebastian.

Alex Binnie, photographed by Jill Westwood, c.1985

Binnie was photographed by his friend Jill Westwood for Tim Coleman's 1985 documentary, *Pigments of the Imagination*. Through art school, Binnie paid his bills by working as a medical illustrator, and by tattooing friends and acquaintances out of London's infamous Crowndale Road squats in the 1980s. Binnie's artistic circle included Grayson Perry, Lee Bowery, Boy George, the fashion designers David Holah and Stevie Stewart (aka BodyMap), and performance artists the Neo-Naturists, fronted by Jennifer and Christine Binnie (no relation). His nipple and pubic tattoos were completed by Mr Sebastian.

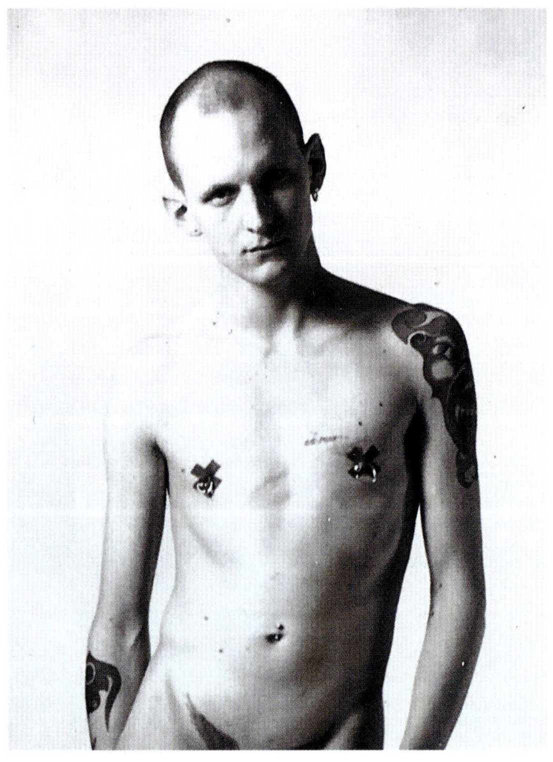

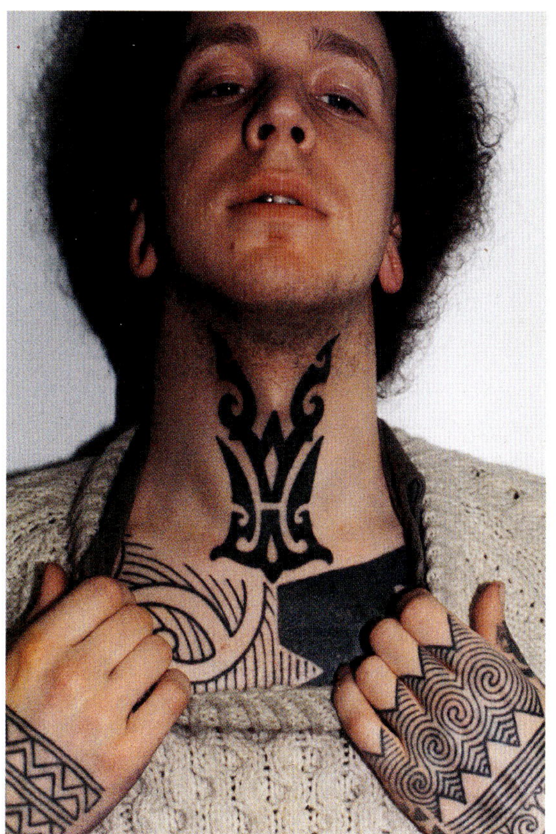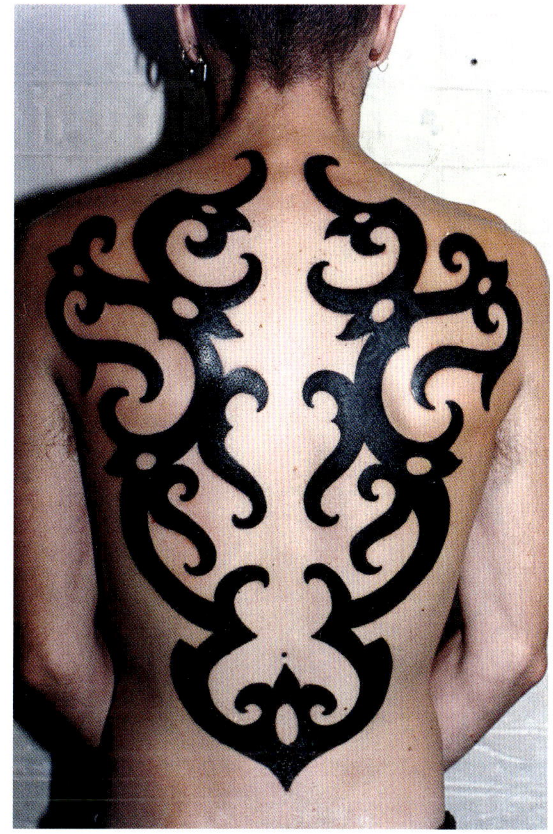

**Tattoos by Alex Binnie on Curly Moore (*left*) and an unnamed client
(*right*), 1990s**

Andreas "Curly" Moore worked with Alex Binnie at Into You for nearly all of its
existence. On the right is the first backpiece Binnie ever produced, tattooed before he
first left London for the US in around 1990. An ambitious, progessive, "Tribal" style
became Binnie's signature, and allowed him to very rapidly ascend in reputation from
backroom scratcher to the spearhead of the transformation of British tattooing in the
last decade of the millennium.

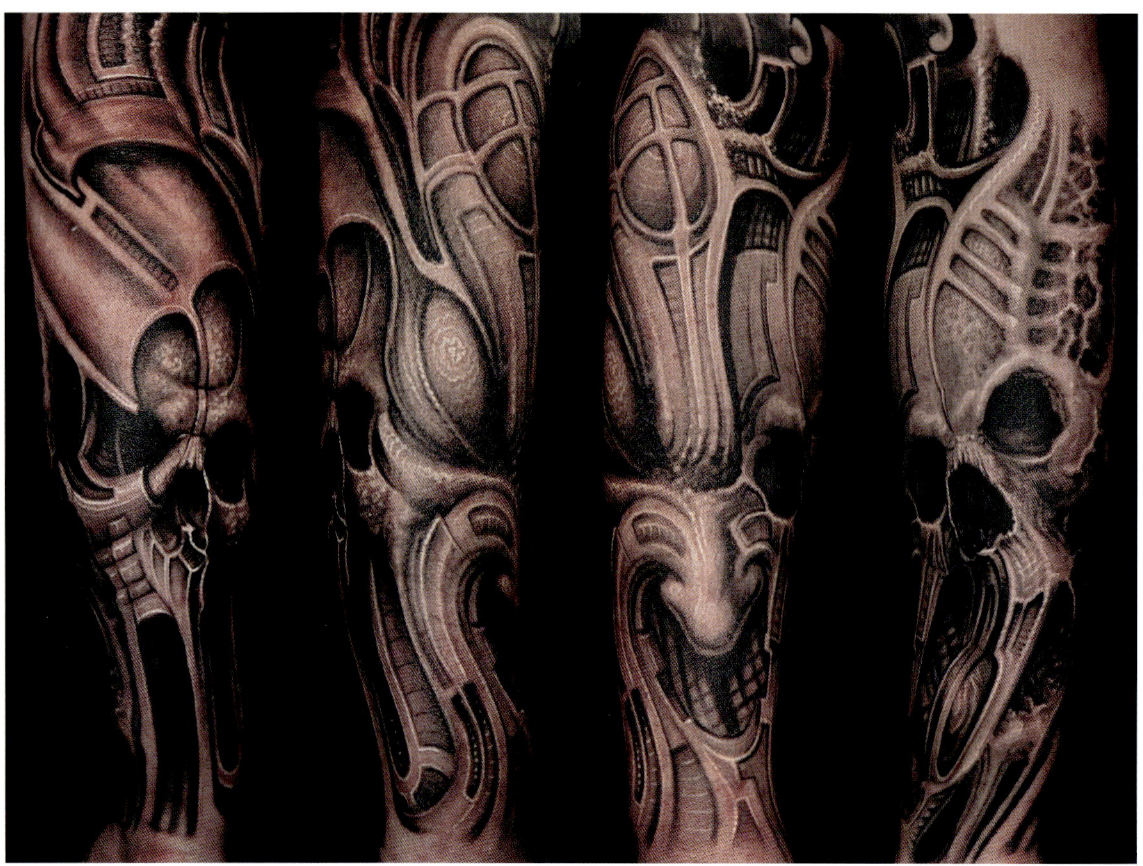

Tattoo series by Paul Booth, c.2020

Booth's most direct influence was Swiss artist H.R. Giger, famous for designing the titular Alien from Ridley Scott's 1979 film. In 1981, Giger had painted models' bodies and faces—including Blondie's Debbie Harry—with transformational biomechanical forms, instantly inspiring a whole generation of aspiring artists who would eventually transpose the style to tattooing. Booth finally met Giger in person in 2007 at an exhibition of Booth's work at the Swiss artist's museum in Gruyeres. Of Giger, he states: "Giger is the reason that light and shade, dimension and texture have always been a major focus for me in my art—whether it be on canvas, skin, or otherwise."

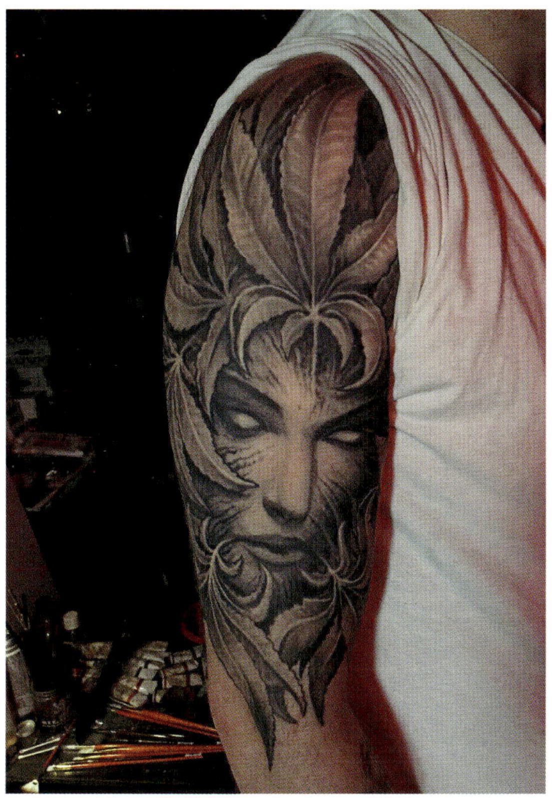

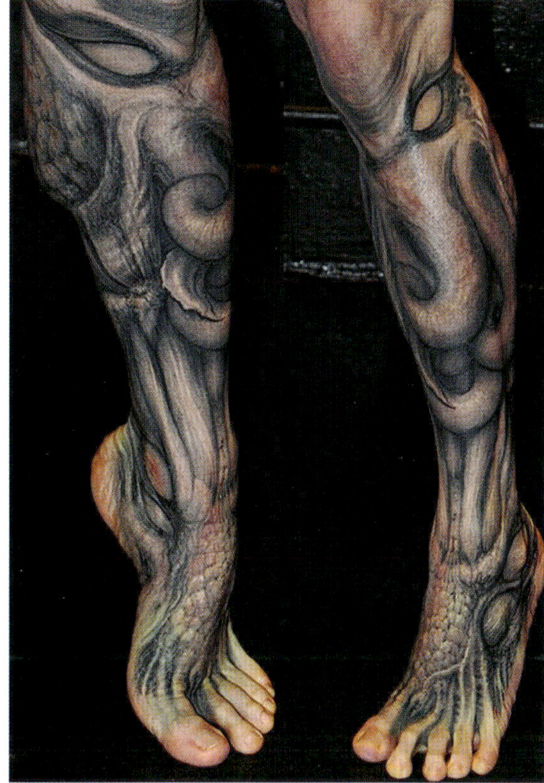

Tattoos by Paul Booth, c.2020

Aside from Giger, gothic illustration has also been a key influence in Booth's instantly recognizable work. In these pieces, Booth draws on the illustrative tradition of pulp horror fiction—think the work of Hugh Rankin, who illustrated many of HP Lovecraft's stories, movie monster great Basil Gogos, or Graham Ingels and Virgil Finlay, the illustrators of many mid-century horror comics. To these pulpy inspirations, Booth adds the grandeur and majesty of grotesque medieval stone-carving, the tonal qualities of etching, and the contrast of black-and-white film.

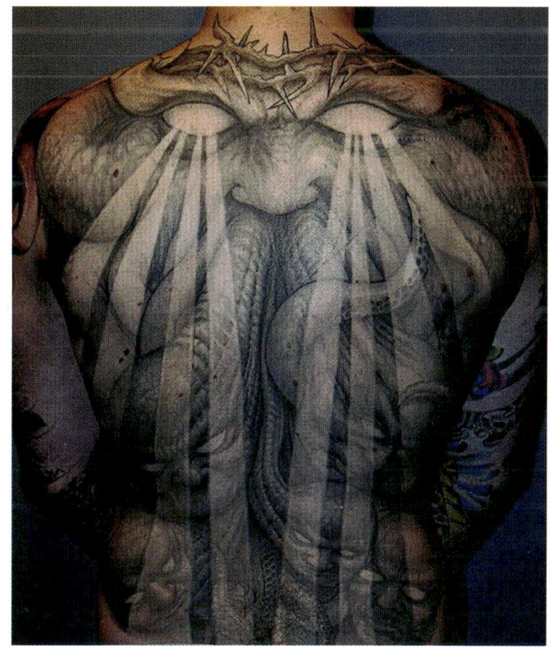

Epilogue

"I see this festival for the body art generation.
The connection between the tattoo artists, bands
and fans is powerful; forged in blood, ink and music . . .
I also want to tie in museums, and academia, and mainstream
sponsors to put tattooing in the forefront."

Scott Alderman, 2022

I n 1997, New York City's prohibition on tattooing, which had held steadfast in the face of repeated attempts to overturn it for nearly four decades, finally gave way. Attempts to ban the importation and sale of *Modern Primitives* in Britain on the grounds of obscenity had been thwarted in 1991 when a jury refused to convict a bookseller who was stocking it. And so, while not exactly a renaissance, by the end of the second millennium the Western tattoo industry had stepped slowly into the light. It was now unrecognizable in comparison to its postwar nadir.

From "Tattoo" brand lipsticks and custom tattooed knitwear in the 1920s, to the rugged tattooed Marlboro man of the 1950s and the appearance of tattooed models on the catwalks in the early 90s, popular culture had long sought to arm itself with the countercultural edge that tattooing could provide. The connection was particularly enmeshed in the summer of 2000, as the Tattoo the Earth music festival toured across the United States, filling enormous venues such as New Jersey's Giants Stadium with thronging crowds of fans eager to see a new wave of heavily tattooed metal bands at the height of their popularity, alongside hugely popular tattoo artists. The tour was headlined by the chaotic costumed energy of nine-man Slipknot, and featured genre titans such as Sepultura, Slayer, and Metallica further down the bill. Fittingly, alongside the glittering roster of bands was a raft of tattoo artists who received equal billing, and whose job was to offer tattooing to attendees.

Festival organizer Scott Alderman had been directly inspired to synthesize tattooing and alternative rock music after having read *Modern Primitives* a decade earlier. He had long been drawn to tattoos, and though he hated piercings, he saw a great business opportunity in the wake of the cultural tide triggered

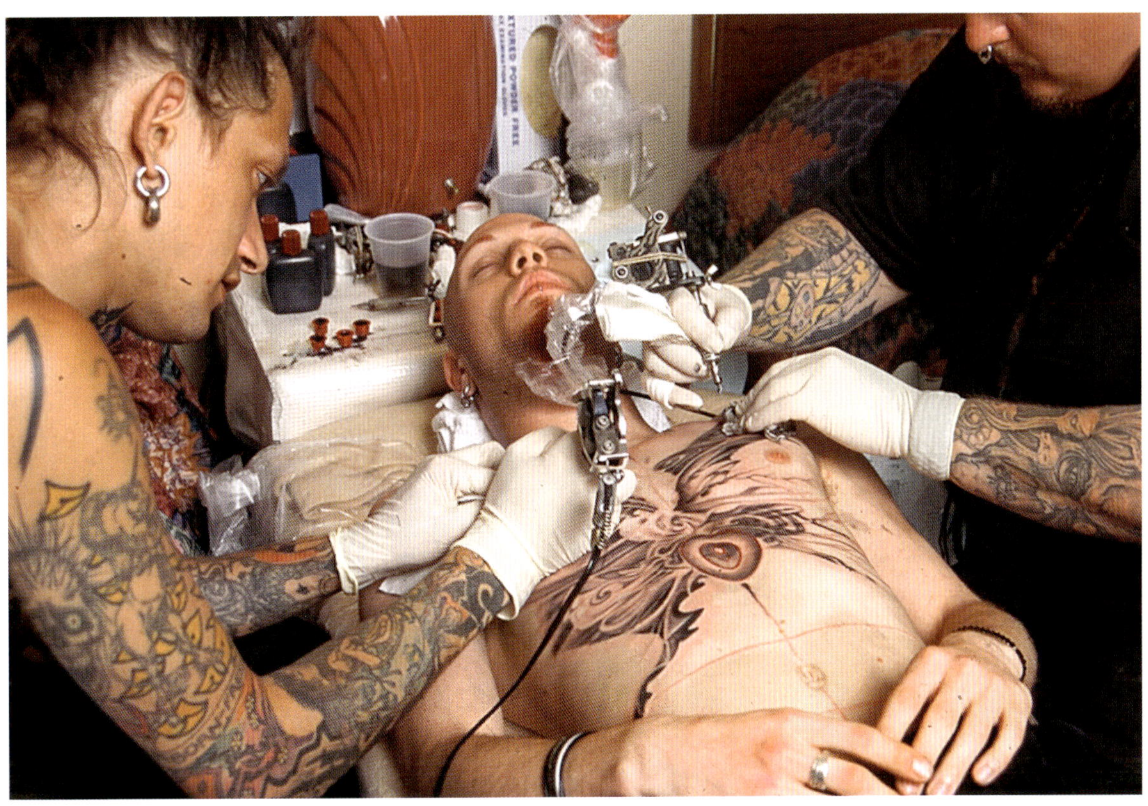

Musical duet Filip Leu and Paul Booth
simultaneously tattoo Ryan Martine, bassist of
Mudvayne, during the Tattoo the Earth tour in 2000.

by the book. It seemed that there was money to be made. His gamble was not simply to use tattooing as branding shorthand for countercultural cool, but to attempt to make tattooing a stadium-filling attraction in its own right.

Alderman's first instinct was to reach out to Lyle Tuttle, the tattooer who was featured on the cover of *Rolling Stone* in 1970 and who still stood for a particular kind of cultural vanguard even three decades later. "I see this festival for the body art generation," Alderman pitched. Tuttle acerbically sent him packing, dismissing him as a poser. "You are completely full of shit," Alderman reports Tuttle having told him. "You think you'll get tattooists to work together, to put aside their egos for something created by an outsider?" Tuttle, and the rest of the industry, remained skeptical of this step into the arms of mainstream corporate entertainment, and Alderman himself was clearly

rather cynical, sensing an opportunity to profit from an industry which was in a period of growing popularity. Such was his desire to court Tuttle and others that he even took to buying a new leather jacket, imagining that it was his outfit rather than his approach that had made the tattoo industry suspicious of him.

Ultimately, though, Alderman was able to persuade a shining pantheon of tattooers to staff the booths at his festival sites. Through a mix of money, buy-in from an impressive roster of bands, and a full charm offensive on industry leaders, enough tattooers were recruited to make the event a reality. Amsterdam's Henk Schiffmacher was initially receptive, but withdrew when told he couldn't bring his dog to the events, however some of the hottest tattooers of the age, including Filip Leu, Paul Booth, and Guy Aitchinson, did work the tour schedule alongside elder statesmen such as Jack Rudy.

The tour got decent reviews from fans and journalists. It was a tense affair, however, and tempers quickly flared, with several bands pulling out. Amongst the tattooers, Paul Booth tired of Alderman's management, and it is clear that the tattooists in general were irritated by the disrespect they felt they were shown at an event that was "ninety percent music, ten percent tattooing." It simply wasn't plausible, efficient, or even hygienic to run a full suite of high-end tattooing alongside a hot, booze-fuelled music event in a traveling caravan of buses and marquees. Alderman himself called the event a "fiasco" and "a successful failure," having been unable to fully corral the industry to the practical and logistical realities of the commercial entertainment industry.

An unassociated event in Europe, Tattoo the Planet, was canceled as it had been due to start on September 13, 2001, just days after the 9/11 terror attacks. Alderman sued the European promoters for infringing upon his branding, and attempted a more tattoo-focussed event in 2002, trying to run three-day tattoo conventions in enormous, corporate-sponsored arenas in Chicago and Oakland. By this stage, even Ed Hardy and the formerly reluctant Tuttle couldn't resist taking part, simply due to the scale of it all, but the events just weren't financially viable and were not repeated. Tattoo conventions may have morphed from Les Skuse's small pub gatherings in Bristol in the early 1950s into stadium-filling mega-productions, but the intimacy, authenticity, and necessarily human scale of tattooing ensured it remained awkwardly incompatible with the financial and practical demands of blockbuster entertainment.

Tattoo the Earth took place at the very moment that tattooing crossed a Rubicon into the new millennium. Its fragility and failures have stood as something of a metaphor for the awkward and uneasy embrace between contemporary culture and tattooing ever since. Though driven by a genuine fascination and appreciation for tattooing, Alderman's interest was ultimately as a branding sheen for his music promotion. Tattooing could lend its cultural capital to the tour, but tattooing itself could not and cannot straightforwardly be commercialized in the same way as bands, for example, can be, given the fact that every tattoo client must be present for every second of their tattoo's production, and that the best tattoo artists in the world have the same amount of hours in a day as everyone else. Despite Alderman's insistence that the troublesome Paul Booth could have been replaced by "any other competent and unknown artist," for example, that is of course not straightforwardly true—at least not in a way that is compatible with the rhetorical elevation of individuals to the status of great artists whose work is specifically and individually coveted and praised.

Though many have tried over the intervening decades, tattooers have always understood that the basic facts of the production of a tattoo renders it robust, and perhaps even impervious, to commercialization of the kind Alderman envisaged. Even as it increases in popularity, and even though it is subject to commercial pressures and the whims of social fashions, tattooing cannot be a business that is like any other. "In a Society dedicated to what Veblin described as 'conspicuous consumption'—that is, using a commodity for a relatively short period of time and either totally consuming it or throwing it away because it has become obsolete—a tattoo represents the antithesis of consumer thinking," Davy

> "It can neither be eaten or thrown away. It is a lifetime gift to the receiver. In short, a tattoo is not a consumable commodity, any more than a man himself is expendable."
>
> *Davy Jones,* 1967

Jones wrote in his 1967 abortive essay, Tattooing as a Business. "It can neither be eaten or thrown away. It is a lifetime gift to the receiver. In short, a tattoo is not a consumable commodity, any more than a man himself is expendable. And because of this, the tattoo shop, the business of tattooing never has and never will be a big business."

Tattooing in the Digital Age

It is true to say that with the diversification and stylistic expansion of tattooing following the innovations of the 1980s and 90s, it ceases to be possible to demarcate chains of stylistic influence through individuals and moments in time in ways that are as neatly discernible as those which this book tracks in the prior decades and centuries. Jack Rudy once claimed that when he started tattooing, "there were essentially two styles: take it, or leave it," but as Hardy himself noted in an interview about the Tattoo the Earth conventions, by the time Alderman was trying to fill stadiums full of tattoo fans, the image bank available was essentially unlimited, opening the floodgates to a world of tattooing in which anything was possible.

There are countless extraordinary artists whose work has been hailed as visionary and extraordinary in the last twenty-five years, but they are too numerous to fully and succinctly account for, and their distinct influence on the stylistic evolution of Western tattooing too diffuse. Instead, the stylistic development of tattooing since the early 2000s has more profoundly been propelled by the technological innovations that have also transformed culture at large. The internet—first through Usenet groups such as rec.arts.bodyart (founded 1991), and then through websites such as

the Body Modification Ezine (bmezine.com; founded 1994)—spread the cultural zeitgeist of Hardy and Musafar's Californian body modification subcultures around the world with much greater alacrity than had been possible with conventional print publications. Through nascent social media sites such as MySpace (launched 2003), Facebook (2004), and later Instagram (2010), tattooed people were able to connect with artists around the world.

In turn, the specific features of social media profiles—and in particular the ubiquitous "profile picture," which conventionally presents a user's face—accelerated the adoption of visible tattooing on the hands and face, as people could present themselves to their friends and to the wider internet as tattooed, even in a small avatar image. So prevalent was this effect that young music fans who had their hands and necks tattooed without first obtaining heavy coverage were often mocked by elder tattoo collectors as wearing a "MySpace bodysuit," giving an appearance of extensive, full-body tattooing in online photos in ways that had been unthinkable in previous decades, when most credible artists would—in the name of social responsibility—refuse to tattoo people's hands and necks unless they were already covered elsewhere.

The internet also facilitated the easier sale of tattoo equipment to amateurs, and the sharing of information on how to tattoo, which industry professionals had tried to guard somewhat jealously for decades. Though tattooing equipment had been on sale to the general public for over a century, since the 1970s, as part of the generalized push for respectability bolstered by self-regulation, tattoo supply companies had attempted to limit the availability of machines, needles, and inks

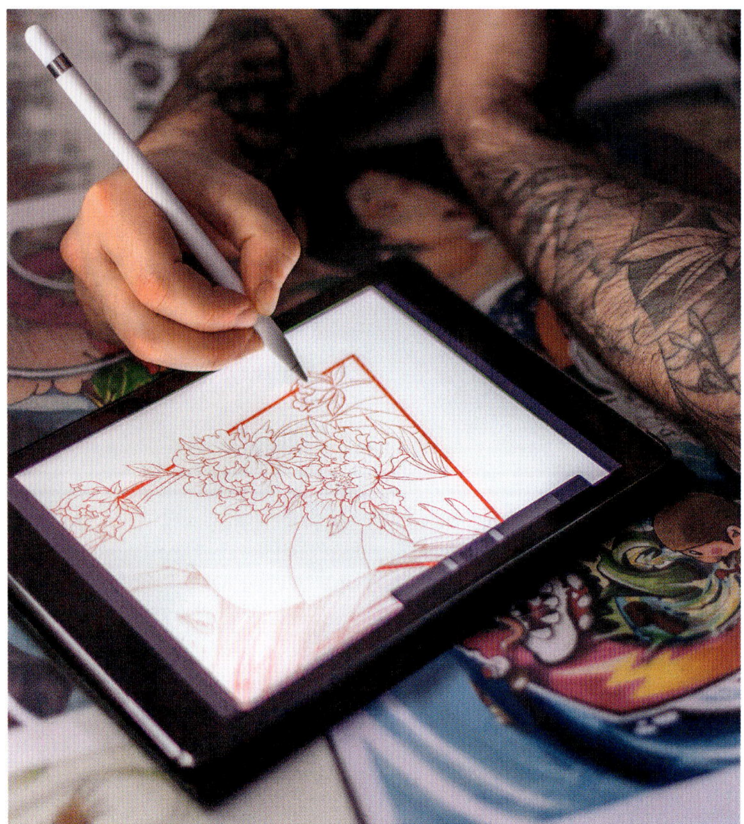

Flexible design tools In the third decade of the twenty-first century, designs for tattoos are increasingly produced on digital tablets. This technology allows artists to easily adjust the size and detail of their design, to overlay it onto a photograph of their client to ensure conformity to the curves of the body, and to send designs to their customers over email or social media prior to an in-person appointment. Most of this utility replicates techniques used in analog form in the past—Victorian tattooists often planned out large-scale projects on physical photographs, for example, and twentieth century artists sometimes sent designs by post—but the uptake of digital tools has made tattooing increasingly flexible for both artist and client alike.

to registered professionals. But sites like eBay and Amazon, coupled with cheap mass manufacturing of shoddy machines, have made start-up kits easy to obtain, especially in the face of impotent regulations and the entry into the market of suppliers who are unfortunately not beholden to the conservative community standards of old.

For designs, too, online image hosting has rapidly replaced traditional flash and the Victorian scrapbook as sources of inspiration, and Facebook groups and then Instagram pages have taken the place of analog photo-trading networks. Flash supply was a multimillion-dollar industry by the late 1990s, but the internet era saw the market dissolve almost entirely. Clients and artists are now able to collect and download pictures from sites such as Tumblr and Pinterest, and thus today's tattoo design trends are influenced as much by the pictures surfaced by search engine algorithms as

they are by designs emerging from within the industry itself. In one hilarious example, in 2023 an anatomist posting on social media noticed that many tattoos appearing online that were supposedly of wolf skulls were actually copies of a popular Pinterest picture of a racoon skull which had been incorrectly tagged. When searching for photographic references, tattoo artists had clearly been searching "wolf skull front view" and tracing the most popular photo in Google Images' results page.

Many artists have also adapted to new technologies for their drawing and stencil preparation practices, using digital tools such as iPads and drawing tablets to produce preparatory sketches. The results of this set of innovations on the skin have been varied—artists working in styles that deploy geometric patterns, for example, have been able to use generative algorithms, clone tools, and custom digital brushes to create precise

> "To those who feel tattooing's allure deeply, in all its romance and mystery, there will always be something profoundly magical about making indelible marks on skin."
>
> *Matt Lodder,* 2024

tessellations which fit perfectly onto their customers' bodies. But in many cases, where tattoo artists have abandoned traditional flash painting using watercolor and spit-shading, the result has been a loss of fluidity in the finished tattoo. Old-school flash painting drew upon the similarities between the migration of pigment in paper with the fugitive nature of ink in skin to ensure that proficient artists could prepare designs that worked well as readable, durable tattoos on the body; a digital drawing tool simply does not analogize to tattooing in the same way, and the resulting tattoos are often unsympathetic and lifeless.

Tattoo machines are often wireless now, and driven by rechargeable batteries; inks are regulated by major consumer safety standards organizations; tattooers no longer solder their own needles but buy them presterilized from mass manufacturers in East Asia. Tattoo artists no longer become famous through glowing, gossipy broadsheet profiles of the rarefied and organic social networks of Edwardian high society or the cover of *Rolling Stone*, or even through glittering television shows like *Miami Ink* and *Ink Master,* but instead through the algorithmic whims of social media sites like Instagram and TikTok. At its root, though, tattooing in the third millennium is fundamentally the same practice as it was at the birth of the professional industry in the late nineteenth century. Despite the influence of the internet on tattoo culture, you cannot, of course, acquire a tattoo online. Every client who is tattooed must still sit and endure their tattoo creation; despite advances in laser technology, tattoos are still essentially permanent; and, despite the undoubtedly steady increase in the popularity of tattooing, mainstream culture still looks upon tattooing slightly

askance. In 2015, London's *Daily Telegraph* newspaper suspected that "we're not going to reach peak tattoo until 2025." In 2024, the *Guardian* suggested that "peak tattoo seems almost certainly behind us," and that it is "safe to say tattoos aren't that rebellious anymore." But these ideas are presented in the same misleading frame as the *Vanity Fair* article that had made the same claim back in 1926: "that tattooing has passed from the savage to the sailor, from the sailor to the landsman, and is now to be found beneath many a tailored shirt." To those who do not fully understand tattooing, its visibility and popularity among anyone but sailors and criminals has always felt like an anomaly. But to those who feel tattooing's allure deeply, in all its romance and mystery, there will always be something profoundly magical about making indelible marks on skin.

References

Chapter One

"Curious Robberies by a 'Gentleman'", *Illustrated London News.* August 17, 1844

"Leeds, Jan 14. 1769," *Virginia Gazette* [Rind]. Williamsburg, January 26, 1769

"Tattooing," *The Literary Gazette*, February 20, 1819

"Who has seen him?" *Punch*, November 25, 1854, 220

Baptista Porta, John. *Natural Magick* XVI. London: John Wright, 1669

Beaglehole, J.C. (ed.). *The Endeavour Journal of Joseph Banks* 1768–1771. Vol. 1. Sydney: Angus & Robertson, 1962.

Cardano, Girolamo, *De Subtilitate* XVIII. Paris : Michaelis Fezendat et Roberti Granjon : Paris, 1550

Carswell, John, *Coptic Tattoo Designs*. Beirut: American University of Beirut, 1958

Criminal Registers of Prisoners in Middlesex and the City. April 13, 1797, pardon of Bisk Jho. alias Tho. Maley. HO26/5/10. National Archives, London

Dauge Roth, Katherine and Craig Koslofsky. *Stigma: Marking Skin in the Early Modern World*. Pennsylvania : Pennsylvania State University Press, 2023

Dauge-Roth, Katherine. *Signing the Body in Early Modern France*. London: Ashgate, 2016

Forrester, John M. *The De Subtilitate of Girolamo Cardano*. Tempe, AZ : ACMRS, 2013

Frank, Michael C., "'A Mark Indelible': Herman Melville and the Cross-Cultural History of Tattooing in the Nineteenth Century." In Sebastian Jobs (ed.), *Embodiments of Cultural Encounters*. Berlin : Waxmann, 2011

Friedman Herhily, Anna Felicity. "Tattooed transculturites: Western expatriates among Amerindian and Pacific Islander societies, 1500–1900." (PhD diss., University of Chicago, 2012)

Grevenbroeck, Jan van. "Gli habiti de Veneziani di quasi ogni età con diligenza raccolti a dipinti nel secolo XVIII", 1760. Museo Correr, Venice

Guerzoni, Guido. "'Notae Divine Ex Arte Compunctae": Prime Impressioni sul Tatuaggio devozionale in Italia (XV–XIX)'", *Micrologus*, No. 13 (2005), 418

Hildebrand, Wolfgang. *Magia naturalis*. Leipzig : Birnstil 1610

Jacobs, Fredrika *Votive Panels and Popular Piety in Early Modern Italy*. Cambridge: Cambridge University Press, 2013

John George Keysler, *Travels through Germany, Bohemia, Hungary, Switzerland, Italy and Lorrain*. London: A. Linde, 1756

Langsdorff, Georg Heinrich von, Voyages and *Travels in Various Parts of the World*. London : Henry Colburn, 1813

Letterbook of Capt Edward Rotherham, 1799-1808. LBK/38. Caird Library, National Maritime Museum London

Lodder, Matt, "'*Things of the sea*': Iconographic continuities between tattooing and handicrafts in Georgian-era maritime culture." *Sculpture Journal* 24/2(2015) : 195-210

Lodder, Matt, *Painted People*. London : William Collins, 2022

Lodder, Matt. "*A Medium, not a Phenomenon*." In James Martell and Erik Larsen, *Tattooed Bodies*. London : Palgrave Macmillan, 2022, 13-42

Mordecai Lewy, "Jerusalem unter der Haut: Zur Geschichte der Jerusalemer Pilgertätowierung," *Zeitschrift für Religions- und Geitesgeschichte*, Vol. 55 (2003): 1–39

Old Bailey Proceedings, February 25, 1719, trial of John Woodward and Thomas Williams (t17190225-33)

Ousterhout, Robert. "Permanent Ephemera: The 'Honourable Stigmatisation' of Jerusalem Pilgrims." In Renana Bartel and Hanna Vorholt, *Between Jerusalem and Europe*. Leiden: Brill, 2015

Parkinson, Sydney. *A Journal of a Voyage to the South Seas, in his Majesty's Ship the Endeavor*. London: Charles Dilly and James Phillips, 1784

Pennsylvania Gazette, Philadelphia, August 14, 1766

Pigorini-Beri, Caterina. "Tatuaggi Sacri e Profani." *In Costumi e superstizioni dell'appennino Marchigiano*. Città di Castello : S. Lapi, 1889

Presciutti, Diana Bullen. "Signs of Belonging: Identifying Foundlings and Orphans in Early Modern Europe." In Nicholas Terpstra (ed.), *Common Children and the Common Good: Locating Foundlings in the Early Modern World* (Florence: Villa I Tatti and Instituto degli Innocenti, 2022

Renaut, Luc. "Marquage Corporel et Signation Religieuse dans L'Antiquité" (PhD diss., École Pratique des Hautes Études, 2004)

Thévenot, Jean de. *The Travels of Monsieur de Thévenot into the Levant*. London: H. Faithorne, J. Adamson, C. Skegnes and T. Newborough, 1687

von Pappenheim, Alexander. *Reisebericht nach Italien und ins Heilige Land*. Hamburg: Verlag Dr. Kovač, 1564

Zuallart, Jean. *Les Tres devot voyage de Ierusalem*. En Anvers: Arnould s'Conincx, 1608

Chapter Two

"A New Custom," *New York Times*, August 16, 1879

"A Visit to a Tattooer," *Marathon Independent* [New York], August 31, 1881

"Designs on Humanity," *The Sun* [New York], June 5, 1881

"One Curiosity Seeking Another," *New York Herald*, October 24, 1885

"Practical Jokes," *The Saturday Review* [London], June 8, 1967

"Practical Receipts," *Reynold's Miscellany*, September 9, 1865

"Tattooing Among Fashionable Folks," *New York Times*, August 20, 1882

"Tattooing in New York," *New York Times*, January 16, 1876

"Tattooing, Savage and Civilised (?)" *Cassell's Magazine*, September 1873

"The Tattooing Artist," *The Sun* [New York], December 18, 1872

"The Tattooing Freak," *National Police Gazette*, November 15, 1879

"The Uses of Tattooing," *The Saturday Review*, March 16, 1879

"Well Marked Man," *The Evening News* [Portsmouth], July 16, 1880

Blanco, Richard L. "Attempts to Abolish Branding and Flogging in the Army of Victorian England Before 1881." Journal of the Society for *Army Historical Research* 46/187 (1968): 137–45

Burroughs, Peter. "Crime and Punishment in the British Army, 1815-1870." *English Historical Review* 100/396 (July 1985) : 545-571

Daily Chronicle and Clerkenwell News, July 18, 1878

Daily Chronicle and Clerkenwell News, June 9, 1873

HC Deb 26 Feb 1876, vol 227, cc929-89

Lodder, Matt, "'Do you tattoo your children yet? : Roger Tichborne, 1871." In Matt Lodder, *Painted People*. London : William Collins, 2022

Lodder, Matt. '"Geijutsu-tekina" Nihon no irezumi to vuikutoria asa Ingurando no shogyo senryaku' ['"Artistic" Japanese Tattoos and Commercial Strategy in Victorian England'], trans. Naho Onuki. In: 身体を彫る、世界を印す イレズミ・タトゥーの人類学 [Sculpting the Body, Marking the World: The Anthropology of Irezumi Tattoo]. Editors: Yamamoto, Y., Kuwabara, M. and Tsumura, F., Tokyo : Shunpusha, 2022

Nyssen, Carmen. "Salon-Tattoo Shops of New York City's 4th Ward." BuzzworthyTattooHistory.com, 31 Jul. 2017. https://web.archive.org/web/20170907022552/https://buzzworthytattoo.com/saloon-tattoo-shops-of-new-york-citys-4th-ward/

Terry Manton, *The Pioneers of British Tattooing*. Britain : Terry Manton, 2023

The Times 26 Jul. 1879

Wilson, H (comp.), *New York City Directory for the Year Ending May 1859*. New York : Trow's, 1858

Wilson, H (comp.), *New York City Directory for the Year Ending May 1871*. New York : Trow's, 1850

Chapter 3

"A chat with a 'Tattooer'", *The Sketch*, January 23, 1895

"A tattooer", *The Gleaner*, March 1897

"An English tattooer: interview with Mr Sutherland Macdonald," *Pall Mall Gazette*, May 1, 1889

"Answers to Correspondents," *The Girl's Own Paper*, October 1, 1881

"Books Literary 1896 Jan–Mar," March 25 1896, COPY1/738. National Archives, London

"Coroner's Inquests," *Liverpool Weekly Courier*, October 16, 1890

"Cycles, Etc.," *Lincolnshire Echo*, June 3, 1897

"Dangers of Tattooing," *Illustrated Police News*, April 15, 1899

"Favorite Heroes of the War Tattooed on the Arms of Enthusiastic Soldiers," *San Francisco Cal*, December 11, 1898

"In a Tattooer's Atelier," *Daily Graphic*, August 2, 1890

"In Japan, 1881: Prince George and the Tattooing Artist," *The Graphic*. July 8, 1893

"Managers, Showmen and Others. Look. Look," *The Era*, January 11, 1890

"New Yorkers Adopt a Startling French Fad," *The World* [New York]. August 29, 1897

"Now 'tis tattooing," *Boston Daily Globe*, May 22, 1893

"Odds and Ends," *Wide World Magazine*, August 1906

"Tattoo Artists at War," *New York Time*, January 1, 1900

"Tattooed Royalty," *Standard* (*London*), January 4, 1899

"Tattooing at Nagasaki," *Illustrated London New*s, December 2, 1882

"The Apelles of Japanese Tattooers", *Pall Mall Gazette*, May 7, 1889

"Westminster," *The Standard* (London), July 16, 1898

「長崎入墨見本帳」 Nagasaki Museum of History and Culture

Angel, Gemma, "Recovering the Nineteenth Century European Tattoo." In Lars Krutak and Aaron Deter-Wolf (eds), *Ancient Ink*. Seattle : University of Washington Press, 2017

Basil Hall Chamberlain and W.B Mason, *A Handbook for Travellers in Japan*. Third Edition New York : Charles Scribner's Sons, 1893

Berchon, Ernst, *Histoire Médicale du tatouage*. Paris : J-B Ballière, 1869

Bolton. Gambier. "Pictures on the human skin," *Strand Magazine*, April 1897, 425–34

Bolton, Gambier. "A tattoo artist," *Pearson's Magazine*, August 1902

British Army WWI Pension Records, Norfolk Infantry Regiment 2109 (1901) / 10574 (1914) (Later: Shropshire Regiment 8057; National Reserve, 20-501)

British Postal Service Appointment Books, 1894, Series: POST 58; Reference Number 94, British Postal Museum and Archive, London

Brooklyn, Pat. "Pictures on the Skin", *English Illustrated Magazine*, April 1903

Burchett, George. *Memoirs of a Tattooists*. Edited by Peter Leighton. London : Oldbourne, 1958

Catalogue of Cruft's Great International Dog Show. London : Charles Cruft, 1904

Census Returns of England and Wales, 1901, 1901, Willesden 41/1221, National Archives, London

Census Returns of England and Wales, 1911, 1911. Kensington South 14 /101. National Archives, London.

Daniel Owen & Co's (Wright's) Cardiff Directory, Cardiff : Daniel Owen & Co, 1983

Derin Bray, *Tattoo, Circus, Sideshow & Curiosities* [catalog], Portsmouth, NH : Bray & Co., 2023

E. H. Cookridge Fonds. 1979-1905. McMaster University, Hamilton, ON, Canada

England and Wales Civil Registration Indexes, Q3 1931, 1b/212, General Register Office

Kiralfy, Imre. *Military Exhibition Earl's Court Official Guide and Catalogue*, London : J.J Keliher, 1901

Koyama, Noboru, "Japanese Tattooists and the British Royal Family During the Meiji Period" in Japan: Biographical

Letter from John Dalton to the Princess of Wales, 31 October 1881. RA VIC/Z 474/9 Royal Archives

Lodder, '"Geijutsu-tekina"

Lodder, Matt, "The Man, the Myth, The Legend," *Total Tattoo Magazine* 100. February 2013 : 66-69

Lodder, Matt. "Macdonald, Sutherland (1860–1942), tattoo artist." *Oxford Dictionary of National Biography*, May 26, 2016

London Electoral Register. West Division, No. 3 Polling District—Ward 2, Lower Holloway, 1896, 126 Entry 3786; Census Returns of England and Wales, 1891, 1891, Islington South West 8/152, Schedule 85. National Archives, London

MacDonald, Sutherland, "Macdonald of the Isle of Skye, and later of Fort George, co. Inverness, Scotland," *Genealogical Quarterly*, 7 (September 1938), 142–4

McCabe, Michael, *New York City Tattoo*. Honolulu, HI : Hardy Marks, 1997

Nyssen, Carmen, "Early Tinkerers of Electric Tattooing." BuzzworthyTattooHistory.com, n.d. https://web.archive.org/web/20170613205308/https://buzzworthytattoo.com/tattoo-history-research-articles/early-tinkerers-of-electric-tattooing/

Ouseley, Mulvey. "Marked for Life." *The Royal Magazine*, Vol. III, 1899

Parry, Albert, *Secrets of a Strange Art*. New York : Simon & Schuster, 1933

Portraits. Vol. VI, ed. Hugh Cortazzi. (Leiden : Global Oritenal, 2007),

Post Office London Directory for 1916 – County Suburbs. London : Kelly's Directories, 1916

Purdy, D.W. *Tattooing: How to Tattoo, What to Use, & How to Use Them*. London: Professor D.W. Purdy, 1896

R. J. Stephens, "Tattooed Royalty. Queer Stories of a Queer Craze," *Harmsworth Magazine,* Vol I, 1898, 472

Reiter, Jon. T*he King of Tattooists*. Milwaukee, WI : Solid State Publishing, 2012

St Pancras Workhouse Admission and Discharge Register 1924 Jan–1925 Jun, 1925 1924, STPBG/282, London Metropolitan Archives

Stephens, "Tattooed Royalty. Queer Stories of a Queer Craze"

Swindon Advertiser, June 12, 1897

War Office: Soldiers' Documents from Pension Claims, First World War (Microfilm Copies), The National Archives Microfilm Publication, 1920 1914, WO364/3110, National Archives, London

War Office: Soldiers' Documents from Pension Claims, First World War (Microfilm Copies), The National Archives, London

Yamamoto, Yoshimi, "Japanese tattooing as souvenirs for foreign travelers in the late 19th and early 20th century." *Nihon kenkyū* 63, 2021

Chapter 4

"Admiralty Description of Deserters from His Majesty's Sea Service," *Police Gazette*, January 26, 1915

"Boom in Tattooing in London," *Morning Oregonian*, October 14, 1919

"Fickle Young Thing," *Punch*, January 12, 1916

"General News," *Edinburgh Evening News*, December 5, 1914

"Have you seen any this year?" *Daily Mail* [Hull], January 16, 1914

"Lady Londonderry's Fashion-Setting Tattooed Legs," *American Weekly*, July 7, 1938

"Little Tattooing Nowadays," *New York Times*, September 28, 1924

"Modern Fashions in Tattooing," *Vanity Fair*, January 1926

"New Craze for Tattooing," *Herald,* November 7, 1931

"Notes on the Collections," *Vogue* [New York], April 13, 1929

"Novel Bathing Suits," *Newcastle Sun* [Newcastle, Australia], October 23, 1929

"Popular with Girls," *Bolton Evening News*, October 12, 1915

"Southend Mystery," *Essex County Chronicle*, July 17, 1914

"Souvenir Tattooing," *Birmingham Mail*, June 29, 1918

"Strange Ways of Acquiring Beauty," *Thomson's Weekly*, January 22, 1910

"Tattooed Marchioness," *Life*, July 18, 1938

"Tattooer in the Trenches," *The Manchester Guardian*, February 12, 1916

"Tattooing à la Mode," *Daily Mail* [Atlantic Edition], March 17, 1930

"Tattooing Craze," *Lancashire Evening Post*, November 2, 1920

"Tattooing is Rage in London Society," *Milwaukee Sentinel*, August 9, 1933

"Tattooing one art not on the bum in Kansas City," *Kansas City Star*, January 17, 1915

"The New Beach Costumes," *San Antonio Light*, June 16, 1929

"The Practice of Tattooing," *The Lethbridge Herald*, November 22, 1935

"The Tattooing Craze," *North Star* [Darlington], November 2, 1915

"You ought to manage to get blown to bits," *Punch*, March 28, 1917

Bioardi, Danielle, *Burchett Treasures*. San Francisco : Lyle Tuttle Tattoo Museum, 2023

Bray, Derin and Margaret Hodges, *Loud, Naked and In Three Colors*. Portsmouth, NH : Rakehouse, 2021

Davis, C.B, *Tattooing Requirements* [catalog], after 1907. Private Collection

Defenders of Egypt [Film]. IWM1178, 1916. Imperial War Museum

Farenholt, A. "Some Statistical Observations concerning Tattooing as seen by the Recruiting Surgeon." In *United States Naval Medical Bulletin*, January 1913

Farenholt, A. "Tattooing in the Navy." In *United States Naval Medical Bulletin*, January 1908

Gamage's of Holborn: A. W. Gamage Ltd Sports, Cycle, Motor and General Outfitters General Catalogue. London: A.W. Gamage, 1911

Govenar, Alan, *Gus Wagner*. Atglen, PA : Schiffer, 2024

Leighton, *Memoirs of a Tattooist*

Letter from Sutherland MacDonald to W.S Brooks. 13 October 1931. 1831.10.1, 1920-1932. Museum of Comparative Zoology, Harvard University

Lodder, Matt, "Tattooing is in Fashion: Elsa Schiaparelli, 1929." In Matt Lodder, *Painted People*. London : William Collins, 2022

Lukas, Judith and Nicholas York, *Professor JT Clark – Tattooing to Perfection*. USA : Emgate Press, 2021

Nordstrom, Jon, *Danish Tattooing*. Copenhagen : Nordstroms, 2009

Parry, *Secrets of a Strange Art*

Reiter, *King of Tattooists*

Richardson, John, *Sorcerer's Apprentice*. Chicago : University of Chicago Press, 2001

Spamer, Adolf, "Die Tätowierung in den deutschen Hafenstädten." In *Niederdeutsche Zeitschrift für Volkskunde* 11 (1934)

Time to Remember, Your Country Needs You [Film]. British Pathe, 1915

Titchener Barnaby, *The Art of Mr Charles Burchett Davis*. Oxford : Tattoo Club of Great Britain, 2016

Vogue [Paris], July 1929

Wittman, Ole, *Karl Finke: Buch 3*. Henstedt-Ulzburg : Nachlass Warlich, 2017

Wittman, Ole, *Christian Warlich: Tattoo Flash Book*. London : Prestel, 2019

Women's War Service 1917. HU082199 & HU10322, 1917. Imperial War Museum

Chapter 5

Boiardi, Danielle. *Uncommon Valor*. San Francisco : Lyle Tuttle Tattoo Museum, 2020

"The barbaric custom of tattooing is spread by British war hysteria," *Philadelphia Enquirer*, November 6, 1938

Scutt and Gotch, *Art, Sex and Symbol*

Govenar, Alan, "The Changing Image of Tattooing in American Culture," *Journal of American Culture* (Spring 1982)

Sinclair, A.T, "Tattooing Oriental and Gypsy", *American Anthropologist* 20 (1908)

Manual for the Medical Department. Washington, DC : Government Printing Office, 1900

Greenleaf, Charles R., An Epitome if Tripler's Manual and other Publications on the Examination of Recruits. Washington, DC : 1890

September Morn [Film]. Pathé, 1914

Banning, Kendall, *The Fleet Today*. New York : Funk & Wagnalls, 1942

Mater Scacheri, Mabel de La, "Millie–Only Lady Tattooist", *The Family Circle*, December 25, 1936

McCabe, *New York City Tattoo.*

McComb, David, *100 Years of Tattoos*. London : Lawrence King, 2015

Partridge, Eric, *A Dictionary of Slang and Unconventional English*. London : Routledge & Kegan Paul, 1937

Hardy, Don Ed, *Bull's Eyes and Black Eyes.* Honolulu, HI : Hardy Marks, 2007

Hardy, Don Ed, *"Lew the Jew" Alber*ts, Honolulu, HI : Hardy Marks, 2015

Lodder, Matt, "From Paper onto Skin." In Edgar Holli, *Tattoo Masters Flash Collection*. Germany : Edition Reuss, 2015

Ackman, Nick, *Lew Alberts Tattoo Pioneer,* Pittsburgh, PA : Blue Letter, 2021

Skuse, Jimme, *The History and Art of Joseph Hartley*, Bristol : Bristol Tattoo Club, 2016

Ackman, Nick, *Designed by Percy Waters*. Olympia, WA : Blue Letter, 2014

Ackman, Nick, *Drawn by Prof Zeis*. Canonsburg, PA : Blue Letter, 2019

Stickler, Andrew, *Tattooing as You Like It: The Legacy of Milton Zeis*. Colorado Springs, CO : Yellow Beak Press, 2012

Zeis, Milton, *Tattooing the World Over*. Rockford, IL : Zeis Studio, 1947 (Second Edition 1951)

"September Morn," *Moving Picture World*, Jan-Mar 1914

Henry, Bruce, "Sailor to Squire," *Esquire*, June 1934

"One out of Ten Americans is Tattooed," *Life*, December 1936

"Girl Tattooist," *Auckland Star*, November 2, 1940

Byelaws: Tattooing Arrangements : Sanitation arrangements. 1942-1950 HO45/24232 National Archives

French, A. "Tattooing – Male and Female," *Salt* 25, May 1942

"Tattooing Stops Sickness," *The Rock Magazine*, November 1, 1942

"Modest Old Man," *Life*, November 30, 1942

"Police Saw Snakes and they were real," *Guinea Gold*, February 26, 1943

"Two Kinds of Bite," *Guinea Gold*, November 21, 1944

"Tattooed ATS Girls," *Nottingham Evening Post*, February 3, 1945

"Now He's Marked for Life," *The Phoenix*, June 23, 1945

"Humor During a Grim War," *Tiger Rag*, September 1, 1945

Knibb, John, "Human Flesh is his Canvas," *Good Morning*, April 11, 1944

Chapter 6

"A Convention of the Tokyo Tattooing Club," *The Sphere*, September 25, 1948

"A Hunt for Most Artistic Tattoo," *Daily Mirror,* July 11, 1955

"Aldershot Tattoo," *Picture Post*, December 13, 1951

"Astounding Savagery by Nazis Alleged by Jews," *Guinea Gold*, June 30, 1944

"Branded Men with Hot Irons," *Guinea Gold*, October 13, 1945

"Buchenwald was a Living Death," *The Stars and Stripes*, April 17, 1945

"Compulsory Tattooing", "A Masterpiece of Art," "Lost Art of Tattooing," *World's Fair*, August 15, 1931

"I was at Auschwitz," *News Guardian*, January 26, 1946

"Les Skuse Jr," *Tattoo International* (Issue 1, 1978)

"Let's Found a Club," *Belfast Newsletter*, June 11, 1955

"No Backing Out of This," *Sunday Dispatch*, September 18, 1955

"On skin or canvas, its all art, says president Skuse," *Western Daily Press & Bristol Mirror*, October 11, 1960

"Sailor Knight is Back". [Clipping. Source publication unknown.] F2021.21.551.5. National Museum of Wales

"Says tattooing is 'savage'," *Adelaide Mail*, June 18, 1949

"Shirts will not be worn," *Sunday Pictorial*, September 12, 1954

"Speaking of Pictures," *Life*, April 3, 1950

"Tattoo Craze Gets Under their Skin," *Reveille*, November 6–8, 1953

"Tattooed Workers with Freed POW," *Eighth Army News,* March 15, 1945

"Tattooing Artists," *World's Fair,* May 23, 1931

"Tattooing Club," *Pix*, August 13, 1949

"Tattooing in US scored by Soviet Sea Captain," *New York Times*, June 13, 1949

"The Lowest Point of Human Degradation," *Union Jack*, May 10, 1945

"Wine Causes Figure to Dance. *Tattoo Art Judging* Cancelled," *Toronto Globe*, August 30, 1948

"Woman tattooist is member of distinguished family." [Clipping. Source publication unknown]. F2021.21.551.6. National Museum of Wales

Ackers, Ron, *Ron Ackers Tattoo Artist*. Bottrop : Peter Pomp, c. 1999

Bagot, Pascal, *The Tattoo Writer*. France : Bagot, 2021

Cogdell, Christina. *Eugenic Design*. Philadelphia, PA : University of Pennsylvania Press, 2004

Gilmore, Eddie, "Tattoos Flourish", *Oregonian*, September 26, 1965

Hardy, Don Ed. *Tattootime* 5: Art from the Heart. Honolulu, HI: Hardy Marks, 1991

Hartley, Joseph, "The Art of Tattooing," *World's Fair*, July 4, 1931

Hughes, Harold, "Harbor's Tattoo Art Colony Vanishes", *Oregonian*, June 15, 1955

Jaguar, Jeff. *The Tattoo: A Pictorial History*. London : Milestone, 1990

Kilbride, Joseph (as 'PAT'), "A Needle Subject," *World's Fair*, November 28, 1931

Kilbride, Joseph (as 'PAT'), "A Needle Subject," *World's Fair,* May 9, 1931

Lodder, Matt. "The New Old Style: Tradition, Archetype and Rhetoric in Contemporary Western Tattooing." *In Revival: Memories, Identities, Utopias*. London : Courtauld Institute, 2015

Lyon, Kathleen, "Slave Girl freed of Nazi Brand," *Daily Mail*, March 2, 1948

Martinetti, Leon, "Art of Tattooing Not Lost," *World's Fair*, April 15, 1931

Martinetti, Leon, "New Interest in Tattooing," *World's Fair*, May 23, 1931

Mifflin, Margot, *Bodies of Subversion*. Brooklyn, NY : Powerhouse Books, 2013

Mingins, Rich. *Press Cutting Scrapbook*. Amsterdam Tattoo Museum

Sayce, Paul, "History of British Tattoo Clubs." *Tattoo International* (Issue 185, c. 2013)

Sayce, Paul, "Jessie Knight." *Tattoo International* (Issue 184, Spring 2013)

Schiffmacher, Henk, *The Mingins Photo Collection*. Amsterdam : ATM Publishing, 2011

Scutt & Gotch, *Art, Sex and Symbol*

Skuse, Jimme, Bristol *Tattoo Club 65th Year*. Bristol : Bristol Tattoo Club, 2018

Skuse, *Joseph Hartley*

Skuse, Les. "Tattooing," *London Life*, c. December 1950

T. Rich, "The Al Schiefley Legacy," *International Tattoo Art*, August 2004

The Jessie Knight Collection. F2021.21 National Museum of Wales

Tuttle, Lyle, "The Doctors Fukushi," *Tattoo Historian* 5 (1984)

Chapter 7

"Porträt: Rudi Inhelder," *Tätowier-Magazin*, August/September, 1994

"TCA The Tattoo Club of America," *Tattoo International* 15 (1979)

Ebensten, Hans. *Pierced Hearts and True Love* (London : Derek Verschoyle, 1953)

Hardy, Don Ed. *Sailor Jerry: American Tattoo Master*. Honolulu, HI : Hardy Marks, 2007

Hill, Amie, "Tattoo Renaissance," *Rolling Stone*, October 1, 1970

King, Paul, *Alan Oversby: Documentary Evidence*. San Francisco : Association of Professional Piercers, 2022

Kitamura, Takahiro, *Tattoo Master Pinky Yun*. St Louis, MO : Scorpion Front, 2022

Kohrs, Manfred, *Horst Helmut "Samy" Streckenbach*. Wedmark : Manfred Kohrs, 2024

Letter from John Lemes to Sailor Sid. Body Piercing Archive, San Fransisco

Michael Berger, "Ein Leben in weiteren Welten: Hans Rudolf Inhelder, Frümsen (1929-2003)", *Werdenberger Jahrbuch* 2004. Werdenberg : Historischer Verein der Region Werdenberg, 2004

Mulderig, Jeremy (ed.), *Phil Sparrow Tells All. Chicago* : University of Chicago Press, 2015

Mulderig, Jeremy, (ed.), T*he Lost Autobiography of Samuel Steward*. Chicago : University of Chicago Press, 2018

National Tattoo Association Magazine 1 (n.d). Collection of Shawn Porter

Schonberger, Nick, *Homeward Bound: The Life and Times of Hori Smoku Sailor Jerry*. USA : Sailor Jerry Ltd, 2010

Spring, Justin, *Secret Historian*. New Yorks : Farrar, Straus & Giroux, 2010

Steward, Samuel, *Bad Boys and Tough Tattoos*. New York : Harrington Park Press, 1990

Steward, Samuel, *Chapters from an Autobiography*. San Francisco : Grey Fox Press, 1981

Tattoo News [Tattoo Club of America]. Collected editions 1964-1966. Body Piercing Archive, San Fransisco

The History of Tattoo Clubs. Winston Salem, NC : Tattoo Archive

Chapter 8

"A Convention where no-one needs a badge", *Chicago Tribune*, January 27, 1976

"A Gallery of People," *Gallery Magazine*. [n.d] Collection of Australian Tattoo Museum

"For the Tattooed: Instant Identity," *Newsday*, October 19, 1971

"Modern Living: Tattoo Renaissance," *Time Magazine*, December 21, 1971

"Psst... Your Epidermis is Showing," *Esquire*, June 1976

"Tat Chat," *Newsletter of the International Tattoo Artists Association*. No. 12. (October 1976)

"Tattoo 77 Opens Today," *Nevada State Journal*, January 24, 1977

"Tattoo art show intends to needle, or does it...?" *Newark Star Ledger*, October 10, 1971

"Tattoo as Art Form," *The Sunday Home News* [New Brunswick, NJ], October 31, 1971

"Tattoo Convention," *Reno Gazette*, January 24, 1977

"Tattoo judging for one and all," *Reno Evening Gazette*, May 19, 1977

"The Renaissance of Tattooing," *This Week*, dir. Ian Fordyce. (Associated Radiodiffusion, 8 May 1958). 389649, British Film Institute

"Weird, Weird, Weird," *Action Magazine*, March 1976

Altman, Jack and Marvin Ziporyn, *Born to Raise Hell: The Untold Story of Richard Speck*. New York : Grove Press, 1967

Archipley, Paul, "Tattoos back, Stigma Remains," *Daily Titan*, October 14, 1976

Black Eyes & Lemonade [ex. cat], Whitechapel Gallery, 1951, Objs. M16–17

Breuer, Karin, *Ed Hardy Deeper than Skin*, San Francisco : Fine Art Museums of San Francisco, 2019

Briony Fer, 'Photographs and Buildings (mainly)' in Ian Borden (ed.), Forty Ways to think about Architecture. Chichester: Wiley & Sons, 2014

Burrell v Harmer 1966 WL 22058 (Divisional Court 1966)

Cartwright, Charlie and Jack Rudy, *Good Time Charlie's*. Los Angeles : CS Con Safos, 2012

Exhibition File: Tattoo. 1971. American Folk Art Museum Archives, New York

Gatewood, Charles, "Spider Webb Rules," *Skin & Ink*, November 1997

Glibert, Steve, *Tattoo History Sourcebook*. San Francisco :RE/Search, 2000

Govenar, Alan. *Ed Hardy Art for Life*. Kempen : teNeues, 2009

Hardy, Don Ed. *Wear Your Dreams* New York : Thomas Dunne, 2013

Introduction of the Tattooing of Minors Bill. BN 29/1427 National Archives, Kew

Jones, Barbara, *Unsophisticated Arts*. London: Little Toller, 2013

Knox, Sanka, "Heyday of Tattooing Recalled at Folk Art Museum," *New York Times*, October 8, 1971

Kohrs, Manfred, "First US Tattoo Convention Houston Texas 1976," *Tattoo Kulture Magazine* 37 (March/April 2020)

Les Skuse The Champion Tattoo Artist of All England, Camden Arts Centre, 13 February–5 March [handbill] (1972), NMWA23777 National Museum of Wales

Letter from Sailor Sid Diller to Roland Loomis. 17 April 1977. Body Piercing Archive

Lodder, Matt. *British Tattoo Art Revealed* [exhibition]. National Maritime Museum Cornwall, 2017

Maciunas, George. *Flux Tattoos*. Fluxus Implosions, Inc, 1967. 2481.2008 Museum of Modern Art, New York

Mifflin, *Bodies of Subversion*

Miller, Russell, "Works of art in the flesh," *The Observer*, February 6, 1972

National: Tattoo Club of the World. February 1977

O'Kane, "Tattoo Parlors are told to Close," *New York Times*, October 10, 1961

*People v. O'Sulliva*n, 96 Misc. 2d 52, 409 N.Y.S.2d 332 (N.Y. App. Term 1978)

Plotsker, Manuel RS (1966) "Tattooing Laws in the United States," *Archives of Environmental Health: An International Journal,* 13:2 (1966), 267

Records & Briefs New York State Appellate Division. New York : The Reporter Company, 1964

Rubin, Arnold (ed.), *Marks of Civilization*. Los Angeles : University of California, 1988

Sanders, Dennis, *Gay Source: A Catalog For Men*. San Fransisco : Berkley Windhover, 1977

Sprinkle, Annie. P*ost-Porn Modernis*t. Jersey City : Cleis, 2001

Stauter, R L. "Tattooing: the protection of the public health." *Health matrix* vol. 6,2 (1988): 51-9

Tattoo, undated. Julia Weissman Papers A0010. Box 8/22. American Folk Art Museum Archives, New York

Taylor, Angela, "Some people just wore their tattoos," *New York Times*, March 25, 1975

Tuttle, Lyle, *Tattoo 70*. San Francisco : Lyle Tuttle, 1970

Vale, V. *Ed Hardy Interviews*. San Francisco : RE/Search, 2013

Van Dellen, Theodore, "How to Keep Well," *Daily Independent*, September 6, 1969

Vanity [ex. cat.], Brighton Museum and Art Gallery, 9 May–31 Aug. 1972, obj A182, 12

Ward, Jim. *Running the Gauntlet*. San Francisco : ReWard, 2013

Webb, Spider and Marco Vassi, *Pushing Ink*. Atlgen, PA : Schiffer, 1979

Yurkew v. Sinclair, 495 F. Supp. 1248 (D. Minn. 1980)

Chapter 9

"Tattoo You?" *City Limits*, February 5–11, 1982

Ackers, *Ron Ackers*

Bubash, Nick. *Thom deVita: deVita Unauthorized*. Honolulu, HI L: Hardy Marks, 2012

Cartwright and Rudy, *Good Time Charlie's*

*Ed Hardy to Lal Hard*y. Letters. Lal Hardy Collection, London

Gilbert, *Tattoo Source Book*

Hardy, *Bull's Eyes and Black Eyes*

Hardy, Don Ed. *Tattootime: Music and the Sea*. Honolulu, HI : Hardy Marks, 1988

Hardy, Don Ed. *TattooTime: New Tribalism*. Permanent Press: Forked River, NJ, 1982

Hardy. *TattooTime: Art from the Heart*

Lodder, Matt "New Old Style"

Lodder, Matt, "The Hardy Boys," *Total Tattoo Magazine* 92, June 2012

Lodder, Matt, "The Myths of Modern Primitivism," *EJAC* 30 (2), 2011

Musafar, Fakir. "Fakir Rants and Raves. Spirit + Flesh: The Energy Pull." 25 Feb 2005. BmeZine.com https://web.archive.org/web/20130119082129/ https://news.bme.com/tag/fakir-rants-raves/

Musafar, Fakir. "Spirt + Flesh." London : Arena, 2002

TATTOO! 7 June -7 August 1977. Archive Materials. Oakland Museum of California

Vale, V and Andrea Juno. *Modern Primitives*. San Fransisco : RE/Search, 1989

Chapter 10

"The Great AIDS Debate," *Tattoo Buzz* (May/Jun, 1985)

Alan Oversby Collection. Jeremy Castle Archive, Bishopsgate Institute, London

Barba, Michael, "The Underground Art of Greg Irons," *Tattoo the World* of Dermagraphics (Winter 1986)

Baxter, Bob, "Guy Aitchison's World of Ink and Paint," *Skin & Ink,* September 2006

Binne, Alex, "The Mother Art", *Body Art* 4 (1988)

Cohen, Nick, "Bookseller cleared of breaching obscenity law," *Independent*, March 8, 1991

Cole, Anna, "Alex Binnie in Interview", *Fashion Theory* 10/3 (2006)

Corfield, Bob, "Ban on gay tattoos," *The Sun* (c.May 1985), reprinted in *Tattoo Buzz* (May/Jun 1985), 33

Eagleton, Terry, "Capitalism, Modernism and Postmodernism," *New Left Review*, July/Aug 1985

Hardy, Don Ed, "Dan Higgs," T*attoo Revue* 25, 1993

Hardy, Don Ed. *Eye Tattooed America*. Honolulu, HI : Hardy Marks, 1993

Irvine, Susan, "My Little Perforation", *Independent*, December 18, 1993

King, *Mr Sebastian*

Leu, Aia, *The Art of the Leu Famil*y. Kenmare : Seed Press, 2012

Leu, Loretta, *Felix Leu: Tattooing—Ask Here*. Kenmare : Seed Press, 2019

Lodder, Matt. "20 Years of Into You," *Total Tattoo* 109 (2013)

Podlichuk Marcus, "Mr Sebastian Ink," *Tattoo International* 52 (1982)

Rosenkranz, Patrick, *You Call this Art?: A Greg Irons Retrospective*. Seattle, WA: Fantagraphics, 2006

Sandercock, James, "The Leu Family's Family Iron," *Total Tattoo* 85 (2011).

Voyle, Susanna, "Tattooing Makes an Indelible Mark at Selfridges," *Financial Times*, June 17, 1993

Ward, Jim, "Meet Mr Sebastian," *Piercing Fans International Quarterly*, No. 4 (Summer 1978)

Index

Acknowledgments

Dedicated to my true love, Layla Boyd, and to the memory of Hans Rudolf Inhelder.

Special thanks to Paul King and Thomas O'Mahony, whose ideas and input have helped shape this project immensely.

In producing this book, amongst other cited collections, I have drawn heavily from primary source material from the following archives and collections and am grateful to them all:

Body Piercing Archive, San Francisco; Jeremy Castle, Alan Oversby and Rudi Inhelder Collections, Bishopsgate Institute, London; Jessie Knight Collection, National Museum of Wales; and the private collections of Stefan Stresnik, Lal Hardy, and Alex Binnie.

Particular thanks to Terry Manton, Manfred Kohrs, Shawn Porter, Nick York, Derin Bray, Loretta Leu, Jimmie Skuse, Willie Robinson, Shotsie Gorman, Doug Hardy, Gideon Schory, and Taki Kitamura for their assistance, kindness, and wisdom.

Image Credits

Key: top = t; bottom = b; left = l; right = r; m = middle

Front cover © Hulton-Deutsch Collection/ CORBIS/Corbis via Getty Images

© Aaron Cain: **p.199**; Courtesy of Adrian Forty: **p.141**; akg-images / Denise Bellon: p.161, akg-images: **p.6**; Akita Prefectural Museum: **p.67**; Alan Oversby Collection. Bishopsgate Institute: **p.157, 178, 194-195, 198**; Alex Binnie: **p.196, 197, 206t, 207**; Alexander Turnbull Library, NZ: **p.22**; Allan Tannenbaum/Getty Images: **p.146**; American Antiquarian Society: **p.43r**; Andy Olenick: **p.18**; Archive Photos / Getty Images: **p.90**; Bodliean Library, University of Oxford: **p.53, 57b**; Courtesy of the Barry Kay Archive / © Hubertus Janssen-Werner: **p.12, 144**; Body Piercing Archive: **p.2, 9, 10, 116t, 123, 125, 130, 133, 134, 137, 142, 152, 162l, 162r, 154-155**; Bridgeman Images: **p.17, 27, 29b, 32**; Chronicle / Alamy Stock Photo: **p.45t**; ClassicStock / Alamy Stock Photo: **p.92**; Images courtesy of the Conservation Center for Art & Historic Artifacts: **p.129**; Cornwall Council | Konsel Kernow: **p.21**; © CSG CIC Glasgow Museums and Libraries Collection: **p.151**; Private Collection, Dr Matt Lodder: **p.14, 58, 62l, 77r, 94-95, 102-103**; Evening Standard / Getty Images: **p.77l**;

From the Ernst Mayr Library and Archives of the Museum of Comparative Zoology, Harvard University: **p.49, 52**; Gideon Schory - Tattoocollection.eu: **p.93, 142t, 170, 171l**; Guy Aitchison: **p.201, 202**; All Right Reserved © 2024, Hardy Marks Publications: **p.175**; Courtesy of Harvard University: **p.37**; Photo: Haywood Magee/Picture Post/Hulton Archive/ Getty Images: **101t**; Heritage Images / Heritage Art / akg-images: **p.33**; IanGreen / Greg Irons Archive: **p.181**; Internet Archive: **p.20, 57t**; © IWM: **p.70, 100b**; Private Collection, Jason Davis Tattoo: **p.177**; Jill Westwood: **p.206b**; © John Deakin / John Deakin Archive / Bridgeman Images: **p.107**; Courtesy of John Wyatt: **p.173**; Lal Hardy: **p.167, 184-185, 186**; Lawrence Schiller / Getty Images: **p.200**; Leather Archives: **p.174, 176r**; Library of Congress Prints and Photographs Division Washington, D.C., USA: **p.30**; Loretta Leu: **p.188, 190-191, 192, 193, 204-205**; © Lyle Tuttle Archive and Collection: **p.147**; Manfred Kohrs / Institute for German Tattoo History: **p.149, 150**; Mary Evans Picture Library: **p.42t**; McMaster University Library: **p.71, 83t, 87, 100, 108-109**; Mirror Pix: **p.59, 84, 86, 153**; Mirrorpix / Getty Images: **p.91, 159**; Nagasaki Museum of History and Culture: **p.66**; Sourced from National Fairground Archives World's Fair Newspaper Collection: **p.68**; © NATIONAL MUSEUM OF WALES: **p.79, 82, 89, 98, 112-113, 114-115, 116b, 117, 119b, 121b, 140**; National Police Gazette: **p.38**; Image courtesy of Neil Hopkin-Thomas/National Maritime Museum Cornwall: **p.80-81**; New image to come: **p.144**; Private Collection Nick York: **p.42b, 43l, 44l, 44r,**

45b, 54b, 56, 64r; © Nigel Henderson Estate / Tate: **p.78b**; OMCA: **p.164, 168, 182-183**; Österreichische Nationalbibliothek: **p.26**; Palace of Westminster Collection: **p.40**; Courtesy of Paul Booth: **p.208-209**; Paul King: **p.172, 187**; © Philadelphia Museum of Art, Pennsylvania, PA, USA / Bridgeman Images: **p.29t**; © Philip Jones Griffiths/ Magnum Photos: **p.158t**; Pitt Rivers Museum: **p.16**; Prismatic Pictures / Bridgeman Images: **p.55**; Robert DOISNEAU / Getty Images: **p.78t**; Rudi Indelder Collection / Bishopsgate Institute: **p.13, 75, 110, 118, 119t, 128, 131, 136b, 163, 171r**; Courtesy of Ryochi Maeda: **p.176l**; Schenking van mevrouw Hansen-van den Brugghen, Den Haag / The Rijksmuseum: **p.19**; Courtesy of Shotsie Gorman, Tattoo Advocate Magazine: **p.160r**; Private Collection, Stephan Strestik: **p.64r, 65, 76, 83b, 97, 120, 121t, 124, 126-127, 138l, 138t, 139, 160l**; Stiftung Historische Museen Hamburg: **p.73, 101b**; Suffolk Gaol Record Book Ipswich: **p.21b**; Courtesy of The Lewis Walpole Library, Yale University: **p.23**; The Mariners' Museum and Park, Newport News, Virginia: **p.88, 99**; The National Archives Image Library: **p.46, 50, 51, 54, 60, 61t, 63b**; The Reading Room / Alamy Stock Photo: **p.35**; © The Trustees of the British Museum: **p.28, 61b**; Topfoto: **p.104**; ullstein bild Dtl. / Getty Images: **p.62r**; University of Edinburgh: **p.41**; Courtesy of William Robinson: **p.158b**; Yale Beneke Library: **p.143**